Thomas Babington
Macaulay

The

History of England

from the Accession of
James II

Volume 1

Elibron Classics
www.elibron.com

Elibron Classics series.

© 2006 Adamant Media Corporation.

ISBN 0-543-93129-3 (paperback)
ISBN 0-543-93128-5 (hardcover)

This Elibron Classics Replica Edition is an unabridged facsimile
of the edition published in 1849 by Bernh.Tauchnitz Jun., Leipzig.

COLLECTION

OF

BRITISH AUTHORS.

VOL. CLXXII.

THE HISTORY OF ENGLAND.

BY

THOMAS BABINGTON MACAULAY.

VOL. I.

THE

HISTORY OF ENGLAND

FROM

THE ACCESSION OF JAMES THE SECOND.

BY

THOMAS BABINGTON MACAULAY.

COPYRIGHT EDITION.

VOL. I.

LEIPZIG

BERNH. TAUCHNITZ JUN.

1849.

CONTENTS

OF

THE FIRST VOLUME.

CHAPTER I.

CHAPTER II.

CHAPTER III.

HISTORY OF ENGLAND.

CHAPTER I.

I PURPOSE to write the history of England from the accession of King James the Second down to a time which is within the memory of men still living. I shall recount the errors which, in a few months, alienated a loyal gentry and priesthood from the House of Stuart. I shall trace the course of that revolution which terminated the long struggle between our sovereigns and their parliaments, and bound up together the rights of the people and the title of the reigning dynasty. I shall relate how the new settlement was, during many troubled years, successfully defended against foreign and domestic enemies; how, under that settlement, the authority of law and the security of property were found to be compatible with a liberty of discussion and of individual action never before known; how, from the auspicious union of order and freedom, sprang a prosperity of which the annals of human affairs had furnished no example; how our country, from a state of ignominious vassalage, rapidly rose to the place of umpire among European powers; how her opulence and her martial glory grew together; how, by wise and resolute good faith, was gradually established a public credit fruitful of marvels which to the statesmen of any former age would have seemed incredible; how a gigantic commerce gave birth to a maritime power, compared with which every other maritime power, ancient or modern, sinks into insignificance; how

Scotland, after ages of enmity, was at length united to England, not merely by legal bonds, but by indissoluble ties of interest and affection; how, in America, the British colonies rapidly became far mightier and wealthier than the realms which Cortes and Pizarro had added to the dominions of Charles the Fifth; how, in Asia, British adventurers founded an empire not less splendid and more durable than that of Alexander.

Nor will it be less my duty faithfully to record disasters mingled with triumphs, and great national crimes and follies far more humiliating than any disaster. It will be seen that even what we justly account our chief blessings were not without alloy. It will be seen that the system which effectually secured our liberties against the encroachments of kingly power gave birth to a new class of abuses from which absolute monarchies are exempt. It will be seen that, in consequence partly of unwise interference, and partly of unwise neglect, the increase of wealth and the extension of trade produced, together with immense good, some evils from which poor and rude societies are free. It will be seen how, in two important dependencies of the crown, wrong was followed by just retribution; how imprudence and obstinacy broke the ties which bound the North American colonies to the parent state; how Ireland, cursed by the domination of race over race, and of religion over religion, remained indeed a member of the empire, but a withered and distorted member, adding no strength to the body politic, and reproachfully pointed at by all who feared or envied the greatness of England.

Yet, unless I greatly deceive myself, the general effect of this chequered narrative will be to excite thankfulness in all religious minds, and hope in the breasts of all patriots. For the history of our country during the last hundred and sixty years is eminently the history of physical, of moral, and of intellectual improvement. Those who compare the age on which their lot has fallen with a golden age which exists only

in their imagination may talk of degeneracy and decay: but CHAP.
I.
no man who is correctly informed as to the past will be disposed to take a morose or desponding view of the present.

I should very imperfectly execute the task which I have
undertaken if I were merely to treat of battles and sieges, of
the rise and fall of administrations, of intrigues in the palace,
and of debates in the parliament. It will be my endeavour to
relate the history of the people as well as the history of the
government, to trace the progress of useful and ornamental
arts, to describe the rise of religious sects and the changes
of literary taste, to portray the manners of successive
generations, and not to pass by with neglect even the revolutions which have taken place in dress, furniture, repasts,
and public amusements. I shall cheerfully bear the reproach
of having descended below the dignity of history, if I can succeed in placing before the English of the nineteenth century
a true picture of the life of their ancestors.

The events which I propose to relate form only a single act
of a great and eventful drama extending through ages, and
must be very imperfectly understood unless the plot of the
preceding acts be well known. I shall therefore introduce my
narrative by a slight sketch of the history of our country from
the earliest times. I shall pass very rapidly over many centuries: but I shall dwell at some length on the vicissitudes of
that contest which the administration of King James the Second brought to a decisive crisis. *

Nothing in the early existence of Britain indicated the Britain
greatness which she was destined to attain. Her inhabitants, under the
Romans.

* In this, and in the next chapter, I have very seldom thought it
necessary to cite authorities: for, in these chapters, I have not detailed
events minutely, or used recondite materials; and the facts which I
mention are for the most part such that a person tolerably well read in
English history, if not already apprised of them, will at least know where
to look for evidence of them. In the subsequent chapters I shall carefully
indicate the sources of my information.

CHAP.
I.

when first they became known to the Tyrian mariners, were little superior to the natives of the Sandwich Islands. She was subjugated by the Roman arms; but she received only a faint tincture of Roman arts and letters. Of the western provinces which obeyed the Cæsars she was the last that was conquered, and the first that was flung away. No magnificent remains of Latian porches and aqueducts are to be found in Britain. No writer of British birth is reckoned among the masters of Latian poetry and eloquence. It is not probable that the islanders were at any time generally familiar with the tongue of their Italian rulers. From the Atlantic to the vicinity of the Rhine the Latin has, during many centuries, been predominant. It drove out the Celtic; it was not driven out by the Teutonic; and it is at this day the basis of the French, Spanish, and Portuguese languages. In our island the Latin appears never to have superseded the old Gaelic speech, and could not stand its ground against the German.

The scanty and superficial civilisation which the Britons had derived from their southern masters was effaced by the calamities of the fifth century. In the continental kingdoms into which the Roman empire was then dissolved, the conquerors learned much from the conquered race. In Britain the conquered race became as barbarous as the conquerors.

Britain
under the
Saxons.

All the chiefs who founded Teutonic dynasties in the continental provinces of the Roman empire, Alaric, Theodoric, Clovis, Alboin, were zealous Christians. The followers of Ida and Cerdic, on the other hand, brought to their settlements in Britain all the superstitions of the Elbe. While the German princes who reigned at Paris, Toledo, Arles, and Ravenna listened with reverence to the instructions of bishops, adored the relics of martyrs, and took part eagerly in disputes touching the Nicene theology, the rulers of Wessex and Mercia were still performing savage rites in the temples of Thor and Woden.

The continental kingdoms which had risen on the ruins of CHAP.
the Western Empire kept up some intercourse with those I.
eastern provinces where the ancient civilisation, though
slowly fading away under the influence of misgovernment,
might still astonish and instruct barbarians, where the court
still exhibited the splendour of Diocletian and Constantine,
where the public buildings were still adorned with the sculp-
tures of Polycletus and the paintings of Apelles, and where
laborious pedants, themselves destitute of taste, sense, and
spirit, could still read and interpret the masterpieces of
Sophocles, of Demosthenes, and of Plato. From this communion Britain was cut off. Her shores were, to the polished
race which dwelt by the Bosporus, objects of a mysterious
horror, such as that with which the Ionians of the age of
Homer had regarded the Straits of Scylla and the city of the
Læstrygonian cannibals.   There was one province of our
island in which, as Procopius had been told, the ground
was covered with serpents, and the air was such that no man
could inhale it and live. To this desolate region the spirits
of the departed were ferried over from the land of the Franks
at midnight.   A strange race of fishermen performed the
ghastly office. The speech of the dead was distinctly heard
by the boatmen: their weight made the keel sink deep in the
water; but their forms were invisible to mortal eye.   Such
were the marvels which an able historian, the contemporary
of Belisarius, of Simplicius, and of Tribonian, gravely related in the rich and polite Constantinople, touching the
country in which the founder of Constantinople had assumed
the imperial purple. Concerning all the other provinces of
the Western Empire we have continuous information. It is
only in Britain that an age of fable completely separates two
ages of truth. Odoacer and Totila, Euric and Thrasimund,
Clovis, Fredegunda, and Brunechild, are historical men and
women. But Hengist and Horsa, Vortigern and Rowena,

Arthur and Mordred are mythical persons, whose very existence may be questioned, and whose adventures must be classed with those of Hercules and Romulus.

Conversion of the Saxons to Christianity.
At length the darkness begins to break; and the country which had been lost to view as Britain reappears as England. The conversion of the Saxon colonists to Christianity was the first of a long series of salutary revolutions. It is true that the Church had been deeply corrupted both by that superstition and by that philosophy against which she had long contended, and over which she had at last triumphed. She had given a too easy admission to doctrines borrowed from the ancient schools, and to rites borrowed from the ancient temples. Roman policy and Gothic ignorance, Grecian ingenuity and Syrian [asceticism, had contributed to deprave her. Yet she retained enough of the sublime theology and benevolent morality of her earlier days to elevate many intellects, and to purify many hearts. Some things also which at a later period were justly regarded as among her chief blemishes were, in the seventh century, and long afterwards, among her chief merits. That the sacerdotal order should encroach on the functions of the civil magistrate would, in our time, be a great evil. But that which in an age of good government is an evil may, in an age of grossly bad government, be a blessing. It is better that mankind should be governed by wise laws well administered, and by an enlightened public opinion, than by priestcraft: but it is better that men should be governed by priestcraft than by brute violence, by such a prelate as Dunstan than by such a warrior as Penda. A society sunk in ignorance, and ruled by mere physical force, has great reason to rejoice when a class, of which the influence is intellectual and moral, rises to ascendency. Such a class will doubtless abuse its power: but mental power, even when abused, is still a nobler and better power than that which consists merely

in corporeal strength. We read in our Saxon chronicles of tyrants, who, when at the height of greatness, were smitten with remorse, who abhorred the pleasures and dignities which they had purchased by guilt, who abdicated their crowns, and who sought to atone for their offences by cruel penances and incessant prayers. These stories have drawn forth bitter expressions of contempt from some writers who, while they boasted of liberality, were in truth as narrow-minded as any monk of the dark ages, and whose habit was to apply to all events in the history of the world the standard received in the Parisian society of the eighteenth century. Yet surely a system which, however deformed by superstition, introduced strong moral restraints into communities previously governed only by vigour of muscle and by audacity of spirit, a system which taught the fiercest and mightiest ruler that he was, like his meanest bondman, a responsible being, might have seemed to deserve a more respectful mention from philosophers and philanthropists.

The same observations will apply to the contempt with which, in the last century, it was fashionable to speak of the pilgrimages, the sanctuaries, the crusades, and the monastic institutions of the middle ages. In times when men were scarcely ever induced to travel by liberal curiosity, or by the pursuit of gain, it was better that the rude inhabitant of the North should visit Italy and the East as a pilgrim, than that he should never see anything but those squalid cabins and uncleared woods amidst which he was born. In times when life and when female honour were exposed to daily risk from tyrants and marauders, it was better that the precinct of a shrine should be regarded with an irrational awe, than that there should be no refuge inaccessible to cruelty and licentiousness. In times when statesmen were incapable of forming extensive political combinations, it was better that the Christian nations should be roused and united for

the recovery of the Holy Sepulchre, than that they should,
one by one, be overwhelmed by the Mahometan power.
Whatever reproach may, at a later period, have been justly
thrown on the indolence and luxury of religious orders, it
was surely good that, in an age of ignorance and violence,
there should be quiet cloisters and gardens, in which the
arts of peace could be safely cultivated, in which gentle and
contemplative natures could find an asylum, in which one
brother could employ himself in transcribing the Æneid of
Virgil, and another in meditating the Analytics of Aristotle,
in which he who had a genius for art might illuminate a marty-
rology or carve a crucifix, and in which he who had a turn
for natural philosophy might make experiments on the properties of plants and minerals. Had not such retreats been
scattered here and there, among the huts of a miserable
peasantry, and the castles of a ferocious aristocracy, European society would have consisted merely of beasts of
burden and beasts of prey. The Church has many times
been compared by divines to the ark of which we read in the
Book of Genesis: but never was the resemblance more perfect than during that evil time when she alone rode, amidst
darkness and tempest, on the deluge beneath which all the
great works of ancient power and wisdom lay entombed,
bearing within her that feeble germ from which a second and
more glorious civilisation was to spring.

Even the spiritual supremacy arrogated by the Pope was,
in the dark ages, productive of far more good than evil.
Its effect was to unite the nations of Western Europe in one
great commonwealth. What the Olympian chariot course
and the Pythian oracle were to all the Greek cities, from
Trebizond to Marseilles, Rome and her Bishop were to all
Christians of the Latin communion, from Calabria to the
Hebrides. Thus grew up sentiments of enlarged benevolence. Races separated from each other by seas and

mountains acknowledged a fraternal tie and a common code of public law. Even in war, the cruelty of the conqueror was not seldom mitigated by the recollection that he and his vanquished enemies were all members of one great federation.

Into this federation our Saxon ancestors were now admitted. A regular communication was opened between our shores and that part of Europe in which the traces of ancient power and policy were yet discernible. Many noble monuments which have since been destroyed or defaced still retained their pristine magnificence; and travellers, to whom Livy and Sallust were unintelligible, might gain from the Roman aqueducts and temples some faint notion of Roman history. The dome of Agrippa, still glittering with bronze, the mausoleum of Adrian, not yet deprived of its columns and statues, the Flavian amphitheatre, not yet degraded into a quarry, told to the Mercian and Northumbrian pilgrims some part of the story of that great civilised world which had passed away. The islanders returned, with awe deeply impressed on their half opened minds, and told the wondering inhabitants of the hovels of London and York that, near the grave of Saint Peter, a mighty race, now extinct, had piled up buildings which would never be dissolved till the judgment day. Learning followed in the train of Christianity. The poetry and eloquence of the Augustan age was assiduously studied in Mercian and Northumbrian monasteries. The names of Bede, of Alcuin, and of John, surnamed Erigena, were justly celebrated throughout Europe. Such was the state of our country when, in the ninth century, began the last great descent of the northern barbarians.

During several generations Denmark and Scandinavia continued to pour forth innumerable pirates, distinguished by strength, by valour, by merciless ferocity, and by hatred of the Christian name. No country suffered so much from these

invaders as England.   Her coast lay near to the ports whence
they sailed; nor was any part of our island so far distant from
the sea as to be secure from attack.   The same atrocities
which had attended the victory of the Saxon over the Celt
were now, after the lapse of ages, suffered by the Saxon at
the hand of the Dane.   Civilisation, just as it began to rise,
was met by this blow, and sank down once more.   Large
colonies of adventurers from the Baltic established themselves
on the eastern shores, spread gradually westward, and, supported by constant reinforcements from beyond the sea,
aspired to the dominion of the whole realm.   The struggle
between the two fierce Teutonic breeds lasted during six
generations.   Each was alternately paramount.   Cruel massacres followed by cruel retribution, provinces wasted, con-
vents plundered, and cities rased to the ground, make up the
greater part of the history of those evil days.   At length the
North ceased to send forth a constant stream of fresh de-
predators, and from that time the mutual aversion of the
races began to subside.   Intermarriage became frequent.
The Danes learned the religion of the Saxons; and thus one
cause of deadly animosity was removed.   The Danish and
Saxon tongues, both dialects of one wide-spread language,
were blended together.   But the distinction between the two
nations was by no means effaced, when an event took place
which prostrated both, in common slavery and degradation,
at the feet of a third people.

The Nor-
mans.
The Normans were then the foremost race of Christendom.
Their valour and ferocity had made them conspicuous among
the rovers whom Scandinavia had sent forth to ravage
Western Europe.   Their sails were long the terror of both
coasts of the channel.   Their arms were repeatedly carried
far into the heart of the Carlovingian empire, and were
victorious under the walls of Maestricht and Paris.   At length
one of the feeble heirs of Charlemagne ceded to the strangers

a fertile province, watered by a noble river, and contiguous CHAP.
to the sea which was their favourite element. In that province ——I.——
they founded a mighty state, which gradually extended its influence over the neighbouring principalities of Britanny and
Maine. Without laying aside that dauntless valour which had
been the terror of every land from the Elbe to the Pyrenees,
the Normans rapidly acquired all, and more than all, the
knowledge and refinement which they found in the country
where they settled. Their courage secured their territory
against foreign invasion. They established internal order,
such as had long been unknown in the Frank empire. They
embraced Christianity, and with Christianity they learned a
great part of what the clergy had to teach. They abandoned
their native speech, and adopted the French tongue, in which
the Latin was the predominant element. They speedily
raised their new language to a dignity and importance which
it had never before possessed. They found it a barbarous
jargon; they fixed it in writing; and they employed it in
legislation, in poetry, and in romance. They renounced that
brutal intemperance to which all the other branches of the
great German family were too much inclined. The polite
luxury of the Norman presented a striking contrast to the
coarse voracity and drunkenness of his Saxon and Danish
neighbours. He loved to display his magnificence, not in
huge piles of food and hogsheads a strong drink, but in large
and stately edifices, rich armour, gallant horses, choice fal-
cons, well ordered tournaments, banquets delicate rather than
abundant, and wines remarkable rather for their exquisite
flavour than for their intoxicating power. That chivalrous
spirit, which has exercised so powerful an influence on the
politics, morals, and manners of all the European nations,
was found in the highest exaltation among the Norman nobles.
Those nobles were distinguished by their graceful bearing
and insinuating address. They were distinguished also by

CHAP. their skill in negotiation, and by a natural eloquence which
I. they assiduously cultivated. It was the boast of one of their
historians that the Norman gentlemen were orators from the
cradle. But their chief fame was derived from their military
exploits. Every country, from the Atlantic Ocean to the
Dead Sea, witnessed the prodigies of their discipline and
valour. One Norman knight, at the head of a handful of
warriors, scattered the Celts of Connaught. Another founded
the monarchy of the Two Sicilies, and saw the emperors both
of the East and of the West fly before his arms. A third, the
Ulysses of the first crusade, was invested by his fellow soldiers
with the sovereignty of Antioch; and a fourth, the Tancred
whose name lives in the great poem of Tasso, was celebrated
through Christendom as the bravest and most generous of the
champions of the Holy Sepulchre.

The vicinity of so remarkable a people early began to produce an effect on the public mind of England. Before the
Conquest, English princes received their education in Normandy. English sees and English estates were bestowed on
Normans. The French of Normandy was familiarly spoken
in the palace of Westminster. The court of Rouen seems to
have been to the court of Edward the Confessor what the court
of Versailles long afterwards was to the court of Charles the
Second.

The Nor-   The battle of Hastings, and the events which followed it,
man Con-   not only placed a Duke of Normandy on the English throne,
quest.
but gave up the whole population of England to the tyranny of
the Norman race. The subjugation of a nation by a nation
has seldom, even in Asia, been more complete. The country
was portioned out among the captains of the invaders. Strong
military institutions, closely connected with the institution of
property, enabled the foreign conquerors to oppress the
children of the soil. A cruel penal code, cruelly enforced,
guarded the privileges, and even the sports, of the alien

tyrants. Yet the subject race, though beaten down and trodden under foot, still made its sting felt. Some bold men, the favourite heroes of our oldest ballads, betook themselves to the woods, and there, in defiance of curfew laws and forest laws, waged a predatory war against their oppressors. Assassination was an event of daily occurrence. Many Normans suddenly disappeared leaving no trace. The corpses of many were found bearing the marks of violence. Death by torture was denounced against the murderers, and strict search was made for them, but generally in vain; for the whole nation was in a conspiracy to screen them. It was at length thought necessary to lay a heavy fine on every Hundred in which a person of French extraction should be found slain; and this regulation was followed up by another regulation, providing that every person who was found slain should be supposed to be a Frenchman, unless he were proved to be a Saxon.

During the century and a half which followed the Conquest, there is, to speak strictly, no English history. The French Kings of England rose, indeed, to an eminence which was the wonder and dread of all neighbouring nations. They conquered Ireland. They received the homage of Scotland. By their valour, by their policy, by their fortunate matrimonial alliances, they became far more powerful on the Continent than their liege lords the Kings of France. Asia, as well as Europe, was dazzled by the power and glory of our tyrants. Arabian chroniclers recorded with unwilling admiration the fall of Acre, the defence of Joppa, and the victorious march to Ascalon; and Arabian mothers long awed their infants to silence with the name of the lion hearted Plantagenet. At one time it seemed that the line of Hugh Capet was about to end as the Merovingian and Carlovingian lines had ended, and that a single great monarchy would spread from the Orkneys to the Pyrenees. So strong an association is established in most

minds between the greatness of a sovereign and the greatness
of the nation which he rules, that almost every historian of
England has expatiated with a sentiment of exultation on the
power and splendour of her foreign masters, and has lamented
the decay of that power and splendour as a calamity to our
country. This is, in truth, as absurd as it would be in a Haytian
negro of our time to dwell with national pride on the greatness
of Lewis the Fourteenth, and to speak of Blenheim and Ra-
milies with patriotic regret and shame.   The Conqueror and
his descendants to the fourth generation were not Englishmen:
most of them were born in France: they spent the greater part
of their lives in France: their ordinary speech was French:
almost every high office in their gift was filled by a Frenchman:
every acquisition which they made on the Continent estranged
them more and more from the population of our island.   One
of the ablest among them indeed attempted to win the hearts
of his English subjects by espousing an English princess. But,
by many of his barons, this marriage was regarded as a marriage between a white planter and a quadroon girl would now
be regarded in Virginia. In history he is known by the honourable surname of Beauclerc; but, in his own time, his own
countrymen called him by a Saxon nickname, in contemptuous
allusion to his Saxon connection.

Had the Plantagenets, as at one time seemed likely, succeeded in uniting all France under their government, it is probable that England would never have had an independent
existence. Her princes, her lords, her prelates, would have
been men differing in race and language from the artisans and
the tillers of the earth. The revenues of her great proprietors
would have been spent in festivities and diversions on the
banks of the Seine. The noble language of Milton and Burke
would have remained a rustic dialect, without a literature, a
fixed grammar, or a fixed orthography, and would have been
contemptuously abandoned to the use of boors. No man of

English extraction would have risen to eminence, except by becoming in speech and habits a Frenchman.

England owes her escape from such calamities to an event which her historians have generally represented as disastrous. Her interest was so directly opposed to the interest of her rulers that she had no hope but in their errors and misfortunes. The talents and even the virtues of her six first French Kings were a curse to her. The follies and vices of the seventh were her salvation. Had John inherited the great qualities of his father, of Henry Beauclerc, or of the Conqueror, nay, had he even possessed the martial courage of Stephen or of Richard, and had the King of France at the same time been as incapable as all the other successors of Hugh Capet had been, the House of Plantagenet must have risen to unrivalled ascendency in Europe. But, just at this conjuncture, France, for the first time since the death of Charlemagne, was governed by a prince of great firmness and ability. On the other hand England which, since the battle of Hastings, had been ruled generally by wise statesmen, always by brave soldiers, fell under the dominion of a trifler and a coward. From that moment her prospects brightened. John was driven from Normandy. The Norman nobles were compelled to make their election between the island and the continent. Shut up by the sea with the people whom they had hitherto oppressed and despised, they gradually came to regard England as their country, and the English as their countrymen. The two races so long hostile, soon found that they had common interests and common enemies. Both were alike aggrieved by the tyranny of a bad king. Both were alike indignant at the favour shown by the court to the natives of Poitou and Aquitaine. The great grandsons of those who had fought under William and the great grandsons of those who had fought under Harold began to draw near to each other in friendship; and the first pledge of their reconciliation was the Great Charter, won

CHAP.
I.

Amal-
gamation
of races.

by their united exertions, and framed for their common benefit.

Here commences the history of the English nation. The history of the preceding events is the history of wrongs inflicted and sustained by various tribes, which indeed all dwelt on English ground, but which regarded each other with aversion such as has scarcely ever existed between communities separated by physical barriers. For even the mutual animosity of countries at war with each other is languid when compared with the animosity of nations which, morally separated, are yet locally intermingled. In no country has the enmity of race been carried farther than in England. In no country has that enmity been more completely effaced. The stages of the process by which the hostile elements were melted down into one homogeneous mass are not accurately known to us. But it is certain that, when John became King, the distinction between Saxons and Normans was strongly marked, and that before the end of the reign of his grandson it had almost disappeared. In the time of Richard the First, the ordinary imprecation of a Norman gentleman was "May I become an Englishman!" His ordinary form of indignant denial was "Do you take me for an Englishman?" The descendant of such a gentleman a hundred years later was proud of the English name.

The sources of the noblest rivers which spread fertility over continents, and bear richly laden fleets to the sea, are to be sought in wild and barren mountain tracts, incorrectly laid down in maps, and rarely explored by travellers. To such a tract the history of our country during the thirteenth century may not unaptly be compared. Sterile and obscure as is that portion of our annals, it is there that we must seek for the origin of our freedom, our prosperity, and our glory. Then it was that the great English people was formed, that the national character began to exhibit those peculiarities which it has ever since retained, and that our fathers became

emphatically islanders, islanders not merely in geographical CHAP.
position, but in their politics, their feelings, and their man- I.
ners. Then first appeared with distinctness that constitution
which has ever since, through all changes, preserved its iden-
tity; that constitution of which all the other free constitutions
in the world are copies, and which, in spite of some defects,
deserves to be regarded as the best under which any great society has ever yet existed during many ages. Then it was
that the House of Commons, the archetype of all the representative assemblies which now meet, either in the old or in
the new world, held its first sittings. Then it was that the
common law rose to the dignity of a science, and rapidly became a not unworthy rival of the imperial jurisprudence.
Then it was that the courage of those sailors who manned the
rude barks of the Cinque Ports first made the flag of England
terrible on the seas. Then it was that the most ancient colleges which still exist at both the great national seats of learning were founded. Then was formed that language, less
musical indeed than the languages of the south, but in force,
in richness, in aptitude for all the highest purposes of the
poet, the philosopher, and the orator, inferior to the tongue
of Greece alone. Then too appeared the first faint dawn of
that noble literature, the most splendid and the most durable
of the many glories of England.

Early in the fourteenth century the amalgamation of the
races was all but complete; and it was soon made manifest,
by signs not to be mistaken, that a people inferior to none
existing in the world had been formed by the mixture of three
branches of the great Teutonic family with each other, and
with the aboriginal Britons. There was, indeed, scarcely
any thing in common between the England to which John had
been chased by Philip Augustus, and the England from which
the armies of Edward the Third went forth to conquer
France.

CHAP.
I.

English
conquests
on the
Conti-
nent.

A period of more than a hundred years followed, during which the chief object of the English was to establish, by force of arms, a great empire on the Continent. The claim of Edward to the inheritance occupied by the House of Valois was a claim in which it might seem that his subjects were little interested. But the passion for conquest spread fast from the prince to the people. The war differed widely from the wars which the Plantagenets of the twelfth century had waged against the descendants of Hugh Capet. For the success of Henry the Second, or of Richard the First, would have made England a province of France. The effect of the successes of Edward the Third and of Henry the Fifth was to make France, for a time, a province of England. The disdain with which, in the twelfth century, the conquerors from the Continent had regarded the islanders, was now retorted by the islanders on the people of the Continent. Every yeoman from Kent to Northumberland valued himself as one of a race born for victory and dominion, and looked down with scorn on the nation before which his ancestors had trembled. Even those knights of Gascony and Guienne who had fought gallantly under the Black Prince were regarded by the English as men of an inferior breed, and were contemptuously excluded from honourable and lucrative commands. In no long time our ancestors altogether lost sight of the original ground of quarrel. They began to consider the crown of France as a mere appendage to the crown of England; and when, in violation of the ordinary law of succession, they transferred the crown of England to the House of Lancaster, they seem to have thought that the right of Richard the Second to the crown of France passed, as of course, to that house. The zeal and vigour which they displayed present a remarkable contrast to the torpor of the French, who were far more deeply interested in the event of the struggle. The greatest victories recorded in the history of the middle ages were gained at this time, against

great odds, by the English armies. Victories indeed they CHAP.
were of which a nation may justly be proud; for they are to be ——I.——
attributed to the moral superiority of the victors, a superiority which was most striking in the lowest ranks. The knights
of England found worthy rivals in the knights of France.
Chandos encountered an equal foe in Du Guesclin. But
France had no infantry that dared to face the English bows
and bills. A French King was brought prisoner to London.
An English King was crowned at Paris. The banner of Saint
George was carried far beyond the Pyrenees and the Alps. On
the south of the Ebro the English won a great battle, which
for a time decided the fate of Leon and Castile; and the English Companies obtained a terrible preeminence among the
bands of warriors who let out their weapons for hire to the
princes and commonwealths of Italy.

Nor were the arts of peace neglected by our fathers during
that stirring period. While France was wasted by war, till
she at length found in her own desolation a miserable defence
against invaders, the English gathered in their harvests,
adorned their cities, pleaded, traded, and studied in security.
Many of our noblest architectural monuments belong to that
age. Then rose the fair chapels of New College and of Saint
George, the nave of Winchester and the choir of York, the
spire of Salisbury and the majestic towers of Lincoln. A copious and forcible language, formed by an infusion of French
into German, was now the common property of the aristocracy
and of the people. Nor was it long before genius began to
apply that admirable machine to worthy purposes. While
English battalions, leaving behind them the devastated provinces of France, entered Valladolid in triumph, and spread
terror to the gates of Florence, English poets depicted in
vivid tints all the wide variety of human manners and fortunes,
and English thinkers aspired to know, or dared to doubt,
where bigots had been content to wonder and to believe. The

same age which produced the Black Prince and Derby, Chandos and Hawkwood, produced also Geoffrey Chaucer and John Wycliffe.

In so splendid and imperial a manner did the English people, properly so called, first take place among the nations of the world. Yet while we contemplate with pleasure the high and commanding qualities which our forefathers displayed, we cannot but admit that the end which they pursued was an end condemned both by humanity and by enlightened policy, and that the reverses which compelled them, after a long and bloody struggle, to relinquish the hope of establishing a great continental empire, were really blessings in the guise of disasters. The spirit of the French was at last aroused: they began to oppose a vigorous national resistance to the foreign conquerors; and from that time the skill of the English captains and the courage of the English soldiers were, happily for mankind, exerted in vain. After many desperate struggles, and with many bitter regrets, our ancestors gave up the contest. Since that age no British government has ever seriously and steadily pursued the design of making great conquests on the Continent. The people, indeed, continued to cherish with pride the recollection of Cressy, of Poitiers, and of Agincourt. Even after the lapse of many years it was easy to fire their blood and to draw forth their subsidies by promising them an expedition for the conquest of France. But happily the energies of our country have been directed to better objects; and she now occupies in the history of mankind a place far more glorious than if she had, as at one time seemed not improbable, acquired by the sword an ascendency similar to that which formerly belonged to the Roman republic.

Wars of theRoses.
Cooped up once more within the limits of the island, the warlike people employed in civil strife those arms which had been the terror of Europe. The means of profuse expendi-

ture had long been drawn by the English barons from the ^{CHAP.} oppressed provinces of France. That source of supply was _{I.} gone; but the ostentatious and luxurious habits which prosperity had engendered still remained; and the great lords, unable to gratify their tastes by plundering the French, were eager to plunder each other. The realm to which they were now confined would not, in the phrase of Comines, the most judicious observer of that time, suffice for them all. Two aristocratical factions, headed by two branches of the royal family, engaged in a long and fierce struggle for supremacy. As the animosity of those factions did not really arise from the dispute about the succession, it lasted long after all ground of dispute about the succession was removed. The party of the Red Rose survived the last prince who claimed the crown in right of Henry the Fourth. The party of the White Rose survived the marriage of Richmond and Elizabeth. Left without chiefs who had any decent show of right, the adherents of Lancaster rallied round a line of bastards, and the adherents of York set up a succession of impostors. When, at length, many aspiring nobles had perished on the field of battle or by the hands of the executioner, when many illustrious houses had disappeared for ever from history, when those great families which remained had been exhausted and sobered by calamities, it was universally acknowledged that the claims of all the contending Plantagenets were united in the house of Tudor.

Meanwhile a change was proceeding infinitely more momentous than the acquisition or loss of any province, than the rise or fall of any dynasty. Slavery and the evils by which slavery is everywhere accompanied were fast disappearing.

It is remarkable that the two greatest and most salutary social revolutions which have taken place in England, that revolution which, in the thirteenth century, put an end to the tyranny of nation over nation, and that revolution which, a few generations later, put an end to the property of man in man, were silently and imperceptibly effected. They struck contemporary observers with no surprise, and have received from historians a very scanty measure of attention. They were brought about neither by legislative regulation nor by physical force. Moral causes noiselessly effaced first the distinction between Norman and Saxon, and then the distinction between master and slave. None can venture to fix the precise moment at which either distinction ceased. Some faint traces of the old Norman feeling might perhaps have been found late in the fourteenth century. Some faint traces of the institution of villenage were detected by the curious so late as the days of the Stuarts; nor has that institution ever, to this hour, been abolished by statute.

Beneficial operation of the Roman Catholic religion. It would be most unjust not to acknowledge that the chief agent in these two great deliverances was religion; and it may perhaps be doubted whether a purer religion might not have been found a less efficient agent. The benevolent spirit of the Christian morality is undoubtedly adverse to distinctions of caste. But to the Church of Rome such distinctions are peculiarly odious; for they are incompatible with other distinctions which are essential to her system. She ascribes to every priest a mysterious dignity which entitles him to the reverence of every layman; and she does not consider any man as disqualified, by reason of his nation or of his family, for the priesthood. Her doctrines respecting the sacerdotal character, however erroneous they may be, have repeatedly mitigated some of the worst evils which can afflict society. That superstition cannot be regarded as unmixedly noxious which, in regions cursed by the tyranny of race over race, creates an aristocracy altogether independent of race, inverts the relation between the oppressor and the oppressed, and compels the hereditary master to kneel before the spiritual

tribunal of the hereditary bondman. To this day, in some
countries where negro slavery exists, Popery appears in advantageous contrast to other forms of Christianity. It is
notorious that the antipathy between the European and
African races is by no means so strong at Rio Janeiro as at
Washington. In our own country this peculiarity of the
Roman Catholic system produced, during the middle ages,
many salutary effects. It is true that, shortly after the battle
of Hastings, Saxon prelates and abbots were violently deposed, and that ecclesiastical adventurers from the Continent
were intruded by hundreds into lucrative benefices. Yet
even then pious divines of Norman blood raised their voices
against such a violation of the constitution of the Church,
refused to accept mitres from the hands of the Conqueror,
and charged him, on the peril of his soul, not to forget that
the vanquished islanders were his fellow Christians. The
first protector whom the English found among the dominant
caste was Archbishop Anselm. At a time when the English
name was a reproach, and when all the civil and military
dignities of the kingdom were supposed to belong exclusively
to the countrymen of the Conqueror, the despised race
learned, with transports of delight, that one of themselves,
Nicholas Breakspear, had been elevated to the papal throne,
and had held out his foot to be kissed by ambassadors sprung
from the noblest houses of Normandy. It was a national as
well as a religious feeling that drew great multitudes to the
shrine of Becket, the first Englishman who, since the Conquest, had been terrible to the foreign tyrants. A successor
of Becket was foremost among those who obtained that
charter which secured at once the privileges of the Norman
barons and of the Saxon yeomanry. How great a part the
Roman Catholic ecclesiastics subsequently had in the abolition of villenage we learn from the unexceptionable testimony
of Sir Thomas Smith, one of the ablest Protestant counsellors

of Elizabeth. When the dying slaveholder asked for the last sacraments, his spiritual attendants regularly adjured him, as he loved his soul, to emancipate his brethren for whom Christ had died. So successfully had the Church used her formidable machinery that, before the Reformation came, she had enfranchised almost all the bondmen in the kingdom except her own, who, to do her justice, seem to have been very tenderly treated.

There can be no doubt, that, when these two great revolutions had been effected, our forefathers were by far the best governed people in Europe. During three hundred years the social system had been in a constant course of improvement. Under the first Plantagenets there had been barons able to bid defiance to the sovereign, and peasants degraded to the level of the swine and oxen which they tended. The exorbitant power of the baron had been gradually reduced. The condition of the peasant had been gradually elevated. Between the aristocracy and the working people had sprung up a middle class, agricultural and commercial. There was still, it may be, more inequality than is favourable to the happiness and virtue of our species: but no man was altogether above the restraints of law; and no man was altogether below its protection.

That the political institutions of England were, at this early period, regarded by the English with pride and affection, and by the most enlightened men of neighbouring nations with admiration and envy, is proved by the clearest evidence. But touching the nature of those institutions, there has been much dishonest and acrimonious controversy.

The early
English
polity
often
misre-
present-
ed. The historical literature of England has indeed suffered grievously from a circumstance which has not a little contributed to her prosperity. The change, great as it is, which her polity has undergone during the last six centuries, has been the effect of gradual development, not of demolition and

reconstruction. ⁊ The present constitution of our country is, to the constitution under which she flourished five hundred years ago, what the tree is to the sapling, what the man is to the boy. The alteration has been great. Yet there never was a moment at which the chief part of what existed was not old. A polity thus formed must abound in anomalies. But for the evils arising from mere anomalies we have ample compensation. Other societies possess written constitutions more symmetrical. But no other society has yet succeeded in uniting revolution with prescription, progress with stability, the energy of youth with the majesty of immemorial antiquity.

This great blessing, however, has its drawbacks: and one of those drawbacks is, that every source of information as to our early history has been poisoned by party spirit. As there is no country where statesmen have been so much under the influence of the past, so there is no country where historians have been so much under the influence of the present. Between these two things, indeed, there is a natural connection. Where history is regarded merely as a picture of life and manners, or as a collection of experiments from which general maxims of civil wisdom may be drawn, a writer lies under no very pressing temptation to misrepresent transactions of ancient date. But where history is regarded as a repository of title-deeds, on which the rights of governments and nations depend, the motive to falsification becomes almost irresistible. A Frenchman is not now impelled by any strong interest either to exaggerate or to underrate the power of the kings of the house of Valois. The privileges of the States General, of the States of Britanny, of the States of Burgundy, are now matters of as little practical importance as the constitution of the Jewish Sanhedrim, or of the Amphictyonic Council. The gulph of a great revolution completely separates the new from the old system. No such chasm divides

the existence of the English nation into two distinct parts.
Our laws and customs have never been lost in general and
irreparable ruin. With us the precedents of the middle ages
are still valid precedents, and are still cited, on the gravest
occasions, by the most eminent statesmen. Thus, when
King George the Third was attacked by the malady which
made him incapable of performing his regal functions, and
when the most distinguished lawyers and politicians differed
widely as to the course which ought, in such circumstances,
to be pursued, the Houses of Parliament would not proceed
to discuss any plan of regency till all the examples which were
to be found in our annals, from the earliest times, had been
collected and arranged. Committees were appointed to examine the ancient records of the realm. The first precedent
reported was that of the year 1217: much importance was
attached to the precedents of 1326, of 1377, and of 1422: but
the case which was justly considered as most in point was that
of 1455. Thus in our country the dearest interests of parties
have frequently been staked on the results of the researches
of antiquaries. The inevitable consequence was, that our
antiquaries conducted their researches in the spirit of par-
tisans.

It is therefore not surprising that those who have written
concerning the limits of prerogative and liberty in the old
polity of England should generally have shown the temper, not
of judges, but of angry and uncandid advocates. For they
were discussing, not a speculative matter, but a matter which
had a direct and practical connection with the most momentous and exciting disputes of their own day. From the commencement of the long contest between the Parliament and the
Stuarts down to the time when the pretensions of the Stuarts
ceased to be formidable, few questions were practically more
important than the question whether the administration of that
family had or had not been in accordance with the ancient

constitution of the kingdom. This question could be decided only by reference to the records of preceding reigns. Bracton and Fleta, the Mirror of Justice and the Rolls of Parliament, were ransacked to find pretexts for the excesses of the Star Chamber on one side, and of the High Court of Justice on the other. During a long course of years every Whig historian was anxious to prove that the old English government was all but republican, every Tory historian to prove that it was all but despotic.

With such feelings, both parties looked into the chronicles of the middle ages. Both readily found what they sought; and both obstinately refused to see anything but what they sought. The champions of the Stuarts could easily point out instances of oppression exercised on the subject. The defenders of the Round-heads could as easily produce instances of determined and successful resistance offered to the Crown. The Tories quoted, from ancient writings, expressions almost as servile as were heard from the pulpit of Mainwaring. The Whigs discovered expressions as bold and severe as any that resounded from the judgment seat of Bradshaw. One set of writers adduced numerous instances in which Kings had extorted money without the authority of Parliament. Another set cited cases in which the Parliament had assumed to itself the power of inflicting punishment on Kings. Those who saw only one half of the evidence would have concluded that the Plantagenets were as absolute as the Sultans of Turkey: those who saw only the other half would have concluded that the Plantagenets had as little real power as the Doges of Venice; and both conclusions would have been equally remote from the truth.

The old English government was one of a class of limited monarchies which sprang up in Western Europe during the middle ages, and which, notwithstanding many diversities, bore to one another a strong family likeness. That there should have been such a likeness is not strange. The countries in

which those monarchies arose had been provinces of the same
great civilised empire, and had been overrun and conquered,
about the same time, by tribes of the same rude and warlike
nation. They were members of the same great coalition against
Islam. They were in communion with the same superb and
ambitious Church. Their polity naturally took the same form.
They had institutions derived partly from imperial Rome,
partly from papal Rome, partly from the old Germany. All
had Kings; and in all the kingly office became by degrees
strictly hereditary. All had nobles bearing titles which had
originally indicated military rank. The dignity of knighthood,
the rules of heraldry, were common to all. All had richly
endowed ecclesiastical establishments, municipal corporations
enjoying large franchises, and senates whose consent was necessary to the validity of some public acts.

Preroga-
tives of
the early
English
Kings.
Of these kindred constitutions the English was, from an
early period, justly reputed the best. The prerogatives of the
sovereign were undoubtedly extensive. The spirit of religion,
and the spirit of chivalry, concurred to exalt his dignity. The
sacred oil had been poured on his head. It was no disparagement to the bravest and noblest knights to kneel at his feet.
His person was inviolable. He alone was entitled to convoke
the Estates of the realm: he could at his pleasure dismiss them;
and his assent was necessary to all their legislative acts. He
was the chief of the executive administration, the sole organ of
communication with foreign powers, the captain of the military and naval forces of the state, the fountain of justice, of
mercy, and of honour. He had large powers for the regulation
of trade. It was by him that money was coined, that weights
and measures were fixed, that marts and havens were appointed. His ecclesiastical patronage was immense. His hereditary revenues, economically administered, sufficed to meet
the ordinary charges of government. His own domains were
of vast extent. He was also feudal lord paramount of the whole

soil of his kingdom, and, in that capacity, possessed many CHAP.
lucrative and many formidable rights, which enabled him to ——
annoy and depress those who thwarted him, and to enrich and
aggrandise, without any cost to himself, those who enjoyed his
favour.

But his power, though ample, was limited by three great Limita-
constitutional principles, so ancient that none can say when the pre-
they began to exist, so potent that their natural development, rogative.
continued through many generations, has produced the order
of things under which we now live.

First, the King could not legislate without the consent of
his Parliament. Secondly, he could impose no taxes without
the consent of his Parliament. Thirdly, he was bound to conduct the executive administration according to the laws of the
land, and, if he broke those laws, his advisers and his agents
were responsible.

No candid Tory will deny that these principles had, five
hundred years ago, acquired the authority of fundamental
rules. On the other hand, no candid Whig will affirm that they
were, till a later period, cleared from all ambiguity, or followed
out to all their consequences. A constitution of the middle
ages was not, like a constitution of the eighteenth or nineteenth
century, created entire by a single act, and fully set forth in a
single document. It is only in a refined and speculative age
that a polity is constructed on system. In rude societies the
progress of government resembles the progress of language
and of versification. Rude societies have language, and often
copious and energetic language: but they have no scientific
grammar, no definitions of nouns and verbs, no names for de-
clensions, moods, tenses, and voices. Rude societies have
versification, and often versification of great power and sweet-
ness: but they have no metrical canons; and the minstrel whose
numbers, regulated solely by his ear, are the delight of his
audience, would himself be unable to say of how many dactyls

CHAP. and trochees each of his lines consists. As eloquence exists
  I.
——— before syntax, and song before prosody, so government may
exist in a high degree of excellence long before the limits of
legislative, executive, and judicial power have been traced with
precision.

It was thus in our country. The line which bounded the
royal prerogative, though in general sufficiently clear, had not
everywhere been drawn with accuracy and distinctness. There
was, therefore, near the border some debatable ground on
which incursions and reprisals continued to take place, till,
after ages of strife, plain and durable landmarks were at length
set up. It may be instructive to note in what way, and to what
extent, our ancient sovereigns were in the habit of violating
the three great principles by which the liberties of the nation
were protected.

No English King has ever laid claim to the general legislative power. The most violent and imperious Plantagenet
never fancied himself competent to enact, without the consent
of his great council, that a jury should consist of ten persons
instead of twelve, that a widow's dower should be a fourth
part instead of a third, that perjury should be a felony, or that
the custom of gavelkind should be introduced into Yorkshire.*
But the King had the power of pardoning offenders; and there
is one point at which the power of pardoning and the power of
legislating seem to fade into each other, and may easily, at least
in a simple age, be confounded. A penal statute is virtually
annulled if the penalties which it imposes are regularly re-
mitted as often as they are incurred. The sovereign was undoubtedly competent to remit penalties without limit. He was
therefore competent to annul virtually a penal statute. It might
seem that there could be no serious objection to his doing formally what he might do virtually. Thus, with the help of

* This is excellently put, by Mr. Hallam in the first chapter of his
Constitutional History.

subtle and courtly lawyers, grew up, on the doubtful frontier which separates executive from legislative functions, that great anomaly known as the dispensing power.

That the King could not impose taxes without the consent of Parliament is admitted to have been, from time immemorial, a fundamental law of England. It was among the articles which John was compelled by the Barons to sign. Edward the First ventured to break through the rule: but, able, powerful, and popular as he was, he encountered an opposition to which he found it expedient to yield. He covenanted accordingly in express terms, for himself and his heirs, that they would never again levy any aid without the assent and goodwill of the Estates of the realm. His powerful and victorious grandson attempted to violate this solemn compact: but the attempt was strenuously withstood. At length the Plantagenets gave up the point in despair; but though they ceased to infringe the law openly, they occasionally contrived, by evading it, to procure an extraordinary supply for a temporary purpose. They were interdicted from taxing; but they claimed the right of begging and borrowing. They therefore sometimes begged in a tone not to be distinguished from that of command, and sometimes borrowed with small thought of repaying. But the fact that it was thought necessary to disguise these exactions under the names of benevolences and loans sufficiently proves that the authority of the great constitutional rule was universally recognised.

The principle that the King of England was bound to conduct the administration according to law, and that, if he did anything against law, his advisers and agents were answerable, was established at a very early period, as the severe judgments pronounced and executed on many royal favourites sufficiently prove. It is, however, certain that the rights of individuals were often violated by the Plantagenets, and that the injured parties were often unable to obtain redress. Ac-

CHAP. cording to law no Englishman could be arrested or detained in
  I.
―――― confinement merely by the mandate of the sovereign. In fact,
persons obnoxious to the government were frequently imprisoned without any other authority than a royal order. According to law, torture, the disgrace of the Roman jurisprudence,
could not, in any circumstances, be inflicted on an English
subject. Nevertheless, during the troubles of the fifteenth
century, a rack was introduced into the Tower, and was occasionally used under the plea of political necessity. But it
would be a great error to infer from such irregularities |that
the English monarchs were, either in theory or in practice,
absolute. We live in a highly civilised society, in which intelligence is so rapidly diffused by means of the press and of
the post office, that any gross act of oppression committed in
any part of our island is, in a few hours, discussed by millions.
If the sovereign were now to immure a subject in defiance of
the writ of Habeas Corpus, or to put a conspirator to the torture, the whole nation would be instantly electrified by the
news. In the middle ages the state of society was widely
different. Rarely and with great difficulty did the wrongs of
individuals come to the knowledge of the public. A man
might be illegally confined during many months in the castle
of Carlisle or Norwich; and no whisper of the transaction
might reach London. It is highly probable that the rack had
been many years in use before the great majority of the nation
had the least suspicion that it was ever employed. Nor were
our ancestors by any means so much alive as we are to the importance of maintaining great general rules. We have been
taught by long experience that we cannot without danger
suffer any breach of the constitution to pass unnoticed. It is
therefore now universally held that a government which un-
necessarily exceeds its powers ought to be visited with severe
parliamentary censure, and that a government which, under
the pressure of a great exigency, and with pure intentions, has

exceeded its powers, ought without delay to apply to Parliament for an act of indemnity. But such were not the feelings
of the Englishmen of the fourteenth and fifteenth centuries.
They were little disposed to contend for a principle merely as
a principle, or to cry out against an irregularity which was not
also felt to be a grievance. As long as the general spirit of the
administration was mild and popular, they were willing to
allow some latitude to their sovereign. If, for ends generally
acknowledged to be good, he exerted a vigour beyond the law,
they not only forgave, but applauded him, and, while they
enjoyed security and prosperity under his rule, were but too
ready to believe that whoever had incurred his displeasure
had deserved it. But to this indulgence there was a limit: nor
was that King wise who presumed far on the forbearance of
the English people. They might sometimes allow him to
overstep the constitutional line; but they also claimed the privilege of overstepping that line themselves, whenever his encroachments were so serious as to excite alarm. If, not content with occasionally oppressing individuals, he dared to
oppress great masses, his subjects promptly appealed to the
laws, and, that appeal failing, appealed as promptly to the God
of battles.

They might indeed safely tolerate a King in a few excesses; Resist-
for they had in reserve a check which soon brought the fiercest ance an
and proudest King to reason, the check of physical force. It tyranny in
is difficult for an Englishman of the nineteenth century to the mid-
image to himself the facility and rapidity with which, four dle ages.
hundred years ago, this check was applied. The people have
long unlearned the use of arms. The art of war has been
carried to a perfection unknown to our forefathers, and the
knowledge of that art is confined to a particular class. A hundred thousand troops, well disciplined and commanded, will
keep down millions of ploughmen and artisans. A few regiments of household troops are sufficient to overawe all the dis

contented spirits of a large capital. In the meantime the
effect of the constant progress of wealth has been to make insurrection far more terrible to thinking men than maladministration. Immense sums have been expended on works
which, if a rebellion broke out, might perish in a few hours.
The mass of moveable wealth collected in the shops and warehouses of London alone exceeds fivehundredfold that which
the whole island contained in the days of the Plantagenets;
and, if the government were subverted by physical force,
all this moveable wealth would be exposed to imminent
risk of spoliation and destruction. Still greater would be the
risk to public credit, on which thousands of families directly
depend for subsistence, and with which the credit of the whole
commercial world is inseparably connected. It is no exaggeration to say that a civil war of a week on English ground
would now produce disasters which would be felt from the
Hoangho to the Missouri, and of which the traces would be
discernible at the distance of a century. In such a state of
society resistance must be regarded as a cure more desperate
than almost any malady which can afflict the state. In the
middle ages, on the contrary, resistance was an ordinary remedy for political distempers, a remedy which was always at
hand, and which, though doubtless sharp at the moment, produced no deep or lasting ill effects. If a popular chief raised
his standard in a popular cause, an irregular army could be
assembled in a day. Regular army there was none. Every
man had a slight tincture of soldiership, and scarcely any man
more than a slight tincture. The national wealth consisted
chiefly in flocks and herds, in the harvest of the year, and in
the simple buildings inhabited by the people. All the furniture, the stock of shops, the machinery which could be found
in the realm was of less value than the property which some
single parishes now contain. Manufactures were rude, credit
almost unknown. Society, therefore, recovered from the shock

as soon as the actual conflict was over. The calamities of civil war were confined to the slaughter on the field of battle, and to a few subsequent executions and confiscations. In a week the peasant was driving his team and the esquire flying his hawks over the field of Towton, or of Bosworth, as if no extraordinary event had interrupted the regular course of human life.

A hundred and sixty years have now elapsed since the English people have by force subverted a government. During the hundred and sixty years which preceded the union of the Roses, nine Kings reigned in England. Six of these nine Kings were deposed. Five lost their lives as well as their crowns. It is evident, therefore, that any comparison between our ancient and our modern polity must lead to most erroneous conclusions, unless large allowance be made for the effect of that restraint which resistance and the fear of resistance constantly imposed on the Plantagenets. As our ancestors had against tyranny a most important security which we want, they might safely dispense with some securities to which we justly attach the highest importance. As we cannot, without the risk of evils from which the imagination recoils, employ physical force as a check on misgovernment, it is evidently our wisdom to keep all the constitutional checks on misgovernment in the highest state of efficiency, to watch with jealousy the first beginnings of encroachment, and never to suffer irregularities, even when harmless in themselves, to pass unchallenged, lest they acquire the force of precedents. Four hundred years ago such minute vigilance might seem unnecessary. A nation of hardy archers and spearmen might, with small risk to its liberties, connive at some illegal acts on the part of a prince whose general administration was good, and whose throne was not defended by a single company of regular soldiers.

Under this system, rude as it may appear when compared with those elaborate constitutions of which the last seventy

3*

years have been fruitful, the English long enjoyed a large measure of freedom and happiness. Though during the feeble reign of Henry the Sixth the state was torn first by factions, and at length by civil war, though Edward the Fourth was a prince of dissolute and imperious character, though Richard the Third has generally been represented as a monster of depravity, though the exactions of Henry the Seventh caused great repining, it is certain that our ancestors, under those Kings, were far better governed than the Belgians under Philip, surnamed the Good, or the French under that Lewis who was styled the Father of his people. Even while the wars of the Roses were actually raging, our country appears to have been in a happier condition than the neighbouring realms during years of profound peace. Comines was one of the most enlightened statesmen of his time. He had seen all the richest and most highly civilised parts of the Continent. He had lived in the opulent towns of Flanders, the Manchesters and Liverpools of the fifteenth century. He had visited Florence, recently adorned by the magnificence of Lorenzo, and Venice, not yet humbled by the confederates of Cambray. This eminent man deliberately pronounced England to be the best governed country of which he had any knowledge. Her constitution he emphatically designated as a just and holy thing, which, while it protected the people, really strengthened the hands of a prince who respected it. In no other country, he said, were men so effectually secured from wrong. The calamities produced by our intestine wars seemed to him to be confined to the nobles and the fighting men, and to leave no traces such as he had been accustomed to see elsewhere, no ruined dwellings, no depopulated cities.

Peculiar
character
of the
English
aristo-
cracy. It was not only by the efficiency of the restraints imposed on the royal prerogative that England was advantageously distinguished from most of the neighbouring countries. A

peculiarity equally important, though less noticed, was the
relation in which the nobility stood here to the commonalty.
There was a strong hereditary aristocracy: but it was of all
hereditary aristocracies the least insolent and exclusive. It
had none of the invidious character of a caste. It was constantly receiving members from the people and constantly
sending down members to mingle with the people. Any
gentleman might become a peer. The younger son of a peer
was but a gentleman. Grandsons of peers yielded precedence to newly made knights. The dignity of knighthood
was not beyond the reach of any man who could by diligence
and thrift realise a good estate, or who could attract notice
by his valour in a battle or a siege. It was regarded as no
disparagement for the daughter of a Duke, nay of a royal
Duke, to espouse a distinguished commoner. Thus, Sir
John Howard married the daughter of Thomas Mowbray
Duke of Norfolk. Sir Richard Pole married the Countess
of Salisbury, daughter of George Duke of Clarence. Good
blood was indeed held in high respect: but between good
blood and the privileges of peerage there was, most fortunately for our country, no necessary connection. Pedigrees
as long, and scutcheons as old, were to be found out of the
House of Lords as in it. There were new men who bore
the highest titles. There were untitled men well known to
be descended from knights who had broken the Saxon ranks
at Hastings, and scaled the walls of Jerusalem. There were
Bohuns, Mowbrays, De Veres, nay kinsmen of the House of
Plantagenet, with no higher addition than that of esquire,
and with no civil privileges beyond those enjoyed by every
farmer and shopkeeper. There was therefore here no line
like that which in some other countries divided the patrician
from the plebeian. The yeoman was not inclined to murmur at dignities to which his own children might rise. The

grandee was not inclined to insult a class into which his own children must descend.

After the wars of York and Lancaster, the links which connected the nobility and the commonalty became closer and more numerous than ever. The extent of the destruction which had fallen on the old aristocracy may be inferred from a single circumstance. In the year 1451 Henry the Sixth summoned fifty-three temporal Lords to parliament. The temporal Lords summoned by Henry the Seventh to the parliament of 1485 were only twenty-nine, and of these twenty-nine several had recently been elevated to the peerage. During the following century the ranks of the nobility were largely recruited from among the gentry. The constitution of the House of Commons tended greatly to promote the salutary intermixture of classes. The knight of the shire was the connecting link between the baron and the shopkeeper. On the same benches on which sate the goldsmiths, drapers, and grocers who had been returned to parliament by the commercial towns, sate also members who, in any other country, would have been called noblemen, hereditary lords of manors, entitled to hold courts and to bear coat armour, and able to trace back an honourable descent through many generations. Some of them were younger sons and brothers of great lords. Others could boast even of royal blood. At length the eldest son of an Earl of Bedford, called in courtesy by the second title of his father, offered himself as candidate for a seat in the House of Commons, and his example was followed by others. Seated in that house, the heirs of the grandees of the realm naturally became as zealous for its privileges as any of the humble burgesses with whom they were mingled. Thus our democracy was, from an early period, the most aristocratic, and our aristocracy the most democratic in the world; a peculiarity which has lasted down

to the present day, and which has produced many important
moral and political effects.

The government of Henry the Seventh, of his son, and of his grandchildren was, on the whole, more arbitrary than that of the Plantagenets. Personal character may in some degree explain the difference; for courage and force of will were common to all the men and women of the House of Tudor. They exercised their power during a period of a hundred and twenty years, always with vigour, often with violence, sometimes with cruelty. They, in imitation of the dynasty which had preceded them, occasionally invaded the rights of the subject, occasionally exacted taxes under the name of loans and gifts, and occasionally dispensed with penal statutes; nay, though they never presumed to enact any permanent law by their own authority, they occasionally took upon themselves, when Parliament was not sitting, to meet temporary exigencies by temporary edicts. It was, however, impossible for the Tudors to carry oppression beyond a certain point: for they had no armed force, and they were surrounded by an armed people. The palace was guarded by a few domestics whom the array of a single shire, or of a single ward of London, could with ease have overpowered. These haughty princes were therefore under a restraint stronger than any which mere laws can impose, under a restraint which did not, indeed, prevent them from sometimes treating an individual in an arbitrary and even in a barbarous manner, but which effectually secured the nation against general and long continued oppression. They might safely be tyrants within the precinct of the court: but it was necessary for them to watch with constant anxiety the temper of the country. Henry the Eighth, for example, encountered no opposition when he wished to send Buckingham and Surrey, Anne Boleyn and Lady Salisbury, to the scaffold. But when, without the consent of Parliament, he demanded of his subjects a contribution amounting to one sixth of their goods, he soon found it necessary to retract. The cry of hundreds of thousands was that they were English and not French, freemen and not slaves. In Kent the royal commissioners fled for their lives. In Suffolk four thousand men appeared in arms. The King's lieutenants in that county vainly exerted themselves to raise an army. Those who did not join in the insurrection declared that they would not fight against their brethren in such a quarrel. Henry, proud and self-willed as he was, shrank, not without reason, from a conflict with the roused spirit of the nation. He had before his eyes the fate of his predecessors who had perished at Berkeley and Pomfret. He not only cancelled his illegal commissions; he not only granted a general pardon to all the malecontents; but he publicly and solemnly apologized for his infraction of the laws.

His conduct, on this occasion, well illustrates the whole policy of his house. The temper of the princes of that line was hot, and their spirit high: but they understood the character of the nation which they governed, and never once, like some of their predecessors, and some of their successors, carried obstinacy to a fatal point. The discretion of the Tudors was such, that their power, though it was often resisted, was never subverted. The reign of every one of them was disturbed by formidable discontents: but the government never failed either to sooth the mutineers, or to conquer and punish them. Sometimes, by timely concessions, it succeeded in averting civil hostilities; but in general it stood firm, and called for help on the nation. The nation obeyed the call, rallied round the sovereign, and enabled him to quell the disaffected minority.

Thus, from the age of Henry the Third to the age of Elizabeth, England grew and flourished under a polity which contained the germ of our present institutions, and which, though not very exactly defined, or very exactly observed,

was yet effectually prevented from degenerating into despotism, by the awe in which the governors stood of the spirit and
strength of the governed.

But such a polity is suited only to a particular stage in the
progress of society. The same causes which produce a division of labour in the peaceful arts must at length make war a
distinct science and a distinct trade. A time arrives when the
use of arms begins to occupy the entire attention of a separate
class. It soon appears that peasants and burghers, however
brave, are unable to stand their ground against veteran soldiers, whose whole life is a preparation for the day of battle,
whose nerves have been braced [by long familiarity with danger, and whose movements have all the precision of clock-
work. It is felt that the defence of nations can no longer be
safely entrusted to warriors taken from the plough or the loom
for a campaign of forty days. If any state forms a great
regular army, the bordering states must imitate the example,
or must submit to a foreign yoke. But, where a great regular
army exists, limited monarchy, such as it was in the middle
ages, can exist no longer. The sovereign is at once emancipated from what had been the chief restraint on his power;
and he inevitably becomes absolute, unless he is subjected to
checks such as would be superfluous in a society where all are
soldiers occasionally, and none permanently.

With the danger came also the means of escape. In the Limited
monar-
monarchies of the middle ages the power of the sword be- chies of
the mid-
longed to the prince, but the power of the purse belonged to dle ages
the nation; and the progress of civilisation, as it made the generally
turned
sword of the prince more and more formidable to the nation, into absolute
made the purse of the nation more and more necessary to the monarchies.
prince. His hereditary revenues would no longer suffice,
even for the expenses of civil government. It was utterly
impossible that, without a regular and extensive system of
taxation, he could keep in constant efficiency a great body of

CHAP.
I.

disciplined troops. The policy which the parliamentary assemblies of Europe ought to have adopted was to take their stand firmly on their constitutional right to give or withhold money, and resolutely to refuse funds for the support of armies, till ample securities had been provided against despotism.

This wise policy was followed in our country alone. In the neighbouring kingdoms great military establishments were formed; no new safeguards for public liberty were devised; and the consequence was, that the old parliamentary institutions everywhere ceased to exist. In France, where they had always been feeble, they languished, and at length died of mere weakness. In Spain, where they had been as strong as in any part of Europe, they struggled fiercely for life, but struggled too late. The mechanics of Toledo and Valladolid vainly defended the privileges of the Castilian Cortes against the veteran battalions of Charles the Fifth. As vainly, in the next generation, did the citizens of Saragossa stand up against Philip the Second, for the old constitution of Aragon. One after another, the great national councils of the continental monarchies, councils once scarcely less proud and powerful than those which sate at Westminster, sank into utter insignificance. If they met, they met merely as our Convocation now meets, to go through some venerable forms.

The English monarchy a singular exception.

In England events took a different course. This singular felicity she owed chiefly to her insular situation. Before the end of the fifteenth century great military establishments were indispensable to the dignity, and even to the safety, of the French and Spanish monarchies. If either of those two powers had disarmed, it would soon have been compelled to submit to the dictation of the other. But England, protected by the sea against invasion, and rarely engaged in warlike operations on the Continent, was not, as yet, under the ne-

cessity of employing regular troops. The sixteenth century,
the seventeenth century, found her still without a standing
army. At the commencement of the seventeenth century
political science had made considerable progress. The fate
of the Spanish Cortes and of the French States General, had
given solemn warning to our Parliaments; and our Parliaments, fully aware of the nature and magnitude of the danger,
adopted, in good time, a system of tactics which, after a
contest protracted through three generations, was at length
successful.

Almost every writer who has treated of that contest has
been desirous to show that his own party was the party which
was struggling to preserve the old constitution unaltered.
The truth however is that the old constitution could not be
preserved unaltered. A law, beyond the control of human
wisdom, had decreed that there should no longer be governments of that peculiar class which, in the fourteenth and
fifteenth centuries, had been common throughout Europe.
The question, therefore, was not whether our polity should
undergo a change, but what the nature of the change should
be. The introduction of a new and mighty force had disturbed the old equilibrium, and had turned one limited monarchy after another into an absolute monarchy. What had
happened elsewhere would assuredly have happened here,
unless the balance had been redressed by a great transfer of
power from the crown to the parliament. Our princes were
about to have at their command means of coercion such as no
Plantagenet or Tudor had ever possessed. They must inevitably have become despots, unless they had been, at the same
time, placed under restraints to which no Plantagenet or
Tudor had ever been subject.

It seems certain, therefore, that, had none but political
causes been at work, the seventeenth century would not have
passed away without a fierce conflict between our Kings and

their Parliaments. But other causes of perhaps greater potency contributed to produce the same effect.   While the government of the Tudors was in its highest vigour took place an
event which has coloured the destinies of all Christian nations,
and in an especial manner the destinies of England.   Twice
durig the middle ages the mind of Europe had risen up against
the domination of Rome.   The first insurrection broke out in
the south of France.   The energy of Innocent the Third, the
zeal of the young orders of Francis and Dominic, and the
ferocity of the Crusaders whom the priesthood let loose on an
unwarlike population, crushed the Albigensian churches.
The second reformation had its origin in England and spread
to Bohemia.   The Council of Constance, by removing some
ecclesiastical disorders which had given scandal to Christendom, and the princes of Europe, by unsparingly using fire
and sword against the heretics, succeeded in arresting and
turning back the movement.   Nor is this much to be regretted. ·
The sympathies of a Protestant, it is true, will naturally be
on the side of the Albigensians and of the Lollards.   Yet an
enlightened and temperate Protestant will perhaps be disposed to doubt whether the success, either of the Albigensians or of the Lollards, would, on the whole, have promoted
the happiness and virtue of mankind.   Corrupt as the Church
of Rome was, there is reason to believe that, if that Church
had been overthrown in the twelfth or even in the fourteenth
century, the vacant space would have been occupied by some
system more corrupt still.   There was then, through the
greater part of Europe, very little knowledge, and that little
was confined to the clergy.   Not one man in five hundred
could have spelled his way through a psalm.   Books were few
and costly.   The art of printing was unknown.   Copies of the
Bible, inferior in beauty and clearness to those which every
cottager may now command, sold for prices which many
priests could not afford to give.   It was obviously impossible

that the laity should search the Scriptures for themselves. It is probable therefore, that, as soon as they had put off one spiritual yoke, they would have put on another, and that the power lately exercised by the clergy of the Church of Rome would have passed to a far worse class of teachers. The sixteenth century was comparatively a time of light. Yet even in the sixteenth century a considerable number of those who quitted the old religion followed the first confident and plausible guide who offered himself, and were soon led into errors far more serious than those which they had renounced. Thus Matthias and Kniperdoling, apostles of lust, robbery, and murder, were able for a time to rule great cities. In a darker age such false prophets might have founded empires; and Christianity might have been distorted into a cruel and licentious superstition, more noxious, not only than Popery, but even than Islamism.

About a hundred years after the rising of the Council of Constance, that great change emphatically called the Reformation began. The fulness of time was now come. The clergy were no longer the sole or the chief depositories of knowledge. The invention of printing had furnished the 'assailants of the Church with a mighty weapon which had been wanting to their predecessors. The study of the ancient writers, the rapid development of the powers of the modern languages, the unprecedented activity which was displayed in every department of literature, the political state of Europe, the vices of the Roman court, the exactions of the Roman chancery, the jealousy with which the wealth and privileges of the clergy were naturally regarded by laymen, the jealousy with which the Italian ascendency was naturally regarded by men born on our side of the Alps, all these things gave to the teachers of the new theology an advantage which they perfectly understood how to use.

Those who hold that the influence of the Church of Rome

CHAP.
I.

in the dark ages was, on the whole, beneficial to mankind may yet with perfect consistency regard the Reformation as an inestimable blessing. The leading strings, which preserve and uphold the infant, would impede the full grown man. And so the very means by which the human mind is, in one stage of its progress, supported and propelled, may, in another stage, be mere hindrances. There is a point in the life both of an individual and of a society, at which submission and faith, such as at a later period would be justly called servility and credulity, are useful qualities. The child who teachably and undoubtingly listens to the instructions of his elders is likely to improve rapidly. But the man who should receive with childlike docility every assertion and dogma uttered by another man no wiser than himself would become contemptible. It is the same with communities. The childhood of the European nations was passed under the tutelage of the clergy. The ascendency of the sacerdotal order was long the ascendency which naturally and properly belongs to intellectual superiority. The priests, with all their faults, were by far the wisest portion of society. It was, therefore, on the whole, good that they should be respected and obeyed. The encroachments of the ecclesiastical power on the province of the civil power produced much more happiness than misery, while the ecclesiastical power was in the hands of the only class that had studied history, philosophy, and public law, and while the civil power was in the hands of savage chiefs, who could not read their own grants and edicts. But a change took place. Knowledge gradually spread among laymen. At the commencement of the sixteenth century many of them were in every intellectual attainment fully equal to the most enlightened of their spiritual pastors. Thenceforward that dominion, which, during the dark ages, had been, in spite of many abuses, a legitimate and a salutary guardianship, became an unjust and noxious tyranny.

From the time when the barbarians overran the Western
Empire to the time of the revival of letters, the influence of
the Church of Rome had been generally favourable to science,
to civilisation, and to good government. But during the last
three centuries, to stunt the growth of the human mind has
been her chief object. Throughout Christendom, whatever
advance has been made in knowledge, in freedom, in wealth,
and in the arts of life, has been made in spite of her, and has
everywhere been in inverse proportion to her power. The
loveliest and most fertile provinces of Europe have, under
her rule, been sunk in poverty, in political servitude, and in
intellectual torpor, while Protestant countries, once proverbial for sterility and barbarism, have been turned by skill and
industry into gardens, and can boast of a long list of heroes
and statesmen, philosophers and poets. Whoever, knowing
what Italy and Scotland naturally are, and what, four hundred years ago, they actually were, shall now compare the
country round Rome with the country round Edinburgh, will
be able to form some judgment as to the tendency of Papal
domination. The descent of Spain, once the first among
monarchies, to the lowest depths of degradation, the elevation of Holland, in spite of many natural disadvantages, to a
position such as no commonwealth so small has ever reached,
teach the same lesson. Whoever passes in Germany from a
Roman Catholic to a Protestant principality, in Switzerland
from a Roman Catholic to a Protestant canton, in Ireland
from a Roman Catholic to a Protestant county, finds that he
has passed from a lower to a higher grade of civilisation. On
the other side of the Atlantic the same law prevails. The
Protestants of the United States have left far behind them the
Roman Catholics of Mexico, Peru, and Brazil. The Roman
Catholics of Lower Canada remain inert, while the whole
continent round them is in a ferment with Protestant activity
and enterprise. The French have doubtless shown an energy

and an intelligence which, even when misdirected, have justly
entitled them to be called a great people. But this apparent
exception, when examined, will be found to confirm the rule;
for in no country that is called Roman Catholic has the Roman
Catholic Church, during several generations, possessed so
little authority as in France.

It is difficult to say whether England owes more to the
Roman Catholic religion or to the Reformation. For the
amalgamation of races and for the abolition of villenage, she
is chiefly indebted to the influence which the priesthood in the
middle ages exercised over the laity. For political and intellectual freedom, and for all the blessings which political and
intellectual freedom have brought in their train, she is chiefly
indebted to the great rebellion of the laity against the priesthood.

The struggle between the old and the new theology in our
country was long, and the event sometimes seemed doubtful. There were two extreme parties, prepared to act with
violence or to suffer with stubborn resolution. Between them
lay, during a considerable time, a middle party, which
blended, very illogically, but by no means unnaturally,
lessons learned in the nursery with the sermons of the modern
evangelists, and, while clinging with fondness to old observances, yet detested abuses with which those observances
were closely connected. Men in such a frame of mind were
willing to obey, almost with thankfulness, the dictation of
an able ruler who spared them the trouble of judging for
themselves, and, raising a firm and commanding voice above
the uproar of controversy, told them how to worship and
what to believe. It is not strange, therefore, that the Tudors
should have been able to exercise a great influence on ecclesiastical affairs; nor is it strange that their influence should,
for the most part, have been exercised with a view to their
own interest.

Henry the Eighth attempted to constitute an Anglican Church differing from the Roman Catholic Church on the point of the supremacy, and on that point alone. His success in this attempt was extraordinary. The force of his character, the singularly favourable situation in which he stood with respect to foreign powers, the immense wealth which the spoliation of the abbeys placed at his disposal, and the support of that class which still halted between two opinions, enabled him to bid defiance to both the extreme parties, to burn as heretics those who avowed the tenets of the Reformers, and to hang as traitors those who owned the authority of the Pope. But Henry's system died with him. Had his life been prolonged, he would have found it difficult to maintain a position assailed with equal fury by all who were zealous either for the new or for the old opinions. The ministers who held the royal prerogatives in trust for his infant son could not venture to persist in so hazardous a policy; nor could Elizabeth venture to return to it. It was necessary to make a choice. The government must either submit to Rome, or must obtain the aid of the Protestants. The government and the Protestants had only one thing in common, hatred of the Papal power. The English reformers were eager to go as far as their brethren on the Continent. They unanimously condemned as Antichristian numerous dogmas and practices to which Henry had stubbornly adhered, and which Elizabeth reluctantly abandoned. Many felt a strong repugnance even to things indifferent which had formed part of the polity or ritual of the mystical Babylon. Thus Bishop Hooper, who died manfully at Gloucester for his religion, long refused to wear the episcopal vestments. Bishop Ridley, a martyr of still greater renown, pulled down the ancient altars of his diocese, and ordered the Eucharist to be administered in the middle of churches, at tables which the Papists irreverently termed oyster boards. Bishop Jewel pronounced the clerical garb to be a stage dress, a fool's coat, a relique of the Amorites, and promised that he would spare no labour to extirpate such degrading absurdities. Archbishop Grindal long hesitated about accepting a mitre from dislike of what he regarded as the mummery of consecration. Bishop Parkhurst uttered a fervent prayer that the Church of England would propose to herself the Church of Zurich as the absolute pattern of a Christian community. Bishop Ponet was of opinion that the word Bishop should be abandoned to the Papists, and that the chief officers of the purified church should be called Superintendents. When it is considered that none of these prelates belonged to the extreme section of the Protestant party, it cannot be doubted that, if the general sense of that party had been followed, the work of reform would have been carried on as unsparingly in England as in Scotland.

But, as the government needed the support of the Protestants, so the Protestants needed the protection of the government. Much was therefore given up on both sides; an union was effected; and the fruit of that union was the Church of England.

To the peculiarities of this great institution, and to the strong passions which it has called forth in the minds both of friends and of enemies, are to be attributed many of the most important events which have, since the Reformation, taken place in our country; nor can the secular history of England be at all understood by us, unless we study it in constant connection with the history of her ecclesiastical polity.

The man who took the chief part in settling the conditions of the alliance which produced the Anglican Church was Thomas Cranmer. He was the representative of both the parties which, at that time, needed each other's assistance. He was at once a divine and a courtier. In his character of divine he was perfectly ready to go as far in the way of change as any

Swiss or Scottish reformer. In his character of courtier he was desirous to preserve that organization which had, during many ages, admirably served the purposes of the Bishops of Rome, and might be expected now to serve equally well the purposes of the English Kings and of their ministers. His temper and his understanding eminently fitted him to act as mediator. Saintly in his professions, unscrupulous in his dealings, zealous for nothing, bold in speculation, a coward and a timeserver in action, a placable enemy and a lukewarm friend, he was in every way qualified to arrange the terms of the coalition between the religious and the worldly enemies of Popery.

To this day the constitution, the doctrines, and the services of the Church, retain the visible marks of the compromise from which she sprang. She occupies a middle position between the Churches of Rome and Geneva. Her doctrinal confessions and discourses, composed by Protestants, set forth principles of theology in which Calvin or Knox would have found scarcely a word to disapprove. Her prayers and thanksgivings, derived from the ancient Breviaries, are very generally such that Cardinal Fisher or Cardinal Pole might have heartily joined in them. A controversialist who puts an Arminian sense on her Articles and Homilies will be pronounced by candid men to be as unreasonable as a controversialist who denies that the doctrine of baptismal regeneration can be discovered in her Liturgy.

The Church of Rome held that episcopacy was of divine institution, and that certain supernatural graces of a high order had been transmitted by the imposition of hands through fifty generations, from the Eleven who received their commission on the Galilean mount, to the bishops who met at Trent. A large body of Protestants, on the other hand, regarded prelacy as positively unlawful, and persuaded them-

4*

CHAP.
I.

selves that they found a very different form of ecclesiastical government prescribed in Scripture. The founders of the Anglican Church took a middle course. They retained episcopacy; but they did not declare it to be an institution essential to the welfare of a Christian society, or to the efficacy of the sacraments. Cranmer, indeed, on one important occasion, plainly avowed his conviction that, in the primitive times, there was no distinction between bishops and priests, and that the laying on of hands was altogether superfluous.

Among the Presbyterians, the conduct of public worship is, to a great extent, left to the minister. Their prayers, therefore, are not exactly the same in any two assemblies on the same day, or on any two days in the same assembly. In one parish they are fervent, eloquent, and full of meaning. In the next parish they may be languid or absurd. The priests of the Roman Catholic Church, on the other hand, have, during many generations, daily chaunted the same ancient confessions, supplications, and thanksgivings, in India and Lithuania, in Ireland and Peru. The service, being in a dead language, is intelligible only to the learned; and the great majority of the congregation may be said to assist as spectators rather than as auditors. Here, again, the Church of England took a middle course. She copied the Roman Catholic forms of prayer, but translated them into the vulgar tongue, and invited the illiterate multitude to join its voice to that of the minister.

In every part of her system the same policy may be traced. Utterly rejecting the doctrine of transubstantiation, and condemning as idolatrous all adoration paid to the sacramental bread and wine, she yet, to the disgust of the Puritan, required her children to receive the memorials of divine love, meekly kneeling upon their knees. Discarding many rich vestments which surrounded the altars of the ancient faith,

she yet retained, to the horror of weak minds, a robe of white
linen, typical of the purity which belonged to her as the mystical spouse of Christ. Discarding a crowd of pantomimic gestures which, in the Roman Catholic worship, are substituted for intelligible words, she yet shocked many rigid Protestants by marking the infant just sprinkled from the font with the sign of the cross. The Roman Catholic addressed his prayers to a multitude of Saints, among whom were numbered many men of doubtful, and some of hateful, character. The Puritan refused the addition of Saint even to the apostle of the Gentiles, and to the disciple whom Jesus loved. The Church of England, though she asked for the intercession of no created being, still set apart days for the commemoration of some who had done and suffered great things for the faith. She retained confirmation and ordination as edifying rites; but she degraded them from the rank of sacraments. Shrift was no part of her system. Yet she gently invited the dying penitent to confess his sins to a divine, and empowered her ministers to sooth the departing soul by an absolution, which breathes the very spirit of the old religion. In general it may be said, that she appeals more to the understanding, and less to the senses and the imagination, than the Church of Rome, and that she appeals less to the understanding, and more to the senses and imagination, than the Protestant Churches of Scotland, France, and Switzerland.

Nothing, however, so strongly distinguished the Church of England from other Churches as the relation in which she stood to the monarchy. The King was her head. The limits of the authority which he possessed, as such, were not traced, and indeed have never yet been traced, with precision. The laws which declared him supreme in ecclesiastical matters were drawn rudely and in general terms. If, for the purpose of ascertaining the sense of those laws, we examine the books and lives of those who founded the English Church, our perplexity will be increased. For the founders of the English Church wrote and acted in an age of violent intellectual fermentation, and of constant action and reaction. They therefore often contradicted each other, and sometimes contradicted themselves. That the King was, under Christ, sole head of the Church, was a doctrine which they all with one voice affirmed: but those words had very different significations in different mouths, and in the same mouth at different conjunctures. Sometimes an authority which would have satisfied Hildebrand was ascribed to the sovereign: then it dwindled down to an authority little more than that which had been claimed by many ancient English princes, who had been in constant communion with the Church of Rome. What Henry and his favourite counsellors meant, at one time, by the supremacy, was certainly nothing less than the whole power of the keys. The King was to be the Pope of his kingdom, the vicar of God, the expositor of Catholic verity, the channel of sacramental graces. He arrogated to himself the right of deciding dogmatically what was orthodox doctrine and what was heresy, of drawing up and imposing confessions of faith, and of giving religious instruction to his people. He proclaimed that all jurisdiction, spiritual as well as temporal, was derived from him alone, and that it was in his power to confer episcopal authority, and to take it away. He actually ordered his seal to be put to commissions by which bishops were appointed, who were to exercise their functions as his deputies, and during his pleasure. According to this system, as expounded by Cranmer, the King was the spiritual as well as the temporal chief of the nation. In both capacities His Highness must have lieutenants. As he appointed civil officers to keep his seal, to collect his revenues, and to dispense justice in his name, so he appointed divines of various ranks to preach the gospel, and to administer the sacraments. It was unnecessary that there should be any imposition of hands. The King — such was the opinion of Cranmer given in the plainest words — might, in virtue of authority derived from God, make a priest; and the priest so made needed no ordination whatever. These opinions Cranmer, in spite of the opposition of less courtly divines, followed out to every legitimate consequence. He held that his own spiritual functions, like the secular functions of the Chancellor and Treasurer, were at once determined by a demise of the crown. When Henry died, therefore, the Archbishop and his suffragans took out fresh commissions, empowering them to ordain and to govern the Church till the new sovereign should think fit to order otherwise. When it was objected that a power to bind and to loose, altogether distinct from temporal power, had been given by our Lord to his apostles, some theologians of this school replied that the power to bind and to loose had descended, not to the clergy, but to the whole body of Christian men, and ought to be exercised by the chief magistrate, as the representative of the society. When it was objected that Saint Paul had spoken of certain persons whom the Holy Ghost had made overseers and shepherds of the faithful, it was answered that King Henry was the very overseer, the very shepherd, whom the Holy Ghost had appointed, and to whom the expressions of Saint Paul applied.*

These high pretensions gave scandal to Protestants as well as to Catholics; and the scandal was greatly increased when the supremacy, which Mary had resigned back to the Pope, was again annexed to the crown, on the accession of Elizabeth. It seemed monstrous that a woman should be the chief bishop of a Church in which an apostle had forbidden her even to let her voice be heard. The Queen, therefore, found it necessary expressly to disclaim that sacerdotal character which her

* See a very curious paper which Strype believed to be in Gardiner's handwriting. Ecclesiastical Memorials, Book I. Chap. xvii.

CHAP. father had assumed, and which, according to Cranmer, had
I.   been inseparably joined, by divine ordinance, to the regal
function. When the Anglican confession of faith was revised
in her reign, the supremacy was explained in a manner somewhat different from that which had been fashionable at the
court of Henry. Cranmer had declared, in emphatic terms,
that God had immediately committed to Christian princes the
whole cure of all their subjects, as well concerning the administration of God's word for the cure of souls, as concerning
the ministration of things political.* The thirty-seventh
article of religion, framed under Elizabeth, declares, in terms
as emphatic, that the ministering of God's word does not
belong to princes. The Queen, however, still had over the
Church a visitatorial power of vast and undefined extent. She
was entrusted by Parliament with the office of restraining and
punishing heresy and every sort of ecclesiastical abuse, and
was permitted to delegate her authority to commissioners.
The Bishops were little more than her ministers. Rather than
grant to the civil magistrate the absolute power of nominating
spiritual pastors, the Church of Rome, in the eleventh century, set all Europe on fire. Rather than grant to the civil
magistrate the absolute power of nominating spiritual pastors,
the ministers of the Church of Scotland, in our own time,
resigned their livings by hundreds. The Church of England
had no such scruples. By the royal authority alone her
prelates were appointed. By the royal authority alone her
Convocations were summoned, regulated, prorogued, and
dissolved. Without the royal sanction her canons had no
force. One of the articles of her faith was that without the
royal consent no ecclesiastical council could lawfully assemble.
From all her judicatures an appeal lay, in the last resort, to
the sovereign, even when the question was whether an opinion

---

* These are Cranmer's own words. See the Appendix to Burnet's
History of the Reformation, Part I. Book III. No. 21. Question 9.

ought to be accounted heretical, or whether the administration of a sacrament had been valid. Nor did the Church grudge this extensive power to our princes. By them she had been called into existence, nursed, through a feeble infancy, guarded from Papists on one side, and from Puritans on the other, protected against Parliaments which bore her no good will, 'and avenged on literary assailants whom she found it hard to answer. Thus gratitude, hope, fear, common attachments, common enmities, bound her to the throne. All her traditions, all her tastes were monarchical. Loyalty became a point of professional honour among her clergy, the peculiar badge which distinguished them at once from Calvinists and from Papists. Both the Calvinists and the Papists, widely as they differed in other respects, regarded with extreme jealousy all encroachments of the temporal power on the domain of the spiritual power. Both Calvinists and Papists maintained that subjects might justifiably draw the sword against ungodly rulers. In France Calvinists resisted Charles the Ninth: Papists resisted Henry the Fourth: both Papists and Calvinists resisted Henry the Third. In Scotland Calvinists led Mary captive. On the north of the Trent Papists took arms against Elizabeth. The Church of England meantime condemned both Calvinists and Papists, and loudly boasted that no duty was more constantly or earnestly inculcated by her than that of submission to princes.

The advantages which the crown derived from this close alliance with the Established Church were great; but they were not without serious drawbacks. The compromise arranged by Cranmer had from the first been considered by a large body of Protestants as a scheme for serving two masters, as an attempt to unite the worship of the Lord with the worship of Baal. In the days of Edward the Sixth the scruples of this party had repeatedly thrown great difficulties in the way of the government. When Elizabeth came to the throne, these difficulties

were much increased. Violence naturally engenders violence.
The spirit of Protestantism was therefore far fiercer and more
intolerant after the cruelties of Mary than before them. Many
persons who were warmly attached to the new opinions had,
during the evil days, taken refuge in Switzerland and Germany.
They had been hospitably received by their brethren in the
faith, had sate at the feet of the great doctors of Strasburg,
Zurich, and Geneva, and had been, during some years,
accustomed to a more simple worship, and to a more democra-
tical form of church government than England had yet seen.
These men returned to their country, convinced that the
reform which had been effected under King Edward had been
far less searching and extensive than the interests of pure
religion required. But it was in vain that they attempted to
obtain any concession from Elizabeth. Indeed her system,
wherever it differed from her brother's, seemed to them to
differ for the worse. They were little disposed to submit, in
matters of faith, to any human authority. They had recently,
in reliance on their own interpretation of Scripture, risen up
against a Church strong in immemorial antiquity and catholic
consent. It was by no common exertion of intellectual energy
that they had thrown off the yoke of that gorgeous and imperial
superstition; and it was vain to expect that, immediately after
such an emancipation, they would patiently submit to a new
spiritual tyranny. Long accustomed, when the priest lifted up
the host, to bow down with their faces to the earth, as before a
present God, they had learned to treat the mass as an idolatrous mummery. Long accustomed to regard the Pope as the
successor of the chief of the apostles, as the bearer of the keys
of earth and heaven, they had learned to regard him as the
Beast, the Antichrist, the Man of Sin. It was not to be expected that they would immediately transfer to an upstart authority the homage which they had withdrawn from the Vatican; that they would submit their private judgment to the

authority of a Church founded on private judgment alone; that they would be afraid to dissent from teachers who themselves dissented from what had lately been the universal faith of western Christendom. It is easy to conceive the indignation which must have been felt by bold and inquisitive spirits, glorying in newly acquired freedom, when an institution younger by many years than themselves, an institution which had, under their own eyes, gradually received its form from the passions and interests of a court, began to mimic the lofty style of Rome.

Since these men could not be convinced, it was determined that they should be persecuted. Persecution produced its natural effects on them. It found them a sect: it made them a faction. To their hatred of the Church was now added hatred *Their re-publican* of the crown. The two sentiments were intermingled; and *spirit.* each embittered the other. The opinions of the Puritan concerning the relation of ruler and subject were widely different from those which were inculcated in the Homilies. His favourite divines had, both by precept and by example, encouraged resistance to tyrants and persecutors. His fellow Calvinists in France, in Holland, and in Scotland, were in arms against idolatrous and cruel princes. His notions, too, respecting the government of the state took a tinge from his notions respecting the government of the Church. Some of the sarcasms which were popularly thrown on episcopacy might, without much difficulty, be turned against royalty; and many of the arguments which were used to prove that spiritual power was best lodged in a synod seemed to lead to the conclusion that temporal power was best lodged in a parliament.

Thus, as the priest of the Established Church was, from interest, from principle, and from passion, zealous for the royal prerogatives, the Puritan was, from interest, from principle, and from passion, hostile to them. The power of the

CHAP.
I.
discontented sectaries was great. They were found in every rank; but they were strongest among the mercantile classes in the towns, and among the small proprietors in the country. Early in the reign of Elizabeth they began to return a majority
No syste-
matic
parlia-
mentary
opposi-
tion of-
fered to
the go-
vernment
of Eliza-
beth.
of the House of Commons. And doubtless, had our ancestors been then at liberty to fix their attention entirely on domestic questions, the strife between the crown and the Parliament would instantly have commenced. But that was no season for internal dissensions. It might, indeed, well be doubted, whether the firmest union among all the orders of the state could avert the common danger by which all were threatened. Roman Catholic Europe and reformed Europe were struggling for death or life. France, divided against herself, had, for a time, ceased to be of any account in Christendom. The English government was at the head of the Protestant interest, and, while persecuting Presbyterians at home, extended a powerful protection to Presbyterian Churches abroad. At the head of the opposite party was the mightiest prince of the age, a prince who ruled Spain, Portugal, Italy, the Netherlands, the East and the West Indies, whose armies repeatedly marched to Paris, and whose fleets kept the coasts of Devonshire and Sussex in alarm. It long seemed probable that Englishmen would have to fight desperately on English ground for their religion and independence. Nor were they ever for a moment free from apprehensions of some great treason at home. For in that age it had become a point of conscience and of honour with many men of generous natures to sacrifice their country to their religion. A succession of dark plots, formed by Roman Catholics against the life of the Queen and the existence of the nation, kept society in constant alarm. Whatever might be the faults of Elizabeth, it was plain that, to speak humanly, the fate of the realm and of all reformed Churches was staked on the security of her person and on the success of her administration. To strengthen her hands was, therefore, the first

duty of a patriot and a Protestant; and that duty was well performed. The Puritans, even in the depths of the prisons to
which she had sent them, prayed, and with no simulated
fervour, that she might be kept from the dagger of the assassin,
that rebellion might be put down under her feet, and that her
arms might be victorious by sea and land. One of the most
stubborn of the stubborn sect, immediately after his hand had
been lopped off for an offence into which he had been hurried
by his intemperate zeal, waved his hat with the hand which was
still left him, and shouted "God save the Queen!" The sentiment with which these men regarded her has descended to
their posterity. The Nonconformists, rigorously as she treated
them, have, as a body, always venerated her memory. *

During the greater part of her reign, therefore, the Puritans in the House of Commons, though sometimes mutinous,
felt no disposition to array themselves in systematic opposition to the government. But, when the defeat of the
Armada, the successful resistance of the United Provinces
to the Spanish power, the firm establishment of Henry the
Fourth on the throne of France, and the death of Philip the
Second, had secured the State and the Church against all
danger from abroad, an obstinate struggle, destined to last
during several generations, instantly began at home.

It was in the Parliament of 1601 that the opposition which
had, during forty years, been silently gathering and hus-
banding strength, fought its first great battle and won its

* The Puritan historian, Neal, after censuring the cruelty with which
she treated the sect to which he belonged, concludes thus: "However,
notwithstanding all these blemishes, Queen Elizabeth stands upon record
as a wise and politic princess, for delivering her kingdom from the difficulties in which it was involved at her accession, for preserving the Protestant reformation against the potent attempts of the Pope, the Emperor,
and King of Spain abroad, and the Queen of Scots and her Popish subjects at home.... She was the glory of the age in which she lived, and
will be the admiration of posterity." — History of the Puritans, Part. I.
Chap. viii.

first victory. The ground was well chosen. The English
sovereigns had always been entrusted with the supreme
direction of commercial police. It was their undoubted prerogative to regulate coin, weights, and measures, and to
appoint fairs, markets, and ports. The line which bounded
their authority over trade had, as usual, been but loosely
drawn. They therefore, as usual, encroached on the province which rightfully belonged to the legislature. The encroachment was as usual, patiently borne, till it became
serious. But at length the Queen took upon herself to grant
patents of monopoly by scores. There was scarcely a family
in the realm which did not feel itself aggrieved by the oppression and extortion which this abuse naturally caused.
Iron, oil, vinegar, coal, saltpetre, lead, starch, yarn, skins,
leather, glass, could be bought only at exorbitant prices.
The House of Commons met in an angry and determined
mood. It was in vain that a courtly minority blamed the
Speaker for suffering the acts of the Queen's Highness to be
called in question. The language of the discontented party
was high and menacing, and was echoed by the voice of the
whole nation. The coach of the chief minister of the crown
was surrounded by an indignant populace, who cursed the
monopolies, and exclaimed that the prerogative should not
be suffered to touch the old liberties of England. There
seemed for a moment to be some danger that the long and
glorious reign of Elizabeth would have a shameful and disastrous end. She, however, with admirable judgment and
temper, declined the contest, put herself at the head of
the reforming party, redressed the grievance, thanked the
Commons, in touching and dignified language, for their
tender care of the general weal, brought back to herself the
hearts of the people, and left to her successors a memorable
example of the way in which it behoves a ruler to deal with
public movements which he has not the means of resisting.

In the year 1603 the great Queen died. That year is, on
many accounts, one of the most important epochs in our
history. It was then that both Scotland and Ireland became
parts of the same empire with England. Both Scotland and
Ireland, indeed, had been subjugated by the Plantagenets;
but neither country had been patient under the yoke. Scotland had, with heroic energy, vindicated her independence,
had, from the time of Robert Bruce, been a separate kingdom, and was now joined to the southern part of the island
in a manner which rather gratified than wounded her national
pride. Ireland had never, since the days of Henry the
Second, been able to expel the foreign invaders; but she
had struggled against them long and fiercely. During the
fourteenth and fifteenth centuries the English power in that
island was constantly declining, and, in the days of Henry
the Seventh, had sunk to the lowest point. The Irish dominions of that prince consisted only of the counties of Dublin
and Louth, of some parts of Meath and Kildare, and of a
few seaports scattered along the coast. A large portion even
of Leinster was not yet divided into counties. Munster,
Ulster, and Connaught were ruled by petty sovereigns, partly
Celts, and partly degenerate Normans, who had forgotten
their origin and had adopted the Celtic language and manners.
But, during the sixteenth century, the English power had
made great progress. The half savage chieftains who reigned
beyond the pale had yielded one after another to the lieutenants of the Tudors. At length, a few weeks before the
death of Elizabeth, the conquest, which had been begun
more than four hundred years before by Strongbow, was
completed by Mountjoy. Scarcely had James the First
mounted the English throne when the last O'Donnell and
O'Neill who have held the rank of independent princes kissed
his hand at Whitehall. Thenceforward his writs ran and his
judges held assizes in every part of Ireland; and the English

CHAP.
1.

law superseded the customs which had prevailed among the aboriginal tribes.

In extent Scotland and Ireland were nearly equal to each other, and were together nearly equal to England, but were much less thickly peopled than England, and were very far behind England in wealth and civilisation. Scotland had been kept back by the sterility of her soil; and, in the midst of light, the thick darkness of the middle ages still rested on Ireland.

The population of Scotland, with the exception of the Celtic tribes which were thinly scattered over the Hebrides and over the mountainous parts of the northern shires, was of the same blood with the population of England, and spoke a tongue which did not differ from the purest English more than the dialects of Somersetshire and Lancashire differed from each other. In Ireland, on the contrary, the population, with the exception of the small English colony near the coast, was Celtic, and still kept the Celtic speech and manners.

In natural courage and intelligence both the nations which now became connected with England ranked high. In perseverance, in self-command, in forethought, in all the virtues which conduce to success in life, the Scots have never been surpassed. The Irish, on the other hand, were distinguished by qualities which tend to make men interesting rather than prosperous. They were an ardent and impetuous race, easily moved to tears or to laughter, to fury or to love. Alone among the nations of northern Europe they had the susceptibility, the vivacity, the natural turn for acting and rhetoric, which are indigenous on the shores of the Mediterranean Sea. In mental cultivation Scotland had an indisputable superiority. Though that kingdom was then the poorest in Christendom, it already vied in every branch of learning with the most favoured countries. Scotsmen, whose dwellings and whose food were as wretched as those of the Icelanders of our time, wrote Latin verse with more than the delicacy of Vida, and made discoveries in science which would have added to the renown of Galileo. Ireland could boast of no Buchanan or Napier. The genius, with which her aboriginal inhabitants were largely endowed, showed itself as yet only in ballads which, wild and rugged as they were, seemed to the judging eye of Spenser to contain a portion of the pure gold of poetry.

Scotland, in becoming part of the British monarchy, preserved all her dignity. Having, during many generations, courageously withstood the English arms, she was now joined to her stronger neighbour on the most honourable terms. She gave a King instead of receiving one. She retained her own constitution and laws. Her tribunals and parliaments remained entirely independent of the tribunals and parliaments which sate at Westminster. The administration of Scotland was in Scottish hands; for no Englishman had any motive to emigrate northward, and to contend with the shrewdest and most pertinacious of all races for what was to be scraped together in the poorest of all treasuries. Meanwhile Scottish adventurers poured southward, and obtained in all the walks of life a prosperity which excited much envy, but which was in general only the just reward of prudence and industry. Nevertheless Scotland by no means escaped the fate ordained for every country which is connected, but not incorporated, with another country of greater resources. Though in name an independent kingdom, she was, during more than a century, really treated, in many respects, as a subject province.

Ireland was undisguisedly governed as a dependency won by the sword. Her rude national institutions had perished. The English colonists submitted to the dictation of the mother country, without whose support they could not exist, and indemnified themselves by trampling on the people among whom they had settled. The parliaments which met at Dublin could pass no law which had not previously been approved by the English Privy Council. The authority of the English legislature extended over Ireland. The executive administration was intrusted to men taken either from England or from the English pale, and, in either case, regarded as foreigners, and even as enemies, by the Celtic population.

But the circumstance which, more than any other, has made Ireland to differ from Scotland remains to be noticed. Scotland was Protestant. In no part of Europe had the movement of the popular mind against the Roman Catholic Church been so rapid and violent. The reformers had vanquished, deposed, and imprisoned their idolatrous sovereign. They would not endure even such a compromise as had been effected in England. They had established the Calvinistic doctrine, discipline, and worship; and they made little distinction between Popery and Prelacy, between the Mass and the Book of Common Prayer. Unfortunately for Scotland, the prince whom she sent to govern a fairer inheritance had been so much annoyed by the pertinacity with which her theologians had asserted against him the privileges of the synod and the pulpit that he hated the ecclesiastical polity to which she was fondly attached as much as it was in his effeminate nature to hate anything, and had no sooner mounted the English throne than he began to show an intolerant zeal for the government and ritual of the English Church.

The Irish were the only people of northern Europe who had remained true to the old religion. This is to be partly ascribed to the circumstance that they were some centuries behind their neighbours in knowledge. But other causes had cooperated. The Reformation had been a national as well as a moral revolt. It had been, not only an insurrection of the laity against the clergy, but also an insurrection of all the branches of the great German race against an alien domination. It is a most significant circumstance that no large society of which the tongue is not Teutonic has ever turned Protestant, and that, wherever a language derived from that of ancient Rome is spoken, the religion of modern Rome to this day prevails. The patriotism of the Irish had taken a peculiar direction. The object of their animosity was not Rome, but England; and they had especial reason to abhor those English sovereigns who had been the chiefs of the great schism, Henry the Eighth and Elizabeth. During the vain struggle which two generations of Milesian princes maintained against the Tudors, religious enthusiasm and national enthusiasm became inseparably blended in the minds of the vanquished race. The new feud of Protestant and Papist inflamed the old feud of Saxon and Celt. The English conquerors, meanwhile, neglected all legitimate means of conversion. No care was taken to provide the vanquished nation with instructors capable of making themselves understood. No translation of the Bible was put forth in the Erse language. The government contented itself with setting up a vast hierarchy of Protestant archbishops, bishops, and rectors, who did nothing, and who, for doing nothing, were paid out of the spoils of a Church loved and revered by the great body of the people.

There was much in the state both of Scotland and of Ireland which might well excite the painful apprehensions of a far-sighted statesman. As yet, however, there was the appearance of tranquillity. For the first time all the British isles were peaceably united under one sceptre.

It should seem that the weight of England among European nations ought, from this epoch, to have greatly increased. The territory which her new King governed was, in extent,

5*

nearly double that which Elizabeth had inherited. His empire
was also the most complete within itself and the most secure
from attack that was to be found in the world. The Plantagenets and Tudors had been repeatedly under the necessity
of defending themselves against Scotland while they were
engaged in continental war. The long conflict in Ireland had
been a severe and perpetual drain on their resources. Yet
even under such disadvantages those sovereigns had been
highly considered throughout Christendom. It might, therefore, not unreasonably be expected that England, Scotland
and Ireland combined would form a state second to none that
then existed.

Diminu-
tion of
the im-
portance
of Eng-
land after
the ac-
cession of
James I. All such expectations were strangely disappointed. On
the day of the accession of James the First our country descended from the rank which she had hitherto held, and began
to be regarded as a power hardly of the second order. During
many years the great British monarchy, under four successive
princes of the House of Stuart, was scarcely a more important
member of the European system than the little kingdom of
Scotland had previously been. This, however, is little to be
regretted. Of James the First, as of John, it may be said
that, if his administration had been able and splendid, it
would probably have been fatal to our country, and that we
owe more to his weakness and meanness than to the wisdom
and courage of much better sovereigns. He came to the
throne at a critical moment. The time was fast approaching
when either the King must become absolute, or the Parliament
must control the whole executive administration. Had James
been, like Henry the Fourth, like Maurice of Nassau, or like
Gustavus Adolphus, a valiant, active, and politic ruler, had
he put himself at the head of the Protestants of Europe, had
he gained great victories over Tilly and Spinola, had he
adorned Westminster with the spoils of Bavarian monasteries
and Flemish cathedrals, had he hung Austrian and Castilian

banners in St. Paul's, and had he found himself, after great
achievements, at the head of fifty thousand troops, brave,
well disciplined, and devotedly attached to his person, the
English Parliament would soon have been nothing more than a
name. Happily he was not a man to play such a part. He
began his administration by putting an end to the war which
had raged during many years between England and Spain;
and from that time he shunned hostilities with a caution which
was proof against the insults of his neighbours and the clamours of his subjects. Not till the last year of his life could
the influence of his son, his favourite, his Parliament and his
people combined, induce him to strike one feeble blow in
defence of his family and of his religion. It was well for those
whom he governed, that he in this matter disregarded their
wishes. The effect of his pacific policy was that, in his time,
no regular troops were needed, and that, while France,
Spain, Italy, Belgium, and Germany swarmed with mercenary
soldiers, the defence of our island was still confided to the
militia.

As the King had no standing army, and did not even
attempt to form one, it would have been wise in him to avoid
any conflict with his people. But such was his indiscretion
that, while he altogether neglected the means which alone
could make him really absolute, he constantly put forward, in
the most offensive form, claims of which none of his predecessors had ever dreamed. It was at this time that those strange
theories which Filmer afterwards formed into a system, and
which became the badge of the most violent class of Tories
and high churchmen, first emerged into notice. It was gravely maintained that the Supreme Being regarded hereditary
monarchy, as opposed to other forms of government, with
peculiar favour; that the rule of succession in order of primogeniture was a divine institution, anterior to the Christian,
and even to the Mosaic dispensation; that no human power,

not even that of the whole legislature, no length of adverse
possession, though it extended to ten centuries, could deprive
the legitimate prince of his rights; that his authority was
necessarily always despotic; that the laws by which, in England and in other countries the prerogative was limited were
to be regarded merely as concessions which the sovereign had
freely made and might at his pleasure resume; and that any
treaty into which a king might enter with his people was
merely a declaration of his present intentions, and not a
contract of which the performance could be demanded. It is
evident that this theory, though intended to strengthen the
foundations of government, altogether unsettles them. Did
the divine and immutable law of primogeniture admit females,
or exclude them? On either supposition half the sovereigns of
Europe must be usurpers, reigning in defiance of the commands of heaven, and liable to be dispossessed by the rightful
heirs. These absurd doctrines received no countenance from
the Old Testament; for in the Old Testament we read that
the chosen people were blamed and punished for desiring a
king, and that they were afterwards commanded to with-
draw their allegiance from him. Their whole history, far
from favouring the notion that primogeniture is of divine
institution, would rather seem to indicate that younger brothers are under the especial protection of heaven. Isaac was
not the eldest son of Abraham, nor Jacob of Isaac, nor Judah
of Jacob, nor David of Jesse, nor Solomon of David. Indeed
the order of seniority among children is seldom strictly regarded in countries where polygamy is practised. Nor did
the system of Filmer receive any countenance from those
passages of the New Testament which describe government as
an ordinance of God: for the government under which the
writers of the New Testament lived was not a hereditary monarchy. The Roman Emperors were republican magistrates,
named by the Senate. None of them pretended to rule by

right of birth; and, in fact, both Tiberius, to whom Christ commanded that tribute should be given, and Nero, whom Paul directed the Romans to obey, were, according to the patriarchal theory of government, usurpers. In the middle ages the doctrine of indefeasible hereditary right would have been regarded as heretical: for it was altogether incompatible with the high pretensions of the Church of Rome. It was a doctrine unknown to the founders of the Church of England. The Homily on Wilful Rebellion had strongly, and indeed too strongly, inculcated submission to constituted authority, but had made no distinction between hereditary and elective monarchies, or between monarchies and republics. Indeed most of the predecessors of James would, from personal motives, have regarded the patriarchal theory of government with aversion. William Rufus, Henry the First, Stephen, John, Henry the Fourth, Henry the Fifth, Henry the Sixth, Richard the Third, and Henry the Seventh, had all reigned in defiance of the strict rule of descent. A grave doubt hung over the legitimacy both of Mary and of Elizabeth. It was impossible that both Catharine of Aragon and Anne Boleyn could have been lawfully married to Henry the Eighth; and the highest authority in the realm had pronounced that neither was so. The Tudors, far from considering the law of succession as a divine and unchangeable institution, were constantly tampering with it. Henry the Eighth obtained an act of parliament, giving him power to leave the crown by will, and actually made a will to the prejudice of the royal family of Scotland. Edward the Sixth, unauthorised by parliament, assumed a similar power, with the full approbation of the most eminent Reformers. Elizabeth, conscious that her own title was open to grave objection, and unwilling to admit even a reversionary right in her rival and enemy the Queen of Scots, induced the Parliament to pass a law, enacting that whoever should deny the competency of the reigning sovereign, with the assent of

the Estates of the realm, to alter the succession, should suffer
death as a traitor.   But the situation of James was widely
different from that of Elizabeth.   Far inferior to her in abilities and in popularity, regarded by the English as an alien,
and excluded from the throne by the testament of Henry the
Eighth, the King of Scots was yet the undoubted heir of
William the Conqueror and of Egbert.   He had, therefore,
an obvious interest in inculcating the superstitious notion that
birth confers rights anterior to law, and unalterable by law.
It was a notion, moreover, well suited to his intellect and
temper.   It soon found many advocates among those who
aspired to his favour, and made rapid progress among the
clergy of the Established Church.

Thus, at the very moment at which a republican spirit
began to manifest itself strongly in the Parliament and in the
country, the claims of the monarch took a monstrous form
which would have disgusted the proudest and most arbitrary
of those who had preceded him on the throne.

James was always boasting of his skill in what he called
kingcraft; and yet it is hardly possible even to imagine a
course more directly opposed to all the rules of kingcraft than
that which he followed.   The policy of wise rulers has always
been to disguise strong acts under popular forms.   It was thus
that Augustus and Napoleon established absolute monarchies,
while the public regarded them merely as eminent citizens invested with temporary magistracies.   The policy of James was
the direct reverse of theirs.   He enraged and alarmed his Parliament by constantly telling them that they held their privileges merely during his pleasure, and that they had no more
business to inquire what he might lawfully do than what the
Deity might lawfully do.   Yet he quailed before them, abandoned minister after minister to their vengeance, and suffered
them to tease him into acts directly opposed to his strongest
inclinations.   Thus the indignation excited by his claims and

the scorn excited by his concessions went on growing together. By his fondness for worthless minions, and by the
sanction which he gave to their tyranny and rapacity, he kept
discontent constantly alive. His cowardice, his childishness,
his pedantry, his ungainly person and manners, his provincial
accent made him an object of derision. Even in his virtues
and accomplishments there was something eminently un-
kingly. Throughout the whole course of his reign, all the
venerable associations by which the throne had long been
fenced were gradually losing their strength. During two
hundred years all the sovereigns who had ruled England, with
the single exception of the unfortunate Henry the Sixth, had
been strong-minded, high-spirited, courageous, and of princely bearing. Almost all had possessed abilities above the
ordinary level. It was no light thing that, on the very eve of
the decisive struggle between our Kings and their Parliaments,
royalty should be exhibited to the world stammering, slob-
bering, shedding unmanly tears, trembling at a drawn sword,
and talking in the style alternately of a buffoon and of a pe-
dagogue.

In the meantime the religious dissensions, by which, from
the days of Edward the Sixth, the Protestant body had been
distracted, had become more formidable than ever. The
interval which had separated the first generation of Puritans
from Cranmer and Jewel was small indeed when compared
with the interval which separated the third generation of Puritans from Laud and Hammond. While the recollection of
Mary's cruelties was still fresh, while the power of the Catholic
party still inspired apprehension, while Spain still retained
ascendency and aspired to universal dominion, all the reformed sects knew that they had a strong common interest and
a deadly common enemy. The animosity which they felt
towards each other was languid when compared with the animosity which they all felt towards Rome. Conformists and

CHAP.
I.

Nonconformists had heartily joined in enacting penal laws of extreme severity against the Papists. But when more than half a century of undisturbed possession had given confidence to the Established Church, when nine tenths of the nation had become heartily Protestant, when England was at peace with all the world, when there was no danger that Popery would be forced by foreign arms on the nation, when the last confessors who had stood before Bonner had passed away, a change took place in the feeling of the Anglican clergy. Their hostility to the Roman Catholic doctrine and discipline was considerably mitigated. Their dislike of the Puritans, on the other hand, increased daily. The controversies which had from the beginning divided the Protestant party took such a form as made reconciliation hopeless; and new controversies of still greater importance were added to the old subjects of dispute.

The founders of the Anglican Church had retained episcopacy as an ancient, a decent, and a convenient ecclesiastical polity, but had not declared that form of church government to be of divine institution. We have already seen how low an estimate Cranmer had formed of the office of a Bishop. In the reign of Elizabeth, Jewel, Cooper, Whitgift, and other eminent doctors defended prelacy as innocent, as useful, as what the state might lawfully establish, as what, when established by the state, was entitled to the respect of every citizen. But they never denied that a Christian community without a Bishop might be a pure Church. On the contrary, they regarded the Protestants of the Continent as of the same household of faith with themselves. Englishmen in England were indeed bound to acknowledge the authority of the Bishop, as they were bound to acknowledge the authority of the Sheriff and of the Coroner: but the obligation was purely local. An English churchman, nay even an English prelate, if he went to Holland, conformed without scruple to the established religion of Holland. Abroad the ambassadors of CHAP. Elizabeth and James went in state to the very worship which I. Elizabeth and James persecuted at home, and carefully abstained from decorating their private chapels after the Anglican fashion, lest scandal should be given to weaker brethren. In the year 1603, the Convocation of the province of Canterbury solemnly recognised the Church of Scotland, a Church in which episcopal control and episcopal ordination were then unknown, as a branch of the Holy Catholic Church of Christ.* It was even held that Presbyterian ministers were entitled to place and voice in œcumenical councils. When the States General of the United Provinces convoked at Dort a synod of doctors not episcopally ordained, an English Bishop and an English Dean, commissioned by the head of the English Church, sate with those doctors, preached to them, and voted with them on the gravest questions of theology.** Nay, many English benefices were held by divines who had been admitted to the ministry in the Calvinistic form used on the Continent; nor was reordination by a Bishop in such cases then thought necessary, or even lawful.

But a new race of divines was already rising in the Church of England. In their view the episcopal office was essential to the welfare of a Christian society and to the efficacy of the most solemn ordinances of religion. To that office belonged certain high and sacred privileges, which no human power could give or take away. A church might as well be without the doctrine of the Trinity, or the doctrine of the Incarnation, as without the apostolical orders; and the Church of Rome, which, in the midst of all her corruptions, had retained the

* Canon 55. of 1603.
** Joseph Hall, then dean of Worcester, and afterwards bishop of Norwich, was one of the commissioners. In his life of himself, he says: "My unworthiness was named for one of the assistants of that honourable, grave, and reverend meeting." To high churchmen this humility will seem not a little out of place.

apostolical orders, was nearer to primitive purity than those reformed societies which had rashly set up, in opposition to the divine model, a system invented by men.

In the days of Edward the Sixth and of Elizabeth, the defenders of the Anglican ritual had generally contented themselves with saying that it might be used without sin, and that, therefore, none but a perverse and undutiful subject would refuse to use it when enjoined to do so by the magistrate. Now, however, that rising party which claimed for the polity of the Church a celestial origin began to ascribe to her services a new dignity and importance. It was hinted that, if the established worship had any fault, that fault was extreme simplicity, and that the Reformers had, in the heat of their quarrel with Rome, abolished many ancient ceremonies which might with advantage have been retained. Days and places were again held in mysterious veneration. Some practices which had long been disused, and which were commonly regarded as superstitious mummeries, were revived. Paintings and carvings, which had escaped the fury of the first generation of Protestants, became the objects of a respect such as to many seemed idolatrous.

No part of the system of the old Church had been more detested by the Reformers than the honour paid to celibacy. They held that the doctrine of Rome on this subject had been prophetically condemned by the Apostle Paul, as a doctrine of devils; and they dwelt much on the crimes and scandals which seemed to prove the justice of this awful denunciation. Luther had evinced his own opinion in the clearest manner, by espousing a nun. Some of the most illustrious bishops and priests who had died by fire during the reign of Mary had left wives and children. Now, however, it began to be rumoured that the old monastic spirit had reappeared in the Church of England; that there was in high quarters a prejudice against married priests; that even laymen, who called

themselves Protestants, had made resolutions of celibacy
which almost amounted to vows; nay, that a minister of the
established religion had set up a nunnery, in which the psalms
were chaunted at midnight, by a company of virgins dedicated
to God. *

Nor was this all. A class of questions as to which the
founders of the Anglican Church and the first generation of
Puritans had differed little or not at all began to furnish matter
for fierce disputes. The controversies which had divided the
Protestant body in its infancy had related almost exclusively
to church government and to ceremonies. There had been
no serious quarrel between the contending parties on points
of metaphysical theology. The doctrines held by the chiefs
of the hierarchy touching original sin, faith, grace, predesti-
nation, and election, were those which are popularly called
Calvinistic. Towards the close of Elizabeth's reign her favourite prelate, Archbishop Whitgift, drew up, in concert
with the Bishop of London and other theologians, the celebrated instrument known by the name of the Lambeth
Articles. In that instrument the most startling of the Calvinistic doctrines are affirmed with a distinctness which would
shock many who, in our age, are reputed Calvinists. One
clergyman, who took the opposite side, and spoke harshly of
Calvin, was arraigned for his presumption by the University
of Cambridge, and escaped punishment only by expressing
his firm belief in the tenets of reprobation and final perseverance, and his sorrow for the offence which he had given to
pious men by reflecting on the great French reformer. The
school of divinity of which Hooker was the chief occupies a
middle place between the school of Cranmer and the school of
Laud; and Hooker has, in modern times, been claimed by

---

* Peckard's Life of Ferrar. The Arminian Nunnery, or a Brief Description of the late erected monastical Place called the Arminian Nunnery, at Little Gidding in Huntingdonshire, 1641.

the Arminians as an ally. Yet Hooker pronounced Calvin to have been a man superior in wisdom to any other divine that France had produced, a man to whom thousands were indebted for the knowledge of divine truth, but who was himself indebted to God alone. When the Arminian controversy arose in Holland, the English government and the English Church lent strong support to the Calvinistic party; nor is the English name altogether free from the stain which has been left on that party by the imprisonment of Grotius and the judicial murder of Barneveldt.

But, even before the meeting of the Dutch synod, that part of the Anglican clergy which was peculiarly hostile to the Calvinistic church government and to the Calvinistic worship had begun to regard with dislike the Calvinistic metaphysics; and this feeling was very naturally strengthened by the gross injustice, insolence, and cruelty of the party which was prevalent at Dort. The Arminian doctrine, a doctrine less austerely logical than that of the early reformers, but more agreeable to the popular notions of the divine justice and benevolence, spread fast and wide. The infection soon reached the court. Opinions which, at the time of the accession of James, no clergyman could have avowed without imminent risk of being stripped of his gown were now the best title to preferment. A divine of that age, who was asked by a simple country gentleman what the Arminians held, answered, with as much truth as wit, that they held all the best bishoprics and deaneries in England.

While a section of the Anglican clergy quitted, in one direction, the position which they had originally occupied, a section of the Puritan body departed, in a direction diametrically opposite, from the principles and practices of their fathers. The persecution which the separatists had undergone had been severe enough to irritate, but not severe enough to destroy. They had not been tamed into submission, but baited into savageness and stubbornness. After the fashion of oppressed sects, they mistook their own vindictive feelings for emotions of piety, encouraged in themselves by reading and meditation a disposition to brood over their wrongs, and, when they had worked themselves up into hating their enemies, imagined that they were only hating the enemies of heaven. In the New Testament there was little indeed which, even when perverted by the most disingenuous exposition, could seem to countenance the indulgence of malevolent passions. But the Old Testament contained the history of a race selected by God to be witnesses of his unity and ministers of his vengeance, and specially commanded by him to do many things which, if done without his special command, would have been atrocious crimes. In such a history it was not difficult for fierce and gloomy spirits to find much that might be distorted to suit their wishes. The extreme Puritans therefore began to feel for the Old Testament a preference, which, perhaps, they did not distinctly avow even to themselves; but which showed itself in all their sentiments and habits. They paid to the Hebrew language a respect which they refused to that tongue in which the discourses of Jesus and the epistles of Paul have come down to us. They baptized their children by the names, not of Christian saints, but of Hebrew patriarchs and warriors. In defiance of the express and reiterated declarations of Luther and Calvin, they turned the weekly festival by which the Church had, from the primitive times, commemorated the resurrection of her Lord, into a Jewish Sabbath. They sought for principles of jurisprudence in the Mosaic law, and for precedents to guide their ordinary conduct in the books of Judges and Kings. Their thoughts and discourse ran much on acts which were assuredly not recorded as examples for our imitation. The prophet who hewed in pieces a captive king, the rebel general who gave the blood of a queen to the

CHAP. dogs, the matron who, in defiance of plighted faith, and of
I.   the laws of eastern hospitality, drove the nail into the brain
of the fugitive ally who had just fed at her board, and who
was sleeping under the shadow of her tent, were proposed as
models to Christians suffering under the tyranny of princes
and prelates. Morals and manners were subjected to a code
resembling that of the synagogue, when the synagogue was in
its worst state. The dress, the deportment, the language,
the studies, the amusements of the rigid sect were regulated
on principles resembling those of the Pharisees who, proud of
their washed hands and broad phylacteries, taunted the
Redeemer as a sabbath-breaker and a wine-bibber. It was a
sin to hang garlands on a Maypole, to drink a friend's health,
to fly a hawk, to hunt a stag, to play at chess, to wear love-
locks, to put starch into a ruff, to touch the virginals, to read
the Fairy Queen. Rules such as these, rules which would
have appeared insupportable to the free and joyous spirit of
Luther, and contemptible to the serene and philosophical intellect of Zwingle, threw over all life a more than monastic
gloom. The learning and eloquence by which the great reformers had been eminently distinguished, and to which they
had been, in no small measure, indebted for their success,
were regarded by the new school of Protestants with suspicion, if not with aversion. Some precisians had scruples
about teaching the Latin grammar because the names of Mars,
Bacchus, and Apollo occurred in it. The fine arts were all
but proscribed. The solemn peal of the organ was superstitious. The light music of Ben Jonson's masques was dissolute. Half the fine paintings in England were idolatrous,
and the other half indecent. The extreme Puritan was at
once known from other men by his gait, his garb, his lank
hair, the sour solemnity of his face, the upturned white of his
eyes, the nasal twang with which he spoke, and, above all,
by his peculiar dialect. He employed, on every occasion, the

imagery and style of Scripture. Hebraisms violently introduced into the English language, and metaphors borrowed
from the boldest lyric poetry of a remote age and country,
and applied to the common concerns of English life, were the
most striking peculiarities of this cant, which moved, not without cause, the derision both of prelatists and libertines.

Thus the political and religious schism which had originated in the sixteenth century was, during the first quarter of
the seventeenth century, constantly widening. Theories tending to Turkish despotism were in fashion at Whitehall. Theories tending to republicanism were in favour with a large
portion of the House of Commons. The violent Prelatists
who were, to a man, zealous for prerogative, and the violent
Puritans who were, to a man, zealous for the privileges of Parliament, regarded each other with animosity more intense than
that which, in the preceding generation, had existed between
Catholics and Protestants.

While the minds of men were in this state, the country,
after a peace of many years, at length engaged in a war which
required strenuous exertions. This war hastened the approach of the great constitutional crisis. It was necessary that
the King should have a large military force. He could not
have such a force without money. He could not legally raise
money without the consent of Parliament. It followed, therefore, that he must either administer the government in conformity with the sense of the House of Commons, or must venture
on such a violation of the fundamental laws of the land as had
been unknown during several centuries. The Plantagenets
and the Tudors had, it is true, occasionallly supplied a deficiency in their revenue by a benevolence or a forced loan: but
these expedients were always of a temporary nature. To
meet the regular charge of a long war by regular taxation, imposed without the consent of the Estates of the realm, was a
course which Henry the Eighth himself would not have dared

to take. It seemed, therefore, that the decisive hour was approaching, and that the English Parliament would soon either share the fate of the senates of the Continent, or obtain supreme ascendency in the state.

Just at this conjuncture James died. Charles the First succeeded to the throne. He had received from nature a far better understanding, a far stronger will, and a far keener and firmer temper than his father's. He had inherited his father's political theories, and was much more disposed than his father to carry them into practice. He was, like his father, a zealous episcopalian. He was, moreover, what his father had never been, a zealous Arminian, and, though no Papist, liked a Papist much better than a Puritan. It would be unjust to deny that Charles had some of the qualities of a good, and even of a great prince. He wrote and spoke, not, like his father, with the exactness of a professor, but after the fashion of intelligent and well educated gentlemen. His taste in literature and art was excellent, his manner dignified though not gracious, his domestic life without blemish. Faithlessness was the chief cause of his disasters, and is the chief stain on his memory. He was, in truth, impelled by an incurable propensity to dark and crooked ways. It may seem strange that his conscience, which, on occasions of little moment, was sufficiently sensitive, should never have reproached him with this great vice. But there is reason to believe that he was perfidious, not only from constitution and from habit, but also on principle. He seems to have learned from the theologians whom he most esteemed that between him and his subjects there could be nothing of the nature of mutual contract; that he could not, even if he would, divest himself of his despotic authority; and that, in every promise which he made, there was an implied reservation that such promise might be broken in case of necessity, and that of the necessity he was the sole judge.

And now began that hazardous game on which were staked CHAP.
the destinies of the English people. It was played on the side I.
of the House of Commons with keenness, but with admirable Tactics of the oppo-
dexterity, coolness, and perseverance. Great statesmen who sition in theHouse
looked far behind them and far before them were at the head of Com-mons.
of that assembly. They were resolved to place the King in
such a situation that he must either conduct the administration
in conformity with the wishes of his Parliament, or make outrageous attacks on the most sacred principles of the constitution. They accordingly doled out supplies to him ¡very sparingly. He found that he must govern either in harmony with
the House of Commons, or in defiance of all law. His choice
was soon made. He dissolved his first Parliament, and levied
taxes by his own authority. He convoked a second Parliament, and found it more intractable than the first. He again
resorted to the expedient of dissolution, raised fresh taxes
without any show of legal right, and threw the chiefs of the opposition into prison. At the same time a new grievance, which
the peculiar feelings and habits of the English nation made insupportably painful, and which seemed to all discerning men
to be of fearful augury, excited general discontent and alarm.
Companies of soldiers were billeted on the people; and
martial law was, in some places, substituted for the ancient
jurisprudence of the realm.

The King called a third Parliament, and soon perceived
that the opposition was stronger and fiercer than ever. He
now determined on a change of tactics. Instead of opposing
an inflexible resistance to the demands of the Commons, he,
after much altercation and many evasions, agreed to a compromise which, if he had faithfully adhered to it, would have averted a long series of calamities. The Parliament granted an
ample supply. The King ratified, in the most solemn manner, Petition
that celebrated law, which is known by the name of the Petition of Right.
of Right, and which is the second Great Charter of the liberties

6 *

of England. By ratifying that law he bound himself never
again to raise money without the consent of the Houses, never
again to imprison any person, except in due course of law, and
never again to subject his people to the jurisdiction of courts
martial.

The day on which the royal sanction was, after many de-
lays, solemnly given to this great act, was a day of joy and
hope. The Commons, who crowded the bar of the House of
Lords, broke forth into loud acclamations as soon as the clerk
had pronounced the ancient form of words by which our
princes have, during many ages, signified their assent to the
wishes of the Estates of the realm. Those acclamations were
reechoed by the voice of the capital and of the nation; but
within three weeks it became manifest that Charles had no intention of observing the compact into which he had entered.
The supply given by the representatives of the nation was collected. The promise by which that supply had been obtained
was broken. A violent contest followed. The Parliament
was dissolved with every mark of royal displeasure. Some of
the most distinguished members were imprisoned; and one of
them, Sir John Eliot, after years of suffering, died in confinement.

Charles, however, could not venture to raise, by his own
authority, taxes sufficient for carrying on war. He accordingly
hastened to make peace with his neighbours, and thenceforth
gave his whole mind to British politics.

Now commenced a new era. Many English Kings had
occasionally committed unconstitutional acts: but none had
ever systematically attempted to make himself a despot, and to
reduce the Parliament to a nullity. Such was the end which
Charles distinctly proposed to himself. From March 1629 to
April 1640, the Houses were not convoked. Never in our
history had there been an interval of eleven years between
Parliament and Parliament. Only once had there been an

interval of even half that length.   This fact alone is suf- CHAP.
I.
ficient to refute those who represent Charles as having merely
trodden in the footsteps of the Plantagenets and Tudors.

It is proved, by the testimony of the King's most strenuous Petition
of Right
violated.
supporters, that, during this part of his reign, the provisions
of the Petition of Right were violated by him, not occasionally,
but constantly, and on system; that a large part of the revenue
was raised without any legal authority; and that persons obnoxious to the government languished for years in prison,
without being ever called upon to plead before any tribunal.

For these things history must hold the King himself chiefly
responsible.   From the time of his third Parliament he was his
own prime minister.   Several persons, however, whose temper
and talents were suited to his purposes, were at the head of
different departments of the administration.

Thomas Wentworth, successively created Lord Wentworth Character
and de-
signs of
Went-
worth.
and Earl of Strafford, a man of great abilities, eloquence, and
courage, but of a cruel and imperious nature, was the coun-
sellor most trusted in political and military affairs.   He had
been one of the most distinguished members of the opposition,
and felt towards those whom he had deserted that peculiar
malignity which has, in all ages, been characteristic of apos-
tates.   He perfectly understood the feelings, the resources,
and the policy of the party to which he had lately belonged,
and had formed a vast and deeply meditated scheme which
very nearly confounded even the able tactics of the statesmen
by whom the House of Commons had been directed.   To this
scheme, in his confidential correspondence, he gave the expressive name of Thorough.   His object was to do in England
all, and more than all, that Richelieu was doing in France; to
make Charles a monarch as absolute as any on the Continent;
to put the estates and the personal liberty of the whole people
at the disposal of the crown; to deprive the courts of law of all

independent authority, even in ordinary questions of civil right
between man and man; and to punish with merciless rigour all
who murmured at the acts of the government, or who applied,
even in the most decent and regular manner, to any tribunal
for relief against those acts. *

This was his end; and he distinctly saw in what manner
alone this end could be attained. There was, in truth, about
all his notions a clearness, coherence, and precision which, if
he had not been pursuing an object pernicious to his country
and to his kind, would have justly entitled him to high admiration. He saw that there was one instrument, and only
one, by which his vast and daring projects could be carried
into execution. That instrument was a standing army. To
the forming of such an army, therefore, he directed all the
energy of his strong mind. In Ireland, where he was viceroy,
he actually succeeded in establishing a military despotism, not
only over the aboriginal population, but also over the English
colonists, and was able to boast that, in that island, the
King was as absolute as any prince in the whole world
could be. **

Character
of Laud.
The ecclesiastical administration was, in the meantime,
principally directed by William Laud, Archbishop of Canterbury. Of all the prelates of the Anglican Church, Laud had
departed farthest from the principles of the Reformation, and
had drawn nearest to Rome. His theology was more remote
than even that of the Dutch Arminians from the theology of
the Calvinists. His passion for ceremonies, his reverence for

* The correspondence of Wentworth seems to me fully to bear out
what I have said in the text. To transcribe all the passages which have
led me to the conclusion at which I have arrived, would be impossible;
nor would it be easy to make a better selection than has already been
made by Mr. Hallam. I may, however, direct the attention of the reader
particularly to the very able paper which Wentworth drew up respecting
the affairs of the Palatinate. The date is March 31. 1637.
** These are Wentworth's own words. See his letter to Laud, dated
Dec. 16. 1634.

holidays, vigils, and sacred places, his ill concealed dislike of
the marriage of ecclesiastics, the ardent and not altogether
disinterested zeal with which he asserted the claims of the
clergy to the reverence of the laity, would have made him an
object of aversion to the Puritans, even if he had used only
legal and gentle means for the attainment of his ends. But his
understanding was narrow, and his commerce with the world
had been small. He was by nature rash, irritable, quick to feel
for his own dignity, slow to sympathize with the sufferings of
others, and prone to the error, common in superstitious men,
of mistaking his own peevish and malignant moods for
emotions of pious zeal. Under his direction every corner of
the realm was subjected to a constant and minute inspection.
Every little congregation of separatists was tracked out and
broken up. Even the devotions of private families could not
escape the vigilance of his spies. Such fear did his rigour
inspire that the deadly hatred of the Church, which festered in
innumerable bosoms, was generally disguised under an outward show of conformity. On the very eve of troubles, fatal to
himself and to his order, the Bishops of several extensive dioceses were able to report to him that not a single dissenter was
to be found within their jurisdiction. *

The tribunals afforded no protection to the subject against
the civil and ecclesiastical tyranny of that period. The judges
of the common law, holding their situations during the pleasure
of the King, were scandalously obsequious. Yet, obsequious
as they were, they were less ready and efficient instruments of
arbitrary power than a class of courts, the memory of which is
still, after the lapse of more than two centuries, held in deep
abhorrence by the nation. Foremost among these courts in Star
power and in infamy were the Star Chamber and the High Com- Chamber and High
mission, the former a political, the latter a religious inquisition. Commis- sion.

* See his report to Charles for the year 1639.

CHAP.
I.

Neither was a part of the old constitution of England. The Star Chamber had been remodelled, and the High Commission created by the Tudors. The power which these boards had possessed before the accession of Charles had been extensive and formidable, but was small indeed when compared with that which they now usurped. Guided chiefly by the violent spirit of the primate, and freed from the control of Parliament, they displayed a rapacity, a violence, a malignant energy, which had been unknown to any former age. The government was able, through their instrumentality, to fine, imprison, pillory, and mutilate without restraint. A separate council which sate at York, under the presidency of Wentworth, was armed, in defiance of law, by a pure act of prerogative, with almost boundless power over the northern counties. All these tribunals insulted and defied the authority of Westminster Hall, and daily committed excesses which the most distinguished Royalists have warmly condemned. We are informed by Clarendon that there was hardly a man of note in the realm who had not personal experience of the harshness and greediness of the Star Chamber, that the High Commission had so conducted itself that it had scarce a friend left in the kingdom, and that the tyranny of the Council of York had made the Great Charter a dead letter north of the Trent.

The government of England was now, in all points but one, as despotic as that of France. But that one point was all important. There was still no standing army. There was, therefore, no security that the whole fabric of tyranny might not be subverted in a single day; and, if taxes were imposed by the royal authority for the support of an army, it was probable that there would be an immediate and irresistible explosion. This was the difficulty which more than any other perplexed Wentworth. The Lord Keeper Finch, in concert with other lawyers who were employed by the government, recommended an expedient, which was eagerly adopted. The ancient princes of

England, as they called on the inhabitants of the counties near
Scotland to arm and array themselves for the defence of the
border, had sometimes called on the maritime counties to furnish ships for the defence of the coast. In the room of ships
money had sometimes been accepted. This old practice it was
now determined, after a long interval, not only to revive but to
extend. Former princes had raised ship-money only in time of
war; it was now exacted in a time of profound peace. Former
princes, even in the most perilous wars, had raised ship-money
only along the coasts; it was now exacted from the inland
shires. Former princes had raised ship-money only for the
maritime defence of the country; it was now exacted, by the
admission of the Royalists themselves, with the object, not of
maintaining a navy, but of furnishing the King with supplies
which might be increased at his discretion to any amount, and
expended at his discretion for any purpose.

The whole nation was alarmed and incensed. John
Hampden, an opulent and well born gentleman of Bucking-
hamshire, highly considered in his own neighbourhood, but as
yet little known to the kingdom generally, had the courage to
step forward, to confront the whole power of the government,
and take on himself the cost and the risk of disputing the prerogative to which the King laid claim. The case was argued
before the judges in the Exchequer Chamber. So strong were
the arguments against the pretensions of the crown that, dependent and servile as the judges were, the majority against
Hampden was the smallest possible. Still there was a majority. The interpreters of the law had pronounced that one
great and productive tax might be imposed by the royal authority. Wentworth justly observed that it was impossible to
vindicate their judgment except by reasons directly leading to
a conclusion which they had not ventured to draw. If money
might legally be raised without the consent of Parliament for
the support of a fleet, it was not easy to deny that money might,

CHAP.   without consent of Parliament, be legally raised for the support
  1.
——— of an army.

The decision of the judges increased the irritation of the people. A century earlier, irritation less serious would have produced a general rising. But discontent did not now so readily as in former ages take the form of rebellion. The nation had been long steadily advancing in wealth and in civilisation. Since the great northern Earls took up arms against Elizabeth seventy years had elapsed; and during those seventy years there had been no civil war. Never, during the whole existence of the English nation, had so long a period passed without intestine hostilities. Men had become accustomed to the pursuits of peaceful industry, and, exasperated as they were, hesitated long before they drew the sword.

This was the conjuncture at which the liberties of the nation were in the greatest peril. The opponents of the government began to despair of the destiny of their country; and many looked to the American wilderness as the only asylum in which they could enjoy civil and spiritual freedom. There a few resolute Puritans, who, in the cause of their religion, feared neither the rage of the ocean nor the hardships of uncivilised life, neither the fangs of savage beasts nor the tomahawks of more savage men, had built, amidst the primeval forest, villages which are now great and opulent cities, but which have, through every change, retained some trace of the character derived from their founders. The government regarded these infant colonies with aversion, and attempted violently to stop the stream of emigration, but could not prevent the population of New England from being largely recruited by stout-hearted and Godfearing men from every part of the old England. And now Wentworth exulted in the near prospect of Thorough. A few years might probably suffice for the execution of his great design. If strict economy were observed, if all collision with foreign powers

were carefully avoided, the debts of the crown would be CHAP.
I.
cleared off: there would be funds available for the support of
a large military force; and that force would soon break the
refractory spirit of the nation.

At this crisis an act of insane bigotry suddenly changed Resist-
ance to
the whole face of public affairs. Had the King been wise, he the Li-
turgy in
would have pursued a cautious and soothing policy towards Scotland.
Scotland till he was master in the South. For Scotland was
of all his kingdoms that in which there was the greatest risk
that a spark might produce a flame, and that a flame might
become a conflagration. Constitutional opposition, indeed,
such as he had encountered at Westminster, he had not to
apprehend at Edinburgh. The Parliament of his northern
kingdom was a very different body from that which bore the
same name in England. It was ill constituted; it was little
considered; and it had never imposed any serious restraint on
any of his predecessors. The three Estates sate in one house.
The commissioners of the burghs were considered merely as
retainers of the great nobles. No act could be introduced
till it had been approved by the Lords of Articles, a committee
which was really, though not in form, nominated by the
crown. But, though the Scottish Parliament was obsequious,
the Scottish people had always been singularly turbulent and
ungovernable. They had butchered their first James in his
bed-chamber: they had repeatedly arrayed themselves in
arms against James the Second: they had slain James the
Third on the field of battle: their disobedience had broken
the heart of James the Fifth: they had deposed and imprisoned Mary: they had led her son captive; and their temper
was still as intractable as ever. Their habits were rude and
martial. All along the southern border, and all along the
line between the highlands and the lowlands, raged an incessant predatory war. In every part of the country men were
accustomed to redress their wrongs by the strong hand.

CHAP.
I.

Whatever loyalty the nation had anciently felt to the Stuarts had cooled during their long absence. The supreme influence over the public mind was divided between two classes of male-contents, the lords of the soil and the preachers; lords animated by the same spirit which had often impelled the old Douglasses to withstand the royal house, and preachers who had inherited the republican opinions and the unconquerable spirit of Knox. Both the national and religious feelings of the population had been wounded. All orders of men complained that their country, that country which had, with so much glory, defended her independence against the ablest and bravest Plantagenets, had, through the instrumentality of her native princes, become in effect, though not in name, a province of England. In no part of Europe had the Calvinistic doctrine and discipline taken so strong a hold on the public mind. The Church of Rome was regarded by the great body of the people with a hatred which might justly be called ferocious; and the Church of England, which seemed to be every day becoming more and more like the Church of Rome, was an object of scarcely less aversion.

The government had long wished to extend the Anglican system over the whole island, and had already, with this view, made several changes highly distasteful to every Presbyterian. One innovation, however, the most hazardous of all, because it was directly cognisable by the senses of the common people, had not yet been attempted. The public worship of God was still conducted in the manner acceptable to the nation. Now, however, Charles and Laud determined to force on the Scots the English liturgy, or rather a liturgy which, wherever it differed from that of England, differed, in the judgment of all rigid Protestants, for the worse.

To this step, taken in the mere wantonness of tyranny, and in criminal ignorance or more criminal contempt of public feeling, our country owes her freedom. The first performance

of the foreign ceremonies produced a riot. The riot rapidly CHAP.
I.
became a revolution. Ambition, patriotism, fanaticism, were
mingled in one headlong torrent. The whole nation was in
arms. The power of England was indeed, as appeared some
years later, sufficient to coerce Scotland: but a large part of
the English people sympathized with the religious feelings of
the insurgents; and many Englishmen who had no scruple
about antiphonies and genuflexions, altars and surplices,
saw with pleasure the progress of a rebellion which seemed
likely to confound the arbitrary projects of the court, and to
make the calling of a Parliament necessary.

For the senseless freak which had produced these effects
Wentworth is not responsible.* It had, in fact, thrown all
his plans into confusion. To counsel submission, however,
was not in his nature. An attempt was made to put down the
insurrection by the sword: but the King's military means and
military talents were unequal to the task. To impose fresh
taxes on England in defiance of law would, at this conjuncture,
have been madness. No resource was left but a Parliament; A Parlia-
ment
and in the spring of 1640 a Parliament was convoked. called and
dissolved.

The nation had been put into good humour by the prospect of seeing constitutional government restored, and
grievances redressed. The new House of Commons was
more temperate and more respectful to the throne than any
which had sate since the death of Elizabeth. The moderation
of this assembly has been highly extolled by the most distinguished royalists, and seems to have caused no small vexation
and disappointment to the chiefs of the opposition: but it
was the uniform practice of Charles, a practice equally im-
politic and ungenerous, to refuse all compliance with the
desires of his people, till those desires were expressed in a
menacing tone. As soon as the Commons showed a disposi-

* See his letter to the Earl of Northumberland, dated July 30. 1638.

tion to take into consideration the grievances under which the country had suffered during eleven years, the King dissolved the Parliament with every mark of displeasure.

Between the dissolution of this short-lived assembly and the meeting of that ever memorable body known by the name of the Long Parliament, intervened a few months, during which the yoke was pressed down more severely than ever on the nation, while the spirit of the nation rose up more angrily than ever against the yoke. Members of the House of Commons were questioned by the Privy Council touching their parliamentary conduct, and thrown into prison for refusing to reply. Ship-money was levied with increased rigour. The Lord Mayor and the Sheriffs of London were threatened with imprisonment for remissness in collecting the payments. Soldiers were enlisted by force. Money for their support was exacted from their counties. Torture, which had always been illegal, and which had recently been declared illegal even by the servile judges of that age, was inflicted for the last time in England in the month of May, 1640.

Everything now depended on the event of the King's military operations against the Scots. Among his troops there was little of that feeling which separates professional soldiers from the mass of a nation, and attaches them to their leaders. His army, composed for the most part of recruits who regretted the plough from which they had been violently taken, and who were imbued with the religious and political sentiments then prevalent throughout the country, was more formidable to himself than to the enemy. The Scots, encouraged by the heads of the English opposition, and feebly resisted by the English forces, marched across the Tweed and the Tyne, and encamped on the borders of Yorkshire. And now the murmurs of discontent swelled into an uproar by which all spirits save one were overawed. But the voice of Strafford was still for Thorough; and he, even in this extremity, showed a nature so cruel and despotic, that his own CHAP. I. pikemen were ready to tear him in pieces.

There was yet one last expedient which, as the King flattered himself, might save him from the misery of facing another House of Commons. To the House of Lords he was less averse. The Bishops were devoted to him; and, though the temporal peers were generally dissatisfied with his administration, they were, as a class, so deeply interested in the maintenance of order, and in the stability of ancient institutions, that they were not likely to call for extensive reforms. Departing from the uninterrupted practice of centuries, he called a Great Council consisting of Lords alone. But the Lords were too prudent to assume the unconstitutional functions with which he wished to invest them. Without money, without credit, without authority even in his own camp, he yielded to the pressure of necessity. The Houses were convoked; and the elections proved that, since the spring, the distrust and hatred with which the government was regarded had made fearful progress.

In November 1640 met that renowned Parliament which, in The Long Parliament. spite of many errors and disasters, is justly entitled to the reverence and gratitude of all who, in any part of the world, enjoy the blessings of constitutional government.

During the year which followed, no very important division of opinion appeared in the Houses. The civil and ecclesiastical administration had, through a period of near twelve years, been so oppressive and so unconstitutional that even those classes of which the inclinations are generally on the side of order and authority were eager to promote popular reforms, and to bring the instruments of tyranny to justice. It was enacted that no interval of more than three years should ever elapse between Parliament and Parliament, and that, if writs under the Great Seal were not issued at the proper time, the returning officers should, without such writs, call the constituent bodies together for the choice of representatives. The Star Chamber, the High Commission, the Council of York were swept away. Men who, after suffering cruel mutilations, had been confined in remote dungeons, regained their liberty. On the chief ministers of the crown the vengeance of the nation was unsparingly wreaked. The Lord Keeper, the Primate, the Lord Lieutenant were impeached. Finch saved himself by flight. Laud was flung into the Tower. Strafford was impeached, and at length put to death by act of attainder. On the same day on which this act passed, the King gave his assent to a law by which he bound himself not to adjourn, prorogue, or dissolve the existing Parliament without its own consent.

After ten months of assiduous toil, the Houses, in September 1641, adjourned for a short vacation, and the King visited Scotland. He with difficulty pacified that kingdom by consenting not only to relinquish his plans of ecclesiastical reform, but even to pass, with a very bad grace, an act declaring that episcopacy was contrary to the word of God.

First appearance of the two great English parties. The recess of the English Parliament lasted six weeks. The day on which the Houses met again is one of the most remarkable epochs in our history. From that day dates the corporate existence of the two great parties which have ever since alternately governed the country. In one sense, indeed, the distinction which then became obvious had always existed, and always must exist. For it has its origin in diversities of temper, of understanding, and of interest, which are found in all societies, and which will be found till the human mind ceases to be drawn in opposite directions by the charm of habit and by the charm of novelty. Not only in politics, but in literature, in art, in science, in surgery and mechanics, in navigation and agriculture, nay, even in mathematics, we find this distinction. Everywhere there is a class of men who cling with fondness to whatever is ancient, and who, even

when convinced by overpowering reasons that innovation
would be beneficial, consent to it with many misgivings and
forebodings. We find also everywhere another class of men
sanguine in hope, bold in speculation, always pressing forward, quick to discern the imperfections of whatever exists,
disposed to think lightly of the risks and inconveniences which
attend improvements, and disposed to give every change
credit for being an improvement. In the sentiments of both
classes there is something to approve. But of both the best
specimens will be found not far from the common frontier.
The extreme section of one class consists of bigoted dotards:
the extreme section of the other consists of shallow and reck-
less empirics.

There can be no doubt that in our very first Parliaments
might have been discerned a body of members anxious to
preserve, and a body eager to reform. But, while the sessions of the legislature were short, these bodies did not take
definite and permanent forms, array themselves under recognised leaders, or assume distinguishing names, badges,
and war cries. During the first months of the Long Parliament, the indignation excited by many years of lawless oppression was so strong and general that the House of Commons acted as one man. Abuse after abuse disappeared without a struggle. If a small minority of the representative body
wished to retain the Star Chamber and the High Commission,
that minority, overawed by the enthusiasm and by the numeri-
cal superiority of the reformers, contented itself with secretly
regretting institutions which could not, with any hope of success, be openly defended. At a later period the Royalists
found it convenient to antedate the separation between themselves and their opponents, and to attribute the Act which
restrained the King from dissolving or proroguing the Parliament, the Triennial Act, the impeachment of the ministers,
and the attainder of Strafford, to the faction which afterwards

made war on the King. But no artifice could be more disingenuous. Every one of those strong measures was actively
promoted by the men who were afterwards foremost among
the Cavaliers. No republican spoke of the long misgovernment of Charles more severely than Colepepper. The most
remarkable speech in favour of the Triennial Bill was made by
Digby. The impeachment of the Lord Keeper was moved by
Falkland. The demand that the Lord Lieutenant should be
kept close prisoner was made at the bar of the Lords by Hyde.
Not till the law attainting Strafford was proposed did the signs
of serious disunion become visible. Even against that law, a
law which nothing but extreme necessity could justify, only
about sixty members of the House of Commons voted. It is
certain that Hyde was not in the minority, and that Falkland
not only voted with the majority, but spoke strongly for the
bill. Even the few who entertained a scruple about inflicting
death by a retrospective enactment thought it necessary to express the utmost abhorrence of Strafford's character and administration.

But under this apparent concord a great schism was latent;
and when, in October 1641, the Parliament reassembled after
a short recess, two hostile parties, essentially the same with
those which, under different names, have ever since contended, and are still contending, for the direction of public
affairs, appeared confronting each other. During some years
they were designated as Cavaliers and Roundheads. They
were subsequently called Tories and Whigs; nor does it seem
that these appellations are likely soon to become obsolete.

It would not be difficult to compose a lampoon or a pane-
gyric on either of these renowned factions. For no man not
utterly destitute of judgment and candour will deny that there
are many deep stains on the fame of the party to which he
belongs, or that the party to which he is opposed may justly
boast of many illustrious names, of many heroic actions, and

of many great services rendered to the State. The truth is
that, though both parties have often seriously erred, England
could have spared neither. If, in her institutions, freedom
and order, the advantages arising from innovation and the
advantages arising from prescription, have been combined to
an extent elsewhere unknown, we may attribute this happy
peculiarity to the strenuous conflicts and alternate victories of
two rival confederacies of statesmen, a confederacy zealous
for authority and antiquity, and a confederacy zealous for
liberty and progress.

It ought to be remembered that the difference between the
two great sections of English politicians has always been a
difference rather of degree than of principle. There were
certain limits on the right and on the left, which were very
rarely overstepped. A few enthusiasts on one side were ready
to lay all our laws and franchises at the feet of our Kings.
A few enthusiasts on the other side were bent on pursuing,
through endless civil troubles, their darling phantom of a
republic. But the great majority of those who fought for the
crown were averse to despotism; and the great majority of the
champions of popular rights were averse to anarchy. Twice,
in the course of the seventeenth century, the two parties
suspended their dissensions, and united their strength in a
common cause. Their first coalition restored hereditary
monarchy. Their second coalition rescued constitutional
freedom.

It is also to be noted that these two parties have never
been the whole nation, nay, that they have never, taken
together, made up a majority of the nation. Between them
has always been a great mass, which has not steadfastly adhered to either, which has sometimes remained inertly neutral,
and has sometimes oscillated to and fro. That mass has more
than once passed in a few years from one extreme to the other,
and back again. Sometimes it has changed sides, merely

7 *

CHAP.
I.

because it was tired of supporting the same men, sometimes because it was dismayed by its own excesses, sometimes because it had expected impossibilities, and had been disappointed. But, whenever it has leaned with its whole weight in either direction, resistance has, for the time, been impossible.

When the rival parties first appeared in a distinct form, they seemed to be not unequally matched. On the side of the government was a large majority of the nobles, and of those opulent and well descended gentlemen to whom nothing was wanting of nobility but the name. These, with the dependents whose support they could command, were no small power in the state. On the same side were the great body of the clergy, both the Universities, and all those laymen who were strongly attached to episcopal government and to the Anglican ritual. These respectable classes found themselves in the company of some allies much less decorous than themselves. The Puritan austerity drove to the King's faction all who made pleasure their business, who affected gallantry, splendour of dress, or taste in the lighter arts. With these went all who live by amusing the leisure of others, from the painter and the comic poet, down to the rope-dancer and the Merry Andrew. For these artists well knew that they might thrive under a superb and luxurious despotism, but must starve under the rigid rule of the precisians. In the same interest were the Roman Catholics to a man. The Queen, a daughter of France, was of their own faith. Her husband was known to be strongly attached to her, and not a little in awe of her. Though undoubtedly a Protestant on conviction, he regarded the professors of the old religion with no ill will, and would gladly have granted them a much larger toleration than he was disposed to concede to the Presbyterians. If the opposition obtained the mastery, it was probable that the sanguinary laws enacted against Papists, in the reign of Elizabeth, would be severely enforced. The Roman Catholics were therefore induced by the strongest motives to espouse the cause of the court. They in general acted with a caution which brought on them the reproach of cowardice and lukewarmness: but it is probable that, in maintaining great reserve, they consulted the King's interest as well as their own. It was not for his service that they should be conspicuous among his friends.

The main strength of the opposition lay among the small freeholders in the country, and among the merchants and shopkeepers of the towns. But these were headed by a formidable minority of the aristocracy, a minority which included the rich and powerful Earls of Northumberland, Bedford, Warwick, Stamford, and Essex, and several other Lords of great wealth and influence. In the same ranks was found the whole body of Protestant Nonconformists, and most of those members of the Established Church who still adhered to the Calvinistic opinions which, forty years before, had been generally held by the prelates and clergy. The municipal corporations took, with few exceptions, the same side. In the House of Commons the opposition preponderated, but not very decidedly.

Neither party wanted strong arguments for the measures which it was disposed to take. The reasonings of the most enlightened Royalists may be summed up thus: — "It is true that great abuses have existed; but they have been redressed. It is true that precious rights have been invaded; but they have been vindicated and surrounded with new securities. The sittings of the Estates of the realm have been, in defiance of all precedent and of the spirit of the constitution, intermitted during eleven years; but it has now been provided that henceforth three years shall never elapse without a Parliament. The Star Chamber, the High Commission, the Council of York, oppressed and plundered us;

but those hateful courts have now ceased to exist. The Lord Lieutenant aimed at establishing military despotism; but he has answered for his treason with his head. The Primate tainted our worship with Popish rites, and punished our scruples with Popish cruelty; but he is awaiting in the Tower the judgment of his peers. The Lord Keeper sanctioned a plan, by which the property of every man in England was placed at the mercy of the crown; but he has been disgraced, ruined, and compelled to take refuge in a foreign land. The ministers of tyranny have expiated their crimes. The victims of tyranny have been compensated for their sufferings. Under such circumstances it would be most unwise to persevere in that course which was justifiable and necessary when we first met, after a long interval, and found the whole administration one mass of abuses. It is time to take heed that we do not so pursue our victory over despotism as to run into anarchy. It was not in our power to overturn the bad institutions which lately afflicted our country, without shocks which have loosened the foundations of government. Now that those institutions have fallen we must hasten to prop the edifice which it was lately our duty to batter. Henceforth it will be our wisdom to look with jealousy on schemes of innovation, and to guard from encroachment all the prerogatives with which the law has, for the public good, armed the sovereign."

Such were the views of those men of whom the excellent Falkland may be regarded as the leader. It was contended on the other side with not less force, by men of not less ability and virtue, that the safety which the liberties of the English people enjoyed was rather apparent than real, and that the arbitrary projects of the court would be resumed as soon as the vigilance of the Commons was relaxed. True it was, — such was the reasoning of Pym, of Hollis, and of Hampden, — that many good laws had been passed: but, if

good laws had been sufficient to restrain the King, his sub- CHAP.
I.
jects would have had little reason ever to complain of his
administration. The recent statutes were surely not of more
authority than the Great Charter or the Petition of Right.
Yet neither the Great Charter, hallowed by the veneration
of four centuries, nor the Petition of Right, sanctioned, after
mature reflection, and for valuable consideration, by Charles
himself, had been found effectual for the protection of the
people. If once the check of fear were withdrawn, if once
the spirit of opposition were suffered to slumber, all the
securities for English freedom resolved themselves into a
single one, the royal word; and it had been proved by a
long and severe experience that the royal word could not be
trusted.

The two parties were still regarding each other with The Irish
cautious hostility, and had not yet measured their strength, Rebel-
when news arrived which inflamed the passions and confirmed
the opinions of both. The great chieftains of Ulster, who,
at the time of the accession of James, had, after a long
struggle, submitted to the royal authority, had not long
brooked the humiliation of dependence. They had con-
spired against the English government, and had been attainted of treason. Their immense domains had been forfeited to the crown, and had soon been peopled by thousands
of English and Scotch emigrants. The new settlers were,
in civilisation and intelligence, far superior to the native
population, and sometimes abused their superiority. The
animosity produced by difference of race was increased by
difference of religion. Under the iron rule of Wentworth,
scarcely a murmur was heard: but, when that strong pressure was withdrawn, when Scotland had set the example of
successful resistance, when England was distracted by internal quarrels, the smothered rage of the Irish broke forth
into acts of fearful violence. On a sudden, the aboriginal

CHAP. population rose on the colonists. A war to which national
1. and theological hatred gave a character of peculiar ferocity
desolated Ulster, and spread to the neighbouring provinces.
The castle of Dublin was scarcely thought secure. Every
post brought to London exaggerated accounts of outrages
which, without any exaggeration, were sufficient to move
pity and horror. These evil tidings roused to the height
the zeal of both the great parties which were marshalled
against each other at Westminster. The Royalists maintained
that it was the first duty of every good Englishman and
Protestant, at such a crisis, to strengthen the hands of the
sovereign. To the opposition it seemed that there were now
stronger reasons than ever for thwarting and restraining him.
That the commonwealth was in danger was undoubtedly a
good reason for giving large powers to a trustworthy magistrate: but it was a good reason for taking away powers from
a magistrate who was at heart a public enemy. To raise
a great army had always been the King's first object. A great
army must now be raised. It was to be feared that, unless
some new securities were devised, the forces levied for the
reduction of Ireland would be employed against the liberties
of England. Nor was this all. A horrible suspicion, unjust
indeed, but not altogether unnatural, had arisen in many
minds. The Queen was an avowed Roman Catholic: the
King was not regarded by the Puritans, whom he had mercilessly persecuted, as a sincere Protestant; and so notorious
was his duplicity, that there was no treachery of which his
subjects might not, with some show of reason, believe him
capable. It was soon whispered that the rebellion of the
Roman Catholics of Ulster was part of a vast work of darkness
which had been planned at Whitehall.

The re-   After some weeks of prelude, the first great parliamentary
mon-
strance. conflict between the parties which have ever since contended,
and are still contending, for the government of the nation,

took place on the twenty-second of November 1641. It was
moved by the opposition, that the House of Commons should
present to the King a remonstrance, enumerating the faults of
his administration from the time of his accession, and expressing the distrust with which his policy was still regarded by his
people. That assembly, which a few months before had been
unanimous in calling for the reform of abuses, was now divided into two fierce and eager factions of nearly equal
strength. After a hot debate of many hours, the remonstrance
was carried by only eleven votes.

The result of this struggle was highly favourable to the
conservative party. It could not be doubted that only some
great indiscretion could prevent them from shortly obtaining
the predominance in the Lower House. The Upper House
was already their own. Nothing was wanting to insure their
success, but that the King should, in all his conduct, show
respect for the laws and scrupulous good faith towards his
subjects.

His first measures promised well. He had, it seemed, at
last discovered that an entire change of system was necessary,
and had wisely made up his mind to what could no longer be
avoided. He declared his determination to govern in harmony
with the Commons, and, for that end, to call to his councils
men in whose talents and character the Commons might place
confidence. Nor was the selection ill made. Falkland, Hyde,
and Colepepper, all three distinguished by the part which
they had taken in reforming abuses and in punishing evil ministers, were invited to become the confidential advisers of the
crown, and were solemnly assured by Charles that he would
take no step in any way affecting the Lower House of Parliament without their privity.

Had he kept this promise, it cannot be doubted that the
reaction which was already in progress would very soon have
become quite as strong as the most respectable Royalists

would have desired. Already the violent members of the opposition had begun to despair of the fortunes of their party, to tremble for their own safety, and to talk of selling their estates and emigrating to America. That the fair prospects which had begun to open before the King were suddenly overcast, that his life was darkened by adversity, and at length shortened by violence, is to be attributed to his own faithlessness and contempt of law.

The truth seems to be that he detested both the parties into which the House of Commons was divided: nor is this strange; for in both those parties the love of liberty and the love of order were mingled, though in different proportions. The advisers whom necessity had compelled him to call round him were by no means men after his own heart. They had joined in condemning his tyranny, in abridging his power, and in punishing his instruments. They were now indeed prepared to defend by strictly legal means his strictly legal prerogatives; but they would have recoiled with horror from the thought of reviving Wentworth's projects of Thorough. They were, therefore, in the King's opinion, traitors who differed only in the degree of their seditious malignity from Pym and Hampden.

Impeachment of the five members.
He accordingly, a few days after he had promised the chiefs of the constitutional Royalists that no step of importance should be taken without their knowledge, formed a resolution the most momentous of his whole life, carefully concealed that resolution from them, and executed it in a manner which overwhelmed them with shame and dismay. He sent the Attorney General to impeach Pym, Hollis, Hampden, and other members of the House of Commons of high treason at the bar of the House of Lords. Not content with this flagrant violation of the Great Charter and of the uninterrupted practice of centuries, he went in person, accompanied by

armed men, to seize the leaders of the opposition within the
walls of Parliament.

The attempt failed. The accused members had left the
House a short time before Charles entered it. A sudden and
violent revulsion of feeling, both in the Parliament and in the
country, followed. The most favourable view that has ever
been taken of the King's conduct on this occasion by his most
partial advocates is that he had weakly suffered himself to be
hurried into a gross indiscretion by the evil counsels of his
wife and of his courtiers. But the general voice loudly charged
him with far deeper guilt. At the very moment at which his
subjects, after a long estrangement produced by his maladministration, were returning to him with feelings of confidence
and affection, he had aimed a deadly blow at all their dearest
rights, at the privileges of Parliament, at the very principle
of trial by jury. He had shown that he considered opposition
to his arbitrary designs as a crime to be expiated only by
blood. He had broken faith, not only with his Great Council
and with his people, but with his own adherents. He had
done what, but for an unforeseen accident, would probably
have produced a bloody conflict round the Speaker's chair.
Those who had the chief sway in the Lower House now felt
that not only their power and popularity, but their lands and
their necks, were staked on the event of the struggle in which
they were engaged. The flagging zeal of the party opposed
to the court revived in an instant. During the night which
followed the outrage the whole City of London was in arms.
In a few hours the roads leading to the capital were covered
with multitudes of yeomen spurring hard to Westminster with
the badges of the parliamentary cause in their hats. In the
House of Commons the opposition became at once irresistible,
and carried, by more than two votes to one, resolutions of
unprecedented violence. Strong bodies of the trainbands,
regularly relieved, mounted guard round Westminster Hall.

The gates of the King's palace were daily besieged by a furious multitude whose taunts and execrations were heard even in the presence chamber, and who could scarcely be kept out of the royal apartments by the gentlemen of the household. Had Charles remained much longer in his stormy capital, it is probable that the Commons would have found a plea for making him, under outward forms of respect, a state prisoner.

Depar-
ture of
Charles
from
London.
He quitted London, never to return till the day of a terrible and memorable reckoning had arrived. A negotiation began which occupied many months. Accusations and recriminations passed backward and forward between the contending parties. All accommodation had become impossible. The sure punishment which waits on habitual perfidy had at length overtaken the King. It was to no purpose that he now pawned his royal word, and invoked heaven to witness the sincerity of his professions. The distrust with which his adversaries regarded him was not to be removed by oaths or treaties. They were convinced that they could be safe only when he was utterly helpless. Their demand, therefore, was, that he should surrender, not only those prerogatives which he had usurped in violation of ancient laws and of his own recent promises, but also other prerogatives which the English Kings had possessed from time immemorial, and continue to possess at the present day. No minister must be appointed, no peer created without the consent of the Houses. Above all, the sovereign must resign that supreme military authority which, from time beyond all memory, had appertained to the regal office.

That Charles would comply with such demands while he had any means of resistance was not to be expected. Yet it will be difficult to show that the Houses could safely have exacted less. They were truly in a most embarrassing position. The great majority of the nation was firmly attached to here-

ditary monarchy. Those who held republican opinions were
as yet few, and did not venture to speak out. It was therefore impossible to abolish kingly government. Yet it was
plain that no confidence could be placed in the King. It would
have been absurd in those who knew, by recent proof, that he
was bent on destroying them, to content themselves with pre-
senting to him another Petition of Right, and receiving from
him fresh promises similar to those which he had repeatedly
made and broken. Nothing but the want of an army had prevented him from entirely subverting the old constitution of
the realm. It was now necessary to levy a great regular army
for the conquest of Ireland; and it would therefore have been
mere insanity to leave him in possession of that plenitude of
military authority which his ancestors had enjoyed.

When a country is in the situation in which England then
was, when the kingly office is regarded with love and veneration, but the person who fills that office is hated and distrusted,
it should seem that the course which ought to be taken is obvious. The dignity of the office should be preserved; the
person should be discarded. Thus our ancestors acted in
1399 an in 1689. Had there been, in 1642, any man occupy-
ing a position similar to that which Henry of Lancaster occupied at the time of the deposition of Richard the Second,
and which the Prince of Orange occupied at the time of the deposition of James the Second, it is probable that the Houses
would have changed the dynasty, and would have made no
formal change in the constitution. The new King, called to
the throne by their choice, and dependent on their support,
would have been under the necessity of governing in conformity with their wishes and opinions. But there was no prince
of the blood royal in the parliamentary party; and, though
that party contained many men of high rank and many men of
eminent ability, there was none who towered so conspicuously
above the rest that he could be proposed as a candidate for

CHAP.   the crown.   As there was to be a King, and as no new King
I.
was to be found, it was necessary to leave the regal title to
Charles.   Only one course, therefore, was left: and that was
to disjoin the regal title from the regal prerogatives.

The change which the Houses proposed to make in our
institutions, though it seems exorbitant, when distinctly set
forth and digested into articles of capitulation, really amounts
to little more than the change which, in the next generation,
was effected by the Revolution.   It is true that, at the Revolution, the sovereign was not deprived by law of the power of
naming his ministers: but it is equally true that, since the
Revolution, no ministry has been able to remain in office six
months in opposition to the sense of the House of Commons.
It is true that the sovereign still possesses the power of crea-
ting peers, and the more important power of the sword: but
it is equally true that in the exercise of these powers the sovereign has, ever since the Revolution, been guided by advisers who possess the confidence of the representatives of
the nation.   In fact, the leaders of the Roundhead party in
1642, and the statesmen who, about half a century later,
effected the Revolution, had exactly the same object in view.
That object was to terminate the contest between the crown
and the Parliament, by giving to the Parliament a supreme
control over the executive administration.   The statesmen of
the Revolution effected this indirectly by changing the
dynasty.   The Roundheads of 1642, being unable to change
the dynasty, were compelled to take a direct course towards
their end.

We cannot, however, wonder that the demands of the
opposition, importing as they did a complete and formal
transfer to the Parliament of powers which had always belonged to the Crown, should have shocked that great party of
which the characteristics are respect for constituted authority
and dread of violent innovation.   That party had recently

been in hopes of obtaining by peaceable means the as- cendency in the House of Commons; but every such hope had been blighted. The duplicity of Charles had made his old enemies irreconcileable, had driven back into the ranks of the disaffected a crowd of moderate men who were in the very act of coming over to his side, and had so cruelly mortified his best friends that they had for a time stood aloof in silent shame and resentment. Now, however, the constitutional Royalists were forced to make their choice between two dangers; and they thought it their duty rather to rally round a prince whose past conduct they condemned, and whose word inspired them with little confidence, than to suffer the regal office to be degraded, and the polity of the realm to be entirely remodelled. With such feelings, many men whose virtues and abilities would have done honour to any cause ranged themselves on the side of the King.

In August 1642 the sword was at length drawn; and soon, in almost every shire of the kingdom, two hostile factions appeared in arms against each other. It is not easy to say which of the contending parties was at first the more formidable. The Houses commanded London and the counties round London, the fleet, the navigation of the Thames, and most of the large towns and seaports. They had at their disposal almost all the military stores of the kingdom, and were able to raise duties, both on goods imported from foreign counries, and on some important products of domestic industry. The King was ill provided with artillery and ammunition. The taxes which he laid on the rural districts occupied by his troops produced, it is probable, a sum far less than that which the Parliament drew from the city of London alone. He relied, indeed, chiefly, for pecuniary aid, on the munificence of his opulent adherents. Many of these mortgaged their land, pawned their jewels, and broke up their silver chargers and christening bowls, in order to assist him. But experience has fully proved that the voluntary liberality of individuals, even in times of the greatest excitement, is a poor financial resource when compared with severe and methodical taxation, which presses on the willing and unwilling alike.

Charles, however, had one advantage, which, if he had used it well, would have more than compensated for the want of stores and money, and which, notwithstanding his mismanagement, gave him, during some months, a superiority in the war. His troops at first fought much better than those of the Parliament. Both armies, it is true, were almost entirely composed of men who had never seen a field of battle. Nevertheless, the difference was great. The parliamentary ranks were filled with hirelings whom want and idleness had induced to enlist. Hampden's regiment was regarded as one of the best; and even Hampden's regiment was described by Cromwell as a mere rabble of tapsters and serving men out of place. The royal army, on the other hand, consisted in great part of gentlemen, high spirited, ardent, accustomed to consider dishonour as more terrible than death, accustomed to fencing, to the use of fire arms, to bold riding, and to manly and perilous sport, which has been well called the image of war. Such gentlemen, mounted on their favourite horses, and commanding little bands, composed of their younger brothers, grooms, gamekeepers and huntsmen, were, from the very first day on which they took the field, qualified to play their part with credit in a skirmish. The steadiness, the prompt obedience, the mechanical precision of movement, which are characteristic of the regular soldier, these gallant volunteers never attained. But they were at first opposed to enemies as undisciplined as themselves, and far less active, athletic, and daring. For a time, therefore, the Cavaliers were successful in almost every encounter.

The Houses had also been unfortunate in the choice of a general. The rank and wealth of the Earl of Essex made

him one of the most important members of the parliamentary
party. He had borne arms on the Continent with credit, and,
when the war began, had as high a military reputation as any
man in the country. But it soon appeared that he was unfit
for the post of Commander in Chief. He had little energy and
no originality. The methodical tactics which he had learned
in the war of the Palatinate did not save him from the disgrace
of being surprised and baffled by such a Captain as Rupert,
who could claim no higher fame than that of an enterprising
partisan.

Nor were the officers who held the chief commissions
under Essex qualified to supply what was wanting in him.
For this, indeed, the Houses are scarcely to be blamed. In
a country which had not, within the memory of the oldest
person living, made war on a great scale by land, generals of
tried skill and valour were not to be found. It was necessary,
therefore, in the first instance, to trust untried men; and the
preference was naturally given to men distinguished either by
their station, or by the abilities which they had displayed in
parliament. In scarcely a single instance, however, was the
selection fortunate. Neither the grandees nor the orators
proved good soldiers. The Earl of Stamford, one of the
greatest nobles of England, was routed by the Royalists at
Stratton. Nathaniel Fiennes, inferior to none of his contemporaries in talents for civil business, disgraced himself by the
pusillanimous surrender of Bristol. Indeed, of all the statesmen who at this juncture accepted high military commands,
Hampden alone appears to have carried into the camp the
capacity and strength of mind which had made him eminent in
politics.

When the war had lasted a year, the advantage was deci- Successes
dedly with the Royalists. They were victorious, both in the of the Royalists.
western and in the northern counties. They had wrested
Bristol, the second city in the kingdom, from the Parliament.

CHAP.
I.

They had won several battles, and had not sustained a single serious or ignominious defeat. Among the Roundheads adversity had begun to produce dissension and discontent. The Parliament was kept in alarm, sometimes by plots, and sometimes by riots. It was thought necessary to fortify London against the royal army, and to hang some disaffected citizens at their own doors. Several of the most distinguished peers who had hitherto remained at Westminster fled to the court at Oxford; nor can it be doubted that, if the operations of the Cavaliers had, at this season, been directed by a sagacious and powerful mind, Charles would soon have marched in triumph to Whitehall.

But the King suffered the auspicious moment to pass away; and it never returned. In August 1643 he sate down before the city of Gloucester. That city was defended by the inhabitants and by the garrison, with a determination such as had not, since the commencement of the war, been shown by the adherents of the Parliament. The emulation of London was excited. The trainbands of the City volunteered to march wherever their services might be required. A great force was speedily collected, and began to move westward. The siege of Gloucester was raised. The Royalists in every part of the kingdom were disheartened: the spirit of the parliamentary party revived; and the apostate Lords, who had lately fled from Westminster to Oxford, hastened back from Oxford to Westminster.

Rise of
the Inde-
pendents.

And now a new and alarming class of symptoms began to appear in the distempered body politic. There had been, from the first, in the parliamentary party, some men whose minds were set on objects from which the majority of that party would have shrunk with horror. These men were, in religion, Independents. They conceived that every Christian congregation had, under Christ, supreme jurisdiction in things spiritual; that appeals to provincial and national synods were scarcely less unscriptural than appeals to the Court of Arches, or to the Vatican; and that Popery, Prelacy, and Presbyterianism were merely three forms of one great apostasy. In politics the Independents were, to use the phrase of their time, root and branch men, or, to use the kindred phrase of our own time, radicals. Not content with limiting the power of the monarch, they were desirous to erect a commonwealth on the ruins of the old English polity. At first they had been inconsiderable, both in numbers and in weight; but before the war had lasted two years they became, not indeed the largest, but the most powerful faction in the country. Some of the old parliamentary leaders had been removed by death; and others had forfeited the public confidence. Pym had been borne, with princely honours, to a grave among the Plantagenets. Hampden had fallen, as became him, while vainly endeavouring, by his heroic example, to inspire his followers with courage to face the fiery cavalry of Rupert. Bedford had been untrue to the cause. Northumberland was known to be lukewarm. Essex and his lieutenants had shown little vigour and ability in the conduct of military operations. At such a conjuncture it was that the Independent party, ardent, resolute, and uncompromising, began to raise its head, both in the camp and in the House of Commons.

The soul of that party was Oliver Cromwell. Bred to Oliver Cromwell. peaceful occupations, he had, at more than forty years of age, accepted a commission in the parliamentary army. No sooner had he become a soldier than he discerned, with the keen glance of genius, what Essex and men like Essex, with all their experience, were unable to perceive. He saw precisely where the strength of the Royalists lay, and by what means alone that strength could be overpowered. He saw that it was necessary to reconstruct the army of the Parliament. He saw also that there were abundant and excellent materials for the purpose, materials less showy, indeed, but more solid, than those

CHAP.
I.
of which the gallant squadrons of the King were composed. It was necessary to look for recruits who were not mere mercenaries, for recruits of decent station and grave character, fearing God and zealous for public liberty. With such men he filled his own regiment, and, while he subjected them to a discipline more rigid than had ever before been known in England, he administered to their intellectual and moral nature stimulants of fearful potency.

The events of the year 1644 fully proved the superiority of his abilities. In the south, where Essex held the command, the parliamentary forces underwent a succession of shameful disasters; but in the north the victory of Marston Moor fully compensated for all that had been lost elsewhere. That victory was not a more serious blow to the Royalists than to the party which had hitherto been dominant at Westminster; for it was notorious that the day, disgracefully lost by the Presbyterians, had been retrieved by the energy of Cromwell, and by the steady valour of the warriors whom he had trained.

Self-
denying
Ordi-
nance.
These events produced the Self-denying Ordinance and the new model of the army. Under decorous pretexts, and with every mark of respect, Essex and most of those who had held high posts under him were removed; and the conduct of the war was intrusted to very different hands. Fairfax, a brave soldier, but of mean understanding und irresolute temper, was the nominal Lord General of the forces; but Cromwell was their real head.

Cromwell made haste to organize the whole army on the same principles on which he had organized his own regiment. As soon as this process was complete, the event of the war was decided. The Cavaliers had now to encounter natural courage equal to their own, enthusiasm stronger than their own, and discipline such as was utterly wanting to them. It soon became a proverb that the soldiers of Fairfax and Cromwell were men of a different breed from the soldiers of Essex. At

Naseby took place the first great encounter between the
Royalists and the remodelled army of the Houses. The
victory of the Roundheads was complete and decisive. It
was followed by other triumphs in rapid succession. In a few
months the authority of the Parliament was fully established
over the whole kingdom. Charles fled to the Scots, and was
by them, in a manner which did not much exalt their national
character, delivered up to his English subjects.

While the event of the war was still doubtful, the Houses
had put the Primate to death, had interdicted, within the
sphere of their authority, the use of the Liturgy, and had required all men to subscribe that renowned instrument known
by the name of the Solemn League and Covenant. When the
struggle was over, the work of innovation and revenge was
pushed on with still greater ardour. The ecclesiastical polity
of the kingdom was remodelled. Most of the old clergy were
ejected from their benefices. Fines, often of ruinous amount,
were laid on the Royalists, already impoverished by large aids
furnished to the King. Many estates were confiscated. Many
proscribed Cavaliers found it expedient to purchase, at an
enormous cost, the protection of eminent members of the
victorious party. Large domains belonging to the crown, to
the bishops, and to the chapters were seized, and either
granted away or put up to auction. In consequence of these
spoliations, a great part of the soil of England was at once
offered for sale. As money was scarce, as the market was
glutted, as the title was insecure, and as the awe inspired by
powerful bidders prevented free competition, the prices were
often merely nominal. Thus many old and honourable families disappeared and were heard of no more; and many new
men rose rapidly to affluence.

But, while the Houses were employing their authority
thus, it suddenly passed out of their hands. It had been
obtained by calling into existence a power which could not be

controlled. In the summer of 1647, about twelve months
after the last fortress of the Cavaliers had submitted to the
Parliament, the Parliament was compelled to submit to its
own soldiers.

Thirteen years followed, during which England was, under
various names and forms, really governed by the sword.
Never before that time, or since that time, was the civil power
in our country subjected to military dictation.

The army which now became supreme in the State was an
army very different from any that has since been seen among
us. At present the pay of the common soldier is not such
as can seduce any but the humblest class of English labourers
from their calling. A barrier almost impassable separates
him from the commissioned officer. The great majority of
those who rise high in the service rise by purchase. So numerous and extensive are the remote dependencies of England,
that every man who enlists in the line must expect to pass
many years in exile, and some years in climates unfavourable
to the health and vigour of the European race. The army of
the Long Parliament was raised for home service. The pay
of the private soldier was much above the wages earned by
the great body of the people; and, if he distinguished himself
by intelligence and courage, he might hope to attain high
commands. The ranks were accordingly composed of persons
superior in station and education to the multitude. These
persons, sober, moral, diligent, and accustomed to reflect,
had been induced to take up arms, not by the pressure of
want, not by the love of novelty and license, not by the
arts of recruiting officers, but by religious and political zeal,
mingled with the desire of distinction and promotion. The
boast of the soldiers, as we find it recorded in their solemn
resolutions, was, that they had not been forced into the service, nor had enlisted chiefly for the sake of lucre, that they
were no janissaries, but freeborn Englishmen, who had, of

their own accord, put their lives in jeopardy for the liberties
and religion of England, and whose right and duty it was to watch over the welfare of the nation which they had saved.

A force thus composed might, without injury to its efficiency, be indulged in some liberties which, if allowed to any other troops, would have proved subversive of all discipline. In general, soldiers who should form themselves into political clubs, elect delegates, and pass resolutions on high questions of state, would soon break loose from all control, would cease to form an army, and would become the worst and most dangerous of mobs. Nor would it be safe, in our time, to tolerate in any regiment religious meetings, at which a corporal versed in Scripture should lead the devotions of his less gifted colonel, and admonish a backsliding major. But such was the intelligence, the gravity, and the self-command of the warriors whom Cromwell had trained, that in their camp a political organization and a religious organization could exist without destroying military organization. The same men, who, off duty, were noted as demagogues and field preachers, were distinguished by steadiness, by the spirit of order, and by prompt obedience on watch, on drill, and on the field of battle.

In war this strange force was irresistible. The stubborn courage characteristic of the English people was, by the system of Cromwell, at once regulated and stimulated. Other leaders have maintained order as strict. Other leaders have inspired their followers with zeal as ardent. But in his camp alone the most rigid discipline was found in company with the fiercest enthusiasm. His troops moved to victory with the precision of machines, while burning with the wildest fanaticism of Crusaders. From the time when the army was remodelled to the time when it was disbanded, it never found, either in the British islands or on the Continent, an enemy who could stand its onset. In England, Scotland, Ireland, Flanders, the Puritan warriors, often surrounded by difficulties, sometimes contending against threefold odds, not only never failed to conquer, but never failed to destroy and break in pieces whatever force was opposed to them. They at length came to regard the day of battle as a day of certain triumph, and marched against the most renowned battalions of Europe with disdainful confidence. Turenne was startled by the shout of stern exultation with which his English allies advanced to the combat, and expressed the delight of a true soldier, when he learned that it was ever the fashion of Cromwell's pikemen to rejoice greatly when they beheld the enemy; and the banished Cavaliers felt an emotion of national pride, when they saw a brigade of their countrymen, outnumbered by foes and abandoned by allies, drive before it in headlong rout the finest infantry of Spain, and force a passage into a counterscarp which had just been pronounced impregnable by the ablest of the Marshals of France.

But that which chiefly distinguished the army of Cromwell from other armies was the austere morality and the fear of God which pervaded all ranks. It is acknowledged by the most zealous Royalists that, in that singular camp, no oath was heard, no drunkenness or gambling was seen, and that, during the long dominion of the soldiery, the property of the peaceable citizen and the honour of woman were held sacred. If outrages were committed, they were outrages of a very different kind from those of which a victorious army is generally guilty. No servant girl complained of the rough gallantry of the redcoats. Not an ounce of plate was taken from the shops of the goldsmiths. But a Pelagian sermon, or a window on which the Virgin and Child were painted, produced in the Puritan ranks an excitement which it required the utmost exertions of the officers to quell. One of Cromwell's chief difficulties was to restrain his musketeers and dragoons from invading by main force the pulpits of ministers whose discourses, to use the language of that time, were not savoury; and too many of our cathedrals still bear the marks of the hatred with which those stern spirits regarded every vestige of Popery.

To keep down the English people was no light task even for that army. No sooner was the first pressure of military tyranny felt, than the nation, unbroken to such servitude, began to struggle fiercely. Insurrections broke out even in those counties which, during the recent war, had been the most submissive to the Parliament. Indeed, the Parliament itself abhorred its old defenders more than its old enemies, and was desirous to come to terms of accommodation with Charles at the expense of the troops. In Scotland, at the same time, a coalition was formed between the Royalists and a large body of Presbyterians who regarded the doctrines of the Independents with detestation. At length the storm burst. There were risings in Norfolk, Suffolk, Essex, Kent, Wales. The fleet in the Thames suddenly hoisted the royal colours, stood out to sea, and menaced the southern coast. A great Scottish force crossed the frontier and advanced into Lancashire. It might well be suspected that these movements were contemplated with secret complacency by a majority both of the Lords and of the Commons.

But the yoke of the army was not to be so shaken off. While Fairfax suppressed the risings in the neighbourhood of the capital, Oliver routed the Welsh insurgents, and, leaving their castles in ruins, marched against the Scots. His troops were few, when compared with the invaders; but he was little in the habit of counting his enemies. The Scottish army was utterly destroyed. A change in the Scottish government followed. An administration, hostile to the King, was formed at Edinburgh; and Cromwell, more than ever the darling of his soldiers, returned in triumph to London.

And now a design, to which, at the commencement of the civil war, no man would have dared to allude, and which was not less inconsistent with the Solemn League and Covenant than with the old law of England, began to take a distinct form. The austere warriors who ruled the nation had, during some months, meditated a fearful vengeance on the captive King. When and how the scheme originated; whether it spread from the general to the ranks, or from the ranks to the general; whether it is to be ascribed to policy using fanaticism as a tool, or to fanaticism bearing down policy with headlong impulse, are questions which, even at this day, cannot be answered with perfect confidence. It seems, however, on the whole, probable that he who seemed to lead was really forced to follow, and that, on this occasion, as on another great occasion a few years later, he sacrificed his own judgment and his own inclinations to the wishes of the army. For the power which he had called into existence was a power which even he could not always control; and, that he might ordinarily command, it was necessary that he should sometimes obey. He publicly protested that he was no mover in the matter, that the first steps had been taken without his privity, that he could not advise the Parliament to strike the blow, but that he submitted his own feelings to the force of circumstances which seemed to him to indicate the purposes of providence. It has been the fashion to consider those professions as instances of the hypocrisy which is vulgarly imputed to him. But even those who pronounce him a hypocrite will scarcely venture to call him a fool. They are therefore bound to show that he had some purpose to serve by secretly stimulating the army to take that course which he did not venture openly to recommend. It would be absurd to suppose that he, who was never by his respectable enemies represented as wantonly cruel or implacably vindictive, would have taken the most important step of his life under the influence of mere malevolence. He was far too wise a man not to know, when he consented to shed CHAP. that august blood, that he was doing a deed which was in- I. expiable, and which would move the grief and horror, not only of the Royalists, but of nine tenths of those who had stood by the Parliament. Whatever visions may have deluded others, he was assuredly dreaming neither of a republic on the antique pattern, nor of the millennial reign of the saints. If he already aspired to be himself the founder of a new dynasty, it was plain that Charles the First was a less formidable competitor than Charles the Second would be. At the moment of the death of Charles the First the loyalty of every Cavalier would be transferred, unimpaired, to Charles the Second. Charles the First was a captive; Charles the Second would be at liberty. Charles the First was an object of suspicion and dislike to a large proportion of those who yet shuddered at the thought of slaying him; Charles the Second would excite all the interest which belongs to distressed youth and innocence. It is impossible to believe that considerations so obvious, and so important, escaped the most profound politician of that age. The truth is that Cromwell had, at one time, meant to mediate between the throne and the Parliament, and to reorganize the distracted State by the power of the sword, under the sanction of the royal name. In this design he persisted till he was compelled to abandon it by the refractory temper of the soldiers, and by the incurable duplicity of the King. A party in the camp began to clamour for the head of the traitor, who was for treating with Agag. Conspiracies were formed. Threats of impeachment were loudly uttered. A mutiny broke out, which all the vigour and resolution of Oliver could hardly quell. And though, by a judicious mixture of severity and kindness, he succeeded in restoring order, he saw that it would be in the highest degree difficult and perilous to contend against the rage of warriors, who regarded the fallen tyrant as their foe, and as the foe of their God.

At the same time it became more evident than ever that the King could not be trusted. The vices of Charles had grown upon him. They were, indeed, vices which difficulties and perplexities generally bring out in the strongest light. Cunning is the natural defence of the weak. A prince, therefore, who is habitually a deceiver when at the height of power, is not likely to learn frankness in the midst of embarrassments and distresses. Charles was not only a most unscrupulous but a most unlucky dissembler. There never was a politician to whom so many frauds and falsehoods were brought home by undeniable evidence. He publicly recognised the Houses at Westminster as a legal Parliament, and, at the same time, made a private minute in council, declaring the recognition null. He publicly disclaimed all thought of calling in foreign aid against his people: he privately solicited aid from France, from Denmark, and from Loraine. He publicly denied that he employed Papists: at the same time he privately sent to his generals directions to employ every Papist that would serve. He publicly took the sacrament at Oxford, as a pledge that he never would even connive at Popery: he privately assured his wife, that he intended to tolerate Popery in England; and he authorised Lord Glamorgan to promise that Popery should be established in Ireland. Then he attempted to clear himself at his agent's expense. Glamorgan received, in the royal hand-writing, reprimands intended to be read by others, and eulogies which were to be seen only by himself. To such an extent, indeed, had insincerity now tainted the King's whole nature, that his most devoted friends could not refrain from complaining to each other, with bitter grief and shame, of his crooked politics. His defeats, they said, gave them less pain than his intrigues. Since he had been a prisoner, there was no section of the victorious party which had not been the object both of his flatteries and of his machinations: but never was he more unfortunate than when he attempted at once to cajole and to undermine Cromwell.

Cromwell had to determine whether he would put to hazard the attachment of his party, the attachment of his army, his own greatness, nay his own life, in an attempt, which would probably have been vain, to save a prince whom no engagement could bind. With many struggles and misgivings, and probably not without many prayers, the decision was made. Charles was left to his fate. The military saints resolved that, in defiance of the old laws of the realm, and of the almost universal sentiment of the nation, the King should expiate his crimes with his blood. He for a time expected a death like that of his unhappy predecessors, Edward the Second and Richard the Second. But he was in no danger of such treason. Those who had him in their gripe were not midnight stabbers. What they did they did in order that it might be a spectacle to heaven and earth, and that it might be held in everlasting remembrance. They enjoyed keenly the very scandal which they gave. That the ancient constitution and the public opinion of England were directly opposed to regicide made regicide seem strangely fascinating to a party bent on effecting a complete political and social revolution. In order to accomplish their purpose, it was necessary that they should first break in pieces every part of the machinery of the government; and this necessity was rather agreeable than painful to them. The Commons passed a vote tending to accommodation with the King. The soldiers excluded the majority by force. The Lords unanimously rejected the proposition that the King should be brought to trial. Their house was instantly closed. No court, known to the law, would take on itself the office of judging the fountain of justice. A revolutionary tribunal was created. That tribunal pronounced Charles a tyrant, a traitor, a murderer, and a public enemy; and his head was severed from his shoulders before thousands of spectators, in front of the banqueting hall of his own palace.

In no long time it became manifest that those political and

religious zealots, to whom this deed is to be ascribed, had committed, not only a crime, but an error. They had given to a prince, hitherto known to his people chiefly by his faults, an opportunity of displaying, on a great theatre, before the eyes of all nations and all ages, some qualities which irresistibly call forth the admiration and love of mankind, the high spirit of a gallant gentleman, the patience and meekness of a penitent Christian. Nay, they had so contrived their revenge that the very man whose whole life had been a series of attacks on the liberties of England now seemed to die a martyr in the cause of those liberties. No demagogue ever produced such an impression on the public mind as the captive King who, retaining in that extremity all his regal dignity, and confronting death with dauntless courage, gave utterance to the feelings of his oppressed people, manfully refused to plead before a court unknown to the law, appealed from military violence to the principles of the constitution, asked by what right the House of Commons had been purged of its most respectable members and the House of Lords deprived of its legislative functions, and told his weeping hearers that he was defending not only his own cause, but theirs. His long misgovernment, his innumerable perfidies, were forgotten. His memory was, in the minds of the great majority of his subjects, associated with those free institutions which he had, during many years, laboured to destroy: for those free institutions had perished with him, and, amidst the mournful silence of a community kept down by arms, had been defended by his voice alone. From that day began a reaction in favour of monarchy and of the exiled house, a reaction which never ceased till the throne had again been set up in all its old dignity.

At first, however, the slayers of the King seemed to have derived new energy from that sacrament of blood by which they had bound themselves closely together, and separated themselves for ever from the great body of their countrymen. England was declared a commonwealth. The House of Commons, reduced to a small number of members, was nominally the supreme power in the State. In fact, the army and its great chief governed every thing. Oliver had made his choice. He had kept the hearts of his soldiers, and had broken with almost every other class of his fellow-citizens. Beyond the limits of his camps and fortresses he could scarcely be said to have a party. Those elements of force which, when the civil war broke out, had appeared arrayed against each other, were combined against him; all the Cavaliers, the great majority of the Roundheads, the Anglican Church, the Presbyterian Church, the Roman Catholic Church, England, Scotland, Ireland. Yet such was his genius and resolution that he was able to overpower and crush everything that crossed his path, to make himself more absolute master of his country than any of her legitimate Kings had been, and to make his country more dreaded and respected than she had been during many generations under the rule of her legitimate Kings.

England had already ceased to struggle. But the two other kingdoms which had been governed by the Stuarts were hostile to the new republic. The Independent party was equally odious to the Roman Catholics of Ireland, and to the Presbyterians of Scotland. Both those countries, lately in rebellion against Charles the First, now acknowledged the authority of Charles the Second.

But everything yielded to the vigour and ability of Cromwell. In a few months he subjugated Ireland, as Ireland had never been subjugated during the five centuries of slaughter which had elapsed since the landing of the first Norman settlers. He resolved to put an end to that conflict of races and religions which had so long distracted the island, by making the English and Protestant population decidedly predominant. For this end he gave the rein to the fierce enthusiasm of his followers, waged war resembling that which Israel waged on the Canaanites, smote the idolaters with the edge of the sword, so that great cities were left without inhabitants, drove many thousands to the Continent, shipped off many thousands to the West Indies, and supplied the void thus made by pouring in numerous colonists, of Saxon blood, and of Calvinistic faith. Strange to say, under that iron rule, the conquered country began to wear an outward face of prosperity. Districts which had recently been as wild as those where the first white settlers of Connecticut were contending with the red men were in a few years transformed into the likeness of Kent and Norfolk. New buildings, roads, and plantations were everywhere seen. The rent of estates rose fast; and soon the English land-owners began to complain that they were met in every market by the products of Ireland, and to clamour for protecting laws.

From Ireland the victorious chief, who was now in name, as he had long been in reality, Lord General of the armies of the Commonwealth, turned to Scotland. The young King was there. He had consented to profess himself a Presbyterian, and to subscribe the Covenant; and, in return for these concessions, the austere Puritans who bore sway at Edinburgh had permitted him to assume the crown, and to hold, under their inspection and control, a solemn and melancholy court. This mock loyalty was of short duration. In two great battles Cromwell annihilated the military force of Scotland. Charles fled for his life, and, with extreme difficulty, escaped the fate of his father. The ancient kingdom of the Stuarts was reduced, for the first time, to profound submission. Of that independence, so manfully defended against the mightiest and ablest of the Plantagenets, no vestige was left. The English Parliament made laws for Scotland. English judges held assizes in Scotland. Even that stubborn Church, which has held its own against so many CHAP. I. governments, scarce dared to utter an audible murmur.

Thus far there had been at least the semblance of harmony Expulsion of the Long Parliament. between the warriors who subjugated Ireland and Scotland and the politicians who sate at Westminster: but the alliance which had been cemented by danger was dissolved by victory. The Parliament forgot that it was but the creature of the army. The army was less disposed than ever to submit to the dictation of the Parliament. Indeed the few members who made up what was contemptuously called the Rump of the House of Commons had no more claim than the military chiefs to be esteemed the representatives of the nation. The dispute was soon brought to a decisive issue. Cromwell filled the House with armed men. The Speaker was pulled out of his chair, the mace taken from the table, the room cleared, and the door locked. The nation, which loved neither of the contending parties, but which was forced, in its own despite, to respect the capacity and resolution of the General, looked on with patience, if not with complacency.

King, Lords, and Commons, had now in turn been vanquished and destroyed; and Cromwell seemed to be left the sole heir of the powers of all three. Yet were certain limitations still imposed on him by the very army to which he owed his immense authority. That singular body of men was, for the most part, composed of zealous republicans. In the act of enslaving their country, they had deceived themselves into the belief that they were emancipating her. The book which they most venerated furnished them with a precedent which was frequently in their mouths. It was true that the ignorant and ungrateful nation murmured against its deliverers. Even so had another chosen nation murmured against the leader who brought it, by painful and dreary paths, from the house of bondage to the land flowing with milk and honey. Yet had that leader rescued his brethren in spite of themselves; nor had he shrunk from making terrible examples of those who contemned the proffered freedom, and pined for the flesh-pots, the task-masters, and the idolatries of Egypt. The object of the warlike saints who surrounded Cromwell was the settlement of a free and pious commonwealth. For that end they were ready to employ, without scruple, any means, however violent and lawless. It was not impossible, therefore, to establish by their aid a monarchy absolute in effect: but it was probable that their aid would be at once withdrawn from a ruler who, even under strict constitutional restraints, should venture to assume the regal name and dignity.

The sentiments of Cromwell were widely different. He was not what he had been; nor would it be just to consider the change which his views had undergone as the effect merely of selfish ambition. When he came up to the Long Parliament, he brought with him from his rural retreat little knowledge of books, no experience of great affairs, and a temper galled by the long tyranny of the government and of the hierarchy. He had, during the thirteen years which followed, gone through a political education of no common kind. He had been a chief actor in a succession of revolutions. He had been long the soul, and at last the head, of a party. He had commanded armies, won battles, negotiated treaties, subdued, pacified, and regulated kingdoms. It would have been strange indeed if his notions had been still the same as in the days when his mind was principally occupied by his fields and his religion, and when the greatest events which diversified the course of his life were a cattle fair or a prayer meeting at Huntingdon. He saw that some schemes of innovation for which he had once been zealous, whether good or bad in themselves, were opposed to the general feeling of the country, and that, if he persevered in those schemes, he had nothing before him but constant troubles, which must

be suppressed by the constant use of the sword. He therefore wished to restore, in all essentials, that ancient constitution which the majority of the people had always loved,
and for which they now pined. The course afterwards taken
by Monk was not open to Cromwell. The memory of one
terrible day separated the great regicide for ever from the
House of Stuart. What remained was that he should mount
the ancient English throne, and reign according to the ancient
English polity. If he could effect this, he might hope that the
wounds of the lacerated State would heal fast. Great numbers of honest and quiet men would speedily rally round him.
Those Royalists whose attachment was rather to institutions
than to persons, to the kingly office than to King Charles
the First or King Charles the Second, would soon kiss the
hand of King Oliver. The peers, who now remained sullenly
at their country houses, and refused to take any part in
public affairs, would, when summoned to their House by the
writ of a King in possession, gladly resume their ancient
functions. Northumberland and Bedford, Manchester and
Pembroke, would be proud to bear the crown and the spurs,
the sceptre and the globe before the restorer of aristocracy.
A sentiment of loyalty would gradually bind the people to
the new dynasty; and, on the decease of the founder of that
dynasty, the royal dignity might descend with general ac-
quiescence to his posterity.

The ablest Royalists were of opinion that these views
were correct, and that, if Cromwell had been permitted to
follow his own judgment, the exiled line would never have
been restored. But his plan was directly opposed to the
feelings of the only class which he dared not offend. The
name of King was hateful to the soldiers. Some of them
were indeed unwilling to see the administration in the hands
of any single person. The great majority, however, were
disposed to support their general, as elective first magistrate

9 *

of a commonwealth, against all factions which might resist his authority: but they would not consent that he should assume the regal title, or that the dignity, which was the just reward of his personal merit, should be declared hereditary in his family. All that was left to him was, to give to the new republic a constitution as like the constitution of the old monarchy as the army would bear. That his elevation to power might not seem to be his own mere act, he convoked a council, composed partly of persons on whose support he could depend, and partly of persons whose opposition he might safely defy. This assembly, which he called a Parliament, and which the populace nicknamed, from one of the most conspicuous members, Barebone's Parliament, after exposing itself during a short time to the public contempt, surrendered back to the General the powers which it had received from him, and left him at liberty to frame a plan of government.

The Protectorate of Oliver Cromwell.
His plan bore, from the first, a considerable resemblance to the old English constitution; but, in a few years, he thought it safe to proceed further, and to restore almost every part of the ancient system under new names and forms. The title of King was not revived; but the kingly prerogatives were intrusted to a Lord High Protector. The sovereign was called not His Majesty, but His Highness. He was not crowned and anointed in Westminster Abbey, but was solemnly enthroned, girt with a sword of state, clad in a robe of purple, and presented with a rich Bible, in Westminster Hall. His office was not declared hereditary: but he was permitted to name his successor; and none could doubt that he would name his son.

A House of Commons was a necessary part of the new polity. In constituting this body, the Protector showed a wisdom and a public spirit which were not duly appreciated

by his contemporaries. The vices of the old representative
system, though by no means so serious as they afterwards
became, had already been remarked by far-sighted men.
Cromwell reformed that system on the same principles on
which Mr. Pitt, a hundred and thirty years later, attempted
to reform it, and on which it was at length reformed in our
own times. Small boroughs were disfranchised even more
unsparingly than in 1832; and the number of county members
was greatly increased. Very few unrepresented towns had
yet grown into importance. Of those towns the most considerable were Manchester, Leeds, and Halifax. Representatives were given to all three. An addition was made to the
number of the members for the capital. The elective fran-
chise was placed on such a footing that every man of substance, whether possessed of freehold estates in land or not,
had a vote for the county in which he resided. A few
Scotchmen and a few of the English colonists settled in Ireland, were summoned to the assembly which was to legislate,
at Westminster, for every part of the British isles.

To create a House of Lords was a less easy task. Democracy does not require the support of prescription. Monarchy
has often stood without that support. But a patrician order is
the work of time. Oliver found already existing a nobility,
opulent, highly considered, and as popular with the commonalty as any nobility has ever been. Had he, as King of
England, commanded the peers to meet him in Parliament
according to the old usage of the realm, many of them would
undoubtedly have obeyed the call. This he could not do;
and it was to no purpose that he offered to the chiefs of illustrious families seats in his new senate. They conceived that
they could not accept a nomination to an upstart assembly
without renouncing their birthright and betraying their order.
The Protector was, therefore, under the necessity of filling
his Upper House with new men who, during the late stirring

times, had made themselves conspicuous. This was the least happy of his contrivances, and displeased all parties. The Levellers were angry with him for instituting a privileged class. The multitude, which felt respect and fondness for the great historical names of the land, laughed without restraint at a House of Lords, in which lucky draymen and shoemakers were seated, to which few of the old nobles were invited, and from which almost all those old nobles who were invited turned disdainfully away.

How Oliver's Parliaments were constituted, however, was practically of little moment: for he possessed the means of conducting the administration without their support, and in defiance of their opposition. His wish seems to have been to govern constitutionally, and to substitute the empire of the laws for that of the sword. But he soon found that, hated as he was, both by Royalists and Presbyterians, he could be safe only by being absolute. The first House of Commons which the people elected by his command, questioned his authority, and was dissolved without having passed a single act. His second House of Commons, though it recognised him as Protector, and would gladly have made him King, obstinately refused to acknowledge his new Lords. He had no course left but to dissolve the Parliament. "God," he exclaimed, at parting, "be judge between you and me!"

Yet was the energy of the Protector's administration in nowise relaxed by these dissensions. Those soldiers who would not suffer him to assume the kingly title stood by him when he ventured on acts of power, as high as any English King has ever attempted. The government, therefore, though in form a republic, was in truth a despotism, moderated only by the wisdom, the sobriety, and the magnanimity of the despot. The country was divided into military districts. Those districts were placed under the command of Major Generals. Every insurrectionary movement was promptly put down and punished. The fear inspired by the power of the sword in so strong, steady, and expert a hand, quelled the spirit both of Cavaliers and Levellers. The loyal gentry declared that they were still as ready as ever to risk their lives for the old government and the old dynasty, if there were the slightest hope of success: but to rush at the head of their serving men and tenants on the pikes of brigades victorious in a hundred battles and sieges, would be a frantic waste of innocent and honourable blood. Both Royalists and Republicans, having no hope in open resistance, began to revolve dark schemes of assassination: but the Protector's intelligence was good: his vigilance was unremitting; and, whenever he moved beyond the walls of his palace, the drawn swords and cuirasses of his trusty bodyguards encompassed him thick on every side.

Had he been a cruel, licentious, and rapacious prince, the nation might have found courage in despair, and might have made a convulsive effort to free itself from military domination. But the grievances which the country suffered, though such as excited serious discontent, were by no means such as impel great masses of men to stake their lives, their fortunes, and the welfare of their families against fearful odds. The taxation, though heavier than it had been under the Stuarts, was not heavy when compared with that of the neighbouring states and with the resources of England. Property was secure. Even the Cavalier, who refrained from giving disturbance to the new settlement, enjoyed in peace whatever the civil troubles had left him. The laws were violated only in cases where the safety of the Protector's person and government was concerned. Justice was administered between man and man with an exactness and purity not before known. Under no English government, since the Reformation, had there been so little religious persecution. The unfortunate Roman Catholics, indeed, were held to be scarcely within the

pale of Christian charity. But the clergy of the fallen Anglican
Church were suffered to celebrate their worship on condition
that they would abstain from preaching about politics. Even
the Jews, whose public worship had, ever since the thirteenth
century, been interdicted, were, in spite of the strong opposition of jealous traders and fanatical theologians, permitted to build a synagogue in London.

The Protector's foreign policy at the same time extorted
the ungracious approbation of those who most detested him.
The Cavaliers could scarcely refrain from wishing that one
who had done so much to raise the fame of the nation had been
a legitimate King; and the Republicans were forced to own
that the tyrant suffered none but himself to wrong his country,
and that, if he had robbed her of liberty, he had at least given
her glory in exchange. After half a century during which
England had been of scarcely more weight in European politics than Venice or Saxony, she at once became the most
formidable power in the world, dictated terms of peace to the
United Provinces, avenged the common injuries of Christendom on the pirates of Barbary, vanquished the Spaniards by
land and sea, seized one of the finest West Indian islands,
and acquired on the Flemish coast a fortress which consoled
the national pride for the loss of Calais. She was supreme on
the ocean. She was the head of the Protestant interest. All
the reformed Churches scattered over Roman Catholic kingdoms acknowledged Cromwell as their guardian. The Huguenots of Languedoc, the shepherds who, in the hamlets of
the Alps, professed a Protestantism older than that of Augs-
burg, were secured from oppression by the mere terror of his
great name. The Pope himself was forced to preach humanity
and moderation to Popish princes. For a voice which seldom
threatened in vain had declared that, unless favour were
shown to the people of God, the English guns should be heard
in the Castle of Saint Angelo. In truth, there was nothing

which Cromwell had, for his own sake and that of his family, CHAP.
so much reason to desire as a general religious war in Europe. I.
In such a war he must have been the captain of the Protestant
armies. The heart of England would have been with him.
His victories would have been hailed with an unanimous
enthusiasm unknown in the country since the rout of the
Armada, and would have effaced the stain which one act,
condemned by the general voice of the nation, has left on his
splendid fame. Unhappily for him he had no opportunity of
displaying his admirable military talents, except against the
inhabitants of the British isles.

While he lived his power stood firm, an object of mingled
aversion, admiration, and dread to his subjects. Few indeed
loved his government; but those who hated it most hated it
less than they feared it. Had it been a worse government, it
might perhaps have been overthrown in spite of all its
strength. Had it been a weaker government, it would certainly
have been overthrown in spite of all its merits. But it had
moderation enough to abstain from those oppressions which
drive men mad; and it had a force and energy which none
but men driven mad by oppression would venture to encounter.

It has often been affirmed, but apparently with little Oliver
reason, that Oliver died at a time fortunate for his renown, succeed-
and that, if his life had been prolonged, it would probably Richard.
have closed amidst disgraces and disasters. It is certain that
he was, to the last, honoured by his soldiers, obeyed by the
whole population of the British islands, and dreaded by all
foreign powers, that he was laid among the ancient sovereigns
of England with funeral pomp such as London had never before seen, and that he was succeeded by his son Richard as
quietly as any King had ever been succeeded by any Prince of
Wales.

During five months, the administration of Richard Cromwell went on so tranquilly and regularly that all Europe be-

lieved him to be firmly established on the chair of state.   In truth his situation was in some respects much more advantageous than that of his father.   The young man had made no enemy.   His hands were unstained by civil blood.   The Cavaliers themselves allowed him to be an honest, good-natured gentleman.   The Presbyterian party, powerful both in numbers and in wealth, had been at deadly feud with the late Protector, but was disposed to regard the present Protector with favour.   That party had always been desirous to see the old civil polity of the realm restored with some clearer definitions and some stronger safeguards for public liberty, but had many reasons for dreading the restoration of the old family.   Richard was the very man for politicians of this description.   His humanity, ingenuousness, and modesty, the mediocrity of his abilities, and the docility with which he submitted to the guidance of persons wiser than himself, admirably qualified him to be the head of a limited monarchy.

For a time it seemed highly probable that he would, under the direction of able advisers, effect what his father had attempted in vain.   A Parliament was called, and the writs were directed after the old fashion.   The small boroughs which had recently been disfranchised regained their lost privilege: Manchester, Leeds, and Halifax ceased to return members; and the county of York was again limited to two knights.   It may seem strange to a generation which has been excited almost to madness by the question of parliamentary reform that great shires and towns should have submitted with patience, and even with complacency, to this change: but though reflecting men could, even in that age, discern the vices of the old representative system, and foresee that those vices would, sooner or later, produce serious practical evil, the practical evil had not yet been much felt.   Oliver's representative system, on the other hand, though constructed on

the soundest principles, was not popular. Both the events in
which it originated, and the effects which it had produced,
prejudiced men against it. It had sprung from military
violence. It had been fruitful of nothing but disputes. The
whole nation was sick of government by the sword, and pined
for government by the law. The restoration, therefore, even
of anomalies and abuses, which were in strict conformity
with the law, and which had been destroyed by the sword,
gave general satisfaction.

Among the Commons there was a strong opposition, consisting partly of avowed Republicans, and partly of concealed
Royalists: but a large and steady majority appeared to be
favourable to the plan of reviving the old civil constitution
under a new dynasty. Richard was solemnly recognised as
first magistrate. The Commons not only consented to transact
business with Oliver's Lords, but passed a vote acknowledging the right of those nobles who had in the late troubles
taken the side of public liberty, to sit in the Upper House of
Parliament without any new creation.

Thus far the statesmen by whose advice Richard acted
had been successful. Almost all the parts of the government
were now constituted as they had been constituted at the
commencement of the civil war. Had the Protector and the
Parliament been suffered to proceed undisturbed, there can
be little doubt that an order of things similar to that which
was afterwards established under the House of Hanover would
have been established under the House of Cromwell. But
there was in the State a power more than sufficient to deal
with Protector and Parliament together. Over the soldiers
Richard had no authority except that which he derived from
the great name which he had inherited. He had never led
them to victory. He had never even borne arms. All his
tastes and habits were pacific. Nor were his opinions and
feelings on religious subjects approved by the military saints.

That he was a good man he evinced by proofs more satisfactory than deep groans or long sermons, by humility and
suavity when he was at the height of human greatness, and by
cheerful resignation under cruel wrongs and misfortunes: but
the cant then common in every guard-room gave him a disgust
which he had not always the prudence to conceal. The officers
who had the principal influence among the troops stationed
near London were not his friends. They were men distinguished by valour and conduct in the field, but destitute of
the wisdom and civil courage which had been conspicuous in
their deceased leader. Some of them were honest, but fanatical, Independents and Republicans. Of this class Fleet-
wood was the representative. Others were impatient to be
what Oliver had been. His rapid elevation, his prosperity
and glory, his inauguration in the Hall, and his gorgeous
obsequies in the Abbey, had inflamed their imagination. They
were as well born as he, and as well educated: they could
not understand why they were not as worthy to wear the
purple robe, and to wield the sword of state; and they pursued
the objects of their wild ambition, not, like him, with patience,
vigilance, sagacity, and determination, but with the restless-
ness and irresolution characteristic of aspiring mediocrity.
Among these feeble copies of a great original the most conspicuous was Lambert.

Fall of
Richard,
and revi-
val of the
Long Par-
liament.
On the very day of Richard's accession the officers began
to conspire against their new master. The good understanding which existed between him and his Parliament hastened
the crisis. Alarm and resentment spread through the camp
Both the religious and the professional feelings of the army
were deeply wounded. It seemed that the Independents were
to be subjected to the Presbyterians, and that the men of the
sword were to be subjected to the men of the gown. A coalition was formed between the military malecontents and the
republican minority of the House of Commons. It may well

be doubted whether Richard could have triumphed over that CHAP. coalition, even if he had inherited his father's clear judgment I. and iron courage. It is certain that simplicity and meekness like his were not the qualities which the conjuncture required. He fell ingloriously, and without a struggle. He was used by the army as an instrument for the purpose of dissolving the Parliament, and was then contemptuously thrown aside. The officers gratified their republican allies by declaring that the expulsion of the Rump had been illegal, and by inviting that assembly to resume its functions. The old Speaker and a quorum of the old members came together and were proclaimed, amidst the scarcely stifled derision and execration of the whole nation, the supreme power in the State. It was at the same time expressly declared that there should be no first magistrate, and no House of Lords.

But this state of things could not last. On the day on which the Long Parliament revived, revived also its old quarrel with the army. Again the Rump forgot that it owed its existence to the pleasure of the soldiers, and began to treat them as subjects. Again the doors of the House of Com- Second mons were closed by military violence; and a provisional expulsion of the government, named by the officers, assumed the direction LongPar-liament. of affairs.

Meanwhile the sense of great evils, and the strong apprehension of still greater evils close at hand, had at length produced an alliance between the Cavaliers and the Presbyterians. Some Presbyterians had, indeed, been disposed to such an alliance even before the death of Charles the First: but it was not till after the fall of Richard Cromwell that the whole party became eager for the restoration of the royal house. There was no longer any reasonable hope that the old constitution could be reestablished under a new dynasty. One choice only was left, the Stuarts or the army. The banished family had committed great faults; but it had dearly

CHAP. expiated those faults, and had undergone a long, and, it
I.
——— might be hoped, a salutary training in the school of adversity.
It was probable that Charles the Second would take warning
by the fate of Charles the First. But, be this as it might,
the dangers which threatened the country were such that, in
order to avert them, some opinions might well be compromised, and some risks might well be incurred. It seemed
but too likely that England would fall under the most odious
and degrading of all kinds of government, under a government uniting all the evils of despotism to all the evils of
anarchy. Anything was preferable to the yoke of a succession
of incapable and inglorious tyrants, raised to power, like the
Deys of Barbary, by military revolutions recurring at short
intervals. Lambert seemed likely to be the first of these
rulers; but within a year Lambert might give place to Desborough, and Desborough to Harrison. As often as the
truncheon was transferred from one feeble hand to another,
the nation would be pillaged for the purpose of bestowing a
fresh donative on the troops. If the Presbyterians obstinately
stood aloof from the Royalists, the State was lost; and men
might well doubt whether, by the combined exertions of
Presbyterians and Royalists, it could be saved. For the dread
of that invincible army was on all the inhabitants of the island;
and the Cavaliers, taught by a hundred disastrous fields how
little numbers can effect against discipline, were even more
completely cowed than the Roundheads.

The army   While the soldiers remained united, all the plots and
of Scot-
land   risings of the malecontents were ineffectual. But a few days
marches   after the second expulsion of the Rump, came tidings which
into Eng-
land.   gladdened the hearts of all who were attached either to
monarchy or to liberty. That mighty force which had, during
many years, acted as one man, and which, while so acting,
had been found irresistible, was at length divided against
itself. The army of Scotland had done good service to the

Commonwealth, and was in the highest state of efficiency. It CHAP.
had borne no part in the late revolutions, and had seen them I.
with indignation resembling the indignation which the Roman
legions posted on the Danube and the Euphrates felt, when
they learned that the empire had been put up to sale by the
Prætorian Guards. It was intolerable that certain regiments
should, merely because they happened to be quartered near
Westminster, take on themselves to make and unmake several
governments in the course of half a year. If it were fit that
the state should be regulated by the soldiers, those soldiers
who upheld the English ascendency on the north of the Tweed
were as well entitled to a voice as those who garrisoned the
Tower of London. There appears to have been less fanaticism
among the troops stationed in Scotland than in any other part
of the army; and their general, George Monk, was himself
the very opposite of a zealot. He had, at the commencement
of the civil war, borne arms for the King, had been made
prisoner by the Roundheads, had then accepted a commission
from the Parliament, and, with very slender pretensions to
saintship, had raised himself to high commands by his courage
and professional skill. He had been an useful servant to both
the Protectors, had quietly acquiesced when the officers at
Westminster pulled down Richard and restored the Long
Parliament, and would perhaps have acquiesced as quietly in
the second expulsion of the Long Parliament, if the provisional government had abstained from giving him cause of
offence and apprehension. For his nature was cautious and
somewhat sluggish; nor was he at all disposed to hazard sure
and moderate advantages for the chance of obtaining even
the most splendid success. He seems to have been impelled
to attack the new rulers of the Commonwealth less by the hope
that, if he overthrew them, he should become great, than
by the fear that, if he submitted to them, he should not even
be secure. Whatever were his motives, he declared him-

CHAP.
I.

self the champion of the oppressed civil power, refused to acknowledge the usurped authority of the provisional government, and, at the head of seven thousand veterans, marched into England.

This step was the signal for a general explosion. The people everywhere refused to pay taxes. The apprentices of the City assembled by thousands and clamoured for a free Parliament. The fleet sailed up the Thames, and declared against the tyranny of the soldiers. The soldiers, no longer under the control of one commanding mind, separated into factions. Every regiment, afraid lest it should be left alone a mark for the vengeance of the oppressed nation, hastened to make a separate peace. Lambert, who had hastened northward to encounter the army of Scotland, was abandoned by his troops, and became a prisoner. During thirteen years the civil power had, in every conflict, been compelled to yield to the military power. The military power now humbled itself before the civil power. The Rump, generally hated and despised, but still the only body in the country which had any show of legal authority, returned again to the house from which it had been twice ignominiously expelled.

In the mean time Monk was advancing towards London. Wherever he came, the gentry flocked round him, imploring him to use his power for the purpose of restoring peace and liberty to the distracted nation. The General, cold-blooded, taciturn, zealous for no polity and for no religion, maintained an impenetrable reserve. What were at this time his plans, and whether he had any plan, may well be doubted. His great object, apparently, was to keep himself, as long as possible, free to choose between several lines of action. Such, indeed, is commonly the policy of men who are, like him, distinguished rather by wariness than by farsightedness. It was probably not till he had been some days in the capital that he made up his mind. The cry of the whole people was for a

free Parliament; and there could be no doubt that a Parliament really free would instantly restore the exiled family.
The Rump and the soldiers were still hostile to the House of
Stuart. But the Rump was universally detested and despised.
The power of the soldiers was indeed still formidable, but
had been greatly diminished by discord. They had no head.
They had recently been, in many parts of the country, arrayed against each other. On the very day before Monk
reached London, there was a fight in the Strand between the
cavalry and the infantry. An united army had long kept down
a divided nation: but the nation was now united, and the
army was divided.

During a short time, the dissimulation or irresolution of
Monk kept all parties in a state of painful suspense. At length Monk de-
he broke silence, and declared for a free Parliament. clares for
a free

As soon as his declaration was known, the whole nation Parlia-
ment.
was wild with delight. Wherever he appeared thousands
thronged round him, shouting and blessing his name. The
bells of all England rang joyously: the gutters ran with ale:
and, night after night, the sky five miles round London was
reddened by innumerable bonfires. Those Presbyterian members of the House of Commons who had many years before
been expelled by the army, returned to their seats, and were
hailed with acclamations by great multitudes, which filled
Westminster Hall and Palace Yard. The Independent leaders
no longer dared to show their faces in the streets, and were
scarcely safe within their own dwellings. Temporary provision was made for the government: writs were issued for a
general election; and then that memorable Parliament, which
had, during twenty eventful years, experienced every variety
of fortune, which had triumphed over its sovereign, which
had been enslaved and degraded by its servants, which had
been twice ejected and twice restored, solemnly decreed its
own dissolution.

The result of the elections was such as might have been expected from the temper of the nation. The new House of Commons consisted, with few exceptions, of persons friendly to the royal family. The Presbyterians formed the majority.

That there would be a restoration now seemed almost certain; but whether there would be a peaceable restoration was matter of painful doubt. The soldiers were in a gloomy and savage mood. They hated the title of King. They hated the name of Stuart. They hated Presbyterianism much, and Prelacy more. They saw with bitter indignation that the close of their long domination was approaching, and that a life of inglorious toil and penury was before them. They attributed their ill fortune to the weakness of some generals, and to the treason of others. One hour of their beloved Oliver might even now restore the glory which had departed. Betrayed, disunited, and left without any chief in whom they could confide, they were yet to be dreaded. It was no light thing to encounter the rage and despair of fifty thousand fighting men, whose backs no enemy had ever seen. Monk, and those with whom he acted, were well aware that the crisis was most perilous. They employed every art to sooth and to divide the discontented warriors. At the same time vigorous preparation was made for a conflict. The army of Scotland, now quartered in London, was kept in good huumor by bribes, praises, and promises. The wealthy citizens grudged nothing to a red coat, and were indeed so liberal of their best wine, that warlike saints were sometimes seen in a condition not very honourable either to their religious or to their military character. Some refractory regiments Monk ventured to disband. In the meantime the greatest exertions were made by the provisional government, with the strenuous aid of the whole body of the gentry and magistracy, to organize the militia. In every county the trainbands were held ready to march; and this force cannot be estimated at less than a hun-

dred and twenty thousand men. In Hyde Park twenty thousand citizens, well armed and accoutred, passed in review,
and showed a spirit which justified the hope that, in case of
need, they would fight manfully for their shops and firesides.
The fleet was heartily with the nation. It was a stirring time,
a time of anxiety, yet of hope. The prevailing opinion was
that England would be delivered, but not without a desperate
and bloody struggle, and that the class which had so long
ruled by the sword would perish by the sword.

Happily the dangers of a conflict were averted. There
was indeed one moment of extreme peril. Lambert escaped
from his confinement, and called his comrades to arms. The
flame of civil war was actually rekindled; but by prompt and
vigorous exertion it was trodden out before it had time to
spread. The luckless imitator of Cromwell was again a prisoner. The failure of his enterprise damped the spirit of the
soldiers; and they sullenly resigned themselves to their fate.

The new Parliament, which, having been called without The Re-
the royal writ, is more accurately described as a Convention, storation.
· met at Westminster. The Lords repaired to the hall, from
which they had, during more than eleven years, been excluded by force. Both Houses instantly invited the King to
return to his country. He was proclaimed with pomp never
before known. A gallant fleet convoyed him from Holland to
the coast of Kent. When he landed, the cliffs of Dover were
covered by thousands of gazers, among whom scarcely one
could be found who was not weeping with delight. The journey to London was a continued triumph. The whole road
from Rochester was bordered by booths and tents, and looked
like an interminable fair. Everywhere flags were flying, bells
and music sounding, wine and ale flowing in rivers to the
health of him whose return was the return of peace, of law,
and of freedom. But in the midst of the general joy, one
spot presented a dark and threatening aspect. On Blackheath

the army was drawn up to welcome the sovereign. He smiled, bowed, and extended his hand graciously to the lips of the colonels and majors. But all his courtesy was vain. The countenances of the soldiers were sad and lowering; and, had they given way to their feelings, the festive pageant of which they reluctantly made a part would have had a mournful and bloody end. But there was no concert among them. Discord and defection had left them no confidence in their chiefs or in each other. The whole array of the City of London was under arms. Numerous companies of militia had assembled from various parts of the realm, under the command of loyal noblemen and gentlemen, to welcome the King. That great day closed in peace; and the restored wanderer reposed safe in the palace of his ancestors.

CHAPTER II.

THE history of England, during the seventeenth century, CHAP. II.
is the history of the transformation of a limited monarchy, Conduct of those who restored the House of Stuart unjustly censured.
constituted after the fashion of the middle ages, into a limited
monarchy suited to that more advanced state of society in
which the public charges can no longer be borne by the
estates of the crown, and in which the public defence can no
longer be entrusted to a feudal militia. We have seen that
the politicians who were at the head of the Long Parliament
made, in 1642, a great effort to accomplish this change by
transferring, directly and formally, to the Estates of the
realm the choice of ministers, the command of the army, and
the superintendence of the whole executive administration.
This scheme was, perhaps, the best that could then be contrived: but it was completely disconcerted by the course
which the civil war took. The Houses triumphed, it is true;
but not till after such a struggle as made it necessary for them
to call into existence a power which they could not control,
and which soon began to domineer over all orders and all
parties. For a time, the evils inseparable from military
government were, in some degree, mitigated by the wisdom
and magnanimity of the great man who held the supreme
command. But, when the sword which he had wielded, with
energy indeed, but with energy always guided by good sense
and generally tempered by good nature, had passed to
captains who possessed neither his abilities nor his virtues,
it seemed too probable that order and liberty would perish in
one ignominious ruin.

That ruin was happily averted. It has been too much the
practice of writers zealous for freedom to represent the
Restoration as a disastrous event, and to condemn the folly or

baseness of that Convention which recalled the royal family without exacting new securities against maladministration. Those who hold this language do not comprehend the real nature of the crisis which followed the deposition of Richard Cromwell. England was in imminent danger of sinking under the tyranny of a succession of small men raised up and pulled down by military caprice. To deliver the country from the domination of the soldiers was the first object of every enlightened patriot: but it was an object which, while the soldiers were united, the most sanguine could scarcely expect to attain. On a sudden a gleam of hope appeared. General was opposed to general, army to army. On the use which might be made of one auspicious moment depended the future destiny of the nation. Our ancestors used that moment well. They forgot old injuries, waved petty scruples, adjourned to a more convenient season all dispute about the reforms which our institutions needed, and stood together, Cavaliers and Roundheads, Episcopalians and Presbyterians, in firm union, for the old laws of the land against military despotism. The exact partition of power among King, Lords, and Commons, might well be postponed till it had been decided whether England should be governed by King, Lords, and Commons, or by cuirassiers and pikemen. Had the statesmen of the Convention taken a different course, had they held long debates on the principles of government, had they drawn up a new constitution and sent it to Charles, had conferences been opened, had couriers been passing and repassing during some weeks between Westminster and the Netherlands, with projects and counterprojects, replies by Hyde and rejoinders by Prynne, the coalition on which the public safety depended would have been dissolved: the Presbyterians and Royalists would certainly have quarrelled: the military factions might possibly have been reconciled: and the misjudging friends of liberty might long have regretted, under a rule worse than

that of the worst Stuart, the golden opportunity which had CHAP.
II.
been suffered to escape.

The old civil polity was, therefore, by the general consent Abolition of te-
of both the great parties, reestablished.   It was again exactly nures by
what it had been when Charles the First, eighteen years be- knight service.
fore, withdrew from his capital.   All those acts of the Long
Parliament which had received the royal assent were admitted
to be still in full force.   One fresh concession, a concession
in which the Cavaliers were even more deeply interested than
the Roundheads, was easily obtained from the restored King.
The military tenure of land had been originally created as a
means of national defence.   But in the course of ages whatever was useful in the institution had disappeared; and nothing was left but ceremonies and grievances.   A landed proprietor who held an estate under the crown by knight service,
— and it was thus that most of the soil of England was
held, — had to pay a large fine on coming to his property.
He could not alienate one acre without purchasing a license.
When he died, if his domains descended to an infant, the
sovereign was guardian, and was not only entitled to great
part of the rents during the minority, but could require the
ward, under heavy penalties, to marry any person of suitable
rank.   The chief bait which attracted a needy sycophant to
the court was the hope of obtaining as the reward of servility
and flattery, a royal letter to an heiress.   These abuses had
perished with the monarchy.   That they should not revive
with it was the wish of every landed gentleman in the kingdom.   They were, therefore, solemnly abolished by statute;
and no relic of the ancient tenures in chivalry was suffered to
remain, except those honorary services which are still, at a
coronation, rendered to the person of the sovereign by some
lords of manors.

The troops were now to be disbanded.   Fifty thousand Disband-
ing of the
men, accustomed to the profession of arms, were at once army.

thrown on the world: and experience seemed to warrant the belief that this change would produce much misery and crime, that the discharged veterans would be seen begging in every street, or that they would be driven by hunger to pillage. But no such result followed. In a few months there remained not a trace indicating that the most formidable army in the world had just been absorbed into the mass of the community. The Royalists themselves confessed that, in every department of honest industry, the discarded warriors prospered beyond other men, that none was charged with any theft or robbery, that none was heard to ask an alms, and that, if a baker, a mason, or a waggoner attracted notice by his diligence and sobriety, he was in all probability one of Oliver's old soldiers.

The military tyranny had passed away; but it had left deep and enduring traces in the public mind. The name of a standing army was long held in abhorrence: and it is remarkable that this feeling was even stronger among the Cavaliers than among the Roundheads. It ought to be considered as a most fortunate circumstance that, when our country was, for the first and last time, ruled by the sword, the sword was in the hands, not of her legitimate princes, but of those rebels who slew the King and demolished the Church. Had a prince, with a title as good as that of Charles, commanded an army as good as that of Cromwell, there would have been little hope indeed for the liberties of England. Happily that instrument by which alone the monarchy could be made absolute became an object of peculiar horror and disgust to the monarchical party, and long continued to be inseparably associated in the imagination of Royalists and Prelatists with regicide and field preaching. A century after the death of Cromwell, the Tories still continued to clamour against every augmentation of the regular soldiery, and to sound the praise of a national militia. So late as the year

1786, a minister who enjoyed no common measure of their
confidence found it impossible to overcome their aversion to his scheme of fortifying the coast: nor did they ever look with entire complacency on the standing army, till the French Revolution gave a new direction to their apprehensions.

The coalition which had restored the King terminated with the danger from which it had sprung; and two hostile parties again appeared ready for conflict. Both indeed were agreed as to the propriety of inflicting punishment on some unhappy men who were, at that moment, objects of almost universal hatred. Cromwell was no more; and those who had fled before him were forced to content themselves with the miserable satisfaction of digging up, hanging, quartering, and burning the remains of the greatest prince that has ever ruled England. Other objects of vengeance, few indeed, yet too many, were found among the republican chiefs. Soon, however, the conquerors, glutted with the blood of the regicides, turned against each other. The Roundheads, while admitting the virtues of the late King, and while condemning the sentence passed upon him by an illegal tribunal, yet maintained that his administration had been, in many things, unconstitutional, and that the Houses had taken arms against him from good motives and on strong grounds. The monarchy, these politicians conceived, had no worse enemy than the flatterer who exalted the prerogative above the law, who condemned all opposition to regal encroachments, and who reviled, not only Cromwell and Harrison, but Pym and Hampden, as traitors. If the King wished for a quiet and prosperous reign, he must confide in those who, though they had drawn the sword in defence of the invaded privileges of Parliament, had yet exposed themselves to the rage of the soldiers in order to save his father, and had taken the chief part in bringing back the royal family.

The feeling of the Cavaliers was widely different. During eighteen years they had, through all vicissitudes, been faithful to the crown. Having shared the distress of their prince, were they not to share his triumph? Was no distinction to be made between them and the disloyal subject who had fought against his rightful sovereign, who had adhered to Richard Cromwell, and who had never concurred in the restoration of the Stuarts, till it appeared that nothing else could save the nation from the tyranny of the army? Grant that such a man had, by his recent services, fairly earned his pardon. Yet were his services, rendered at the eleventh hour, to be put in comparison with the toils and sufferings of those who had borne the burden and heat of the day? Was he to be ranked with men who had no need of the royal clemency, with men who had, in every part of their lives, merited the royal gratitude? Above all, was he to be suffered to retain a fortune raised out of the substance of the ruined defenders of the throne? Was it not enough that his head and his patrimonial estate, a hundred times forfeited to justice, were secure, and that he shared, with the rest of the nation, in the blessings of that mild government of which he had long been the foe? Was it necessary that he should be rewarded for his treason at the expense of men whose only crime was the fidelity with which they had observed their oath of allegiance? And what interest had the King in gorging his old enemies with prey torn from his old friends? What confidence could be placed in men who had opposed their sovereign, made war on him, imprisoned him, and who, even now, instead of hanging down their heads in shame and contrition, vindicated all that they had done, and seemed to think that they had given an illustrious proof of loyalty by just stopping short of regicide? It was true that they had lately assisted to set up the throne: but it was not less true that they had previously pulled it down, and that they still avowed principles which might impel them to pull it down again. Undoubtedly it might be fit that marks of royal approbation should be bestowed on some converts who had been eminently useful: but policy, as well as justice and gratitude, enjoined the CHAP. King to give the highest place in his regard to those who, from first to last, through good and evil, had stood by his house. On these grounds the Cavaliers very naturally demanded indemnity for all that they had suffered, and preference in the distribution of the favours of the crown. Some violent members of the party went further, and clamoured for large categories of proscription.

The political feud was, as usual, exasperated by a religious Religious feud. The King found the Church in a singular state. A short time before the commencement of the civil war, his father had given a reluctant assent to a bill, strongly supported by Falkland, which deprived the Bishops of their seats in the House of Lords: but Episcopacy and the Liturgy had never been abolished by law. The Long Parliament, however, had passed ordinances which had made a complete revolution in Church government and in public worship. The new system was, in principle, scarcely less Erastian than that which it displaced. The Houses, guided chiefly by the counsels of the accomplished Selden, had determined to keep the spiritual power strictly subordinate to the temporal power. They had refused to declare that any form of ecclesiastical polity was of divine origin; and they had provided that, from all the Church courts, an appeal should lie in the last resort to Parliament. With this highly important reservation it had been resolved to set up in England a hierarchy closely resembling that which now exists in Scotland. The authority of councils, rising one above another in regular gradation, was substituted for the authority of Bishops and Archbishops. The Liturgy gave place to the Presbyterian directory. But scarcely had the new regulations been framed, when the Independents rose to supreme influence in the state. The Independents had no disposition to enforce the ordinances touching classical, provincial, and national synods. Those ordinances, therefore, were never carried into full execution.   The Presbyterian system was fully established nowhere but in Middlesex and Lancashire.   In the other fifty counties, almost every parish seems to have been unconnected with the neighbouring parishes.   In some districts, indeed, the ministers formed themselves into voluntary associations, for the purpose of mutual help and counsel; but these associations had no coercive power.   The patrons of livings, being now checked by neither Bishop nor Presbytery, would have been at liberty to confide the cure of souls to the most scandalous of mankind, but for the arbitrary intervention of Oliver.   He established, by his own authority, a board of commissioners, called Triers.   Most of these persons were Independent divines; but a few Presbyterian ministers and a few laymen had seats.   The certificate of the Triers stood in the place both of institution and of induction; and without such a certificate no person could hold a benefice.   This was undoubtedly one of the most despotic acts ever done by any English ruler.   Yet, as it was generally felt that, without some such precaution, the country would be overrun by ignorant and drunken reprobates, bearing the name and receiving the pay of ministers, some highly respectable persons, who were not in general friendly to Cromwell, allowed that, on this occasion, he had been a public benefactor. The presentees whom the Triers had approved took possession of the rectories, cultivated the glebe lands, collected the tithes, prayed without book or surplice, and administered the Eucharist to communicants seated at long tables.

Thus the ecclesiastical polity of the realm was in inextricable confusion.   Episcopacy was the form of government prescribed by the old law which was still unrepealed.   The form of government prescribed by parliamentary ordinance was Presbyterian.   But neither the old law nor the parliamentary ordinance was practically in force.   The Church actually established may be described as an irregular body made up of a few Presbyteries, and of many Independent congregations, which were all held down and held together by the authority of the government.

Of those who had been active in bringing back the King, many were zealous for synods and for the directory, and many were desirous to terminate by a compromise the religious dissensions which had long agitated England. Between the bigoted followers of Laud and the bigoted followers of Calvin there could be neither peace nor truce: but it did not seem impossible to effect an accommodation between the moderate Episcopalians of the school of Usher and the moderate Presbyterians of the school of Baxter. The moderate Episcopalians would admit that a Bishop might lawfully be assisted by a council. The moderate Presbyterians would not deny that each provincial assembly might lawfully have a permanent president, and that this president might lawfully be called a Bishop. There might be a revised Liturgy which should not exclude extemporaneous prayer, a baptismal service in which the sign of the cross might be used or omitted at discretion, a communion service at which the faithful might sit if their consciences forbade them to kneel. But to no such plan could the great body of the Cavaliers listen with patience. The religious members of that party were conscientiously attached to the whole system of their Church. She had been dear to their murdered King. She had consoled them in defeat and penury. Her service, so often whispered in an inner chamber during the season of trial, had such a charm for them that they were unwilling to part with a single response. Other Royalists, who made little pretence to piety, yet loved the episcopal Church because she was the foe of their foes. They valued a prayer or a ceremony, not on account of the comfort which it conveyed to themselves, but on account of the vexation which it gave to the Roundheads, and were so far from being disposed to purchase union by concession that

they objected to concession chiefly because it tended to produce union.

Such feelings, though blamable, were natural and not
wholly inexcusable. The Puritans in the day of their power
had undoubtedly given cruel provocation. They ought to
have learned, if from nothing else, yet from their own discontents, from their own struggles, from their own victory, from
the fall of that proud hierarchy by which they had been so
heavily oppressed, that, in England, and in the seventeenth century, it was not in the power of the civil magistrate to drill the
minds of men into conformity with his own system of theology.
They proved, however, as intolerant and as meddling as ever
Laud had been. They interdicted under heavy penalties the
use of the Book of Common Prayer, not only in churches, but
even in private houses. It was a crime in a child to read by the
bedside of a sick parent one of those beautiful collects which
had soothed the griefs of forty generations of Christians.
Severe punishments were denounced against such as should
presume to blame the Calvinistic mode of worship. Clergymen
of respectable character were not only ejected from their benefices by thousands, but were frequently exposed to the outrages of a fanatical rabble. Churches and sepulchres, fine
works of art and curious remains of antiquity, were brutally
defaced. The Parliament resolved that all pictures in the
royal collection which contained representations of Jesus or
of the Virgin Mother should be burned. Sculpture fared as
ill as painting. Nymphs and Graces, the work of Ionian
chisels, were delivered over to Puritan stone-masons to be
made decent. Against the lighter vices the ruling faction
waged war with a zeal little tempered by humanity or by
common sense. Sharp laws were passed against betting. It
was enacted that adultery should be punished with death.
The illicit intercourse of the sexes, even where neither violence nor seduction was imputed, where no public scandal was

given, where no conjugal right was violated, was made a misdemeanour. Public amusements, from the masques which were exhibited at the mansions of the great down to the wrestling matches and grinning matches on village greens, were vigorously attacked. One ordinance directed that all the Maypoles in England should forthwith be hewn down. Another proscribed all theatrical diversions. The play-houses were to be dismantled, the spectators fined, the actors whipped at the cart's tail. Rope-dancing, puppet-shows, bowls, horse-racing, were regarded with no friendly eye. But bear-baiting, then a favourite diversion of high and low, was the abomination which most strongly stirred the wrath of the austere sectaries. It is to be remarked that their antipathy to this sport had nothing in common with the feeling which has, in our own time, induced the legislature to interfere for the purpose of protecting beasts against the wanton cruelty of men. The Puritan hated bear-baiting, not because it gave pain to the bear, but because it gave pleasure to the spectators. Indeed, he generally contrived to enjoy the double pleasure of tormenting both spectators and bear. *

* How little compassion for the bear had to do with the matter is sufficiently proved by the following extract from a paper entitled. A perfect Diurnal of some Passages of Parliament, and from other Parts of the Kingdom, from Monday July 24th, to Monday July 31st, 1643. "Upon the queen's coming from Holland, she brought with her, besides a company of savagelike ruffians, a company of savage bears, to what purpose you may judge by the sequel. Those bears were left about Newark, and were brought into country towns constantly on the Lord's day to be baited, such is the religion those here related would settle amongst us; and, if any went about to hinder or but speak against their damnable profanations, they were presently noted as Roundheads and Puritans, and sure to be plundered for it. But some of Colonel Cromwell's forces coming by accident into Uppingham town, in Rutland, on the Lord's day, found these bears playing there in the usual manner, and, in the height of their sport, caused them to be seized upon, tied to a tree and shot." This was by no means a solitary instance. Colonel Pride, when Sheriff of Surrey, ordered the beasts in the bear garden of Southwark to be killed. He is represented by a loyal satirist as defending the act thus: — "The first thing that is upon my spirits is the killing of the bears, for which the

CHAP.
II.
　　Perhaps no single circumstance more strongly illustrates the temper of the precisians than their conduct respecting Christmas day. Christmas had been, from time immemorial, the season of joy and domestic affection, the season when families assembled, when children came home from school, when quarrels were made up, when carols were heard in every street, when every house was decorated with evergreens, and every table was loaded with good cheer. At that season all hearts not utterly destitute of kindness were enlarged and softened. At that season the poor were admitted to partake largely of the overflowings of the wealth of the rich, whose bounty was peculiarly acceptable on account of the shortness of the days and of the severity of the weather. At that season the interval between landlord and tenant, master and servant, was less marked than through the rest of the year. Where there is much enjoyment there will be some excess: yet, on the whole, the spirit in which the holiday was kept was not unworthy of a Christian festival. The Long Parliament gave orders, in 1644, that the twenty-fifth of December should be strictly observed as a fast, and that all men should pass it in humbly bemoaning the great national sin which they and their fathers had so often committed on that day by romping under the mistletoe, eating boar's head, and drinking ale flavoured with roasted apples. No public act of that time seems to have irritated the common people more. On the next anniversary of the festival formidable riots broke out in many places. The constables were resisted, the magistrates insulted, the houses of noted zealots attacked, and the proscribed service of the day openly read in the churches.

　　Such was the spirit of the extreme Puritans, both Presbyterian and Independent. Oliver, indeed, was little disposed

---

people hate me, and call me all the names in the rainbow. But did not David kill a bear? Did not the Lord Deputy Ireton kill a bear? Did not another lord of ours kill five bears?" — Last Speech and dying Words of Thomas Pride.

to be either a persecutor or a meddler. But Oliver, the head of a party, and consequently, to a great extent, the slave of a party, could not govern altogether according to his own inclinations. Even under his administration many magistrates, within their own jurisdiction, made themselves as odious as Sir Hudibras, interfered with all the pleasures of the neighbourhood, dispersed festive meetings, and put fiddlers in the stocks. Still more formidable was the zeal of the soldiers. In every village where they appeared there was an end of dancing, bell-ringing, and hockey. In London they several times interrupted theatrical performances at which the Protector had the judgment and good nature to connive.

With the fear and hatred inspired by such a tyranny contempt was largely mingled. The peculiarities of the Puritan, his look, his dress, his dialect, his strange scruples, had been, ever since the time of Elizabeth, favourite subjects with mockers. But these peculiarities appeared far more grotesque in a faction which ruled a great empire than in obscure and persecuted congregations. The cant which had moved laughter when it was heard on the stage from Tribulation Wholesome, and Zeal-of-the-Land Busy, was still more laughable when it proceeded from the lips of Generals and Councillors of state. It is also to be noted that during the civil troubles several sects had sprung into existence, whose eccentricities surpassed anything that had before been seen in England. A mad tailor, named Lodowick Muggleton, wandered from pot-house to pot-house, tippling ale, and denouncing eternal torments against those who refused to believe, on his testimony, that the Supreme Being was only six feet high, and that the sun was just four miles from the earth. * George Fox had raised a tempest of derision by

* See Penn's New Witnesses proved Old Heretics, and Muggleton's works, *passim.*

proclaiming that it was a violation of Christian sincerity to designate a single person by a plural pronoun, and that it was an idolatrous homage to Janus and Woden to talk about January and Wednesday. His doctrine, a few years later, was embraced by some eminent men, and rose greatly in the public estimation. But at the time of the Restoration the Quakers were popularly regarded as the most despicable of fanatics. By the Puritans they were treated with severity here, and were persecuted to the death in New England. Nevertheless the public, which seldom makes nice distinctions, often confounded the Puritan with the Quaker. Both were schismatics. Both hated episcopacy and the Liturgy. Both had what seemed extravagant whimsies about dress, diversions, and postures. Widely as the two differed in opinion, they were popularly classed together as canting schismatics; and whatever was ridiculous or odious in either increased the scorn and aversion which the multitude felt for both.

Before the civil wars, even those who most disliked the opinions and manners of the Puritan were forced to admit that his moral conduct was generally, in essentials, blameless; but this praise was now no longer bestowed, and, unfortunately, was no longer deserved. The general fate of sects is to obtain a high reputation for sanctity while they are oppressed, and to lose it as soon as they become powerful: and the reason is obvious. It is seldom that a man inrolls himself in a proscribed body from any but conscientious motives. Such a body, therefore, is composed, with scarcely an exception, of sincere persons. The most rigid discipline that can be enforced within a religious society is a very feeble instrument of purification, when compared with a little sharp persecution from without. We may be certain that very few persons, not seriously impressed by religious convictions, applied for baptism while Diocletian was vexing the Church, or joined themselves to Protestant congregations at the risk of being burned by Bonner. But, when a sect becomes powerful, when its favour is the road to riches and dignities, worldly and ambitious men crowd into it, talk its language, conform strictly to its ritual, mimic its peculiarities, and frequently go beyond its honest members in all the outward indications of zeal. No discernment, not watchfulness, on the part of ecclesiastical rulers, can prevent the intrusion of such false brethren. The tares and the wheat must grow together. Soon the world begins to find out that the godly are not better than other men, and argues, with some justice, that, if not better, they must be much worse. In no long time all those signs which were formerly regarded as characteristic of a saint are regarded as characteristic of a knave.

Thus it was with the English Nonconformists. They had been oppressed; and oppression had kept them a pure body. They then became supreme in the state. No man could hope to rise to eminence and command but by their favour. Their favour was to be gained only by exchanging with them the signs and pass-words of spiritual fraternity. One of the first resolutions adopted by Barebone's Parliament, the most intensely Puritanical of all our political assemblies, was that no person should be admitted into the public service till the House should be satisfied of his real godliness. What were then considered as the signs of real godliness, the sad coloured dress, the sour look, the straight hair, the nasal whine, the speech interspersed with quaint texts, the abhorrence of comedies, cards, and hawking, were easily counterfeited by men to whom all religions were the same. The sincere Puritans soon found themselves lost in a multitude, not merely of men of the world, but of the very worst sort of men of the world. For the most notorious libertine who had fought under the royal standard might justly be thought

11*

virtuous when compared with some of those who, while they
talked about sweet experiences and comfortable scriptures,
lived in the constant practice of fraud, rapacity, and secret
debauchery. The people, with a rashness which we may
justly regret, but at which we cannot wonder, formed their
estimate of the whole body from these hypocrites. The
theology, the manners, the dialect of the Puritan were thus
associated in the public mind with the darkest and meanest
vices. As soon as the Restoration had made it safe to avow
enmity to the party which had so long been predominant in
the state, a general outcry against Puritanism rose from every
corner of the kingdom, and was often swollen by the voices
of those very dissemblers whose villany had brought disgrace
on the Puritan name.

Thus the two great parties, which, after a long contest,
had for a moment concurred in restoring monarchy, were,
both in politics and in religion, again opposed to each other.
The great body of the nation leaned to the Royalists. The
crimes of Strafford and Laud, the excesses of the Star
Chamber and of the High Commission, the great services
which the Long Parliament had, during the first year of its
existence, rendered to the state, had faded from the minds
of men. The execution of Charles the First, the sullen
tyranny of the Rump, the violence of the army, were remembered with loathing; and the multitude was inclined to
hold all who had withstood the late King responsible for his
death and for the subsequent disasters.

The House of Commons, having been elected while the
Presbyterians were dominant, by no means represented the
general sense of the people, and showed a strong disposition
to check the intolerant loyalty of the Cavaliers. One member,
who ventured to declare that all who had drawn the sword
against Charles the First were as much traitors as those who
cut off his head, was called to order, placed at the bar, and

reprimanded by the Speaker. The general wish of the House undoubtedly was to settle the ecclesiastical disputes in a manner satisfactory to the moderate Puritans. But to such a settlement both the court and the nation were averse.

The restored King was at this time more loved by the people than any of his predecessors had ever been. The calamities of his house, the heroic death of his father, his own long sufferings and romantic adventures, made him an object of tender interest. His return had delivered the country from an intolerable bondage. Recalled by the voice of both the contending factions, he was in a position which enabled him to arbitrate between them; and in some respects he was well qualified for the task. He had received from nature excellent parts and á happy temper. His education had been such as might have been expected to develope his understanding, and to form him to the practice of every public and private virtue. He had passed through all varieties of fortune, and had seen both sides of human nature. He had, while very young, been driven forth from a palace to a life of exile, penury, and danger. He had, at the age when the mind and body are in their highest perfection, and when the first effervescence of boyish passions should have subsided, been recalled from his wanderings to wear a crown. He had been taught by bitter experience how much baseness, perfidy, and ingratitude may lie hid under the obsequious demeanour of courtiers. He had found, on the other hand, in the huts of the poorest, true nobility of soul. When wealth was offered to any who would betray him, when death was denounced against all who should shelter him, cottagers and serving men had kept his secret truly, and had kissed his hand under his mean disguises with as much reverence as if he had been seated on his ancestral throne. From such a school it might have been expected that a young man who wanted neither abilities nor amiable qualities would have come forth a great and good King. Charles came forth from that school with social habits, with polite and engaging manners, and with some talent for lively conversation, addicted beyond measure to sensual indulgence, fond of sauntering and of frivolous amusements, incapable of self-denial and of exertion, without faith in human virtue or in human attachment, without desire of renown, and without sensibility to reproach. According to him, every person was to be bought: but some people haggled more about their price than others; and when this haggling was very obstinate and very skilful it was called by some fine name. The chief trick by which clever men kept up the price of their abilities was called integrity. The chief trick by which handsome women kept up the price of their beauty was called modesty. The love of God, the love of country, the love of family, the love of friends, were phrases of the same sort, delicate and convenient synonymes for the love of self. Thinking thus of mankind, Charles naturally cared very little what they thought of him. Honour and shame were scarcely more to him than light and darkness to the blind. His contempt of flattery has been highly commended, but seems, when viewed in connection with the rest of his character, to deserve no commendation. It is possible to be below flattery as well as above it. One who trusts nobody will not trust sycophants. One who does not value real glory will not value its counterfeit.

It is creditable to Charles's temper that, ill as he thought of his species, he never became a misanthrope. He saw little in men but what was hateful. Yet he did not hate them. Nay, he was so far humane that it was highly disagreeable to him to see their sufferings or to hear their complaints. This however is a sort of humanity which, though amiable and laudable in a private man whose power to help or hurt is bounded by a narrow circle, has in princes often been rather a vice than a virtue. More than one well disposed ruler has given up whole provinces to rapine and oppression, merely from a wish to see none but happy faces round his own board and in his own walks. No man is fit to govern great societies who hesitates about disobliging the few who have access to him for the sake of the many whom he will never see. The facility of Charles was such as has perhaps never been found in any man of equal sense. He was a slave without being a dupe. Worthless men and women to the very bottom of whose hearts he saw, and whom he knew to be destitute of affection for him and undeserving of his confidence, could easily wheedle him out of titles, places, domains, state secrets and pardons. He bestowed much; yet he neither enjoyed the pleasure nor acquired the fame of beneficence. He never gave spontaneously; but it was painful to him to refuse. The consequence was that his bounty generally went, not to those who deserved it best, nor even to those whom he liked best, but to the most shameless and importunate suitor who could obtain an audience.

The motives which governed the political conduct of Charles the Second differed widely from those by which his predecessor and his successor were actuated. He was not a man to be imposed upon by the patriarchal theory of government and the doctrine of divine right. He was utterly without ambition. He detested business, and would sooner have abdicated his crown than have undergone the trouble of really directing the administration. Such was his aversion to toil, and such his ignorance of affairs, that the very clerks who attended him when he sate in council could not refrain from sneering at his frivolous remarks, and at his childish impatience. Neither gratitude nor revenge had any share in determining his course; for never was there a mind on which both services and injuries left such faint and transitory impressions. He wished merely to be a King such as Lewis the Fifteenth of France afterwards was; a King who could

CHAP.
II.
draw without limit on the treasury for the gratification of his private tastes, who could hire with wealth and honours persons capable of assisting him to kill the time, and who, even when the state was brought by maladministration to the depths of humiliation and to the brink of ruin, could still exclude unwelcome truth from the purlieus of his own seraglio, and refuse to see and hear whatever might disturb his luxurious repose. For these ends, and for these ends alone, he wished to obtain arbitrary power, if it could be obtained without risk or trouble. In the religious disputes which divided his Protestant subjects his conscience was not at all interested. For his opinions oscillated in a state of contented suspense between infidelity and Popery. But,! though his conscience was neutral in the quarrel between the Episcopalians and the Presbyterians, his taste was by no means so. His favourite vices were precisely those to which the Puritans were least indulgent. He could not get through one day without the help of diversions which the Puritans regarded as sinful. As a man eminently well bred, and keenly sensible of the ridiculous, he was moved to contemptuous mirth by the Puritan oddities. He had indeed some reason to dislike the rigid sect. He had, at the age when the passions are most impetuous and when levity is most pardonable, spent some months in Scotland, a King in name, but in fact a state prisoner in the hands of austere Presbyterians. Not content with requiring him to conform to their worship and to subscribe their Covenant, they had watched all his motions, and lectured him on all his youthful follies. He had been compelled to give reluctant attendance at endless prayers and sermons, and might think himself fortunate when he was not insolently reminded from the pulpit of his own frailties, of his father's tyranny, and of his mother's idolatry. Indeed he had been so miserable during this part of his life that the defeat which made him again a wanderer might be regarded

as a deliverance rather than as a calamity. Under the influence of such feelings as these Charles was desirous to
depress the party which had resisted his father.

The King's brother, James Duke of York, took the same
side. Though a libertine, James was diligent, methodical,
and fond of authority and business. His understanding was
singularly slow and narrow, and his temper obstinate, harsh,
and unforgiving. That such a prince should have looked with
no good will on the free institutions of England, and on the
party which was peculiarly zealous for those institutions, can
excite no surprise. As yet the Duke professed himself a
member of the Anglican Church: but he had already shown
inclinations which had seriously alarmed good Protestants.

The person on whom devolved at this time the greatest
part of the labour of governing was Edward Hyde, Chancellor
of the realm, who was soon created Earl of Clarendon. The
respect which we justly feel for Clarendon as a writer must not
blind us to the faults which he committed as a statesman.
Some of those faults, however, are explained and excused
by the unfortunate position in which he stood. He had,
during the first year of the Long Parliament, been honourably
distinguished among the senators who laboured to redress the
grievances of the nation. One of the most odious of those
grievances, the Council of York, had been removed in consequence chiefly of his exertions. When the great schism took
place, when the reforming party and the conservative party
first appeared marshalled against each other, he with many
wise and good men took the conservative side. He thenceforward followed the fortunes of the court, enjoyed as large a
share of the confidence of Charles the First as the reserved
nature and tortuous policy of that prince allowed to any
minister, and subsequently shared the exile and directed the
political conduct of Charles the Second. At the Restoration
Hyde became chief minister. In a few months it was an-

CHAP.
II.
nounced that he was closely related by affinity to the royal house. His daughter had become, by a secret marriage, Duchess of York. His grandchildren might perhaps wear the crown. He was raised by this illustrious connection over the heads of the old nobility of the land, and was for a time supposed to be all powerful. In some respects he was well fitted for his great place. No man wrote abler state papers. No man spoke with more weight and dignity in Council and in Parliament. No man was better acquainted with general maxims of statecraft. No man observed the varieties of character with a more discriminating eye. It must be added that he had a strong sense of moral and religious obligation, a sincere reverence for the laws of his country, and a conscientious regard for the honour and interest of the crown. But his temper was sour, arrogant, and impatient of opposition. Above all, he had been long an exile; and this circumstance alone would have completely disqualified him for the supreme direction of affairs. It is scarcely possible that a politician, who has been compelled by civil troubles to go into banishment, and to pass many of the best years of his life abroad, can be fit, on the day on which he returns to his native land, to be at the head of the government. Clarendon was no exception to this rule. He had left England with a mind heated by a fierce conflict which had ended in the downfall of his party and of his own fortunes. From 1646 to 1660 he had lived beyond sea, looking on all that passed at home from a great distance, and through a false medium. His notions of public affairs were necessarily derived from the reports of plotters, many of whom were ruined and desperate men. Events naturally seemed to him auspicious, not in proportion as they increased the prosperity and glory of the nation, but in proportion as they tended to hasten the hour of his own return. His wish, a wish which he has not disguised, was that, till his countrymen brought back the old line, they might

never enjoy quiet or freedom. At length he returned; and, without having a single week to look about him, to mix with society, to note the changes which fourteen eventful years had produced in the national character and feelings, he was at once set to rule the state. In such circumstances, a minister of the greatest tact and docility would probably have fallen into serious errors. But tact and docility made no part of the character of Clarendon. To him England was still the England of his youth; and he sternly frowned down every theory and every practice which had sprung up during his own exile. Though he was far from meditating any attack on the ancient and undoubted power of the House of Commons, he saw with extreme uneasiness the growth of that power. The royal prerogative, for which he had long suffered, and by which he had at length been raised to wealth and dignity, was sacred in his eyes. The Roundheads he regarded both with political and with personal aversion. To the Anglican Church he had always been strongly attached, and had repeatedly, where her interests were concerned, separated himself with regret from his dearest friends. His zeal for Episcopacy and for the Book of Common Prayer was now more ardent than ever, and was mingled with a vindictive hatred of the Puritans, which did him little honour either as a statesman or as a Christian.

While the House of Commons which had recalled the royal family was sitting, it was impossible to effect the reestablishment of the old ecclesiastical system. Not only were the intentions of the court strictly concealed, but assurances which quieted the minds of the moderate Presbyterians were given by the King in the most solemn manner. He had promised, before his restoration, that he would grant liberty of conscience to his subjects. He now repeated that promise, and added a promise to use his best endeavours for the purpose of effecting a compromise between the contending sects. He wished, he said, to see the spiritual jurisdiction divided

between bishops and synods.   The Liturgy should be revised
by a body of learned divines, one half of whom should be
Presbyterians.   The questions respecting the surplice, the
posture at the Eucharist, and the sign of the cross in baptism,
should be settled in a way which would set tender consciences
at ease.*   When the King had thus laid asleep the vigilance of
those whom he most feared, he dissolved the Parliament.   He
had already given his assent to an act by which an amnesty
was granted, with few exceptions, to all who, during the late
troubles, had been guilty of political offences.   He had also
obtained from the Commons a grant for life of taxes, the
annual produce of which was estimated at twelve hundred
thousand pounds.   The actual income, indeed, during some
years, amounted to little more than a million: but this sum,
together with the hereditary revenue of the crown, was then
sufficient to defray the expenses of the government in time of
peace.   Nothing was allowed for a standing army.   The
nation was sick of the very name; and the least mention of
such a force would have incensed and alarmed all parties.

General
election
of 1661.
Early in 1661 took place a general election.   The people
were mad with loyal enthusiasm.   The capital was excited by
preparations for the most splendid coronation that had ever
been known.   The result was that a body of representatives
was returned, such as England had never yet seen.   A large
proportion of the successful candidates were men who had
fought for the crown and the Church, and whose minds had
been exasperated by many injuries and insults suffered at the
hands of the Roundheads.   When the members met, the
passions which animated each individually acquired new
strength from sympathy.   The House of Commons was,
during some years, more zealous for royalty than the King,
more zealous for Episcopacy than the Bishops.   Charles and
Clarendon were almost terrified at the completeness of their
own success.   They found themselves in a situation not unlike

that in which Lewis the Eighteenth and the Duke of Richelieu CHAP. were placed while the Chamber of 1815 was sitting. Even if—— the King had been desirous to fulfil the promises which he had made to the Presbyterians, it would have been out of his power to do so. It was indeed only by the strong exertion of his influence that he could prevent the victorious Cavaliers from rescinding the act of indemnity, and retaliating without mercy all that they had suffered.

The Commons began by resolving that every member Violence should, on pain of expulsion, take the sacrament according Cavaliers to the form prescribed by the old Liturgy, and that the Cove- in the nant should be burned by the hangman in Palace Yard. An liament. act was passed, which not only acknowledged the power of the sword to be solely in the King, but declared that in no extremity whatever could the two Houses be justified in withstanding him by force. Another act was passed which required every officer of a corporation to swear that he held resistance to the King's authority to be in all cases unlawful. A few hot-headed men wished to bring in a bill, which should at once annul all the statutes passed by the Long Parliament, and should restore the Star Chamber and the High Commission; but the reaction, violent as it was, did not proceed quite to this length. It still continued to be the law that a Parliament should be held every three years: but the stringent clauses which directed the returning officers to proceed to election at the proper time, even without the royal writ, were repealed. The Bishops were restored to their seats in the Upper House. The old ecclesiastical polity and the old Liturgy were revived without any modification which had any tendency to conciliate even the most reasonable Presbyterians. Episcopal ordination was now, for the first time, made an indispensable qualification for church preferment. About two thousand ministers of religion, whose conscience did not suffer them to conform, were driven from their benefices in

one day. The dominant party exultingly reminded the sufferers that the Long Parliament, when at the height of power,
had turned out a still greater number of Royalist divines. The
reproach was but too well founded: but the Long Parliament
had at least allowed to the divines whom it ejected a provision
sufficient to keep them from starving; and this example the
Cavaliers, intoxicated with animosity, had not the justice and
humanity to follow.

Persecu-
tion of
the Puri-
tans.
Then came penal statutes against Nonconformists, statutes
for which precedents might too easily be found in the Puritan
legislation, but to which the King could not give his assent
without a breach of promises publicly made, in the most important crisis of his life, to those on whom his fate depended.
The Presbyterians, in extreme distress and terror, fled to
the foot of the throne, and pleaded their recent services and
the royal faith solemnly and repeatedly plighted. The King
wavered. He could not deny his own hand and seal. He
could not but be conscious that he owed much to the petitioners. He was little in the habit of resisting importunate soli-
citation. His temper was not that of a persecutor. He disliked the Puritans indeed; but in him dislike was a languid
feeling, very little resembling the energetic hatred which had
burned in the heart of Laud. He was, moreover, partial to
the Roman Catholic religion; and he knew that it would be
impossible to grant liberty of worship to the professors of that
religion without extending the same indulgence to Protestant
dissenters. He therefore made a feeble attempt to restrain
the intolerant zeal of the House of Commons; but that House
was under the influence of far deeper convictions, and far
stronger passions than his own. After a faint struggle he
yielded, and passed, with the show of alacrity, a series of
odious acts against the separatists. It was made a crime to
attend a dissenting place of worship. A single justice of the
peace might convict without a jury, and might, for the third

offence, pass sentence for transportation beyond sea for seven years. With refined cruelty it was provided that the offender should not be transported to New England, where he was likely to find sympathizing friends. If he returned to his own country before the expiration of his term of exile, he was liable to capital punishment. A new and most unreasonable test was imposed on divines who had been deprived of their benefices for nonconformity; and all who refused to take it were prohibited from coming within five miles of any town which was governed by a corporation, of any town which was represented in Parliament, or of any town where they had themselves resided as ministers. The magistrates, by whom these rigorous statutes were to be enforced, were in general men inflamed by party spirit and [by the remembrance of wrongs which they had themselves suffered in the time of the Commonwealth. The gaols were therefore soon crowded with dissenters; and, among the sufferers, were some of whose genius and virtue any Christian society might well be proud.

The Church of England was not ungrateful for the pro- tection which she received from the government. From the first day of her existence, she had been attached to monarchy. But, during the quarter of a century which followed the Restoration, her zeal for royal authority and hereditary right passed all bounds. She had suffered with the House of Stuart. She had been restored with that House. She was connected with it by common interests, friendships, and enmities. It seemed impossible that a day could ever come when the ties which bound her to the children of her august martyr would be sundered, and when the loyalty in which she gloried would cease to be a pleasing and profitable duty. She accordingly magnified in fulsome phrase that prerogative which was constantly employed to defend and to aggrandise her, and reprobated, much at her ease, the depravity of those whom oppression, from which she was exempt, had goaded to rebellion.

Her favourite theme was the doctrine of nonresistance.   That
doctrine she taught without any qualification, and followed
out to all its extreme consequences.   Her disciples were never
weary of repeating that in no conceivable case, not even if
England were cursed with a King resembling Busiris or Phalaris, who, in defiance of law, and without the pretence of
justice, should daily doom hundreds of innocent victims to
torture and death, would all the Estates of the realm united
be justified in withstanding his tyranny by physical force.
Happily the principles of human nature afford abundant security that such theories will never be more than theories.   The
day of trial came: and the very men who had most loudly and
most sincerely professed this extravagant loyalty were, in
almost every county of England, arrayed in arms against the
throne.

Property all over the kingdom was now again changing
hands.   The national sales, not having been confirmed by
Parliament, were regarded by the tribunals as nullities.   The
sovereign, the bishops, the deans, the chapters, the royalist
nobility and gentry, reentered on their confiscated estates,
and ejected even purchasers who had given fair prices.   The
losses which the Cavaliers had sustained during the ascendency of their opponents were thus in part repaired; but in
part only. All actions for mesne profits were effectually barred
by the general amnesty; and the numerous Royalists who, in
order to discharge fines imposed by the Parliament, or in
order to purchase the favour of powerful Roundheads, had
sold lands for much less than the real value, were not relieved
from the legal consequences of their own acts.

Change
in the
morals of
the com-
munity.
While these changes were in progress, a change still more
important took place in the morals and manners of the community.   Those passions and tastes which, under the rule of
the Puritans, had been sternly repressed, and, if gratified
at all, had been gratified by stealth, broke forth with un-

governable violence as soon as the check was withdrawn. CHAP.
Men flew to frivolous amusements and to criminal pleasures ——II.——
with the greediness which long and enforced abstinence naturally produces. Little restraint was imposed by public
opinion. For the nation, nauseated with cant, suspicious of
all pretensions to sanctity, and still smarting from the recent
tyranny of rulers austere in life and powerful in prayer, looked
for a time with complacency on the softer and gayer vices.
Still less restraint was imposed by the government. Indeed
there was no excess which was not encouraged by the ostentatious profligacy of the King and of his favourite courtiers.
A few counsellors of Charles the First, who were now no
longer young, retained the decorous gravity which had been
thirty years before in fashion at Whitehall. Such were
Clarendon himself, and his friends, Thomas Wriothesley,
Earl of Southampton, Lord Treasurer, and James Butler,
Duke of Ormond, who, having through many vicissitudes
struggled gallantly for the royal cause in Ireland, now governed that kingdom as Lord Lieutenant. But neither the
memory of the services of these men, nor their great power in
the state, could protect them from the sarcasms which modish
vice loves to dart at obsolete virtue. The praise of politeness
and vivacity could now scarcely be obtained except by some
violation of decorum. Talents great and various assisted to
spread the contagion. Ethical philosophy had recently taken
a form well suited to please a generation equally devoted to
monarchy and to vice. Thomas Hobbes had, in language
more precise and luminous than has ever been employed by
any other metaphysical writer, maintained that the will of the
prince was the standard of right and wrong, and that every
subject ought to be ready to profess Popery, Mahometanism,
or Paganism at the royal command. Thousands who were
incompetent to appreciate what was really valuable in his
speculations, eagerly welcomed a theory which, while it

exalted the kingly office, relaxed the obligations of morality, and degraded religion into a mere affair of state. Hobbism soon became an almost essential part of the character of the fine gentleman. All the lighter kinds of literature were deeply tainted by the prevailing licentiousness. Poetry stooped to be the pandar of every low desire. Ridicule, instead of putting guilt and error to the blush, turned her formidable shafts against innocence and truth. The restored Church contended indeed against the prevailing immorality, but contended feebly, and with half a heart. It was necessary to the decorum of her character that she should admonish her erring children. But her admonitions were given in a somewhat perfunctory manner. Her attention was elsewhere engaged. Her whole soul was in the work of crushing the Puritans, and of teaching her disciples to give unto Cæsar the things which were Cæsar's. She had been pillaged and oppressed by the party which preached an austere morality. She had been restored to opulence and honour by libertines. Little as the men of mirth and fashion were disposed to shape their lives according to her precepts, they were yet ready to fight knee deep in blood for her cathedrals and palaces, for every line of her rubric and every thread of her vestments. If the debauched Cavalier haunted brothels and gambling houses, he at least avoided conventicles. If he never spoke without uttering ribaldry and blasphemy, he made some amends by his eagerness to send Baxter and Howe to gaol for preaching and praying. Thus the clergy, for a time, made war on schism with so much vigour that they had little leisure to make war on vice. The ribaldry of Etherege and Wycherley was, in the presence and under the special sanction of the head o the Church, publicly recited by female lips in female ears, while the author of the Pilgrim's Progress languished in a dungeon for the crime of proclaiming the gospel to the poor. It is an unquestionable and a most instructive fact that the

years during which the political power of the Anglican hie- CHAP. .
rarchy was in the zenith were precisely the years during which ——II.——
national virtue was at the lowest point.

Scarcely any rank or profession escaped the infection of Profligacy
of politi-
the prevailing immorality; but those persons who made po- cians.
litics their business were perhaps the most corrupt part of the
corrupt society. For they were exposed not only to the same
noxious influences which affected the nation generally, but
also to a taint of a peculiar and of a most malignant kind.
Their character had been formed amidst frequent and violent
revolutions and counterrevolutions. In the course of a few
years they had seen the ecclesiastical and civil polity of their
country repeatedly changed. They had seen an Episcopal
Church persecuting Puritans, a Puritan Church persecuting
Episcopalians, and an Episcopal Church persecuting Puritans
again. They had seen hereditary monarchy abolished and
restored. They had seen the Long Parliament thrice supreme
in the state and thrice dissolved amidst the curses and
laughter of millions. They had seen a new dynasty rapidly
rising to the height of power and glory, and then on a sudden
hurled down from the chair of state without a struggle. They
had seen a new representative system devised, tried, and
abandoned. They had seen a new House of Lords created
and scattered. They had seen great masses of property
violently transferred from Cavaliers to Roundheads, and from
Roundheads back to Cavaliers. During these events no man
could be a stirring and thriving politician who was not prepared to change with every change of fortune. It was only
in retirement that any person could long keep the character
either of a steady Royalist or of a steady Republican. One
who, in such an age, is determined to attain civil greatness
must renounce all thought of consistency. Instead of affecting immutability in the midst of endless mutation, he must be
always on the watch for the indications of a coming reaction.

12*

He must seize the exact moment for deserting a falling cause.
Having gone all lengths with a faction while it was uppermost,
he must suddenly extricate himself from it when its difficulties
begin, must assail it, must persecute it, must enter on a new
career of power and prosperity in company with new associates. His situation naturally developes in him to the highest degree a peculiar class of abilities and a peculiar class of
vices. He becomes quick of observation and fertile of resource. He catches without effort the tone of any sect or
party with which he chances to mingle. He discerns the signs
of the times with a sagacity which to the multitude appears
miraculous, with a sagacity resembling that with which a
veteran police officer pursues the faintest indications of crime,
or with which a Mohawk warrior follows a track through the
woods. But we shall seldom find in a statesman so trained,
integrity, constancy, any of the virtues of the noble family of
Truth. He has no faith in any doctrine, no zeal for any
cause. He has seen so many old institutions swept away,
that he has no reverence for prescription. He has seen so
many new institutions from which much had been expected
produce mere disappointment, that he has no hope of improvement. He sneers alike at those who are anxious to
preserve and at those who are eager to reform. There is
nothing in the state which he could not, without a scruple
or a blush, join in defending or in destroying. Fidelity to
opinions and to friends seems to him mere dulness and wrong-
headedness. Politics he regards, not as a science of which
the object is the happiness of mankind, but as an exciting
game of mixed chance and skill, at which a dexterous and
lucky player may win an estate, a coronet, perhaps a crown,
and at which one rash move may lead to the loss of fortune
and of life. Ambition, which, in good times, and in good
minds, is half a virtue, now, disjoined from every elevated
and philanthropic sentiment, becomes a selfish cupidity scarce-

ly less ignoble than avarice. Among those politicians who, from the Restoration to the accession of the House of Hanover, were at the head of the great parties in the state, very few can be named whose reputation is not stained by what, in our age, would be called gross perfidy and corruption. It is scarcely an exaggeration to say that the most unprincipled public men who have taken part in affairs within our memory would, if tried by the standard which was in fashion during the latter part of the seventeenth century, deserve to be regarded as scrupulous and disinterested.

While these political, religious, and moral changes were taking place in England, the royal authority had been without difficulty reestablished in every other part of the British islands. In Scotland the restoration of the Stuarts had been hailed with delight; for it was regarded as the restoration of national independence. And true it was that the yoke which Cromwell had imposed was, in appearance, taken away, that the Estates again met in their old hall at Edinburgh, and that the Senators of the College of Justice again administered the Scottish law according to the old forms. Yet was the independence of the little kingdom necessarily rather nominal than real: for, as long as the King had England on his side, he had nothing to apprehend from disaffection in his other dominions. He was now in such a situation that he could renew the attempt which had proved destructive to his father without any danger of his father's fate. Charles the First had tried to force his own religion by his regal power on the Scots at a moment when both his religion and his regal power were unpopular in England; and he had not only failed, but had raised troubles which had ultimately cost him his crown and his head. Times had now changed: England was zealous for monarchy and prelacy; and therefore the scheme which in the preceding generation had been in the highest degree imprudent might be resumed with little risk to the throne. The government resolved to set up a

prelatical church in Scotland. The design was disapproved by
every Scotchman whose judgment was entitled to respect.
Some Scottish statesmen who were zealous for the King's prerogative had been bred Presbyterians. Though little troubled
with scruples, they retained a preference for the religion of
their childhood; and they well knew how strong a hold that
religion had on the hearts of their countrymen. They re-
monstrated strongly: but, when they found that they remon-
strated in vain, they had not virtue enough to persist in an
opposition which would have given offence to their master;
and several of them stooped to the wickedness and baseness of
persecuting what in their consciences they believed to be the
purest form of Christianity. The Scottish Parliament was so
constituted that it had scarcely ever offered any serious opposition even to Kings much weaker than Charles then was.
Episcopacy, therefore, was established by law. As to the form
of worship, a large discretion was left to the clergy. In some
churches the English Liturgy was used. In others, the ministers selected from that Liturgy such prayers and thanksgivings as were likely to be least offensive to the people. But
in general the doxology was sung at the close of public worship, and the Apostles' Creed was recited when baptism was
administered. By the great body of the Scottish nation the
new Church was detested both as superstitious and as foreign;
as tainted with the corruptions of Rome, and as a mark of the
predominance of England. There was, however, no general
insurrection. The country was not what it had been twenty-
two years before. Disastrous war and alien domination had
tamed the spirit of the people. The aristocracy, which was
held in great honour by the middle class and by the populace,
had put itself at the head of the movement against Charles the
First, but proved obsequious to Charles the Second. From
the English Puritans no aid was now to be expected. They
were a feeble party, proscribed both by law and by public

opinion. The bulk of the Scottish nation, therefore, sullenly submitted, and, with many misgivings of conscience, attended the ministrations of the Episcopal clergy, or of Presbyterian divines who had consented to accept from the government a half toleration, known by the name of the Indulgence. But there were, particularly in the western lowlands, many fierce and resolute men, who held that the obligation to observe the Covenant was paramount to the obligation to obey the magistrate. These people, in defiance of the law, persisted in meeting to worship God after their own fashion. The Indulgence they regarded, not as a partial reparation of the wrongs inflicted by the magistrate on the Church, but as a new wrong, the more odious because it was disguised under the appearance of a benefit. Persecution, they said, could only kill the body; but the black Indulgence was deadly to the soul. Driven from the towns, they assembled on heaths and mountains. Attacked by the civil power, they without scruple repelled force by force. At every conventicle they mustered in arms. They repeatedly broke out into open rebellion. They were easily defeated, and mercilessly punished: but neither defeat nor punishment could subdue their spirit. Hunted down like wild beasts, tortured till their bones were beaten flat, imprisoned by hundreds, hanged by scores, exposed at one time to the license of soldiers from England, abandoned at another time to the mercy of bands of marauders from the Highlands, they still stood at bay in a mood so savage that the boldest and mightiest oppressor could not but dread the audacity of their despair.

Such was, during the reign of Charles the Second, the state of Scotland. Ireland was not less distracted. In that island existed feuds, compared with which the hottest animosities of English politicians were lukewarm. The enmity between the Irish Cavaliers and the Irish Roundheads was almost forgotten in the fiercer enmity which raged between the English and the

CHAP.
II.

State of
Ireland.

Celtic races.   The interval between the Episcopalian and the Presbyterian seemed to vanish, when compared with the interval which separated both from the Papist.   During the late civil troubles the greater part of the Irish soil had been transferred from the vanquished nation to the victors.   To the favour of the crown few either of the old or of the new occupants had any pretensions.   The despoilers and the despoiled had, for the most part, been rebels alike.   The government was soon perplexed and wearied by the conflicting claims and mutual accusations of the two incensed factions.   Those colonists among whom Cromwell had portioned out the conquered territory, and whose descendants are still called Cromwellians, represented that the aboriginal inhabitants were deadly enemies of the English nation under every dynasty, and of the Protestant religion in every form.   They described and exaggerated the atrocities which had disgraced the insurrection of Ulster: they urged the King to follow up with resolution the policy of the Protector; and they were not ashamed to hint that there would never be peace in Ireland till the old Irish race should be extirpated.   The Roman Catholics extenuated their offence as they best might, and expatiated in piteous language on the severity of their punishment, which, in truth, had not been lenient.   They implored Charles not to confound the innocent with the guilty, and reminded him that many of the guilty had atoned for their fault by returning to their allegiance, and by defending his rights against the murderers of his father.   The court, sick of the importunities of two parties, neither of which it had any reason to love, at length relieved itself from trouble by dictating a compromise.   That cruel, but most complete and energetic system, by which Oliver had proposed to make the island thoroughly English, was abandoned. The Cromwellians were induced to relinquish a third part of their acquisitions.   The land thus surrendered was capriciously divided among claimants whom the government chose to favour. But great numbers who protested that they were CHAP.
II. innocent of all disloyalty, and some persons who boasted that their loyalty had been signally displayed, obtained neither restitution nor compensation, and filled France and Spain with outcries against the injustice and ingratitude of the House of Stuart.

Meantime the government had, even in England, ceased to be popular. The Royalists had begun to quarrel with the court and with each other; and the party which had been vanquished, trampled down, and, as it seemed, annihilated, but which had still retained a strong principle of life, again raised its head, and renewed the interminable war. The government becomes unpopular in England.

Had the administration been faultless, the enthusiasm with which the return of the King and the termination of the military tyranny had been hailed could not have been permanent. For it is the law of our nature that such fits of excitement shall always be followed by remissions. The manner in which the court abused its victory made the remission speedy and complete. Every moderate man was shocked by the insolence, cruelty and perfidy with which the Nonconformists were treated. The penal laws had effectually purged the oppressed party of those insincere members whose vices had disgraced it, and had made it again an honest and pious body of men. The Puritan, a conqueror, a ruler, a persecutor, a sequestrator, had been detested. The Puritan, betrayed and evil intreated, deserted by all the time-servers who, in his prosperity, had claimed brotherhood with him, hunted from his home, forbidden under severe penalties to pray or receive the sacrament according to his conscience, yet still firm in his resolution to obey God rather than man, was, in spite of some unpleasing recollections, an object of pity and respect to well constituted minds. These feelings became stronger when it was noised abroad that the court was not disposed to treat Papists with the same rigour which had been shown to Presbyterians. A

vague suspicion that the King and the Duke were not sincere
Protestants sprang up in many quarters. Many persons too
who had been disgusted by the austerity and hypocrisy of the
Pharisees of the Commonwealth began to be still more disgusted by the open profligacy of the court and of the Cavaliers, and were disposed to doubt whether the sullen precise-
ness of Praise God Barebone might not be preferable to the
outrageous profaneness and licentiousness of the Bucking-
hams and Sedleys. Even immoral men, who were not utterly
destitute of sense and public spirit, complained that the
government treated the most serious matters as trifles, and
made trifles its serious business. A King might be pardoned
for amusing his leisure with wine, wit, and beauty. But it was
intolerable that he should sink into a mere saunterer and vo-
luptuary, that the gravest affairs of state should be neglected,
and that the public service should be starved and the finances deranged in order that harlots and parasites might grow
rich.

A large body of Royalists joined in these complaints, and
added many sharp reflections on the King's ingratitude. His
whole revenue, indeed, would not have sufficed to reward
them all in proportion to their own consciousness of desert.
For to every distressed gentleman who had fought under
Rupert or Derby his own services seemed eminently meritorious, and his own sufferings eminently severe. Every one
had flattered himself that, whatever became of the rest, he
should be largely recompensed for all that he had lost during
the civil troubles, and that the restoration of the monarchy
would be followed by the restoration of his own dilapidated
fortunes. None of these expectants could restrain his indignation, when he found that he was as poor under the King as
he had been under the Rump or the Protector. The negligence and extravagance of the court excited the bitter indignation of these loyal veterans. They justly said that one half

of what His Majesty squandered on concubines and buffoons would gladden the hearts of hundreds of old Cavaliers who, after cutting down their oaks and melting their plate to help his father, now wandered about in threadbare suits, and did not know where to turn for a meal.

At the same time a sudden fall of rents took place. The income of every landed proprietor was diminished by five shillings in the pound. The cry of agricultural distress rose from every shire in the kingdom; and for that distress the government was, as usual, held accountable. The gentry, compelled to retrench their expenses for a period, saw with indignation the increasing splendour and profusion of White-hall, and were immovably fixed in the belief that the money which ought to have supported their households had, by some inexplicable process, gone to the favourites of the King.

The minds of men were now in such a temper that every public act excited discontent. Charles had taken to wife Catharine Princess of Portugal. The marriage was generally disliked; and the murmurs became loud when it appeared that the King was not likely to have any legitimate posterity. Dunkirk, won by Oliver from Spain, was sold to Lewis the Fourteenth, King of France. This bargain excited general indignation. Englishmen were already beginning to observe with uneasiness the progress of the French power, and to regard the House of Bourbon with the same feeling with which their grandfathers had regarded the House of Austria. Was it wise, men asked, at such a time, to make any addition to the strength of a monarchy already too formidable? Dunkirk was, moreover, prized by the people, not merely as a place of arms, and as a key to the Low Countries, but also as a trophy of English valour. It was to the subjects of Charles what Calais had been to an earlier generation, and what the rock of Gibraltar, so manfully defended, through disastrous and perilous years, against the fleets and armies of a mighty

CHAP. II. coalition, is to ourselves. The plea of economy might have had some weight, if it had been urged by an economical government. But it was notorious that the charges of Dunkirk fell far short of the sums which were wasted at court in vice and folly. It seemed insupportable that a sovereign, profuse beyond example in all that regarded his own pleasures, should be niggardly in all that regarded the safety and honour of the state.

The public discontent was heightened, when it was found that, while Dunkirk was abandoned on the plea of economy, the fortress of Tangier, which was part of the dower of Queen Catharine, was repaired and kept up at an enormous charge. That place was associated with no recollections gratifying to the national pride: it could in no way promote the national interests: it involved us in inglorious, unprofitable, and interminable wars with tribes of half savage Mussulmans; and it was situated in a climate singularly unfavourable to the health and vigour of the English race.

War with the Dutch. But the murmurs excited by these errors were faint, when compared with the clamours which soon broke forth. The government engaged in war with the United Provinces. The House of Commons readily voted sums unexampled in our history, sums exceeding those which had supported the fleets and armies of Cromwell at the time when his power was the terror of all the world. But such was the extravagance, dishonesty, and incapacity of those who had succeeded to his authority, that this liberality proved worse than useless. The sycophants of the court, ill qualified to contend against the great men who then directed the arms of Holland, against such a statesman as De Witt, and such a commander as De Ruyter, made fortunes rapidly, while the sailors mutinied from very hunger, while the dockyards were unguarded, while the ships were leaky and without rigging. It was at length determined to abandon all schemes of offensive war;

and it soon appeared that even a defensive war was a task too hard for that administration. The Dutch fleet sailed up the Thames, and burned the ships of war which lay at Chatham. It was said that, on the very day of that great humiliation, the King feasted with the ladies of his seraglio, and amused himself with hunting a moth about the supper room. Then, at length, tardy justice was done to the memory of Oliver. Everywhere men magnified his valour, genius, and patriotism. Everywhere it was remembered how, when he ruled, all foreign powers had trembled at the name of England, how the States General, now so haughty, had crouched at his feet, and how, when it was known that he was no more, Amsterdam was lighted up as for a great deliverance, and children ran along the canals, shouting for joy that the devil was dead. Even Royalists exclaimed that the State could be saved only by calling the old soldiers of the Commonwealth to arms. Soon the capital began to feel the miseries of a blockade. Fuel was scarcely to be procured. Tilbury Fort, the place where Elizabeth had, with manly spirit, hurled foul scorn at Parma and Spain, was insulted by the invaders. The roar of foreign guns was heard, for the first and last time, by the citizens of London. In the Council it was seriously proposed that, if the enemy advanced, the Tower should be abandoned. Great multitudes of people assembled in the streets crying out that England was bought and sold. The houses and carriages of the ministers were attacked by the populace; and it seemed likely that the government would have to deal at once with an invasion and with an insurrection. The extreme danger, it is true, soon passed by. A treaty was concluded, very different from those which Oliver had been in the habit of signing; and the nation was once more at peace, but was in a mood scarcely less fierce and sullen than in the days of ship-money.

The discontent engendered by maladministration was

CHAP. II. heightened by calamities which the best administration could not have averted. While the ignominious war with Holland was raging, London suffered two great disasters, such as never, in so short a space of time, befell one city. A pestilence, surpassing in horror any that during three centuries had visited the island, swept away, in six months, more than a hundred thousand human beings. And scarcely had the dead cart ceased to go its rounds, when a fire, such as had not been known in Europe since the conflagration of Rome under Nero, laid in ruins the whole City, from the Tower to the Temple, and from the river to the purlieus of Smithfield.

Opposition in the House of Commons. Had there been a general election while the nation was smarting under so many disgraces and misfortunes, it is probable that the Roundheads would have regained ascendency in the state. But the Parliament was still the Cavalier Parliament, chosen in the transport of loyalty which had followed the Restoration. Nevertheless it soon became evident that no English legislature, however loyal, would now consent to be merely what the legislature had been under the Tudors. From the death of Elizabeth to the eve of the civil war, the Puritans, who predominated in the representative body, had been constantly, by a dexterous use of the power of the purse, encroaching on the province of the executive government. The gentlemen who, after the Restoration, filled the Lower House, though they abhorred the Puritan name, were well pleased to inherit the fruit of the Puritan policy. They were indeed most willing to employ the power which they possessed in the state for the purpose of making their King mighty and honoured, both at home and abroad: but with the power itself they were resolved not to part. The great English revolution of the seventeenth century, that is to say, the transfer of the supreme control of the executive administration from the crown to the House of Commons, was,

through the whole long existence of this Parliament, proceeding noiselessly, but rapidly and steadily. Charles, kept
poor by his follies and vices, wanted money. The Commons
alone could legally grant him money. They could not be
prevented from putting their own price on their grants. The
price which they put on their grants was this, that they should
be allowed to interfere with every one of the King's prerogatives, to wring from him his consent to laws which he
disliked, to break up cabinets, to dictate the course of foreign
policy, and even to direct the administration of war. To
the royal office, and the royal person, they loudly and sincerely professed the strongest attachment. But to Clarendon
they owed no allegiance; and they fell on him as furiously as
their predecessors had fallen on Strafford. The minister's
virtues and vices alike contributed to his ruin. He was the
ostensible head of the administration, and was therefore held
responsible even for those acts which he had strongly, but
vainly, opposed in Council. He was regarded by the Puritans, and by all who pitied them, as an implacable bigot, a
second Laud, with much more than Laud's understanding.
He had on all occasions maintained that the Act of Indemnity
ought to be strictly observed; and this part of his conduct,
though highly honourable to him, made him hateful to all
those Royalists who wished to repair their ruined fortunes
by suing the Roundheads for damages and mesne profits.
The Presbyterians of Scotland attributed to him the downfall
of their Church. The Papists of Ireland attributed to him
the loss of their lands. As father of the Duchess of York,
he had an obvious motive for wishing that there might be a
barren Queen; and he was therefore suspected of having pur-
posely recommended one. The sale of Dunkirk was justly
imputed to him. For the war with Holland he was, with less
justice, held accountable. His hot temper, his arrogant deportment, the indelicate eagerness with which he grasped

at riches, the ostentation with which he squandered
them, his picture gallery, filled with master-pieces of
Vandyke which had once been the property of ruined Cavaliers, his palace, which reared its long and stately front
right opposite to the humbler residence of our Kings, drew
on him much deserved, and some undeserved, censure.
When the Dutch fleet was in the Thames, it was against the
Chancellor that the rage of the populace was chiefly directed.
His windows were broken, the trees of his garden cut down,
and a gibbet set up before his door. But nowhere was he
more detested than in the House of Commons. He was
unable to perceive that the time was fast approaching when
that House, if it continued to exist at all, must be supreme
in the state, when the management of that House would be
the most important department of politics, and when, without
the help of men possessing the ear of that House, it would
be impossible to carry on the government. He obstinately
persisted in considering the Parliament as a body in no respect
differing from the Parliament which had been sitting when,
forty years before, he first began to study law at the Temple.
He did not wish to deprive the legislature of those powers
which were inherent in it by the old constitution of the realm:
but the new development of those powers, though a development natural, inevitable, and to be prevented only by utterly
destroying the powers themselves, disgusted and alarmed
him. Nothing would have induced him to put the great seal
to a writ for raising ship-money, or to give his voice in Council
for committing a member of Parliament to the Tower, on
account of words spoken in debate: but, when the Commons
began to inquire in what manner the money voted for the
war had been wasted, and to examine into the maladministration of the navy, he flamed with indignation. Such inquiry,
according to him, was out of their province. He admitted
that the House was a most loyal assembly, that it had done

good service to the crown, and that its intentions were excellent. But, both in public and in the closet, he, on every
occasion, expressed his concern that gentlemen so sincerely
attached to mornarchy should unadvisedly incroach on the
prerogative of the monarch. Widely as they differed in spirit
from the members of the Long Parliament, they yet, he said,
imitated that Parliament in meddling with matters which
lay beyond the sphere of the Estates of the realm, and
which were subject to the authority of the crown alone. The
country, he maintained, would never be well governed till
the knights of shires and the burgesses were content to be
what their predecessors had been in the days of Elizabeth.
All the plans which men more observant than himself of the
signs of that time proposed, for the purpose of maintaining a
good understanding between the Court and the Commons, he
disdainfully rejected as crude projects, inconsistent with the
old polity of England. Towards the young orators, who
were rising to distinction and authority in the Lower House,
his deportment was ungracious; and he succeeded in making
them, with scarcely an exception, his deadly enemies. Indeed one of his most serious faults was an inordinate contempt for youth: and this contempt was the more unjusti-
fiable, because his own experience in English politics was by
no means proportioned to his age. For so great a part of his
life had been passed abroad that he knew less of that world
in which he found himself on his return than many who might
have been his sons.

For these reasons he was disliked by the Commons. For
very different reasons he was equally disliked by the Court.
His morals as well as his politics were those of an earlier
generation. Even when he was a young law student, living
much with men of wit and pleasure, his natural gravity and
his religious principles had to a great extent preserved him
from the contagion of fashionable debauchery; and he was

CHAP.
II.

by no means likely, in advanced years and in declining health, to turn libertine. On the vices of the young and gay he looked with an aversion almost as bitter and contemptuous as that which he felt for the theological errors of the sectaries. He missed no opportunity of showing his scorn of the mimics, revellers, and courtesans who crowded the palace; and the admonitions which he addressed to the King himself were very sharp, and, what Charles disliked still more, very long. Scarcely any voice was raised in favour of a minister loaded with the double odium of faults which roused the fury of the people, and of virtues which annoyed and importuned the sovereign. Southampton was no more. Ormond performed the duties of friendship manfully and faithfully, but in vain. The Chancellor fell with a great ruin. The seal was taken from him: the Commons impeached him: his head was not safe; he fled from the country: an act was passed which doomed him to perpetual exile; and those who had assailed and undermined him began to struggle for the fragments of his power.

The sacrifice of Clarendon in some degree took off the edge of the public appetite for revenge. Yet was the anger excited by the profusion and negligence of the government, and by the miscarriages of the late war, by no means extinguished. The counsellors of Charles, with the fate of the Chancellor before their eyes, were anxious for their own safety. They accordingly advised their master to soothe the irritation which prevailed both in the Parliament and throughout the country, and for that end, to take a step which has no parallel in the history of the House of Stuart, and which was worthy of the prudence and magnanimity of Oliver.

State of European politics, and ascendency of France.

We have now reached a point at which the history of the great English revolution begins to be complicated with the history of foreign politics. The power of Spain had, during many years, been declining. She still, it is true, held in

Europe the Milanese and the two Sicilies, Belgium, and Franche Comté. In America her dominions still spread, on both sides of the equator, far beyond the limits of the torrid zone. But this great body had been smitten with palsy, and was not only incapable of giving molestation to other states, but could not, without assistance, repel aggression. France was now, beyond all doubt, the greatest power in Europe. Her resources have, since those days, absolutely increased, but have not increased so fast as the resources of England. It must also be remembered that, a hundred and eighty years ago, the empire of Russia, now a monarchy of the first class, was as entirely out of the system of European politics as Abyssinia or Siam, that the House of Brandenburg was then hardly more powerful than the House of Saxony, and that the republic of the United States had not then begun to exist. The weight of France, therefore, though still very considerable, has relatively diminished. Her territory was not in the days of Lewis the Fourteenth quite so extensive as at present: but it was large, compact, fertile, well placed both for attack and for defence, situated in a happy climate, and inhabited by a brave, active, and ingenious people. The state implicitly obeyed the direction of a single mind. The great fiefs which, three hundred years before, had been, in all but name, independent principalities, had been annexed to the crown. Only a few old men could remember the last meeting of the States General. The resistance which the Huguenots, the nobles, and the parliaments had offered to the kingly power, had been put down by the two great Cardinals who had ruled the nation during forty years. The government was now a despotism, but, at least in its dealings with the upper classes, a mild and generous despotism, tempered by courteous manners and chivalrous sentiments. The means at the disposal of the sovereign were, for that age, truly formidable. His revenue, raised, it is true, by a severe and

CHAP.
II.
unequal taxation which pressed heavily on the cultivators of the soil, far exceeded that of any other potentate. His army, excellently disciplined, and commanded by the greatest generals then living, already consisted of more than a hundred and twenty thousand men. Such an array of regular troops had not been seen in Europe since the downfall of the Roman empire. Of maritime powers France was not the first. But, though she had rivals on the sea, she had not yet a superior. Such was her strength during the last forty years of the seventeenth century, that no enemy could singly withstand her, and that two great coalitions, in which half Christendom was united against her, failed of success.

Character
of Lewis
XIV.
The personal qualities of the French King added to the respect inspired by the power and importance of his kingdom. No sovereign has ever represented the majesty of a great state with more dignity and grace. He was his own prime minister, and performed the duties of that arduous situation with an ability and an industry which could not be reasonably expected from one who had in infancy succeeded to a crown, and who had been surrounded by flatterers before he could speak. He had shown, in an eminent degree, two talents invaluable to a prince, the talent of choosing his servants well, and the talent of appropriating to himself the chief part of the credit of their acts. In his dealings with foreign powers he had some generosity, but no justice. To unhappy allies who threw themselves at his feet, and had no hope but in his compassion, he extended his protection with a romantic disinterestedness, which seemed better suited to a knight errant than to a statesman. But he broke through the most sacred ties of public faith without scruple or shame, whenever they interfered with his interest, or with what he called his glory. His perfidy and violence, however, excited less enmity than the insolence with which he constantly reminded his neighbours of his own greatness and of their littleness. He did

not at this time profess the austere devotion which, at a later period, gave to his court the aspect of a monastery. On the contrary, he was as licentious, though by no means as frivolous and indolent, as his brother of England. But he was a sincere Roman Catholic; and both his conscience and his vanity impelled him to use his power for the defence and propagation of the true faith, after the example of his renowned predecessors, Clovis, Charlemagne, and Saint Lewis.

Our ancestors naturally looked with serious alarm on the growing power of France. This feeling, in itself perfectly reasonable, was mingled with other feelings less praiseworthy. France was our old enemy. It was against France that the most glorious battles recorded in our annals had been fought. The conquest of France had been twice effected by the Plantagenets. The loss of France had been long remembered as a great national disaster. The title of King of France was still borne by our sovereigns. The lilies of France still appeared, mingled with our own lions, on the shield of the House of Stuart. In the sixteenth century the dread inspired by Spain had suspended the animosity of which France had anciently been the object. But the dread inspired by Spain had given place to contemptuous compassion; and France was again regarded as our national foe. The sale of Dunkirk to France had been the most generally unpopular act of the restored King. Attachment to France had been prominent among the crimes imputed by the Commons to Clarendon. Even in trifles the public feeling showed itself. When a brawl took place in the streets of Westminster between the retinues of the French and Spanish embassies, the populace, though forcibly prevented from interfering, had given unequivocal proofs that the old antipathy was not extinct.

France and Spain were now engaged in a more serious contest. One of the chief objects of the policy of Lewis throughout his life was to extend his dominions towards the Rhine. For this end he had engaged in war with Spain, and he was now in the full career of conquest. The United Provinces saw with anxiety the progress of his arms. That renowned federation had reached the height of power, prosperity, and glory. The Batavian territory, conquered from the waves, and defended against them by human art, was in extent little superior to the principality of Wales. But all that narrow space was a busy and populous hive, in which new wealth was every day created, and in which vast masses of old wealth were hoarded. The aspect of Holland, the rich cultivation, the innumerable canals, the ever whirling mills, the endless fleets of barges, the quick succession of great towns, the ports bristling with thousands of masts, the large and stately mansions, the trim villas, the richly furnished apartments, the picture galleries, the summer houses, the tulip beds, produced on English travellers in that age an effect similar to the effect which the first sight of England now produces on a Norwegian or a Canadian. The States General had been compelled to humble themselves before Cromwell. But after the Restoration they had taken their revenge, had waged war with success against Charles, and had concluded peace on honourable terms. Rich, however, as the Republic was, and highly considered in Europe, she was no match for the power of Lewis. She apprehended, not without good cause, that his kingdom might soon be extended to her frontiers; and she might well dread the immediate vicinity of a monarch so great, so ambitious, and so unscrupulous. Yet it was not easy to devise any expedient which might avert the danger. The Dutch alone could not turn the scale against France. On the side of the Rhine no help was to be expected. Several German princes had been gained by Lewis; and the Emperor himself was embarrassed by the discontents of Hungary. England was separated from the United Provinces by the recollection of cruel injuries CHAP.
II. recently inflicted and endured; and her policy had, since the Restoration, been so devoid of wisdom and spirit, that it was scarcely possible to expect from her any valuable assistance.

But the fate of Clarendon and the growing ill humour of the Parliament determined the advisers of Charles to adopt on a sudden a policy which amazed and delighted the nation.

The English resident at Brussels, Sir William Temple, The Triple Alliance. one of the most expert diplomatists and most pleasing writers of that age, had already represented to his court that it was both desirable and practicable to enter into engagements with the States General for the purpose of checking the progress of France. For a time his suggestions had been slighted; but it was now thought expedient to act on them. He was commissioned to negotiate with the States General. He proceeded to the Hague, and soon came to an understanding with John De Witt, then the chief minister of Holland. Sweden, small as her resources were, had, forty years before, been raised by the genius of Gustavus Adolphus to a high rank among European powers, and had not yet descended to her natural position. She was induced to join on this occasion with England and the States. Thus was formed that coalition known as the Triple Alliance. Lewis showed signs of vexation and resentment, but did not think it politic to draw on himself the hostility of such a confederacy in addition to that of Spain. He consented, therefore, to relinquish a large part of the territory which his armies had occupied. Peace was restored to Europe; and the English government, lately an object of general contempt, was, during a few months, regarded by foreign powers with respect scarcely less than that which the Protector had inspired.

At home the Triple Alliance was popular in the highest

degree. It gratified alike national animosity and national pride. It put a limit to the encroachments of a powerful and ambitious neighbour. It bound the leading Protestant states together in close union. Cavaliers and Roundheads rejoiced in common: but the joy of the Roundhead was even greater than that of the Cavalier. For England had now allied herself strictly with a country republican in government and Presbyterian in religion, against a country ruled by an arbitrary prince and attached to the Roman Catholic Church. The House of Commons loudly applauded the treaty; and some uncourtly grumblers described it as the only good thing that had been done since the King came in.

The Country Party.

The King, however, cared little for the approbation of his Parliament or of his people. The Triple Alliance he regarded merely.as a temporary expedient for quieting discontents which had seemed likely to become serious. The independence, the safety, the dignity of the nation over which he presided were nothing to him. He had begun to find constitutional restraints galling. Already had been formed in the Parliament a strong connection known by the name of the Country Party. That party included all the public men who leaned towards Puritanism and Republicanism, and many who, though attached to the Church and to hereditary monarchy, had been driven into opposition by dread of Popery, by dread of France, and by disgust at the extravagance, dissoluteness, and faithlessness of the court. The power of this band of politicians was constantly growing. Every year some of those members who had been returned to Parliament during the loyal excitement of 1661 dropped off; and the vacant seats were generally filled by persons less tractable. Charles did not think himself a King while an assembly of subjects could call for his accounts before paying his debts, and could insist on knowing which of his mistresses or boon companions had intercepted the money destined for the equipping and man-

ning of the fleet. Though not very studious of fame, he was
galled by the taunts which were sometimes uttered in the discussions of the Commons, and on one occasion attempted to restrain the freedom of speech by disgraceful means. Sir John Coventry, a country gentleman, had, in debate, sneered at the profligacy of the court. In any former reign he would probably have been called before the Privy Council and committed to the Tower. A different course was now taken. A gang of bullies was secretly sent to slit the nose of the offender. This ignoble revenge, instead of quelling the spirit of opposition, raised such a tempest that the King was compelled to submit to the cruel humiliation of passing an act which attainted the instruments of his revenge, and which took from him the power of pardoning them.

But, impatient as he was of constitutional restraints, how was he to emancipate himself from them? He could make himself despotic only by the help of a great standing army; and such an army was not in existence. His revenues did indeed enable him to keep up some regular troops: but these troops, though numerous enough to excite great jealousy and apprehension in the House of Commons and in the country, were scarcely numerous enough to protect Whitehall and the Tower against a rising of the mob of London. Such risings were, indeed, to be dreaded; for it was calculated that in the capital and its suburbs dwelt not less than twenty thousand of Oliver's old soldiers.

Since the King was bent on emancipating himself from the control of Parliament, and since, in such an enterprise, he could not hope for effectual aid at home, it followed that he must look for aid abroad. The power and wealth of the King of France might be equal to the arduous task of establishing absolute monarchy in England. Such an ally would undoubtedly expect substantial proofs of gratitude for such a service. Charles must descend to the rank of a great vassal, *Connection between Charles II. and France.*

and must make peace and war according to the directions of
the government which protected him. His relation to Lewis
would closely resemble that in which the Rajah of Nagpore
and the King of Oude now stand to the British government.
Those princes are bound to aid the East India Company in all
hostilities, defensive and offensive, and to have no diplomatic
relations but such as the East India Company shall sanction.
The Company in return guarantees them against insurrection.
As long as they faithfully discharge their obligations to the
paramount power, they are permitted to dispose of large
revenues, to fill their palaces with beautiful women, to besot
themselves in the company of their favourite revellers, and to
oppress with impunity any subject who may incur their displeasure. Such a life would be insupportable to a man of high
spirit and of powerful understanding. But to Charles, sensual,
indolent, unequal to any strong intellectual exertion, and
destitute alike of all patriotism and of all sense of personal
dignity, the prospect had nothing unpleasing.

That the Duke of York should have concurred in the
design of degrading that crown which it was probable that he
would himself one day wear may seem more extraordinary.
For his nature was haughty and imperious; and, indeed,
he continued to the very last to show, by occasional starts and
struggles, his impatience of the French yoke. But he was
almost as much debased by superstition as his brother by
indolence and vice. James was now a Roman Catholic.
Religious bigotry had become the dominant sentiment of his
narrow and stubborn mind, and had so mingled itself with his
love of rule, that the two passions could hardly be distinguished from each other. It seemed highly improbable that,
without foreign aid, he would be able to obtain ascendency or
even toleration for his own faith: and he was in a temper to
see nothing humiliating in any step which might promote the
interests of the true Church.

A negotiation was opened which lasted during several months. The chief agent between the English and French courts was the beautiful, graceful, and intelligent Henrietta, Duchess of Orleans, sister of Charles, sister-in-law of Lewis, and a favourite with both. The King of England offered to declare himself a Roman Catholic, to dissolve the Triple Alliance, and to join with France against Holland, if France would engage to lend him such military and pecuniary aid as might make him independent of his Parliament. Lewis at first affected to receive these propositions coolly, and at length agreed to them with the air of a man who is conferring a great favour: but in truth, the course which he had resolved to take was one by which he might gain and could not lose.

It seems certain that he never seriously thought of establishing despotism and Popery in England by force of arms. He must have been aware that such an enterprise would be in the highest degree arduous and hazardous, that it would task to the utmost all the energies of France during many years, and that it would be altogether incompatible with more promising schemes of aggrandisement, which were dear to his heart. He would indeed willingly have acquired the merit and the glory of doing a great service on reasonable terms to the Church of which he was a member. But he was little disposed to imitate his ancestors who, in the twelfth and thirteenth centuries, had led the flower of French chivalry to die in Syria and Egypt; and he well knew that a crusade against Protestantism in Great Britain would not be less perilous than the expeditions in which the armies of Lewis the Seventh and of Lewis the Ninth had perished. He had no motive for wishing the Stuarts to be absolute. He did not regard the English constitution with feelings at all resembling those which have in later times induced princes to make war on the free institutions of neighbouring nations. At present a great party zealous for popular government has ramifications in every civilised country. Any important advantage gained anywhere by that party is almost certain to be the signal for general commotion. It is not wonderful that governments threatened by a common danger should combine for the purpose of mutual insurance. But in the seventeenth century no such danger existed. Between the public mind of England and the public mind of France, there was a great gulph. Our institutions and our factions were as little understood at Paris as at Constantinople. It may be doubted whether any one of the forty members of the French Academy had an English volume in his library, or knew Shakspeare, Jonson, or Spenser, even by name. A few Huguenots, who had inherited the mutinous spirit of their ancestors, might perhaps have a fellow feeling with their brethren in the faith, the English Roundheads: but the Huguenots had ceased to be formidable. The French, as a body, attached to the Church of Rome, and proud of the greatness of their King, and of their own loyalty, looked on our struggles against Popery and arbitrary power, not only without admiration or sympathy, but with strong disapprobation and disgust. It would therefore be a great error to ascribe the conduct of Lewis to apprehensions at all resembling those which, in our age, induced the Holy Alliance to interfere in the internal troubles of Naples and Spain.

Nevertheless, the propositions made by the court of Whitehall were most welcome to him. He already meditated gigantic designs, which were destined to keep Europe in constant fermentation during more than forty years. He wished to humble the United Provinces, and to annex Belgium, Franche Comté and Loraine to his dominions. Nor was this all. The King of Spain was a sickly child. It was likely that he would die without issue. His eldest sister was Queen of France. A day would almost certainly come, and might come very soon, when the House of Bourbon might lay claim to that

vast empire on which the sun never set. The union of two
great monarchies under one head would doubtless be opposed
by a continental coalition. But for any continental coalition
France single handed was a match. England could turn the
scale. On the course which, in such a crisis, England might
pursue, the destinies of the world would depend; and it was
notorious that the English Parliament and nation were strongly
attached to the policy which had dictated the Triple Alliance.
Nothing, therefore, could be more gratifying to Lewis than
to learn that the princes of the House of Stuart needed his
help, and were willing to purchase that help by unbounded
subserviency. He determined to profit by the opportunity,
and laid down for himself a plan to which, without deviation,
he adhered, till the Revolution of 1688 disconcerted all his
politics. He professed himself desirous to promote the designs of the English court. He promised large aid. He from
time to time doled out such aid as might serve to keep hope
alive, and as he could without risk or inconvenience spare.
In this way, at an expense very much less than that which he
incurred in building and decorating Versailles or Marli, he
succeeded in making England, during nearly twenty years,
almost as insignificant a member of the political system of
Europe as the republic of San Marino.

His object was not to destroy our constitution, but to keep
the various elements of which it was composed in a perpetual
state of conflict, and to set irreconcilable enmity between
those who had the power of the purse and those who had the
power of the sword. With this view he bribed and stimulated
both parties in turn, pensioned at once the ministers of the
crown and the chiefs of the opposition, encouraged the court
to withstand the seditious encroachments of the Parliament,
and conveyed to the Parliament intimations of the arbitrary
designs of the court.

One of the devices to which he resorted for the purpose of

obtaining an ascendency in the English counsels deserves especial notice. Charles, though incapable of love in the highest sense of the word, was the slave of any woman whose person excited his desires, and whose airs and prattle amused his leisure. Indeed a husband would be justly derided who should bear from a wife of exalted rank and spotless virtue half the insolence which the King of England bore from concubines who, while they owed everything to his bounty, caressed his courtiers almost before his face. He had patiently endured the termagant passions of Barbara Palmer and the pert vivacity of Eleanor Gwynn. Lewis thought that the most useful envoy who could be sent to London, would be a handsome, licentious, and crafty Frenchwoman. Such a woman was Louisa, a lady of the House of Querouaille, whom our rude ancestors called Madam Carwell. She was soon triumphant over all her rivals, was created Duchess of Portsmouth, was loaded with wealth, and obtained a dominion which ended only with the life of Charles.

Treaty of Dover.   The most important conditions of the alliance between the crowns were digested into a secret treaty which was signed at Dover in May 1670, just ten years after the day on which Charles had landed at that very port amidst the acclamations and joyful tears of a too confiding people.

By this treaty Charles bound himself to make public profession of the Roman Catholic religion, to join his arms to those of Lewis for the purpose of destroying the power of the United Provinces, and to employ the whole strength of England, by land and sea, in support of the rights of the House of Bourbon to the vast monarchy of Spain. Lewis, on the other hand, engaged to pay a large subsidy, and promised that, if any insurrection should break out in England, he would send an army at his own charge to support his ally.

This compact was made with gloomy auspices. Six weeks after it had been signed and sealed, the charming princess, whose influence over her brother and brother-in-law had been so pernicious to her country, was no more. Her death gave rise to horrible suspicions which, for a moment, seemed likely to interrupt the newly formed friendship between the Houses of Stuart and Bourbon: but in a short time fresh assurances of undiminished good will were exchanged between the confederates.

The Duke of York, too dull to apprehend danger, or too fanatical to care about it, was impatient to see the article touching the Roman Catholic religion carried into immediate execution: but Lewis had the wisdom to perceive that, if this course were taken, there would be such an explosion in England as would probably frustrate those parts of the plan which he had most at heart. It was therefore determined that Charles should still call himself a Protestant, and should still, at high festivals, receive the sacrament according to the ritual of the Church of England. His more scrupulous brother ceased to appear in the royal chapel.

About this time died the Duchess of York, daughter of the banished Earl of Clarendon. She had been, during some years, a concealed Roman Catholic. She left two daughters, Mary and Anne, afterwards successively Queens of Great Britain. They were bred Protestants by the positive command of the King, who knew that it would be vain for him to profess himself a member of the Church of England, if children who seemed likely to inherit his throne were, by his permission, brought up as members of the Church of Rome.

The principal servants of the crown at this time were men whose names have justly acquired an unenviable notoriety. We must take heed, however, that we do not load their memory with infamy which of right belongs to their master. For the treaty of Dover the King himself is chiefly answerable. He held conferences on it with the French agents: he wrote many letters concerning it with his own hand: he was the per-

CHAP.
II.

Nature of
the Eng-
lish Ca-
binet.

The
Cabal.

son who first suggested the most disgraceful articles which it contained; and he carefully concealed some of those articles from the majority of his Cabinet.

Few things in our history are more curious than the origin and growth of the power now possessed by the Cabinet. From an early period the Kings of England had been assisted by a Privy Council to which the law assigned many important functions and duties. During several centuries this body deliberated on the gravest and most delicate affairs. But by degrees its character changed. It became too large for despatch and secrecy. The rank of Privy Councillor was often bestowed as an honorary distinction on persons to whom nothing was confided, and whose opinion was never asked. The sovereign, on the most important occasions, resorted for advice to a small knot of leading ministers. The advantages and disadvantages of this course were early pointed out by Bacon, with his usual judgment and sagacity: but it was not till after the Restoration that the interior council began to attract general notice. During many years old fashioned politicians continued to regard the Cabinet as an unconstitutional and dangerous board. Nevertheless, it constantly became more and more important. It at length drew to itself the chief executive power, and has now been regarded, during several generations, as an essential part of our polity. Yet, strange to say, it still continues to be altogether unknown to the law. The names of the noblemen and gentlemen who compose it are never officially announced to the public. No record is kept of its meetings and resolutions; nor has its existence ever been recognised by any Act of Parliament.

During some years the word Cabal was popularly used as synonymous with Cabinet. But it happened by a whimsical coincidence that, in 1671, the Cabinet consisted of five persons the initial letters of whose names made up the word Cabal, Clifford, Arlington, Buckingham, Ashley, and Lau-

derdale.   These ministers were therefore emphatically called
the Cabal; and they soon made that appellation so infamous
that it has never since their time been used except as a term of
reproach.

Sir Thomas Clifford was a Commissioner of the Treasury,
and had greatly distinguished himself in the House of Commons.   Of the members of the Cabal he was the most respectable.   For, with a fiery and imperious temper, he had a
strong though a lamentably perverted sense of duty and
honour.

Henry Bennet, Lord Arlington, then Secretary of State,
had, since he came to manhood, resided principally on the
Continent, and had learned that cosmopolitan indifference to
constitutions and religions which is often observable in persons whose life has been passed in vagrant diplomacy.   If
there was any form of government which he liked, it was that
of France.   If there was any Church for which he felt a preference, it was that of Rome.   He had some talent for conversation, and some talent also for transacting the ordinary
business of office.   He had learned, during a life passed in
travelling and negotiating, the art of accommodating his language and deportment to the society in which he found himself.   His vivacity in the closet amused the King: his gravity
in debates and conferences imposed on the public: and he
had succeeded in attaching to himself, partly by services
and partly by hopes, a considerable number of personal retainers.

Buckingham, Ashley, and Lauderdale, were men in whom
the immorality which was epidemic among the politicians of
that age appeared in its most malignant type, but variously
modified by great diversities of temper and understanding.
Buckingham was a sated man of pleasure, who had turned to
ambition as to a pastime.   As he had tried to amuse himself
with architecture and music, with writing farces and with

seeking for the philosopher's stone, so he now tried to amuse
himself with a secret negotiation and a Dutch war. He had
already, rather from fickleness and love of novelty than from
any deep design, been faithless to every party. At one time
he had ranked among the Cavaliers. At another time warrants
had been out against him for maintaining a treasonable correspondence with the remains of the Republican party in the
city. He was now again a courtier, and was eager to win the
favour of the King by services from which the most illustrious
of those who had fought and suffered for the royal house
would have recoiled with horror.

Ashley, with a far stronger head, and with a far fiercer and
more earnest ambition, had been equally versatile. But Ashley's versatility was the effect, not of levity, but of deliberate
selfishness. He had served and betrayed a succession of
governments. But he had timed all his treacheries so well
that, through all revolutions, his fortunes had constantly been
rising. The multitude, struck with admiration by a prosperity which, while everything else was constantly changing,
remained unchangeable, attributed to him a prescience almost
miraculous, and likened him to the Hebrew statesman of whom
it is written that his counsel was as if a man had inquired of the
oracle of God.

Lauderdale, loud and coarse both in mirth and anger, was
perhaps, under the outward show of boisterous frankness, the
most dishonest man in the whole Cabal. He had been conspicuous among the Scotch insurgents of 1638, and zealous for the
Covenant. He was accused of having been deeply concerned
in the sale of Charles the First to the English Parliament, and
was therefore, in the estimation of good Cavaliers, a traitor, if
possible, of a worse description than those who had sate in the
High Court of Justice. He often talked with noisy jocularity
of the days when he was a canter and a rebel. He was now the
chief instrument employed by the court in the work of forcing

Episcopacy on his reluctant countrymen; nor did he in that cause shrink from the unsparing use of the sword, the halter, and the boot. Yet those who knew him knew that thirty years had made no change in his real sentiments, that he still hated the memory of Charles the First, and that he still preferred the Presbyterian form of church government to every other.

Unscrupulous as Buckingham, Ashley, and Lauderdale were, it was not thought safe to entrust to them the King's intention of declaring himself a Roman Catholic. A false treaty, in which the article concerning religion was omitted, was shown to them. The names and seals of Clifford and Arlington are affixed to the genuine treaty. Both these statesmen had a partiality for the old Church, a partiality which the brave and vehement Clifford in no long time manfully avowed, but which the colder and meaner Arlington concealed, till the near approach of death scared him into sincerity. The three other cabinet ministers, however, were not men to be easily kept in the dark, and probably suspected more than was distinctly avowed to them. They were certainly privy to all the political engagements contracted with France, and were not ashamed to receive large gratifications from Lewis.

The first object of Charles was to obtain from the Commons supplies which might be employed in executing the secret treaty. The Cabal, holding power at a time when our government was in a state of transition, united in itself two different kinds of vices belonging to two different ages and to two different systems. As those five evil counsellors were among the last English statesmen who seriously thought of destroying the Parliament, so they were the first English statesmen who attempted extensively to corrupt it. We find in their policy at once the latest trace of the Thorough of Strafford, and the earliest trace of that methodical bribery which was afterwards practised by Walpole. They soon perceived, however, that,

14*

though the House of Commons was chiefly composed of Cavaliers, and though places and French gold had been lavished on
the members, there was no chance that even the least odious
parts of the scheme arranged at Dover would be supported by
a majority. It was necessary to have recourse to fraud. The
King accordingly professed great zeal for the principles of the
Triple Alliance, and pretended that, in order to hold the ambition of France in check, it would be necessary to augment
the fleet. The Commons fell into the snare, and voted a grant
of eight hundred thousand pounds. The Parliament was instantly prorogued; and the court, thus emancipated from control, proceeded to the execution of the great design.

Shutting
of the Ex-
chequer. The financial difficulties were serious. A war with Holland
could be carried on only at enormous cost. The ordinary
revenue was not more than sufficient to support the government in time of peace. The eight hundred thousand pounds
out of which the Commons had just been tricked would not
defray the naval and military charge of a single year of hostilities. After the terrible lesson given by the Long Parliament,
even the Cabal did not venture to recommend benevolences or
ship-money. In this perplexity Ashley and Clifford proposed
a flagitious breach of public faith. The goldsmiths of London
were then not only dealers in the precious metals, but also
bankers, and were in the habit of advancing large sums of
money to the government. In return for these advances they
received assignments on the revenue, and were repaid with interest as the taxes came in. About thirteen hundred thousand
pounds had been in this way entrusted to the honour of the
state. On a sudden it was announced that it was not convenient to pay the principal, and that the lenders must content
themselves with interest. They were consequently unable to
meet their own engagements. The Exchange was in an uproar: several great mercantile houses broke; and dismay and
distress spread through all society. Meanwhile rapid strides

were made towards despotism. Proclamations, dispensing
with Acts of Parliament or enjoining what only Parliament
could lawfully enjoin, appeared in rapid succession. Of these
edicts the most important was the Declaration of Indulgence.
By this instrument the penal laws against Roman Catholics
were set aside by royal authority; and, that the real object of
the measure might not be perceived, the laws against Protestant Nonconformists were also suspended.

A few days after the appearance of the Declaration of Indulgence, war was proclaimed against the United Provinces.
By sea the Dutch maintained the struggle with honour; but on
land they were at first borne down by irresistible force. A
great French army passed the Rhine. Fortress after fortress
opened its gates. Three of the seven provinces of the federation were occupied by the invaders. The fires of the
hostile camp were seen from the top of the Stadthouse of
Amsterdam. The Republic, thus fiercely assailed from without, was torn at the same time by internal dissensions. The
government was in the hands of a close oligarchy of powerful
burghers. There were numerous self-elected town councils,
each of which exercised, within its own sphere, many of the
rights of sovereignty. These councils sent delegates to the
Provincial States, and the Provincial States again sent delegates to the States General. A hereditary first magistrate was
no essential part of this polity. Nevertheless one family, singularly fertile of great men, had gradually obtained a large and
somewhat indefinite authority. William, first of the name,
Prince of Orange Nassau, and Stadtholder of Holland, had
headed the memorable insurrection against Spain. His son
Maurice had been Captain General and first minister of the
States, had, by eminent abilities and public services, and by
some treacherous and cruel actions, raised himself to almost
kingly power, and had bequeathed a great part of that power
to his family. The influence of the Stadtholders was an object

of extreme jealousy to the municipal oligarchy. But the army,
and that great body of citizens which was excluded from all
share in the government, looked on the Burgomasters and Deputies with a dislike resembling the dislike with which the
legions and the common people of Rome regarded the Senate,
and were as zealous for the House of Orange as the legions and
the common people of Rome for the House of Cæsar.   The
Stadtholder commanded the forces of the commonwealth, disposed of all military commands, had a large share of the civil
patronage, and was surrounded by pomp almost regal.

Prince William the Second had been strongly opposed by
the oligarchical party.   His life had terminated in the year
1650, amidst great civil troubles.   He died childless : the
adherents of his house were left for a short time without a
head; and the powers which he had exercised were divided
among the town councils, the Provincial States, and the States
General.

But, a few days after William's death, his widow, Mary,
daughter of Charles the First, King of Great Britain, gave
birth to a son, destined to raise the glory and authority of the
House of Nassau to the highest point, to save the United
Provinces from slavery, to curb the power of France, and to
establish the English constitution on a lasting foundation.

William,
Prince of
Orange.
This Prince, named William Henry, was from his birth
an object of serious apprehension to the party now supreme
in Holland, and of loyal attachment to the old friends of his
line.   He enjoyed high consideration as the possessor of a
splendid fortune, as the chief of one of the most illustrious
houses in Europe, as a sovereign prince of the German empire, as a prince of the blood royal of England, and, above
all, as the descendant of the founders of Batavian liberty.
But the high office which had once been considered as hereditary in his family, remained in abeyance; and the intention
of the aristocratical party was that there should never be

another Stadtholder. The want of a first magistrate was, to a great extent, supplied by the Grand Pensionary of the Province of Holland, John de Witt, whose abilities, firmness, and integrity had raised him to unrivalled authority in the counsels of the municipal oligarchy.

The French invasion produced a complete change. The suffering and terrified people raged fiercely against the government. In their madness they attacked the bravest captains and the ablest statesmen of the distressed commonwealth. De Ruyter was insulted by the rabble. De Witt was torn in pieces before the gate of the palace of the States General at the Hague. The Prince of Orange, who had no share in the guilt of the murder, but who, on this occasion, as on another lamentable occasion twenty years later, extended to crimes perpetrated in his cause an indulgence which has left a stain on his glory, became chief of the government without a rival. Young as he was, his ardent and unconquerable spirit, though disguised by a cold and sullen manner, soon roused the courage of his dismayed countrymen. It was in vain that both his uncle and the French King attempted by splendid offers to seduce him from the cause of the republic. To the States General he spoke a high and inspiriting language. He even ventured to suggest a scheme which has an aspect of antique heroism, and which, if it had been accomplished, would have been the noblest subject for epic song that is to be found in the whole compass of modern history. He told the deputies that, even if their natal soil and the marvels with which human industry had covered it were buried under the ocean, all was not lost. The Hollanders might survive Holland. Liberty and pure religion, driven by tyrants and bigots from Europe, might take refuge in the farthest isles of Asia. The shipping in the ports of the republic would suffice to carry two hundred thousand emigrants to the Indian Archipelago. There the Dutch commonwealth might com-

CHAP. mence a new and more glorious existence, and might rear,
 II.
————— under the Southern Cross, amidst the sugar canes and nutmeg
trees, the Exchange of a wealthier Amsterdam, and the
schools of a more learned Leyden. The national spirit swelled
and rose high. The terms offered by the allies were firmly
rejécted. The dykes were opened. The whole country was
one great lake, from which the cities, with their ramparts
and steeples, rose like islands. The invaders were forced to
save themselves from destruction by a precipitate retreat.
Lewis, who, though he sometimes thought it necessary to
appear at the head of his troops, greatly preferred a palace
to a camp, had already returned to enjoy the adulation of
· poets and the smiles of ladies in the newly planted alleys of
Versailles.

   And now the tide turned fast. The event of the maritime
war had been doubtful : by land the United Provinces had
obtained a respite; and a respite, though short, was of in-
finite importance.   Alarmed by the vast designs of Lewis,
both the branches of the |great House of Austria sprang to
arms. Spain and Holland, divided by the memory of ancient
wrongs and humiliations, were reconciled by the nearness of
the common danger. From every part of Germany troops
poured towards the Rhine. The English government had
already expended all the funds which had been obtained by
pillaging the public creditor. No loan could be expected
from the City. An attempt to raise taxes by the royal authority
would have at once produced a rebellion; and Lewis, who
had now to maintain a contest against half Europe, was in no
condition to furnish the means of coercing the people of England. It was necessary to convoke the Parliament.

Meeting   In the spring of 1673, therefore, the Houses reassembled
of the
Parlia-   after a recess of near two years. Clifford, now a peer and
ment.   Lord Treasurer, and Ashley, now Earl of Shaftesbury and
Lord Chancellor, were the persons on whom the King chiefly

relied as Parliamentary managers. The Country Party instantly began to attack the policy of the Cabal. The attack
was made, not in the way of storm, but by slow and scientific
approaches. The Commons at first held out hopes that they
would give support to the King's foreign policy, but insisted
that he should purchase that support by abandoning his whole
system of domestic policy. Their first object was to obtain
the revocation of the Declaration of Indulgence. Of all the
many unpopular steps taken by the government the most unpopular was the publishing of this Declaration. The most
opposite sentiments had been shocked by an act so liberal,
done in a manner so despotic. All the enemies of religious
freedom, and all the friends of civil freedom, found themselves on the same side; and these two classes made up
nineteen twentieths of the nation. The zealous Churchman
exclaimed against the favour which had been shown both to
the Papist and to the Puritan. The Puritan, though he might
rejoice in the suspension of the persecution by which he had
been harassed, felt little gratitude for a toleration which he
was to share with Antichrist. And all Englishmen who
valued liberty and law, saw with uneasiness the deep inroad
which the prerogative had made into the province of the legislature.

It must in candour be admitted that the constitutional
question was then not quite free from obscurity. Our ancient
Kings had undoubtedly claimed and exercised the right of
suspending the operation of penal laws. The tribunals had
recognised that right. Parliaments had suffered it to pass
unchallenged. That some such right was inherent in the
crown, few even of the Country Party ventured, in the face
of precedent and authority, to deny. Yet it was clear that,
if this prerogative were without limit, the English government
could scarcely be distinguished from a pure despotism. That
there was a limit was fully admitted by the King and his mi-

nisters. Whether the Declaration of Indulgence lay within or without the limit was the question ; and neither party could succeed in tracing any line which would bear examination. Some opponents of the government complained that the Declaration suspended not less than forty statutes. But why not forty as well as one? There was an orator who gave it as his opinion that the King might constitutionally dispense with bad laws, but not with good laws. The absurdity of such a distinction it is needless to expose. The doctrine which seems to have been generally received in the House of Commons was, that the dispensing power was confined to secular matters, and did not extend to laws enacted for the security of the established religion. Yet, as the King was supreme head of the Church, it should seem that, if he possessed the dispensing power at all, he might well possess that power where the Church was concerned. When the courtiers on the other side attempted to point out the bounds of this prerogative, they were not more successful than the opposition had been. *

The truth is that the dispensing power was a great anomaly in politics.   It was utterly inconsistent in theory with the principles of mixed government: but it had grown up in times when people troubled themselves little about theories.   It had not been very grossly abused in practice. It had therefore been tolerated, and had gradually acquired a kind of prescription. At length it was employed, after a long interval, in an enlightened age, and at an important conjuncture, to an extent never before known, and for a purpose generally abhorred. It was instantly subjected to a severe scrutiny. Men did not, indeed, at first, venture to pronounce it altogether unconstitutional. But they began to perceive that it was at direct va-

* The most sensible thing said in the House of Commons, on this subject, came from Sir William Coventry: — "Our ancestors never did draw a line to circumscribe prerogative and liberty."

riance with the spirit of the constitution, and would, if left CHAP.
unchecked, turn the English government from a limited into ――――
an absolute monarchy.

Under the influence of such apprehensions, the Commons It is can-
denied the King's right to dispense, not indeed with all penal and the
statutes, but with penal statutes in matters ecclesiastical, and passed.
gave him plainly to understand that, unless he renounced that
right, they would grant no supply for the Dutch war. He, for
a moment, showed some inclination to put everything to
hazard: but he was strongly advised by Lewis to submit to
necessity, and to wait for better times, when the French
armies, now employed in an arduous struggle on the continent,
might be available for the purpose of suppressing discontent
in England. In the Cabal itself the signs of disunion and
treachery began to appear. Shaftesbury, with his proverbial
sagacity, saw that a violent reaction was at hand, and that all
things were tending towards a crisis resembling that of 1640.
He was determined that such a crisis should not find him in the
situation of Strafford. He therefore turned suddenly round,
and acknowledged, in the House of Lords, that the Declaration was illegal. The King, thus deserted by his ally and by
his Chancellor, yielded, cancelled the Declaration, and solemnly promised that it should never be drawn into precedent.

Even this concession was insufficient. The Commons, not
content with having forced their sovereign to annul the Indulgence, next extorted his unwilling consent to a celebrated
law, which continued in force down to the reign of George the
Fourth. This law, known as the Test Act, provided that all
persons holding any office, civil or military, should take the
oath of supremacy, should subscribe a declaration against
transubstantiation, and should publicly receive the sacrament
according to the rites of the Church of England. The
preamble expressed hostility only to the Papists: but the

CHAP. enacting clauses were scarcely more unfavourable to the
II. Papists than to the most rigid class of Puritans. The Puritans, however, terrified at the evident leaning of the court towards Popery, and encouraged by some churchmen to hope
that, as soon as the Roman Catholics should have been
effectually disarmed, relief would be extended to Protestant
Nonconformists, made little opposition; nor could the King,
who was in extreme want of money, venture to withhold his
assent. The act was passed; and the Duke of York was consequently under the necessity of resigning the great place of
Lord High Admiral.

The Cabal dissolved. Hitherto the Commons had not declared against the Dutch
war. But, when the King had, in return for money cautiously
doled out, relinquished his whole plan of domestic policy, they
fell impetuously on his foreign policy. They requested him
to dismiss Buckingham and Lauderdale from his councils for
ever, and appointed a committee to consider the propriety of
impeaching Arlington. In a short time the Cabal was no
more. Clifford, who, alone of the five, had any claim to be
regarded as an honest man, refused to take the new test, laid
down his white staff, and retired to his country seat. Arlington quitted the post of Secretary of State for a quiet and dignified employment in the royal household. Shaftesbury and
Buckingham made their peace with the opposition, and appeared at the head of the stormy democracy of the city. Lauderdale, however, still continued to be minister for Scotch
affairs, with which the English Parliament could not interfere.

And now the Commons urged the King to make peace with
Holland, and expressly declared that no more supplies should
be granted for the war, unless it should appear that the enemy
obstinately refused to consent to reasonable terms. Charles
found it necessary to postpone to a more convenient season all
thought of executing the treaty of Dover, and to cajole the

nation by pretending to return to the policy of the Triple CHAP.
II.
Alliance. Temple, who, during the ascendency of the Cabal,
had lived in seclusion among his books and flower beds, was
called forth from his hermitage. By his instrumentality a se- Peace
with the
parate peace was concluded with the United Provinces; and United
he again became ambassador at the Hague, where his presence Provinces.
was regarded as a sure pledge for the sincerity of his court.

The chief direction of affairs was now entrusted to Sir Administration of
Thomas Osborn, a Yorkshire baronet, who had, in the House Danby.
of Commons, shown eminent talents for business and debate.
Osborn became Lord Treasurer, and was soon created Earl of
Danby. He was not a man whose character, if tried by any
high standard of morality, would appear to merit approbation.
He was greedy of wealth and honours, corrupt himself, and a
corrupter of others. The Cabal had bequeathed to him the
art of bribing Parliaments, an art still rude, and giving little
promise of the rare perfection to which it was brought in the
following century. He improved greatly on the plan of the
first inventors. They had merely purchased orators: but
every man who had a vote, might sell himself to Danby. Yet
the new minister must not be confounded with the negotiators
of Dover. He was not without the feelings of an Englishman
and a Protestant; nor did he, in his solicitude for his own interests, ever wholly forget the interests of his country and of
his religion. He was desirous, indeed, to exalt the prerogative: but the means by which he proposed to exalt it were
widely different from those which had been contemplated by
Arlington and Clifford. The thought of establishing arbitrary
power, by calling in the aid of foreign arms, and by reducing
the kingdom to the rank of a dependent principality, never
entered into his mind. His plan was to rally round the monarchy those classes which had been the firm allies of the monarchy during the troubles of the preceding generation, and
which had been disgusted by the recent crimes and errors of

the court. With the help of the old Cavalier interest, of the nobles, of the country gentlemen, of the clergy, and of the Universities, it might, he conceived, be possible to make Charles, not indeed an absolute sovereign, but a sovereign scarcely less powerful than Elizabeth had been.

Prompted by these feelings, Danby formed the design of securing to the Cavalier party the exclusive possession of all political power, both executive and legislative. In the year 1675, accordingly, a bill was offered to the Lords which provided that no person should hold any office, or should sit in either House of Parliament, without first declaring on oath that he considered resistance to the kingly power as in all cases criminal, and that he would never endeavour to alter the government either in Church or State. During several weeks the debates, divisions, and protests caused by this proposition kept the country in a state of excitement. The opposition in the House of Lords, headed by two members of the Cabal who were desirous to make their peace with the nation, Buckingham and Shaftesbury, was beyond all precedent vehement and pertinacious, and at length proved successful. The bill was not indeed rejected, but was retarded, mutilated, and at length suffered to drop.

So arbitrary and so exclusive was Danby's scheme of domestic policy. His opinions touching foreign policy did him more honour. They were in truth directly opposed to those of the Cabal, and differed little from those of the Country Party. He bitterly lamented the degraded situation to which England was reduced, and declared, with more energy than politeness, that his dearest wish was to cudgel the French into a proper respect for her. So little did he disguise his feelings, that, at a great banquet where the most illustrious dignitaries of the State and of the Church were assembled, he not very decorously filled his glass to the confusion of all who were against a war with France. He would indeed most gladly have seen his country united with the powers which were then combined against Lewis, and was for that end bent on placing Temple, the author of the Triple Alliance, at the head of the department which directed foreign affairs. But the power of the prime minister was limited. In his most confidential letters he complained that the infatuation of his master prevented England from taking her proper place among European nations. Charles was insatiably greedy of French gold: he had by no means relinquished the hope that he might, at some future day, be able to establish absolute monarchy by the help of the French arms; and for both reasons he wished to maintain a good understanding with the Court of Versailles.

Thus the sovereign leaned towards one system of foreign politics, and the minister towards a system diametrically opposite. Neither the sovereign nor the minister, indeed, was of a temper to pursue any object with undeviating constancy. Each occasionally yielded to the importunity of the other; and their jarring inclinations and mutual concessions gave to the whole administration a strangely capricious character. Charles sometimes, from levity and indolence, suffered Danby to take steps which Lewis resented as mortal injuries. Danby, on the other hand, rather than relinquish his great place, sometimes stooped to compliances which caused him bitter pain and shame. The King was brought to consent to a marriage between the Lady Mary, eldest daughter and presumptive heiress of the Duke of York, and William of Orange, the deadly enemy of France, and the hereditary champion of the Reformation. Nay, the brave Earl of Ossory, son of Ormond, was sent to assist the Dutch with some British troops, who, on the most bloody day of the whole war, signally vindicated the national reputation for stubborn courage. The Treasurer, on the other hand, was induced, not only to connive at some scandalous pecu-

CHAP.
II.

niary transactions which took place between his master and the court of Versailles, but to become, unwillingly indeed and ungraciously, an agent in those transactions.

Embar-
rassing
situation
of the
Country
Party.

Meanwhile, the Country Party was driven by two strong feelings in two opposite directions. The popular leaders were afraid of the greatness of Lewis, who was not only making head against the whole strength of the continental alliance, but was even gaining ground. Yet they were afraid to entrust their own King with the means of curbing France, lest those means should be used to destroy the liberties of England. The conflict between these apprehensions, both of which were perfectly legitimate, made the policy of the Opposition seem as eccentric and fickle as that of the Court. The Commons called for a war with France, till the King, pressed by Danby to comply with their wish, seemed disposed to yield, and began to raise an army. But, as soon as they saw that the recruiting had commenced, their dread of Lewis gave place to a nearer dread. They began to fear that the new levies might be employed on a service in which Charles took much more interest than in the defence of Flanders. They therefore refused supplies, and clamoured for disbanding as loudly as they had just before clamoured for arming. Those historians who have severely reprehended this inconsistency do not appear to have made sufficient allowance for the embarrassing situation of subjects who have reason to believe that their prince is conspiring with a foreign and hostile power against their liberties. To refuse him military resources is to leave the state defenceless. Yet to give him military resources may be only to arm him against the state. In such circumstances vacillation cannot be considered as a proof of dishonesty or even of weakness.

Dealings
of that
party with
the
French
embassy.

These jealousies were studiously fomented by the French King. He had long kept England passive by promising to support the throne against the Parliament. He now, alarmed at finding that the patriotic counsels of Danby seemed likely CHAP.
II. to prevail in the closet, began to inflame the Parliament against the throne. Between Lewis and the Country Party there was one thing, and one only, in common, profound distrust of Charles. Could the Country Party have been certain that their sovereign meant only to make war on France, they would have been eager to support him. Could Lewis have been certain that the new levies were intended only to make war on the constitution of England, he would have made no attempt to stop them. But the unsteadiness and faithlessness of Charles were such that the French government and the English opposition, agreeing in nothing else, agreed in disbelieving his protestations, and were equally desirous to keep him poor and without an army. Communications were opened between Barillon, the Ambassador of Lewis, and those English politicians who had always professed, and who indeed sincerely felt, the greatest dread and dislike of the French ascendency. The most upright member of the Country Party, William Lord Russell, son of the Earl of Bedford, did not scruple to concert with a foreign mission schemes for embarrassing his own sovereign. This was the whole extent of Russell's offence. His principles and his fortune alike raised him above all temptations of a sordid kind: but there is too much reason to believe that some of his associates were less scrupulous. It would be unjust to impute to them the extreme wickedness of taking bribes to injure their country. On the contrary, they meant to serve her: but it is impossible to deny that they were mean and indelicate enough to let a foreign prince pay them for serving her. Among those who cannot be acquitted of this degrading charge was one man who is popularly considered as the personification of public spirit, and who, in spite of some great moral and intellectual faults, has a just claim to be called a hero, a philosopher, and a patriot. It is im-

CHAP.   possible to see without pain such a name in the list of the pen-
II.
————   sioners of France. Yet it is some consolation to reflect that,
in our time, a public man would be thought lost to all sense
of duty and of shame, who should not spurn from him a
temptation which conquered the virtue and the pride of
Algernon Sidney.

Peace of   The effect of these intrigues was that England, though
Nime-
guen.   she occasionally took a menacing attitude, remained inactive
till the continental war, having lasted near seven years, was
terminated, in 1678, by the treaty of Nimeguen. The United
Provinces, which in 1672 had seemed to be on the verge of
utter ruin, obtained honourable and advantageous terms.
This narrow escape was generally ascribed to the ability and
courage of the young Stadtholder. His fame was great
throughout Europe, and especially among the English, who
regarded him as one of their own princes, and rejoiced to see
him the husband of their future Queen. France retained
many important towns in the Low Countries and the great
province of Franche Comté. Almost the whole loss was
borne by the decaying monarchy of Spain.

Violent   A few months after the termination of hostilities on the
discon-
tents in continent came a great crisis in English politics. Towards
England. such a crisis things had been tending during eighteen years.
The whole stock of popularity, great as it was, with which
the King had commenced his administration, had long been
expended. To loyal enthusiasm had succeeded profound disaffection. The public mind had now measured back again
the space over which it had passed between 1640 and 1660,
and was once more in the state in which it had been when the
Long Parliament met.

The prevailing discontent was compounded of many feelings. One of these was wounded national pride. That generation had seen England, during a few years, allied on equal
terms with France, victorious over Holland and Spain, the

mistress of the sea, the terror of Rome, the head of the Protestant interest. Her resources had not diminished; and it might have been expected that she would have been at least as highly considered in Europe under a legitimate King, strong in the affection and willing obedience of his subjects, as she had been under an usurper whose utmost vigilance and energy were required to keep down a mutinous people. Yet she had, in consequence of the imbecility and meanness of her rulers, sunk so low that any German or Italian principality which brought five thousand men into the field was a more important member of the commonwealth of nations.

With the sense of national humiliation was mingled anxiety for civil liberty. Rumours, indistinct indeed, but perhaps the more alarming by reason of their indistinctness, imputed to the court a deliberate design against all the constitutional rights of Englishmen. It had even been whispered that this design was to be carried into effect by the intervention of foreign arms. The thought of such intervention made the blood, even of the Cavaliers, boil in their veins. Some who had always professed the doctrine of nonresistance in its full extent were now heard to mutter that there was one limitation to that doctrine. If a foreign force were brought over to coerce the nation, they would not answer for their own patience.

But neither national pride nor anxiety for public liberty had so great an influence on the popular mind as hatred of the Roman Catholic religion. That hatred had become one of the ruling passions of the community, and was as strong in the ignorant and profane as in those who were Protestants from conviction. The cruelties of Mary's reign, cruelties which even in the most accurate and sober narrative excite just detestation, and which were neither accurately nor soberly related in the popular martyrologies, the conspiracies against Elizabeth, and above all the Gunpowder Plot, had

left in the minds of the vulgar a deep and bitter feeling which
was kept up by annual commemorations, prayers, bonfires,
and processions. It should be added that those classes which
were peculiarly distinguished by attachment to the throne,
the clergy and the landed gentry, had peculiar reasons for
regarding the Church of Rome with aversion. The clergy
trembled for their benefices; the landed gentry for their
abbeys and great tithes. While the memory of the reign of
the Saints was still recent, hatred of Popery had in some
degree given place to hatred of Puritanism: but, during the
eighteen years which had elapsed since the Restoration, the
hatred of Puritanism had abated, and the hatred of Popery
had increased. The stipulations of the treaty of Dover were
accurately known to very few: but some hints had got abroad.
The general impression was that a great blow was about to be
aimed at the Protestant religion. The King was suspected by
many of a leaning towards Rome. His brother and heir presumptive was known to be a bigoted Roman Catholic. The
first Duchess of York had died a Roman Catholic. James
had then, in defiance of the remonstrances of the House of
Commons, taken to wife the Princess Mary of Modena, another Roman Catholic. If there should be sons by this marriage, there was reason to fear that they might be bred
Roman Catholics, and that a long succession of princes,
hostile to the established faith, might sit on the English
throne. The constitution had recently been violated for the
purpose of protecting the Roman Catholics from the penal
laws. The ally by whom the policy of England had, during
many years, been chiefly governed was not only a Roman
Catholic, but a persecutor of the reformed Churches. Under
such circumstances it is not strange that the common people
should have been inclined to apprehend a return of the times
of her whom they called Bloody Mary.

Thus the nation was in such a temper that the smallest

spark might raise a flame. At this conjuncture fire was set in two places at once to the vast mass of combustible matter; —— and in a moment the whole was in a blaze.

The French court, which knew Danby to be its mortal enemy, artfully contrived to ruin him by making him pass for its friend. Lewis, by the instrumentality of Ralph Montague, a faithless and shameless man who had resided in France as minister from England, laid before the House of Commons proofs that the Treasurer had been concerned in an application made by the court of Whitehall to the court of Versailles for a sum of money. This discovery produced its natural effect. The Treasurer was, in truth, exposed to the vengeance of Parliament, not on account of his delinquencies, but on account of his merits; not because he had been an accomplice in a criminal transaction, but because he had been a most unwilling and unserviceable accomplice. But of the circumstances, which have, in the judgment of posterity, greatly extenuated his fault, his contemporaries were ignorant. In their view he was the broker who had sold England to France. It seemed clear that his greatness was at an end, and doubtful whether his head could be saved.

Yet was the ferment excited by this discovery slight, when compared with the commotion which arose when it was noised abroad that a great Popish plot had been detected. One Titus Oates, a clergyman of the Church of England, had, by his disorderly life and heterodox doctrine, drawn on himself the censure of his spiritual superiors, had been compelled to quit his benefice, and had ever since led an infamous and vagrant life. He had once professed himself a Roman Catholic, and had passed some time on the Continent in English colleges of the order of Jesus. In those seminaries he had heard much wild talk about the best means of bringing England back to the true Church. From hints thus furnished he constructed a hideous romance, resembling rather the

dream of a sick man than any transaction which ever took
place in the real world. The Pope, he said, had entrusted
the government of England to the Jesuits. The Jesuits had,
by commissions under the seal of their society, appointed
Catholic clergymen, noblemen, and gentlemen, to all the
highest offices in Church and State. The Papists had burned
down London once. They had tried to burn it down again.
They were at that moment planning a scheme for setting fire
to all the shipping in the Thames. They were to rise at a
signal and massacre all their Protestant neighbours. A French
army was at the same time to land in Ireland. All the leading
statesmen and divines of England were to be murdered.
Three or four schemes had been formed for assassinating the
King. He was to be stabbed. He was to be poisoned in his
medicine. He was to be shot with silver bullets. The public
mind was so sore and excitable that these lies readily found
credit with the vulgar; and two events which speedily took
place led even some reflecting men to suspect that the tale,
though evidently distorted and exaggerated, might have some
foundation.

Edward Coleman, a very busy, and not very honest,
Roman Catholic intriguer, had been among the persons accused. Search was made for his papers. It was found that
he had just destroyed the greater part of them. But a few
which had escaped contained some passages which, to minds
strongly prepossessed, might seem to confirm the evidence
of Oates. Those passages indeed, when candidly construed,
appear to express little more than the hopes which the posture
of affairs, the predilections of Charles, the still stronger predilections of James, and the relations existing between the
French and English courts, might naturally excite in the mind
of a Roman Catholic strongly attached to the interests of his
Church. But the country was not then inclined to construe
the letters of Papists candidly; and it was urged, with some

show of reason, that, if papers which had been passed over
as unimportant were filled with matter so suspicious, some
great mystery of iniquity must have been contained in those
documents which had been carefully committed to the flames.

A few days later it was known that Sir Edmondsbury Godfrey, an eminent justice of the peace who had taken the
depositions of Oates against Coleman, had disappeared.
Search was made; and Godfrey's corpse was found in a field
near London. It was clear that he had died by violence. It
was equally clear that he had not been set upon by robbers.
His fate is to this day a secret. Some think that he perished
by his own hand; some, that he was slain by a private enemy.
The most improbable supposition is that he was murdered by
the party hostile to the court, in order to give colour to the
story of the plot. The most probable supposition seems, on
the whole, to be that some hot-headed Roman Catholic, driven
to frenzy by the lies of Oates and by the insults of the multitude, and not nicely distinguishing between the perjured
accuser and the innocent magistrate, had taken a revenge of
which the history of persecuted sects furnishes but too many
examples. If this were so, the assassin must have afterwards
bitterly execrated his own wickedness and folly. The capital
and the whole nation went mad with hatred and fear. The
penal laws, which had begun to lose something of their edge,
were sharpened anew. Everywhere justices were busied in
searching houses and seizing papers. All the gaols were
filled with Papists. London had the aspect of a city in a state
of siege. The trainbands were under arms all night. Preparations were made for barricading the great thoroughfares.
Patroles marched up and down the streets. Cannon were
planted round Whitehall. No citizen thought himself safe
unless he carried under his coat a small flail loaded with lead
to brain the Popish assassins. The corpse of the murdered
magistrate was exhibited during several days to the gaze of

great multitudes, and was then committed to the grave with
strange and terrible ceremonies which indicated rather fear
and the thirst of vengeance than sorrow or religious hope.
The Houses insisted that a guard should be placed in the
vaults over which they sate, in order to secure them against a
second Gunpowder Plot.   All their proceedings were of a
piece with this demand.   Ever since the reign of Elizabeth
the oath of supremacy had been exacted from members of the
House of Commons.   Some Roman Catholics, however, had
contrived so to interpret this oath that they could take it without scruple.   A more stringent test was now added, and the
Roman Catholic Lords were for the first time excluded from
their seats in Parliament.   Strong resolutions were adopted
against the Queen.   The Commons threw one of the Secretaries of State into prison for having countersigned commissions directed to gentlemen who were not good Protestants.
They impeached the Lord Treasurer of high treason.   Nay,
they so far forgot the doctrine which, while the memory of
the civil war was still recent, they had loudly professed, that
they even attempted to wrest the command of the militia out
of the King's hands.   To such a temper had eighteen years of
misgovernment brought the most loyal Parliament that had
ever met in England.

Yet it may seem strange that, even in that extremity, the
King should have ventured to appeal to the people; for the
people were more excited than their representatives.   The
Lower House, discontented as it was, contained a larger
number of Cavaliers than were likely to find seats again.   But
it was thought that a dissolution would put a stop to the prosecution of the Lord Treasurer, a prosecution which might
probably bring to light all the guilty mysteries of the French
alliance, and might thus cause extreme personal annoyance
and embarrassment to Charles.   Accordingly, in January
1679, the Parliament, which had been in existence ever since

the beginning of the year 1661, was dissolved; and writs were issued for a general election.

During some weeks the contention over the whole country was fierce and obstinate beyond example. Unprecedented sums were expended. New tactics were employed. It was remarked by the pamphleteers of that time as something extraordinary that horses were hired at a great charge for the conveyance of electors. The practice of splitting freeholds for the purpose of multiplying votes dates from this memorable struggle. Dissenting preachers, who had long hidden themselves in quiet nooks from persecution, now emerged from their retreats, and rode from village to village, for the purpose of rekindling the zeal of the scattered people of God. The tide ran strong against the government. Most of the new members came up to Westminster in a mood little differing from that of their predecessors who had sent Strafford and Laud to the Tower.

Meanwhile the courts of justice, which ought to be, in the midst of political commotions, sure places of refuge for the innocent of every party, were disgraced by wilder passions and fouler corruptions than were to be found even on the hustings. The tale of Oates, though it had sufficed to convulse the whole realm, would not, until confirmed by other evidence, suffice to destroy the humblest of those whom he had accused. For, by the old law of England, two witnesses are necessary to establish a charge of treason. But the success of the first impostor produced its natural consequences. In a few weeks he had been raised from penury and obscurity to opulence, to power which made him the dread of princes and nobles, and to notoriety such as has for low and bad minds all the attractions of glory. He was not long without coadjutors and rivals. A wretch named Carstairs, who had earned a living in Scotland by going disguised to conventicles and then informing against the preachers, led the way.

Bedloe, a noted swindler, followed; and soon, from all the
brothels, gambling houses, and spunging houses of London,
false witnesses poured forth to swear away the lives of Roman
Catholics. One came with a story about an army of thirty
thousand men who were to muster in the disguise of pilgrims
at Corunna, and to sail thence to Wales. Another had been
promised canonization and five hundred pounds to murder
the King. A third had stepped into an eating house in Covent
Garden and had there heard a great Roman Catholic banker
vow, in the hearing of all the guests and drawers, to kill the
heretical tyrant. Oates, that he might not be eclipsed by his
imitators, soon added a large supplement to his original narrative. He had the portentous impudence to affirm, among
other things, that he had once stood behind a door which
was ajar, and had there overheard the Queen declare that
she had resolved to give her consent to the assassination of
her husband. The vulgar believed, and the highest magistrates pretended to believe, even such fictions as these.
The chief judges of the realm were corrupt, cruel, and timid.
The leaders of the Country Party encouraged the prevailing
delusion. The most respectable among them, indeed, were
themselves so far deluded as to believe the greater part of
the evidence of the plot to be true. Such men as Shaftesbury
and Buckingham doubtless perceived that the whole was a
romance. But it was a romance which served their turn; and
to their seared consciences the death of an innocent man
gave no more uneasiness than the death of a partridge. The
juries partook of the feelings then common throughout the
nation, and were encouraged by the bench to indulge those
feelings without restraint. The multitude applauded Oates
and his confederates, hooted and pelted the witnesses who
appeared on behalf of the accused, and shouted with joy
when the verdict of Guilty was pronounced. It was in vain
that the sufferers appealed to the respectability of their past

lives: for the public mind was possessed with a belief that the more conscientious a Papist was, the more likely he must be to plot against a Protestant government. It was in vain that, just before the cart passed from under their feet, they resolutely affirmed their innocence: for the general opinion was that a good Papist considered all lies which were serviceable to his Church as not only excusable but meritorious.

While innocent blood was shedding under the forms of justice, the new Parliament met; and such was the violence of the predominant party that even men whose youth had been passed amidst revolutions, men who remembered the attainder of Strafford, the attempt on the five members, the abolition of the House of Lords, the execution of the King, stood aghast at the aspect of public affairs. The impeachment of Danby was resumed. He pleaded the royal pardon. But the Commons treated the plea with contempt, and insisted that the trial should proceed. Danby, however, was not their chief object. They were convinced that the only effectual way of securing the liberties and religion of the nation was to exclude the Duke of York from the throne.

The King was in great perplexity. He had insisted that his brother, the sight of whom inflamed the populace to madness, should retire for a time to Brussels: but this concession did not seem to have produced any favourable effect. The Roundhead party was now decidedly preponderant. Towards that party leaned millions who had, at the time of the Restoration, leaned towards the side of prerogative. Of the old Cavaliers many participated in the prevailing fear of Popery, and many, bitterly resenting the ingratitude of the prince for whom they had sacrificed so much, looked on his distress as carelessly as he had looked on theirs. Even the Anglican clergy, mortified and alarmed by the apostasy of the Duke of York, so far countenanced the opposition as to join cordially in the outcry against the Roman Catholics.

CHAP.
II.

Temple's
plan of
govern-
ment.

The King in this extremity had recourse to Sir William Temple. Of all the official men of that age Temple had preserved the fairest character. The Triple Alliance had been his work. He had refused to take any part in the politics of the Cabal, and had, while that administration directed affairs, lived in strict privacy. He had quitted his retreat at the call of Danby, had made peace between England and Holland, and had borne a chief part in bringing about the marriage of the Lady Mary to her cousin the Prince of Orange. Thus he had the credit of every one of the few good things which had been done by the government since the Restoration. Of the numerous crimes and blunders of the last eighteen years none could be imputed to him. His private life, though not austere, was decorous: his manners were popular; and he was not to be corrupted either by titles or by money. Something, however, was wanting to the character of this respectable statesman. The temperature of his patriotism was lukewarm. He prized his ease and his personal dignity too much, and shrank from responsibility with a pusillanimous fear. Nor indeed had his habits fitted him to bear a part in the conflicts of our domestic factions. He had reached his fiftieth year without having sate in the English Parliament; and his official experience had been almost entirely acquired at foreign courts. He was justly esteemed one of the first diplomatists in Europe: but the talents and accomplishments of a diplomatist are widely different from those which qualify a politician to lead the House of Commons in agitated times.

The scheme which he proposed showed considerable ingenuity. Though not a profound philosopher, he had thought more than most busy men of the world on the general principles of government; and his mind had been enlarged by historical studies and foreign travel. He seems to have discerned more clearly than most of his contemporaries one cause of the difficulties by which the government was beset. The character of the English polity was gradually changing. The Parliament was slowly, but constantly, gaining ground on the prerogative. The line between the legislative and executive powers was in theory as strongly marked as ever, but in practice was daily becoming fainter and fainter. The theory of the constitution was that the King might name his own ministers. But the House of Commons had driven Clarendon, the Cabal, and Danby successively from the direction of affairs. The theory of the constitution was that the King alone had the power of making peace and war. But the House of Commons had forced him to make peace with Holland, and had all but forced him to make war with France. The theory of the constitution was that the King was the sole judge of the cases in which it might be proper to pardon offenders. Yet he was so much in dread of the House of Commons that, at that moment, he could not venture to rescue from the gallows men whom he well knew to be the innocent victims of perjury.

Temple, it should seem, was desirous to secure to the legislature its undoubted constitutional powers, and yet to prevent it, if possible, from encroaching further on the province of the executive administration. With this view he determined to interpose between the sovereign and the Parliament a body which might break the shock of their collision. There was a body, ancient, highly honourable, and recognised by the law, which, he thought, might be so remodelled as to serve this purpose. He determined to give to the Privy Council a new character and office in the government. The number of Councillors he fixed at thirty. Fifteen of them were to be the chief ministers of state, of law, and of religion. The other fifteen were to be unplaced noblemen and gentlemen of ample fortune and high character. There was to be no interior cabinet. All the thirty were to be entrusted with every political secret, and summoned to every meeting; and the King was to declare that he would, on every occasion, be guided by their advice.

Temple seems to have thought that, by this contrivance, he could at once secure the nation against the tyranny of the crown, and the crown against the encroachments of the Parliament. It was, on one hand, highly improbable that schemes such as had been formed by the Cabal would be even propounded for discussion in an assembly consisting of thirty eminent men, fifteen of whom were bound by no tie of interest to the court. On the other hand, it might be hoped that the Commons, content with the guarantee against misgovernment which such a Privy Council furnished, would confine themselves more than they had of late done to their strictly legislative functions, and would no longer think it necessary to pry into every part of the executive administration.

This plan, though in some respects not unworthy of the abilities of its author, was in principle vicious. The new board was half a cabinet and half a Parliament, and, like almost every other contrivance, whether mechanical or political, which is meant to serve two purposes altogether different, failed of accomplishing either. It was too large and too divided to be a good administrative body. It was too closely connected with the crown to be a good checking body. It contained just enough of popular ingredients to make it a bad council of state, unfit for the keeping of secrets, for the conducting of delicate negotiations, and for the administration of war. Yet were these popular ingredients by no means sufficient to secure the nation against misgovernment. The plan, therefore, even if it had been fairly tried, could scarcely have succeeded; and it was not fairly tried. The King was fickle and perfidious: the Parliament was excited and unreasonable; and the materials out of which the new Council was made, though perhaps the best which that age afforded, were still bad.

The commencement of the new system was, however, hailed with general delight; for the people were in a temper to think any change an improvement. They were also pleased by some of the new nominations. Shaftesbury, now their favourite, was appointed Lord President. Russell and some other distinguished members of the Country Party were sworn of the Council. But in a few days all was again in confusion. The inconveniences of having so numerous a cabinet were such that Temple himself consented to infringe one of the fundamental rules which he had laid down, and to become one of a small knot which really directed everything. With him were joined three other ministers, Arthur Capel, Earl of Essex, George Savile, Viscount Halifax, and Robert Spencer, Earl of Sunderland.

Of the Earl of Essex, then First Commissioner of the Treasury, it is sufficient to say that he was a man of solid, though not brilliant parts, and of grave and melancholy character, that he had been connected with the Country Party, and that he was at this time honestly desirous to effect, on terms beneficial to the State, a reconciliation between that party and the throne.

Among the statesmen of that age Halifax was, in genius, the first. His intellect was fertile, subtle, and capacious. His polished, luminous, and animated eloquence, set off by the silver tones of his voice, was the delight of the House of Lords. His conversation overflowed with thought, fancy, and wit. His political tracts well deserve to be studied for their literary merit, and fully entitle him to a place among English classics. To the weight derived from talents so great and various he united all the influence which belongs to rank and ample possessions. Yet he was less successful in politics than many who enjoyed smaller advantages. Indeed, those intellectual peculiarities which make his writings valuable frequently impeded him in the contests of active life. For he always saw passing events, not in the point of view in which they commonly appear to one who bears a part in them, but in the point of view in which, after the lapse of many years, they appear to the philosophic historian. With such a turn of mind, he could not long continue to act cordially with any body of men. All the prejudices, all the exaggerations of both the great parties in the State moved his scorn. He despised the mean arts and unreasonable clamours of demagogues. He despised still more the doctrines of divine right and passive obedience. He sneered impartially at the bigotry of the Churchman and at the bigotry of the Puritan. He was equally unable to comprehend how any man should object to Saints' days and surplices, and how any man should persecute any other man for objecting to them. In temper he was what, in our time, is called a Conservative. In theory he was a Republican. Even when his dread of anarchy and his disdain for vulgar delusions led him to side for a time with the defenders of arbitrary power, his intellect was always with Locke and Milton. Indeed, his jests upon hereditary monarchy were sometimes such as would have better become a member of the Calf's Head Club than a Privy Councillor of the Stuarts. In religion he was so far from being a zealot that he was called by the uncharitable an atheist: but this imputation he vehemently repelled; and in truth, though he sometimes gave scandal by the way in which he exerted his rare powers both of argumentation and of ridicule on serious subjects, he seems to have been by no means unsusceptible of religious impressions.

He was the chief of those politicians whom the two great parties contemptuously called Trimmers. Instead of quarrelling with this nickname, he assumed it as a tittle of honour, and vindicated, with great vivacity, the dignity of the appellation. Every thing good, he said, trims between extremes. The temperate zone trims between the climate in which men are roasted and the climate in which they are frozen. The English Church trims between the Anabaptist madness and

the Papist lethargy. The English constitution trims between
Turkish despotism and Polish anarchy. Virtue is nothing but
a just temper between propensities any one of which, if indulged to excess, becomes vice. Nay, the perfection of the
Supreme Being himself consists in the exact equilibrium of
attributes, none of which could preponderate without disturb-
ing the whole moral and physical order of the world.* Thus
Halifax was a Trimmer on principle. He was also a Trimmer
by the constitution both of his head and of his heart. His
understanding was keen, sceptical, inexhaustibly fertile in
distinctions and objections; his taste refined; his sense of the
ludicrous exquisite; his temper placid and forgiving, but
fastidious, and by no means prone either to malevolence or to
enthusiastic admiration. Such a man could not long be constant to any band of political allies. He must not, however,
be confounded with the vulgar crowd of renegades. For
though, like them, he passed from side to side, his transition
was always in the direction opposite to theirs. He had nothing
in common with those who fly from extreme to extreme, and
who regard the party which they have deserted with an animosity far exceeding that of consistent enemies. His place was
between the hostile divisions of the community, and he never
wandered far beyond the frontier of either. The party to
which he at any moment belonged was the party which, at
that moment, he liked least, because it was the party of which
at that moment he had the nearest view. He was therefore
always severe upon his violent associates, and was always in
friendly relations with his moderate opponents. Every faction
in the day of its insolent and vindictive triumph incurred his
censure; and every faction, when vanquished and persecuted,
found in him a protector. To his lasting honour it must be

* It will be seen that I believe Halifax to have been the author, or at
least one of the authors, of the "Character of a Trimmer," which, for
a time, went under the name of his kinsman, Sir William Coventry.

CHAP. mentioned that he attempted to save those victims whose fate
II.
has left the deepest stain both on the Whig and on the Tory
name.

He had greatly distinguished himself in opposition, and
had thus drawn on himself the royal displeasure, which was
indeed so strong, that he was not admitted into the Council of
Thirty without much difficulty and long altercation. As soon,
however, as he had obtained a footing at court, the charms
of his manner and of his conversation made him a favourite.
He was seriously alarmed by the violence of the public discontent. He thought that liberty was for the present safe, and
that order and legitimate authority were in danger. He therefore, as was his fashion, joined himself to the weaker side.
Perhaps his conversion was not wholly disinterested. For
study and reflection, though they had emancipated him from
many vulgar prejudices, had left him a slave to vulgar desires.
Money he did not want; and there is no evidence that he
ever obtained it by any means which, in that age, even severe
censors considered as dishonourable; but rank and power had
strong attractions for him. He pretended, indeed, that he
considered titles and great offices as baits which could allure
none but fools, that he hated business, pomp, and pageantry,
and that his dearest wish was to escape from the bustle and
glitter of Whitehall to the quiet woods which surrounded his
ancient mansion at Rufford: but his conduct was not a little at
variance with his professions. In truth he wished to command
the respect at once of courtiers and of philosophers, to be admired for attaining high dignities, and to be at the same time
admired for despising them.

Character   Sunderland was Secretary of State. In this man the poli-
of Sun-
derland. tical immorality of his age was personified in the most lively
manner. Nature had given him a keen understanding, a
restless and mischievous temper, a cold heart, and an abject
spirit. His mind had undergone a training by which all his

vices had been nursed up to the rankest maturity. At his
entrance into public life, he had passed several years in diplomatic posts abroad, and had been, during some time, minister in France. Every calling has its peculiar temptations.
There is no injustice in saying that diplomatists, as a class,
have always been more distinguished by their address, by the
art with which they win the confidence of those with whom
they have to deal, and by the ease with which they catch the
tone of every society into which they are admitted, than by
generous enthusiasm or austere rectitude; and the relations
between Charles and Lewis were such that no English noble-
man could long reside in France as envoy, and retain any patriotic or honourable sentiment. Sunderland came forth from
the bad school in which he had been brought up, cunning,
supple, shameless, free from all prejudices, and destitute of
all principles. He was, by hereditary connection, a Cavalier: but with the Cavaliers he had nothing in common.
They were zealous for monarchy, and condemned in theory
all resistance. Yet they had sturdy English hearts which
would never have endured real despotism. He, on the contrary, had a languid speculative liking for republican institutions, which was compatible with perfect readiness to be in
practice the most servile instrument of arbitrary power. Like
many other accomplished flatterers and negotiators, he was
far more skilful in the art of reading the characters and
practising on the weaknesses of individuals, than in the art of
discerning the feelings of great masses, and of foreseeing the
approach of great revolutions. He was adroit in intrigue;
and it was difficult even for shrewd and experienced men who
had been amply forewarned of his perfidy to withstand the
fascination of his manner, and to refuse credit to his professions of attachment. But he was so intent on observing and
courting particular persons, that he forgot to study the temper
of the nation. He therefore miscalculated grossly with respect

16 *

to all the most momentous events of his time.   Every important movement and rebound of the public mind took him by
surprise; and the world, unable to understand how so clever
a man could be blind to what was clearly discerned by the politicians of the coffee houses, sometimes attributed to deep
design what were in truth mere blunders.

It was only in private conference that his eminent abilities
displayed themselves.   In the royal closet, or in a very small
circle, he exercised great influence.   But at the Council board
he was taciturn; and in the House of Lords he never opened
his lips.

The four confidential advisers of the crown soon found
that their position was embarrassing and invidious.   The other
members of the Council murmured at a distinction inconsistent with the King's promises; and some of them, with
Shaftesbury at their head, again betook themselves to strenuous opposition in Parliament.   The agitation, which had
been suspended by the late changes, speedily became more
violent than ever.   It was in vain that Charles offered to grant
to the Commons any security for the Protestant religion
which they could devise, provided only that they would not
touch the order of succession.   They would hear of no compromise.   They would have the Exclusion Bill and nothing
but the Exclusion Bill.   The King, therefore, a few weeks
after he had publicly promised to take no step without the
advice of his new Council, went down to the House of Lords
without mentioning his intention in Council, and prorogued
the Parliament.

Proroga-
tion of
the Par-
liament.
The day of that prorogation, the twenty-sixth of May
1679, is a great era in our history.   For on that day the
Habeas Corpus Act received the royal assent.   From the time
of the Great Charter, the substantive law respecting the personal liberty of Englishmen had been nearly the same as at
present: but it had been inefficacious for want of a stringent

system of procedure. What was needed was not a new right, but a prompt and searching remedy; and such a remedy the —— Habeas Corpus Act supplied. The King would gladly have refused his consent to that measure: but he was about to appeal from his Parliament to his people on the question of the succession; and he could not venture, at so critical a moment, to reject a bill which was in the highest degree popular.

On the same day, the press of England became for a short time free. In old times printers had been strictly controlled by the Court of Star Chamber. The Long Parliament had abolished the Star Chamber, but had, in spite of the philosophical and eloquent expostulation of Milton, established and maintained a censorship. Soon after the Restoration, an Act had been passed which prohibited the printing of unlicensed books; and it had been provided that this Act should continue in force till the end of the firt session of the next Parliament. That moment had now arrived; and the King, in the very act of dismissing the Houses, emancipated the press.

Shortly after the prorogation came a dissolution and another general election. The zeal and strength of the opposition were at the height. The cry for the Exclusion Bill was louder than ever; and with this cry was mingled another cry, which fired the blood of the multitude, but which was heard with regret and alarm by all judicious friends of freedom. Not only the rights of the Duke of York, an avowed Papist, but those of his two daughters, sincere and zealous Protestants, were assailed. It was confidently affirmed that the eldest natural son of the King had been born in wedlock, and was lawful heir to the crown.

Charles, while a wanderer on the Continent, had fallen in at the Hague with Lucy Walters, a Welsh girl of great beauty, but of weak understanding and dissolute manners. She

became his mistress, and presented him with a son. A suspicious lover might have had his doubts; for the lady had
several admirers, and was not supposed to be cruel to any.
Charles, however, readily took her word, and poured forth
on little James Crofts, as the boy was then called, an over-
flowing fondness, such as seemed hardly to belong to that cool
and careless nature. Soon after the Restoration, the young
favourite, who had learned in France the exercises then considered necessary to a fine gentleman, made his appearance
at Whitehall. He was lodged in the palace, attended by
pages, and permitted to enjoy several distinctions which
had till then been confined to princes of the blood royal. He
was married, while still in tender youth, to Anne Scott,
heiress of the noble house of Buccleuch. He took her name,
and received with her hand possession of her ample domains.
The estate which he acquired by this match was popularly
estimated at not less than ten thousand pounds a year. Titles,
and favours more substantial than titles, were lavished on
him. He was made Duke of Monmouth in England, Duke of
Buccleuch in Scotland, a Knight of the Garter, Master of the
Horse, Commander of the first troop of Life Guards, Chief
Justice of Eyre south of Trent, and Chancellor of the University of Cambridge. Nor did he appear to the public unworthy of his high fortunes. His countenance was eminently
handsome and engaging, his temper sweet, his manners polite
and affable. Though a libertine, he won the hearts of the
Puritans. Though he was known to have been privy to the
shameful attack on Sir John Coventry, he easily obtained the
forgiveness of the Country Party. Even austere moralists
owned that, in such a court, strict conjugal fidelity was scarcely to be expected from one who, while a child, had been
married to another child. Even patriots were willing to
excuse a headstrong boy for visiting with immoderate vengeance an insult offered to his father. And soon the stain left

by loose amours and midnight brawls was effaced by honourable exploits. When Charles and Lewis united their forces
against Holland, Monmouth commanded the English auxiliaries who were sent to the Continent, and approved himself
a gallant soldier and a not unintelligent officer. On his
return he found himself the most popular man in the kingdom.
Nothing was withheld from him but the crown; nor did even
the crown seem to be absolutely beyond his reach. The
distinction which had most injudiciously been made between
him and the highest nobles had produced evil consequences.
When a boy he had been invited to put on his hat in the
presence chamber, while Howards and Seymours stood un-
covered round him. When foreign princes died, he had
mourned for them in the long purple cloak, which no other
subject, except the Duke of York and Prince Rupert, was
permitted to wear. It was natural that these things should
lead him to regard himself as a legitimate prince of the House
of Stuart. Charles, even at a ripe age, was devoted to his
pleasures and regardless of his dignity. It could hardly be
thought incredible that he should at twenty have secretly gone
through the form of espousing a lady whose beauty had
fascinated him, and who was not to be won on easier terms.
While Monmouth was still a child, and while the Duke of
York still passed for a Protestant, it was rumoured throughout the country, and even in circles which ought to have been
well informed, that the King had made Lucy Walters his
wife, and that, if every one had his right, her son would be
Prince of Wales. Much was said of a certain black box which,
according to the vulgar belief, contained the contract of
marriage. When Monmouth had returned from the Low
Countries with a high character for valour and conduct, and
when the Duke of York was known to be a member of a
church detested by the great majority of the nation, this idle
story became important. For it there was not the slightest

CHAP.
II.

evidence. Against it there was the solemn asseveration of
the King, made before his Council, and by his order communicated to his people. But the multitude, always fond of
romantic adventures, drank in eagerly the tale of the secret
espousals and the black box. Some chiefs of the opposition
acted on this occasion as they acted with respect to the more
odious fable of Oates, and countenanced a story which they
must have despised. The interest which the populace took
in him whom they regarded as the champion of the true religion, and the rightful heir of the British throne, was kept up
by every artifice. When Monmouth arrived in London at
midnight, the watchmen were ordered by the magistrates to
proclaim the joyful event through the streets of the City: the
people left their beds: bonfires were lighted: the windows
were illuminated: the churches were opened; and a merry
peal rose from all the steeples. When he travelled, he was
everywhere received with not less pomp, and with far more
enthusiasm, than had been displayed when Kings had made
progresses through the realm. He was escorted from mansion
to mansion by long cavalcades of armed gentlemen and
yeomen. Cities poured forth their whole population to receive
him. Electors thronged round him, to assure him that their
votes were at his disposal. To such a height were his pretensions carried, that he not only exhibited on his escutcheon
the lions of England and the lilies of France without the
baton sinister under which, according to the law of heraldry,
they were debruised in token of his illegitimate birth, but
ventured to touch for the king's evil. At the same time, he
neglected no art of condescension by which the love of the
multitude could be conciliated. He stood godfather to the
children of the peasantry, mingled in every rustic sport,
wrestled, played at quarterstaff, and won foot-races in his
boots against fleet runners in shoes.

It is a curious circumstance that, at two of the greatest con-

junctures in our history, the chiefs of the Protestant party
should have committed the same error, and should by that error have greatly endangered their country and their religion. At the death of Edward the Sixth they set up the Lady Jane, without any show of birthright, in opposition, not only to their enemy Mary, but also to Elizabeth, the true hope of England and of the Reformation. Thus the most respectable Protestants, with Elizabeth at their head, were forced to make common cause with the Papists. In the same manner, a hundred and thirty years later, a part of the opposition, by setting up Monmouth as a claimant of the crown, attacked the rights, not only of James, whom they justly regarded as an implacable foe of their faith and their liberties, but also of the Prince and Princess of Orange, who were eminently marked out, both by situation and by personal qualities, as the defenders of all free governments and of all reformed Churches.

In a few years the folly of this course became manifest. At present the popularity of Monmouth constituted a great part of the strength of the opposition. The elections went against the court: the day fixed for the meeting of the Houses drew near; and it was necessary that the King should determine on some line of conduct. Those who advised him discerned the first faint signs of a change of public feeling, and hoped that, by merely postponing the conflict, he would be able to secure the victory. He therefore, without even asking the opinion of the Council of the Thirty, resolved to prorogue the new Parliament before it entered on business. At the same time the Duke of York, who had returned from Brussels, was ordered to retire to Scotland, and was placed at the head of the administration of that kingdom.

Temple's plan of government was now avowedly abandoned and very soon forgotten. The Privy Council again became what it had been. Shaftesbury and those who were connected with him in politics resigned their seat. Temple himself, as was his wont in unquiet times, retired to his garden and his library. Essex quitted the board of Treasury, and cast in his lot with the opposition. But Halifax, disgusted and alarmed by the violence of his old associates, and Sunderland, who never quitted place while he could hold it, remained in the King's service.

In consequence of the resignations which took place at this conjuncture, the way to greatness was left clear to a new set of aspirants. Two statesmen, who subsequently rose to the highest eminence which a British subject can reach, soon began to attract a large share of the public attention. These were Lawrence Hyde and Sidney Godolphin.

Lawrence Hyde.
Lawrence Hyde was the second son of the Chancellor Clarendon, and was brother of the first Duchess of York. He had excellent parts, which had been improved by parliamentary and diplomatic experience; but the infirmities of his temper detracted much from the effective strength of his abilities. Negotiator and courtier as he was, he never learned the art of governing or of concealing his emotions. When prosperous, he was insolent and boastful: when he sustained a check, his undisguised mortification doubled the triumph of his enemies: very slight provocations sufficed to kindle his anger; and when he was angry he said bitter things which he forgot as soon as he was pacified, but which others remembered many years. His quickness and penetration would have made him a consummate man of business but for his self-sufficiency and impatience   His writings prove that he had many of the qualities of an orator: but his irritability prevented him from doing himself justice in debate: for nothing was easier than to goad him into a passion; and, from the moment when he went into a passion, he was at the mercy of opponents far inferior to him in capacity.

Unlike most of the leading politicians of that generation he was a consistent, dogged, and rancorous party man, a Cavalier

of the old school, a zealous champion of the crown and of the CHAP. II.
Church, and a hater of Republicans and Nonconformists. He
had consequently a great body of personal adherents. The
clergy especially looked on him as their own man, and extended to his foibles an indulgence of which, to say the truth,
he stood in some need: for he drank deep; and when he was
in a rage, — and he very often was in a rage, — he swore like
a porter.

He now succeeded Essex at the Treasury. It is to be observed that the place of First Lord of the Treasury had not
then the importance and dignity which now belong to it.
When there was a Lord Treasurer, that great officer was
generally prime minister: but, when the white staff was in
commission, the chief commissioner did not rank so high as a
Secretary of State. It was not till the time of Walpole that
the First Lord of the Treasury was considered as the head of
the executive administration.

Godolphin had been bred a page at Whitehall, and had Sidney
early acquired all the flexibility and the self-possession of a phin.
veteran courtier. He was laborious, clear-headed, and profoundly versed in the details of finance. Every government,
therefore, found him an useful servant; and there was
nothing in his opinions or in his character which could prevent
him from serving any government. "Sidney Godolphin,"
said Charles, "is never in the way, and never out of the way."
This pointed remark goes far to explain Godolphin's extraordinary success in life.

He acted at different times with both the great political
parties: but he never shared in the passions of either. Like
most men of cautious tempers and prosperous fortunes, he
had a strong disposition to support whatever existed. He
disliked revolutions; and, for the same reason for which he
disliked revolutions, he disliked counterrevolutions. His
deportment was remarkably grave and reserved: but his

personal tastes were low and frivolous; and most of the time which he could save from public business was spent in racing, card-playing, and cock-fighting. He now sate below Rochester at the board of Treasury, and distinguished himself there by assiduity and intelligence.

Before the new Parliament was suffered to meet for despatch of business, a whole year elapsed, an eventful year, which has left lasting traces in our manners and language. Never before had political controversy been carried on with so much freedom. Never before had political clubs existed with so elaborate an organisation, or so formidable an influence. The one question of the exclusion occupied the public mind. All the presses and pulpits of the realm took part in the conflict. On one side it was maintained that the constitution and religion of the State would never be secure under a Popish King; on the other, that the right of James to wear the crown in his turn was derived from God, and could not be annulled, even by the consent of all the branches of the legislature. Every county, every town, every family, was in agitation. The civilities and hospitalities of neighbourhood were interrupted. The dearest ties of friendship and of blood were sundered. Even schoolboys were divided into angry parties; and the Duke of York and the Earl of Shaftesbury had zealous adherents on all the forms of Westminster and Eton. The theatres shook with the roar of the contending factions. Pope Joan was brought on the stage by the zealous Protestants. Pensioned poets filled their prologues and epilogues with eulogies on the King and the Duke. The malecontents besieged the throne with petitions, demanding that Parliament might be forthwith convened. The loyalists sent up addresses, expressing the utmost abhorrence of all who presumed to dictate to the sovereign. The citizens of London assembled by tens of thousands to burn the Pope in effigy. The government posted cavalry at Temple Bar,

Violence
of fac-
tions on
the sub-
ject of the
Exclusion
Bill.

and placed ordnance round Whitehall.   In that year our CHAP. II.
tongue was enriched with two words, Mob and Sham, remarkable memorials of a season of tumult and imposture.*
Opponents of the court were called Birminghams, Petitioners,
and Exclusionists.   Those who took the King's side were
Antibirminghams, Abhorrers, and Tantivies.   These appellations soon became obsolete: but at this time were first heard   Names of
two nicknames which, though originally given in insult, were   Whig and
Tory.
soon assumed with pride, which are still in daily use, which
have spread as widely as the English race, and which will
last as long as the English literature.   It is a curious circumstance that one of these nicknames was of Scotch, and the
other of Irish, origin.   Both in Scotland and in Ireland, misgovernment had called into existence bands of desperate
men whose ferocity was heightened by religious enthusiasm.
In Scotland, some of the persecuted Covenanters, driven
mad by oppression, had lately murdered the Primate, had
taken arms against the government, had obtained some advantages against the King's forces, and had not been put
down till Monmouth, at the head of some troops from England, had routed them at Bothwell Bridge.   These zealots
were most numerous among the rustics of the western lowlands, who were vulgarly called Whigs.   Thus the appellation of Whig was fastened on the Presbyterian zealots of Scotland, and was transferred to those English politicians who
showed a disposition to oppose the court, and to treat Protestant Nonconformists with indulgence.   The bogs of Ire-
and, at the same time, afforded a refuge to Popish outlaws,
much resembling those who were afterwards known as
Whiteboys.   These men were then called Tories.   The name
of Tory was therefore given to Englishmen who refused to
concur in excluding a Roman Catholic prince from the
throne.

* North's Examen, 231. 574.

The rage of the hostile factions would have been sufficiently violent, if it had been left to itself. But it was studiously exasperated by the common enemy of both. Lewis
still continued to bribe and flatter both court and opposition.
He exhorted Charles to be firm: he exhorted James to raise
a civil war in Scotland: he exhorted the Whigs not to flinch,
and to rely with confidence on the protection of France.

Through all this agitation a discerning eye might have
perceived that the public opinion was gradually changing.
The persecution of the Roman Catholics went on; but convictions were no longer matters of course. A new brood of
false witnesses, among whom a villain named Dangerfield
was the most conspicuous, infested the courts: but the stories
of these men, though better constructed than that of Oates,
found less credit. Juries were no longer so easy of belief as
during the panic which had followed the murder of Godfrey;
and Judges who, while the popular frenzy was at the height,
had been its most obsequious instruments, now ventured to
express some part of what they had from the first thought.

Meeting
of Parlia-
ment; the
Exclusion
Bill
passes the
Com-
mons.
At length, in October 1680, the Parliament met. The
Whigs had so great a majority in the Commons that the Exclusion Bill went through all its stages there without difficulty.
The King scarcely knew on what members of his own cabinet
he could reckon. Hyde had been true to his Tory opinions,
and had steadily supported the cause of hereditary monarchy.
But Godolphin, anxious for quiet, and believing that quiet
could be restored only by concession, wished the bill to pass.
Sunderland, ever false and ever short-sighted, unable to
discern the signs of approaching reaction, and anxious to
conciliate the party which he believed to be irresistible,
determined to vote against the court. The Duchess of Portsmouth implored her royal lover not to rush headlong to
destruction. If there were any point on which he had a
scruple of conscience or of honour, it was the question of

the succession; but during some days it seemed that he would CHAP. II.
submit. He wavered, asked what sum the Commons would
give him if he yielded, and suffered a negotiation to be
opened with the leading Whigs. But a deep mutual distrust
which had been many years growing, and which had been
carefully nursed by the arts of France, made a treaty impossible. Neither side would place confidence in the other.
The whole nation now looked with breathless anxiety to the
House of Lords. The assemblage of peers was large. The
King himself was present. The debate was long, earnest,
and occasionally furious. Some hands were laid on the pom-
mels of swords, in a manner which revived the recollection
of the stormy Parliaments of Henry the Third and Richard
the Second. Shaftesbury and Essex were joined by the Exclusion
treacherous Sunderland. But the genius of Halifax bore Bill re-jected by
down all opposition. Deserted by his most important col- theLords.
leagues, and opposed to a crowd of able antagonists, he defended the cause of the Duke of York, in a succession of
speeches which, many years later, were remembered as
masterpieces of reasoning, of wit, and of eloquence. It is
seldom that oratory changes votes. Yet the attestation of
contemporaries leaves no doubt that, on this occasion, votes
were changed by the oratory of Halifax. The Bishops, true
to their doctrines, supported the principle of hereditary right,
and the bill was rejected by a great majority. *

* 'A peer who was present has described the effect of Halifax's oratory
in words which I will quote, because, though they have been long in
print, they are probably known to few even of the most curious and diligent readers of history.
"Of powerful eloquence and great parts were the Duke's enemies who
did assert the bill; but a noble Lord appeared against it who, that day,
in all the force of speech, in reason, in arguments of what could concern
the public or the private interests of men, in honour, in conscience, in
estate, did outdo himself and every other man; and in fine his conduct
and his parts were both victorious, and by him all the wit and malice of
that party was overthrown."
، This passage is taken from a memoir of Henry Earl of Peterborough,

CHAP.
II.

Execution
of Staf-
ford.
The party which preponderated in the House of Commons, bitterly mortified by this defeat, found some consolation in shedding the blood of Roman Catholics. William Howard, Viscount Stafford, one of the unhappy men who had been accused of a share in the plot, was brought before the bar of his peers; and on the testimony of Oates and of two other false witnesses, Dugdale and Turberville, was found guilty of high treason, and suffered death. But the circumstances of his trial and execution ought to have given an useful warning to the Whig leaders. A large and respectable minority of the House of Lords pronounced the prisoner not guilty. The multitude, which a few months before had received the dying declarations of Oates's victims with mockery and execrations, now loudly expressed a belief that Stafford was a murdered man. When he with his last breath protested his innocence, the cry was, "God bless you, my Lord! We believe you, my Lord." A judicious observer might easily have predicted that the blood then shed would shortly have blood.

General
election
of 1681.
The King determined to try once more the experiment of a dissolution. A new Parliament was summoned to meet at Oxford, in March 1681. Since the days of the Plantagenets the Houses had constantly sate at Westminster, except when the plague was raging in the capital: but so extraordinary a conjuncture seemed to require extraordinary precautions. If the Parliament were held in its usual place of assembling, the House of Commons might declare itself permanent, and might call for aid on the magistrates and citizens of London. The trainbands might rise to defend Shaftesbury as they had risen forty years before to defend Pym and Hampden. The Guards

---

in a volume entitled "Succinct Genealogies, by Robert Halstead," fol. 1685. The name of Halstead is fictitious. The real authors were the Earl of Peterborough himself and his chaplain. The book is extremely rare. Only twenty-four copies were printed, two of which are now in the British Museum. Of these two one belonged to George the Fourth, and the other to Mr. Grenville.

might be overpowered, the palace forced, the King a prisoner in the hands of his mutinous subjects. At Oxford there was no such danger. The University was devoted to the crown; and the gentry of the neighbourhood were generally Tories. Here, therefore, the opposition had more reason than the King to apprehend violence.

The elections were sharply contested. The Whigs still composed a majority of the House of Commons: but it was plain that the Tory spirit was fast rising throughout the country. It should seem that the sagacious and versatile Shaftesbury ought to have foreseen the coming change, and to have consented to the compromise which the court offered: but he appears to have utterly forgotten his old tactics. Instead of making dispositions which, in the worst event, would have secured his retreat, he took up a position in which it was necessary that he should either conquer or perish. Perhaps his head, strong as it was, had been turned by popularity, by success, and by the excitement of conflict. Perhaps he had spurred his party till he could no longer curb it, and was really hurried on headlong by those whom he seemed to guide.

The eventful day arrived. The meeting at Oxford resembled rather that of a Polish Diet than that of an English Parliament. The Whig members were escorted by great numbers of their armed and mounted tenants and serving men, who exchanged looks of defiance with the royal Guards. The slightest provocation might, under such circumstances, have produced a civil war; but neither side dared to strike the first blow. The King again offered to consent to any thing but the Exclusion Bill. The Commons were determined to accept nothing but the Exclusion Bill. In a few days the Parliament was again dissolved.

Parliament held at Oxford, and dissolved.

The King had triumphed. The reaction, which had begun some months before the meeting of the Houses at Oxford, now went rapidly on. The nation, indeed, was still hostile to

Tory reaction.

Popery: but, when men reviewed the whole history of the plot, they felt that their Protestant zeal had hurried them into folly and crime, and could scarcely believe that they had been induced by nursery tales to clamour for the blood of fellow subjects and fellow Christians. The most loyal, indeed, could not deny that the administration of Charles had often been highly blamable. But men who had not the full information which we possess touching his dealings with France, and who were disgusted by the violence of the Whigs, enumerated the large concessions which, during the last few years, he had made to his Parliaments, and the still larger concessions which he had declared himself willing to make. He had consented to the laws which excluded Roman Catholics from the House of Lords, from the Privy Council, and from all civil and military offices. He had passed the Habeas Corpus Act. If securities yet stronger had not been provided against the dangers to which the constitution and the Church might be exposed under a Roman Catholic sovereign, the fault lay, not with Charles who had invited the Parliament to propose such securities, but with those Whigs who had refused to hear of any substitute for the Exclusion Bill. One thing only had the King denied to his people. He had refused to take away his brother's birthright. And was there not good reason to believe that this refusal was prompted by laudable feelings? What selfish motive could faction itself impute to the royal mind? The Exclusion Bill did not curtail the reigning King's prerogatives, or diminish his income. Indeed, by passing it, he might easily have obtained an ample addition to his own revenue. And what was it to him who ruled after him? Nay, if he had personal predilections, they were known to be rather in favour of the Duke of Monmouth than of the Duke of York. The most natural explanation of the King's conduct therefore seemed to be that, careless as was his temper, and loose as were his morals, he had, on this occasion, acted from a sense of duty and honour.

And, if so, would the nation compel him to do what he thought criminal and disgraceful? To apply, even by strictly constitutional means, a violent pressure to his conscience, seemed to zealous Royalists ungenerous and undutiful. But strictly constitutional means were not the only means which the Whigs were disposed to employ. Signs were already discernible which portended the approach of great troubles. Men, who in the time of the civil war and of the Commonwealth had acquired an odious notoriety, had emerged from the obscurity in which, after the Restoration, they had hidden themselves from the general hatred, showed their confident and busy faces everywhere, and appeared to anticipate a second reign of the Saints. Another Naseby, another High Court of Justice, another usurper on the throne, the Lords again ejected from their hall by violence, the Universities again purged, the Church again robbed and persecuted, the Puritans again dominant, to such results did the desperate policy of the opposition seem to tend.

Animated by such feelings, the majority of the upper and middle classes hastened to rally round the throne. The situation of the King bore, at this time, a great resemblance to that in which his father stood just after the Remonstrance had been voted. But the reaction of 1641 had not been suffered to run its course. Charles the First, at the very moment when his people, long estranged, were returning to him with hearts disposed to reconciliation, had, by a perfidious violation of the fundamental laws of the realm, forfeited their confidence for ever. Had Charles the Second taken a similar course, had he arrested the Whig leaders in an irregular manner, and impeached them of high treason before a tribunal which had no legal jurisdiction over them, it is highly probable that they would speedily have regained the ascendency which they had lost. Fortunately for himself he was induced, at this crisis, to adopt a policy which, for his ends,

17 *

CHAP.
II.

was singularly judicious. He determined to conform to the law, but at the same time to make vigorous and unsparing use of the law against his adversaries. He was not bound to convoke a Parliament till three years should have elapsed. He was not much distressed for money. The produce of the taxes which had been settled on him for life exceeded the estimate. He was at peace with all the world. He could retrench his expenses by giving up the costly and useless settlement of Tangier; and he might hope for pecuniary aid from France. He had, therefore, ample time and means for a systematic attack on the opposition under the forms of the constitution. The Judges were removable at his pleasure: the juries were nominated by the Sheriffs; and, in almost all the counties of England, the Sheriffs were nominated by himself. Witnesses, of the same class with those who had recently sworn away the lives of Papists, were ready to swear away the lives of Whigs.

Persecution of the Whigs.

The first victim was College, a noisy and violent demagogue of mean birth and education. He was by trade a joiner, and was celebrated as the inventor of the Protestant flail. * He had been at Oxford when the Parliament sate there, and was accused of having planned a rising and an attack on the King's guards. Evidence was given against him by Dugdale and Turberville, the same infamous men who had, a few months earlier, borne false witness against Stafford. In the sight of a jury of country squires no Exclusionist was likely to find favour. College was convicted. The verdict was received by the crowd which filled the court house of Oxford with a roar of exultation, as barbarous as that which he and his friends had been in the habit of raising when innocent Papists were doomed to the gallows. His

* This is mentioned in the curious work entitled "Ragguaglio della solenne Comparsa fatta in Roma gli otto di Gennaio, 1687, dall' illustrissimo et excellentissimo signor Conte di Castlemaine."

execution was the beginning of a new judicial massacre, CHAP. II.
not less atrocious than that in which he had himself borne
a share.

The government, emboldened by this first victory, now
aimed a blow at an enemy of a very different class. It was
resolved that Shaftesbury should be brought to trial for his
life. Evidence was collected which, it was thought, would
support a charge of treason. But the facts which it was necessary to prove were alleged to have been committed in
London. The Sheriffs of London, chosen by the citizens,
were zealous Whigs. They named a Whig grand jury, which
threw out the bill. This defeat, far from discouraging those
who advised the King, suggested to them a new and daring
scheme. Since the charter of the capital was in their way, Charter
of the
that charter must be annulled. It was pretended, therefore, City confiscated.
that the City of London had by some irregularities forfeited
its municipal privileges; and proceedings were instituted
against the corporation in the Court of King's Bench. At the
same time those laws which had, soon after the Restoration,
been enacted against Nonconformists, and which had remained dormant during the ascendency of the Whigs, were
enforced all over the kingdom with extreme rigour.

Yet the spirit of the Whigs was not subdued. Though in Whig
conspira-
evil plight, they were still a numerous and powerful party; cies.
and, as they mustered strong in the large towns, and especially
in the capital, they made a noise and a show more than proportioned to their real force. Animated by the recollection
of past triumphs, and by the sense of present oppression, they
overrated both their strength and their wrongs. It was not in
their power to make out that clear and overwhelming case
which can alone justify so violent a remedy as resistance to
an established government. Whatever they might suspect,
they could not prove that their sovereign had entered into a
treaty with France against the religion and liberties of Eng-

land. What was apparent was not sufficient to warrant an appeal to the sword. If the Exclusion Bill had been thrown out, it had been thrown out by the Lords in the exercise of a right coeval with the constitution. If the King had dissolved the Oxford Parliament, he had done so by virtue of a prerogative which had never been questioned. If the court had, since the dissolution, done some harsh things, still those things were in strict conformity with the letter of the law, and with the recent practice of the malecontents themselves. If the King had prosecuted his opponents, he had prosecuted them according to the proper forms, and before the proper tribunals. The evidence now produced for the crown was at least as worthy of credit as the evidence on which the noblest blood of England had lately been shed by the opposition. The treatment which an accused Whig had now to expect from judges, advocates, sheriffs, juries, and spectators, was no worse than the treatment which had lately been thought by the Whigs good enough for an accused Papist. If the privileges of the City of London were attacked, they were attacked, not by military violence or by any disputable exercise of prerogative, but according to the regular practice of Westminster Hall. No tax was imposed by royal authority. No law was suspended. The Habeas Corpus Act was respected. Even the Test Act was enforced. The opposition therefore could not bring home to the King that species of misgovernment which alone could justify insurrection. And, even had his misgovernment been more flagrant than it was, insurrection would still have been criminal, because it was almost certain to be unsuccessful. The situation of the Whigs in 1682 differed widely from that of the Roundheads forty years before. Those who took up arms against Charles the First acted under the authority of a Parliament which had been legally assembled, and which could not, without its own consent, be legally dissolved. The opponents of Charles the Second were

private men.   Almost all the military and naval resources of
the kingdom had been at the disposal of those who resisted
Charles the First.   All the military and naval resources of the
kingdom were at the disposal of Charles the Second.   The
House of Commons had been supported by at least half the
nation against Charles the First.   But those who were disposed
to levy war against Charles the Second were certainly a minority.   It could not reasonably be doubted, therefore, that,
if they attempted a rising, they would fail.   Still less could it
be doubted that their failure would aggravate every evil of
which they complained.   The true policy of the Whigs was
to submit with patience to adversity which was the natural
consequence and the just punishment of their errors, to wait
patiently for that turn of public feeling which must inevitably
come, to observe the law, and to avail themselves of the protection, imperfect indeed, but by no means nugatory, which
the law afforded to innocence.   Unhappily they took a very
different course.   Unscrupulous and hot-headed chiefs of the
party formed and discussed schemes of resistance, and were
heard, if not with approbation, yet with the show of acquies-
cence, by much better men than themselves.   It was proposed
that there should be simultaneous insurrections in London,
in Cheshire, at Bristol, and at Newcastle.   Communications
were opened with the discontented Presbyterians of Scotland,
who were suffering under a tyranny such as England, in the
worst times, had never known.   While the leaders of the
opposition thus revolved plans of open rebellion, but were
still restrained by fears or scruples from taking any decisive
step, a design of a very different kind was meditated by some
of their accomplices.   To fierce spirits, unrestrained by principle, or maddened by fanaticism, it seemed that to waylay
and murder the King and his brother was the shortest and
surest way of vindicating the Protestant religion and the
liberties of England.   A place and a time were named; and

CHAP.
II.

the details of the butchery were frequently discussed, if not definitively arranged. This scheme was known but to few, and was concealed with especial care from the upright and humane Russell, and from Monmouth, who, though not a man of delicate conscience, would have recoiled with horror from the guilt of parricide. Thus there were two plots, one within the other. The object of the great Whig plot was to raise the nation in arms against the government. The lesser plot, commonly called the Rye House Plot, in which only a few desperate men were concerned, had for its object the assassination of the King and of the heir presumptive.

Detection of the Whig conspiracies.

Both plots were soon discovered. Cowardly traitors hastened to save themselves, by divulging all, and more than all, that had passed in the deliberations of the party. That only a small minority of those who meditated resistance had admitted into their minds the thought of assassination is fully established: but, as the two conspiracies ran into each other,

Severity of the government.

it was not difficult for the government to confound them together. The just indignation excited by the Rye House Plot was extended for a time to the whole Whig body. The King was now at liberty to exact full vengeance for years of restraint and humiliation. Shaftesbury, indeed, had escaped the fate which his manifold perfidy had well deserved. He had seen that the ruin of his party was at hand, had in vain endeavoured to make his peace with the royal brothers, had fled to Holland, and had died there, under the generous protection of a government which he had cruelly wronged. Monmouth threw himself at his father's feet and found mercy, but soon gave new offence, and thought it prudent to go into voluntary exile. Essex perished by his own hand in the Tower. Russell, who appears to have been guilty of no offence falling within the definition of high treason, and Sidney, of whose guilt no legal evidence could be produced, were beheaded in defiance of law and justice. Russell died with the fortitude of a Christian, Sidney with the fortitude of a Stoic. Some active politicians of meaner rank were sent to the gallows. Many quitted the country. Numerous prosecutions for misprision of treason, for libel, and for conspiracy were instituted. Convictions were obtained without difficulty from Tory juries, and rigorous punishments were inflicted by courtly judges. With these criminal proceedings were joined civil proceedings scarcely less formidable. Actions were brought against persons who had defamed the Duke of York; and damages tantamount to a sentence of perpetual imprisonment were demanded by the plaintiff, and without difficulty obtained. The Court of King's Bench pronounced that the franchises of the City of London were forfeited to the crown. Flushed with this great victory, the government proceeded to attack the constitutions of other corporations which were governed by Whig officers, and which had been in the habit of returning Whig members to Parliament. Borough after borough was compelled to surrender its privileges; and new charters were granted which gave the ascendency everywhere to the Tories.

Seizure of charters.

These proceedings, however reprehensible, had yet the semblance of legality. They were also accompanied by an act intended to quiet the uneasiness with which many loyal men looked forward to the accession of a Popish sovereign. The Lady Anne, younger daughter of the Duke of York by his first wife, was married to George, a prince of the orthodox House of Denmark. The Tory gentry and clergy might now flatter themselves that the Church of England had been effectually secured without any violation of the order of succession. The King and his heir were nearly of the same age. Both were approaching the decline of life. The King's health was good. It was therefore probable that James, if he ever came to the throne, would have but a short reign. Beyond his reign there was the gratifying prospect of a long series of Protestant sovereigns.

The liberty of unlicensed printing was of little or no use to the vanquished party; for the temper of judges and juries was such that no writer whom the government prosecuted for a libel had any chance of escaping. The dread of punishment therefore did all that a censorship could have done. Meanwhile, the pulpits resounded with harangues against the sin of rebellion. The treatises in which Filmer maintained that hereditary despotism was the form of government ordained by God, and that limited monarchy was a pernicious absurdity, had recently appeared, and had been favourably received by a large section of the Tory party. The University of Oxford, on the very day on which Russell was put to death, adopted by a solemn public act these strange doctrines, and ordered the political works of Buchanan, Milton, and Baxter to be publicly burned in the court of the Schools.

Thus emboldened, the King at length ventured to overstep the bounds which he had during some years observed, and to violate the plain letter of the law. The law was that not more than three years should pass between the dissolving of one Parliament and the convoking of another. But, when three years had elapsed after the dissolution of the Parliament which sate at Oxford, no writs were issued for an election. This infraction of the constitution was the more reprehensible, because the King had little reason to fear a meeting with a new House of Commons. The counties were generally on his side; and many boroughs in which the Whigs had lately held sway had been so remodelled that they were certain to return none but courtiers.

Influence of the Duke of York. In a short time the law was again violated in order to gratify the Duke of York. That prince was, partly on account of his religion, and partly on account of the sternness and harshness of his nature, so unpopular that it had been thought necessary to keep him out of sight while the Exclusion Bill was before Parliament, lest his public appearance should give an advantage to the party which was struggling to deprive him of his birthright. He had therefore been sent to govern Scotland, where the savage old tyrant Lauderdale was sinking into the grave. Even Lauderdale was now outdone. The administration of James was marked by odious laws, by barbarous punishments, and by judgments to the iniquity of which even that age furnished no parallel. The Scottish Privy Council had power to put state prisoners to the question. But the sight was so dreadful that, as soon as the boots appeared, even the most servile and hard-hearted courtiers hastened out of the chamber. The board was sometimes quite deserted: and it was at length found necessary to make an order that the members should keep their seats on such occasions. The Duke of York, it was remarked, seemed to take pleasure in the spectacle which some of the worst men then living were unable to contemplate without pity and horror. He not only came to Council when the torture was to be inflicted, but watched the agonies of the sufferers with that sort of interest and complacency with which men observe a curious experiment in science. Thus he employed himself at Edinburgh, till the event of the conflict between the court and the Whigs was no longer doubtful. He then returned to England: but he was still excluded by the Test Act from all public employment; nor did the King at first think it safe to violate a statute which the great majority of his most loyal subjects regarded as one of the chief securities of their religion and of their civil rights. When, however, it appeared, from a succession of trials, that the nation had patience to endure almost anything that the government had courage to do, Charles ventured to dispense with the law in his brother's favour. The Duke again took his seat in the Council, and resumed the direction of naval affairs.

These breaches of the constitution excited, it is true, some He is opposed by Halifax. murmurs among the moderate Tories, and were not unani-

CHAP.
II.

mously approved even by the King's ministers. Halifax in particular, now a Marquess and Lord Privy Seal, had, from the very day on which the Tories had by his help gained the ascendant, begun to turn Whig. As soon as the Exclusion Bill had been thrown out, he had pressed the House of Lords to make provision against the danger to which, in the next reign, the liberties and religion of the nation might be exposed. He now saw with alarm the violence of that reaction which was, in no small measure, his own work. He did not try to conceal the scorn which he felt for the servile doctrines of the University of Oxford. He detested the French alliance. He disapproved of the long intermission of Parliaments. He regretted the severity with which the vanquished party was treated. He who, when the Whigs were predominant, had ventured to pronounce Stafford not guilty, ventured, when they were vanquished and helpless, to intercede for Russell. At one of the last councils which Charles held a remarkable scene took place. The charter of Massachusetts had been forfeited. A question arose how, for the future, the colony should be governed. The general opinion of the board was that the whole power, legislative as well as executive, should abide in the crown. Halifax took the opposite side, and argued with great energy against absolute monarchy, and in favour of representative government. It was vain, he said, to think that a population, sprung from the English stock, and animated by English feelings, would long bear to be deprived of English institutions. Life, he exclaimed, would not be worth having in a country where liberty and property were at the mercy of one despotic master. The Duke of York was greatly incensed by this language, and represented to his brother the danger of retaining in office a man who appeared to be infected with all the worst notions of Marvell and Sidney.

Some modern writers have blamed Halifax for continuing

in the ministry while he disapproved of the manner in which both domestic and foreign affairs were conducted. But this censure is unjust. Indeed it is to be remarked that the word ministry, in the sense in which we use it, was then unknown.* The thing itself did not exist; for it belongs to an age in which parliamentary government is fully established. At present the chief servants of the crown form one body. They are understood to be on terms of friendly confidence with each other, and to agree as to the main principles on which the executive administration ought to be conducted. If a slight difference of opinion arises among them, it is easily compromised: but, if one of them differs from the rest on a vital point, it is his duty to resign. While he retains his office, he is held responsible even for steps which he has tried to dissuade his colleagues from taking. In the seventeenth century, the heads of the various branches of the administration were bound together in no such partnership. Each of them was accountable for his own acts, for the use which he made of his own official seal, for the documents which he signed, for the counsel which he gave to the King. No statesman was held answerable for what he had not himself done, or induced others to do. If he took care not to be the agent in what was wrong, and if, when consulted, he recommended what was right, he was blameless. It would have been thought strange scrupulosity in him to quit his post, because his advice as to matters not strictly within his own department was not taken by his master; to leave the board of Admiralty, for example, because the finances were in disorder, or the board of Treasury because the foreign relations of the kingdom were in an unsatisfactory state. It was, therefore, by no means unusual to see in high office, at the same time, men who avowedly differed from one another as widely as ever Pulteney differed from Walpole, or Fox from Pitt.

* North's Examen, 69.

The moderate and constitutional counsels of Halifax were timidly and feebly seconded by Francis North, Lord Guildford, who had lately been made Keeper of the Great Seal. The character of Guildford has been drawn at full length by his brother Roger North, a most intolerant Tory, a most affected and pedantic writer, but a vigilant observer of all those minute circumstances which throw light on the dispositions of men. It is remarkable that the biographer, though he was under the influence of the strongest fraternal partiality, and though he was evidently anxious to produce a flattering likeness, was yet unable to portray the Lord Keeper otherwise than as the most ignoble of mankind. Yet the intellect of Guildford was clear, his industry great, his proficiency in letters and science respectable, and his legal learning more than respectable. His faults were selfishness, cowardice, and meanness. He was not insensible to the power of female beauty, nor averse from excess in wine. Yet neither wine nor beauty could ever seduce the cautious and frugal libertine, even in his earliest youth, into one fit of indiscreet generosity. Though of noble descent, he rose in his profession by paying ignominious homage to all who possessed influence in the courts. He became Chief Justice of the Common Pleas, and as such was party to some of the foulest judicial murders recorded in our history. He had sense enough to perceive from the first that Oates and Bedloe were impostors: but the Parliament and the country were greatly excited; the government had yielded to the pressure; and North was not a man to risk a good place for the sake of justice and humanity. Accordingly, while he was in secret drawing up a refutation of the whole romance of the Popish plot, he declared in public that the truth of the story was as plain as the sun in heaven, and was not ashamed to browbeat, from the seat of judgment, the unfortunate Roman Catholics who were arraigned before him for their lives. He had at length reached

the highest post in the law. But a lawyer, who, after many
years devoted to professional labour, engages in politics for
the first time at an advanced period of life, seldom distin-
guishes himself as a statesman, and Guildford was no exception to the general rule. He was indeed so sensible of his
deficiencies that he never attended the meetings of his colleagues on foreign affairs. Even on questions relating to his
own profession his opinion had less weight at the Council
board than that of any man who has ever held the Great Seal.
Such as his influence was, however, he used it, as far as he
dared, on the side of the laws.

The chief opponent of Halifax was Lawrence Hyde, who
had recently been created Earl of Rochester. Of all Tories,
Rochester was the most intolerant and uncompromising. The
moderate members of his party complained that the whole
patronage of the Treasury, while he was First Commissioner
there, went to noisy zealots, whose only claim to promotion
was that they were always drinking confusion to Whiggery,
and lighting bonfires to burn the Exclusion Bill. The Duke
of York, pleased with a spirit which so much resembled
his own, supported his brother-in-law passionately and obstinately.

The attempts of the rival ministers to surmount and sup-
plant each other kept the court in incessant agitation. Halifax pressed the King to summon a Parliament, to grant a
general amnesty, to deprive the Duke of York of all share
in the government, to recall Monmouth from banishment, to
break with Lewis, and to form a close union with Holland on
the principles of the Triple Alliance. The Duke of York, on
the other hand, dreaded the meeting of a Parliament, regarded the vanquished Whigs with undiminished hatred, still
flattered himself that the design formed fourteen years before
at Dover might be accomplished, daily represented to his
brother the impropriety of suffering one who was at heart a

CHAP.
II.

Republican to hold the Privy Seal, and strongly recommended
Rochester for the great place of Lord Treasurer.

While the two factions were struggling, Godolphin, cautious, silent, and laborious, observed a neutrality between
them. Sunderland, with his usual restless perfidy, intrigued
against them both. He had been turned out of office in disgrace for having voted in favour of the Exclusion Bill, but
had made his peace by employing the good offices of the
Duchess of Portsmouth and by cringing to the Duke of York,
and was once more Secretary of State.

Policy of
Lewis.

Nor was Lewis negligent or inactive. Every thing at that
moment favoured his designs. He had nothing to apprehend
from the German empire, which was then contending against
the Turks on the Danube. Holland could not, unsupported,
venture to oppose him. He was therefore at liberty to indulge
his ambition and insolence without restraint. He seized Dix-
mude and Courtray. He bombarded Luxemburg. He exacted from the republic of Genoa the most humiliating submissions. The power of France at that time reached a higher
point than it ever before or ever after attained, during the
ten centuries which separated the reign of Charlemagne and
the reign of Napoleon. It was not easy to say where her
acquisitions would stop, if only England could be kept in a
state of vassalage. The first object of the court of Versailles
was therefore to prevent the calling of a Parliament and the
reconciliation of English parties. For this end bribes, promises, and menaces were unsparingly employed. Charles
was sometimes allured by the hope of a subsidy, and sometimes frightened by being told that, if he convoked the
Houses, the secret articles of the treaty of Dover should be
published. Several Privy Councillors were bought; and
attempts were made to buy Halifax, but in vain. When he
had been found incorruptible, all the art and influence of the
French embassy were employed to drive him from office: but

his polished wit and his various accomplishments had made
him so agreeable to his master, that the design failed. *

Halifax was not content with standing on the defensive.
He openly accused Rochester of malversation. An inquiry
took place. It appeared that forty thousand pounds had been
lost to the public by the mismanagement of the First Lord of
the Treasury. In consequence of this discovery he was not
only forced to relinquish his hopes of the white staff, but was
removed from the direction of the finances to the more dignified but less lucrative and important post of Lord President.
"I have seen people kicked down stairs before," said Halifax;
"but my Lord Rochester is the first person that I ever saw
kicked up stairs." Godolphin, now a peer, became First
Commissioner of the Treasury.

Still, however, the contest continued. The event de- State of
pended wholly on the will of Charles; and Charles could not in the
come to a decision. In his perplexity he promised everything Charles
to everybody. He would stand by France: he would break time of
with France: he would never meet another Parliament: he his death.
would order writs for a Parliament to be issued without delay.
He assured the Duke of York that Halifax should be dismissed
from office, and Halifax that the Duke should be sent to Scotland. In public he affected implacable resentment against
Monmouth, and in private conveyed to Monmouth assurances
of unalterable affection. How long, if the King's life had
been protracted, his hesitation might have lasted, and what

---

* Lord Preston, who was envoy at Paris, wrote thence to Halifax as
follows: — "I find that your lordship lies still under the same misfortune of being no favourite to this court; and Monsieur Barillon dare not
do you the honour to shine upon you, since his master frowneth. They
know very well your lordship's qualifications, which make them fear and
consequently hate you: and be assured, my lord, if all their strength can
send you to Rufford, it shall be employed for that end. Two things, I
hear, they particularly object against you, your secrecy, and your being
incapable of being corrupted. Against these two things I know they have
declared." The date of the letter is October 5. N. s. 1683.

would have been his resolve, can only be conjectured. Early
in the year 1685, while hostile parties were anxiously awaiting
his determination, he died, and a new scene opened.   In a few
months the excesses of the government obliterated the impression which had been made on the public mind by the excesses of the opposition.   The violent reaction which had laid
the Whig party prostrate was followed by a still more violent
reaction in the opposite direction; and signs not to be mistaken indicated that the great conflict between the prerogatives of the crown and the privileges of the Parliament, was
about to be brought to a final issue.

CHAPTER III.

I INTEND, in this chapter, to give a description of the state CHAP.
in which England was at the time when the crown passed from III.
Charles the Second to his brother. Such a description, composed from scanty and dispersed materials, must necessarily
be very imperfect. Yet it may perhaps correct some false
notions which would make the subsequent narrative unintelligible or uninstructive.

If we would study with profit the history of our ancestors,
we must be constantly on our guard against that delusion which
the well known names of families, places, and offices naturally
produce, and must never forget that the country of which we
read was a very different country from that in which we live.
In every experimental science there is a tendency towards
perfection. In every human being there is a wish to ame-
liorate his own condition. These two principles have often
sufficed, even when counteracted by great public calamities
and by bad institutions, to carry civilisation rapidly forward.
No ordinary misfortune, no ordinary misgovernment, will do
so much to make a nation wretched, as the constant progress
of physical knowledge and the constant effort of every man to
better himself will do to make a nation prosperous. It has
often been found that profuse expenditure, heavy taxation,
absurd commercial restrictions, corrupt tribunals, disastrous
wars, seditions, persecutions, conflagrations, inundations,
have not been able to destroy capital so fast as the exertions
of private citizens have been able to create it. It can easily be
proved that, in our own land, the national wealth has, during
at least six centuries, been almost uninterruptedly increasing;
that it was greater under the Tudors than under the Plantagenets; that it was greater under the Stuarts than under the

18*

Tudors; that, in spite of battles, sieges, and confiscations, it was greater on the day of Restoration than on the day when the Long Parliament met; that, in spite of maladministration, of extravagance, of public bankruptcy, of two costly and unsuccessful wars, of the pestilence and of the fire, it was greater on the day of the death of Charles the Second than on the day of his Restoration. This progress, having continued during many ages, became at length, about the middle of the eighteenth century, portentously rapid, and has proceeded, during the nineteenth, with accelerated velocity. In consequence partly of our geographical and partly of our moral position, we have, during several generations, been exempt from evils which have elsewhere impeded the efforts and destroyed the fruits of industry. While every part of the Continent, from Moscow to Lisbon, has been the theatre of bloody and devastating wars, no hostile standard has been seen here but as a trophy. While revolutions have taken place all around us, our government has never once been subverted by violence. During a hundred years there has been in our island no tumult of sufficient importance to be called an insurrection. The law has never been borne down either by popular fury or by regal tyranny. Public credit has been held sacred. The administration of justice has been pure. Even in times which might by Englishmen be justly called evil times, we have enjoyed what almost every other nation in the world would have considered as an ample measure of civil and religious freedom. Every man has felt entire confidence that the state would protect him in the possession of what had been earned by his diligence and hoarded by his self-denial. Under the benignant influence of peace and liberty, science has flourished, and has been applied to practical purposes on a scale

Great change in the state of England since 1685.
never before known. The consequence is that a change to which the history of the old world furnishes no parrallel has taken place in our country. Could the England of 1685 be, by

some magical process, set before our eyes, we should not know one landscape in a hundred or one building in ten thousand. The country gentleman would not recognise his own fields. The inhabitant of the town would not recognise his own street. Everything has been changed, but the great features of nature, and a few massive and durable works of human art. We might find out Snowdon and Windermere, the Cheddar Cliffs and Beachy Head. We might find out here and there a Norman minster, or a castle which witnessed the wars of the Roses. But, with such rare exceptions, everything would be strange to us. Many thousands of square miles which are now rich corn land and meadow, intersected by green hedge-rows, and dotted with villages and pleasant country seats, would appear as moors overgrown with furze, or fens abandoned to wild ducks. We should see straggling huts built of wood and covered with thatch, where we now see manufacturing towns and seaports renowned to the farthest ends of the world. The capital itself would shrink to dimensions not much exceeding those of its present suburb on the south of the Thames. Not less strange to us would be the garb and manners of the people, the furniture and the equipages, the interior of the shops and dwellings. Such a change in the state of a nation seems to be at least as well entitled to the notice of a historian as any change of the dynasty or of the ministry.

One of the first objects of an inquirer, who wishes to form a correct notion of the state of a community at a given time, must be to ascertain of how many persons that community then consisted. Unfortunately the population of England in 1685 cannot be ascertained with perfect accuracy. For no great state had then adopted the wise course of periodically numbering the people. All men were left to conjecture for themselves; and, as they generally conjectured without examining facts, and under the influence of strong passions and prejudices, their guesses were often ludicrously absurd.

Even intelligent Londoners ordinarily talked of London as containing several millions of souls. It was confidently asserted by many that, during the thirty-five years which had elapsed between the accession of Charles the First and the Restoration, the population of the city had increased by two millions.* Even while the ravages of the plague and fire were recent, it was the fashion to say that the capital still had a million and a half of inhabitants.** Some persons, disgusted by these exaggerations, ran violently into the opposite extreme. Thus Isaac Vossius, a man of undoubted parts and learning, strenuously maintained that there were only two millions of human beings in England, Scotland, and Ireland taken together. ***

We are not, however, left without the means of correcting the wild blunders into which some minds were hurried by national vanity and others by a morbid love of paradox. There are extant three computations which seem to be entitled to peculiar attention. They are entirely independent of each other: they proceed on different principles; and yet there is little difference in the results.

One of these computations was made in the year 1696 by Gregory King, Lancaster herald, a political arithmetician of great acuteness and judgment. The basis of his calculations was the number of houses returned in 1690 by the officers who made the last collection of the hearth money. The conclusion at which he arrived was that the population of England was nearly five millions and a half. †

* Observations on the Bills of Mortality, by Captain John Graunt (Sir William Petty), chap. xi.
**   ''She doth comprehend
     Full fifteen hundred thousand which do spend
     Their days within.''   Great Britain's Beauty, 1671.
*** Isaac Vossius, De Magnitudine Urbium Sinarum, 1685. Vossius, as we learn from St. Evremond, talked on this subject oftener and longer than fashionable circles cared to listen.
† King's Natural and Political Observations, 1696. This valuable treatise, which ought to be read as the author wrote it, and not as garbled by Davenant, will be found in some editions of Chalmers's Estimate.

About the same time King William the Third was desirous to ascertain the comparative strength of the religious sects into which the community was divided. An inquiry was instituted; and reports were laid before him from all the dioceses of the realm. According to these reports the number of his English subjects must have been about five million two hundred thousand. *

Lastly, in our own days, Mr. Finlaison, an actuary of eminent skill, subjected the ancient parochial registers to all the tests which the modern improvements in statistical science enabled him to apply. His opinion was, that, at the close of the seventeenth century, the population of England was a little under five million two hundred thousand souls.**

Of these three estimates, framed without concert by different persons from different sets of materials, the highest, which is that of King, does not exceed the lowest, which is that of Finlaison, by one twelfth. We may, therefore, with confidence pronounce that, when James the Second reigned, England contained between five million and five million five hundred thousand inhabitants. On the very highest supposition she then had less than one third of her present population, and less than three times the population which is now collected in her gigantic capital.

The increase of the people has been great in every part Increase of popu- lation greater in the north than in the south. of the kingdom, but generally much greater in the northern than in the southern shires. In truth a large part of the country beyond Trent was, down to the eighteenth century, in a state of barbarism. Physical and moral causes had concurred to prevent civilisation from spreading to that region.

---

* Dalrymple's Appendix to Part II. Book I. The practice of reckoning the population by sects was long fashionable. Gulliver says of the King of Brobdingnag, "He laughed at my odd arithmetic, as he was pleased to call it, in reckoning the numbers of our people by a computation drawn from the several sects among us in religion and politics."

** Preface to the Population Returns of 1831.

The air was inclement; the soil was generally such as required skilful and industrious cultivation; and there could be little skill or industry in a tract which was often the theatre of war, and which, even when there was nominal peace, was constantly desolated by bands of Scottish marauders. Before the union of the two British crowns, and long after that union, there was as great a difference between Middlesex and Northumberland as there now is between Massachusetts and the settlements of those squatters who, far to the west of the Mississippi, administer a rude justice with the rifle and the dagger. In the reign of Charles the Second, the traces left by ages of slaughter and pillage were still distinctly perceptible, many miles south of the Tweed, in the face of the country and in the lawless manners of the people. There was still a large class of moss-troopers, whose calling was to plunder dwellings and to drive away whole herds of cattle. It was found necessary, soon after the Restoration, to enact laws of great severity for the prevention of these outrages. The magistrates of Northumberland and Cumberland were authorised to raise bands of armed men for the defence of property and order; and provision was made for meeting the expense of these levies by local taxation.* The parishes were required to keep bloodhounds for the purpose of hunting the freebooters. Many old men who were living in the middle of the eighteenth century could well remember the time when those ferocious dogs were common.** Yet, even with such auxiliaries, it was often found impossible to track the robbers to their retreats among the hills and morasses. For the geography of that wild country was very imperfectly known. Even after the accession of George the Third, the path over the fells from Borrowdale to Ravenglas

---

* Statutes 14 Car. II. c. 22.; 18 & 19 Car. II. c. 3.; 29 & 30 Car. II. c. 2.
** Nicholson and Bourne, Discourse on the Ancient State of the Border, 1777.

was still a secret carefully kept by the dalesmen, some of whom had probably in their youth escaped from the pursuit of justice by that road.* The seats of the gentry and the larger farm-houses were fortified. Oxen were penned at night beneath the overhanging battlements of the residence, which was known by the name of the Peel. The inmates slept with arms at their sides. Huge stones and boiling water were in readiness to crush and scald the plunderer who might venture to assail the little garrison. No traveller ventured into that country without making his will. The Judges on circuit, with the whole body of barristers, attorneys, clerks, and serving men, rode on horseback from Newcastle to Carlisle, armed and escorted by a strong guard under the command of the Sheriffs. It was necessary to carry provisions; for the country was a wilderness which afforded no supplies. The spot where the cavalcade halted to dine, under an immense oak, is not yet forgotten. The irregular vigour with which criminal justice was administered shocked observers whose life had been passed in more tranquil districts. Juries, animated by hatred and by a sense of common danger, convicted housebreakers and cattle stealers with the promptitude of a court martial in a mutiny; and the convicts were hurried by scores to the gallows.** Within the memory of some whom this generation has seen, the sportsman who wandered in pursuit of game to the sources of the Tyne found the heaths round Keeldar Castle peopled by a race scarcely less savage than the Indians of California, and heard with surprise the half naked women chaunting a wild measure, while the men with brandished dirks danced a war dance.***

Slowly and with difficulty peace was established on the

* Gray's Journal of a Tour in the Lakes, Oct. 3. 1769.
** North's Life of Guildford. Hutchinson's History of Cumberland, parish of Brampton.
*** See Sir Walter Scott's Journal, Oct. 7. 1827, in his Life by Mr. Lockhart.

border. In the train of peace came industry and all the arts of life. Meanwhile it was discovered that the regions north of the Trent possessed in their coal beds a source of wealth far more precious than the gold mines of Peru. It was found that, in the neighbourhood of these beds, almost every manufacture might be most profitably carried on. A constant stream of emigrants began to roll northward. It appeared by the returns of 1841 that the ancient archiepiscopal province of York contained two sevenths of the population of England. At the time of the Revolution that province was believed to contain only one seventh of the population. * In Lancashire the number of inhabitants appears to have increased ninefold, while in Norfolk, Suffolk, and Northamptonshire it has hardly doubled.**

Revenue
in 1685.
Of the taxation we can speak with more confidence and precision than of the population. The revenue of England, when Charles the Second died, was small, when compared with the resources which she even then possessed, or with the sums which were raised by the governments of the neighbouring countries. It had, from the time of the Restoration, been almost constantly increasing: yet it was little more than three fourths of the revenue of the United Provinces, and was hardly one fifth of the revenue of France.

The most important head of receipt was the excise, which, in the last year of the reign of Charles, produced five hundred and eighty-five thousand pounds, clear of all deductions. The net proceeds of the customs amounted in the same year to five hundred and thirty thousand pounds. These burdens did not

---

* Dalrymple, Appendix to Part II. Book I. The returns of the hearth money lead to nearly the same conclusion. The hearths in the province of York were not a sixth of the hearths of England.

** I do not, of course, pretend to strict accuracy here; but I believe that whoever will take the trouble to compare the last returns of hearth money in the reign of William the Third with the census of 1841, will come to a conclusion not very different from mine.

lie very heavy on the nation. The tax on chimneys, though CHAP.
III. less productive, raised far louder murmurs. The discontent excited by direct imposts is, indeed, almost always out of proportion to the quantity of money which they bring into the Exchequer; and the tax on chimneys was, even among direct imposts, peculiarly odious: for it could be levied only by means of domiciliary visits; and of such visits the English have always been impatient to a degree which the people of other countries can but faintly conceive. The poorer householders were frequently unable to pay their hearth money to the day. When this happened, their furniture was distrained without mercy: for the tax was farmed; and a farmer of taxes is, of all creditors, proverbially the most rapacious. The collectors were loudly accused of performing their unpopular duty with harshness and insolence. It was said that, as soon as they appeared at the threshold of a cottage, the children began to wail, and the old women ran to hide their earthenware. Nay, the single bed of a poor family had sometimes been carried away and sold. The net annual receipt from this tax was two hundred thousand pounds. *

* There are in the Pepysian Library, some ballads of that age on the chimney money. I will give a specimen or two: —
"The good old dames, whenever they the chimney man espied,
Unto their nooks they haste away, their pots and pipkins hide.
There is not one old dame in ten, and search the nation through,
But, if you talk of chimney men, will spare a curse or two."
Again,
"Like plundering soldiers they'd enter the door,
And make a distress on the goods of the poor,
While frighted poor children distractedly cried:
This nothing abated their insolent pride."
In the British Museum there are doggrel verses composed on the same subject and in the same spirit:
"Or, if through poverty it be not paid,
For cruelty to tear away the single bed,
On which the poor man rests his weary head,
At once deprives him of his rest and bread."
I take this opportunity, the first which occurs, of acknowledging most gratefully the kind and liberal manner in which the Master and Vicemaster of Magdalene College, Cambridge, gave me access to the valuable collections of Pepys.

When to the three great sources of income which have
been mentioned we add the royal domains, then far more extensive than at present, the first fruits and tenths, which had
not yet been surrendered to the Church, the Duchies of Cornwall and Lancaster, the forfeitures and the fines, we shall find
that the whole annual revenue of the crown may be fairly
estimated at about fourteen hundred thousand pounds. Of
this revenue part was hereditary: the rest had been granted to
Charles for life; and he was at liberty to lay out the whole
exactly as he thought fit. Whatever he could save by re-
trenching the expenditure of the public departments was an
addition to his privy purse. Of the Post Office, more will here-
after be said. The profits of that establishment had been
appropriated by Parliament to the Duke of York.

The King's revenue was, or rather ought to have been,
charged with the payment of about eighty thousand pounds a
year, the interest of the sum fraudulently detained in the Exchequer by the Cabal. While Danby was at the head of the
finances, the creditors had received their dividends, though
not with the strict punctuality of modern times: but those who
had succeeded him at the Treasury had been less expert, or
less solicitous to maintain public faith. Since the victory won
by the court over the Whigs, not a farthing had been paid;
and no redress was granted to the sufferers, till a new dynasty
had established a new system. There can be no greater error
than to imagine that the device of meeting the exigencies of
the state by loans was imported into our island by William the
Third. From a period of immemorial antiquity it had been the
practice of every English government to contract debts. What
the Revolution introduced was the practice of honestly paying
them. *

* My chief authorities for this financial statement will be found in
the Commons' Journals, March 1. and March 20. 168⅚.

By plundering the public creditor, it was possible to make an income of about fourteen hundred thousand pounds, with some occasional help from France, support the necessary charges of the government and the wasteful expenditure of the court. For that load which pressed most heavily on the finances of the great continental states was here scarcely felt. In France, Germany, and the Netherlands, armies, such as Henry the Fourth and Philip the Second had never employed in time of war, were kept up in the midst of peace. Bastions and ravelins were everywhere rising, constructed on principles unknown to Parma or Spinola. Stores of artillery and ammunition were accumulated, such as even Richelieu, whom the preceding generation had regarded as a worker of prodigies, would have pronounced [fabulous. No man could journey many leagues in those countries without hearing the drums of a regiment on march, or being challenged by the sentinels on the draw-bridge of a fortress. In our island, on the contrary, Military system. it was possible to live long and to travel far, without being once reminded, by any martial sight or sound, that the defence of nations had become a science and a calling. The majority of Englishmen who were under twenty-five years of age had probably never seen a company of regular soldiers. Of the cities which, in the civil war, had valiantly repelled hostile armies, scarce one was now capable of sustaining a siege. The gates stood open night and day. The ditches were dry. The ramparts had been suffered to fall into decay, or were repaired only that the townsfolk might have a pleasant walk on summer evenings. Of the old baronial keeps many had been shattered by the cannon of Fairfax and Cromwell, and lay in heaps of ruin, overgrown with ivy. Those which remained had lost their martial character, and were now rural palaces of the aristocracy. The moats were turned into preserves of carp and pike. The mounds were planted with fragrant shrubs, through which spiral walks ran up to summer houses adorned with mirrors and paintings. * On the capes of the sea coast, and on many inland hills, were still seen tall posts, surmounted by barrels. Once those barrels had been filled with pitch. Watchmen had been set round them in seasons of danger; and, within a few hours after a Spanish sail had been discovered in the Channel, or after a thousand Scottish mosstroopers had crossed the Tweed, the signal fires were blazing fifty miles off, and whole counties were rising in arms. But many years had now elapsed since the beacons had been lighted; and they were regarded rather as curious relics of ancient manners than as parts of a machinery necessary to the safety of the state.**

The only army which the law recognised was the militia. That force had been remodelled by two Acts of Parliament passed shortly after the Restoration. Every man who possessed five hundred pounds a year derived from land, or six thousand pounds of personal estate, was bound to provide, equip, and pay, at his own charge, one horseman. Every man who had fifty pounds a year derived from land, or six hundred pounds of personal estate, was charged in like manner with one pikeman or musketeer. Smaller proprietors were joined together in a kind of society, for which our language does not afford a special name, but which an Athenian would have called a Synteleia; and each society was required to furnish, according to its means, a horse soldier or a foot soldier. The whole number of cavalry and infantry thus maintained was popularly estimated at a hundred and thirty thousand men. ***

The King was, by the ancient constitution of the realm, and by the recent and solemn acknowledgment of both Houses of Parliament, the sole Captain General of this large

* See for example the picture of the mound at Marlborough, in Stukeley's Itinerarium Curiosum.
** Chamberlayne's State of England, 1684.
*** 13 & 14 Car. II. c. 3.; 15 Car. II. c. 4. Chamberlayne's State of England, 1684.

force. The Lords Lieutenants and their Deputies held the
command under him, and appointed meetings for drilling and
inspection. The time occupied by such meetings, however,
was not to exceed fourteen days in one year. The Justices
of the Peace were authorised to inflict slight penalties for
breaches of discipline. Of the ordinary cost no part was paid
by the crown: but, when the train-bands were called out
against an enemy, their subsistence became a charge on the
general revenue of the state, and they were subject to the
utmost rigour of martial law.

There were those who looked on the militia with no
friendly eye. Men who had travelled much on the Continent,
who had marvelled at the stern precision with which every
sentinel moved and spoke in the citadels built by Vauban,
who had seen the mighty armies which poured along all the
roads of Germany to chase the Ottoman from the gates of
Vienna, and who had been dazzled by the well ordered pomp
of the household troops of Lewis, sneered much at the way in
which the peasants of Devonshire and Yorkshire marched and
wheeled, shouldered muskets and ported pikes. The enemies
of the liberties and religion of England looked with aversion
on a force which could not, without extreme risk, be employed against those liberties and that religion, and missed
no opportunity of throwing ridicule on the rustic soldiery. *
Enlightened patriots, when they contrasted these rude levies

** Dryden, in his Cymon and Iphigenia, expressed, with his usual
keenness and energy, the sentiments which had been fashionable among
the sycophants of James the Second: —
> " The country rings around with loud alarms,
> And raw in fields the rude militia swarms;
> Mouths without hands, maintained at vast expense,
> In peace a charge, in war a weak defence.
> Stout once a month they march, a blustering band,
> And ever, but in time of need, at hand.
> This was the morn when, issuing on the guard,
> Drawn up in rank and file, they stood prepared
> Of seeming arms to make a short essay,
> Then hasten to be drunk, the business of the day."

with the battalions which, in time of war, a few hours might bring to the coast of Kent or Sussex, were forced to acknowledge that, dangerous as it might be to keep up a permanent military establishment, it might be more dangerous still to stake the honour and independence of the country on the result of a contest between ploughmen officered by Justices of the Peace, and veteran warriors led by Marshals of France. In Parliament, however, 'it was necessary to express such opinions with some reserve; for the militia was an institution eminently popular. Every reflection thrown on it excited the indignation of both the great parties in the state, and especially of that party which was distinguished by peculiar zeal for monarchy and for the Anglican Church. The array of the counties was commanded almost exclusively by Tory noblemen and gentlemen. They were proud of their military rank, and considered an insult offered to the service to which they belonged as offered to themselves. They were also perfectly aware that whatever was said against a militia was said in favour of a standing army; and the name of standing army was hateful to them. One such army had held dominion in England; and under that dominion the King had been murdered, the nobility degraded, the landed gentry plundered, the Church persecuted. There was scarce a rural grandee who could not tell a story of wrongs and insults suffered by himself, or by his father, at the hands of the parliamentary soldiers. One old Cavalier had seen half his manor house blown up. The hereditary elms of another had been hewn down. A third could never go into his parish church without being reminded by the defaced scutcheons and headless statues of his ancestry, that Oliver's redcoats had once stabled their horses there. The consequence was that those very Royalists, who were most ready to fight for the King themselves, were the last persons whom he could venture to ask for the means of hiring regular troops.

Charles, however, had, a few months after his Restoration, begun to form a small standing army. He felt that,
without some better protection than that of the train-bands
and beef-eaters, his palace and person would hardly be secure, in the vicinity of a great city swarming with warlike
Fifth Monarchy men who had just been disbanded. He therefore, careless and profuse as he was, contrived to spare from
his pleasures a sum sufficient to keep up a body of guards
With the increase of trade and of public wealth his revenues
increased; and he was thus enabled, in spite of the occasional
murmurs of the Commons, to make gradual additions to his
regular forces. One considerable addition was made a few
months before the close of his reign. The costly, useless,
and pestilential settlement of Tangier was abandoned to the
barbarians who dwelt around it; and the garrison, consisting
of one regiment of horse and two regiments of foot, was
brought to England.

The little army thus formed by Charles the Second was
the germ of that great and renowned army which has, in the
present century, marched triumphant into Madrid and Paris,
into Canton and Candahar. The Life Guards, who now form
two regiments, were then distributed into three troops, each
of which consisted of two hundred carabineers, exclusive or
officers. This corps, to which the safety of the King and
royal family was confided, had a very peculiar character.
Even the privates were designated as gentlemen of the Guard.
Many of them were of good families, and had held commissions in the civil war. Their pay was far higher than that
of the most favoured regiment of our time, and would in that
age have been thought a respectable provision for the younger
son of a country squire. Their fine horses, their rich housings,
their cuirasses, and their buff coats adorned with ribands,
velvet, and gold lace, made a splendid appearance in St.
James's Park. A small body of grenadier dragoons, who

came from a lower class and received lower pay, was attached to each troop. Another body of household cavalry distinguished by blue coats and cloaks, and still called the Blues, was generally quartered in the neighbourhood of the capital. Near the capital lay also the corps which is now designated as the first regiment of dragoons, but which was then the only regiment of dragoons on the English establishment. It had recently been formed out of the cavalry who had returned from Tangier. A single troop of dragoons, which did not form part of any regiment, was stationed near Berwick, for the purpose of keeping the peace among the moss-troopers of the border. For this species of service the dragoon was then thought to be peculiarly qualified. He has since become a mere horse soldier. But in the seventeenth century he was accurately described by Montecuculi as a foot soldier who used a horse only in order to arrive with more speed at the place where military service was to be performed.

The household infantry consisted of two regiments, which were then, as now, called the first regiment of Foot Guards, and the Coldstream Guards. They generally did duty near Whitehall and St. James's Palace. As there were then no barracks, and as, by the Petition of Right, soldiers could not be quartered on private families, the redcoats filled all the alehouses of Westminster and the Strand.

There were five other regiments of foot. One of these, called the Admiral's Regiment, was especially destined to service on board of the fleet. The remaining four still rank as the first four regiments of the line. Two of these represented two brigades which had long sustained on the Continent the fame of British valour. The first, or Royal regiment, had, under the great Gustavus, borne a conspicuous part in the deliverance of Germany. The third regiment, distinguished by flesh coloured facings, from which it derived the well known name of the Buffs, had, under Maurice of

Nassau, fought not less bravely for the deliverance of the CHAP. III. Netherlands. Both these gallant bands had at length, after many vicissitudes, been recalled from foreign service by Charles the Second, and had been placed on the English establishment.

The regiments which now rank as the second and fourth of the line had, in 1685, just returned from Tangier, bringing with them cruel and licentious habits contracted in a long course of warfare with the Moors. A few companies of infantry which had not been regimented lay in garrison at Tilbury Fort, at Portsmouth, at Plymouth, and at some other important stations on or near the coast.

Since the beginning of the seventeenth century a great change had taken place in the arms of the infantry. The pike had been gradually giving place to the musket; and, at the close of the reign of Charles the Second, most of his foot were musketeers. Still, however, there was a large intermixture of pikemen. Each class of troops was occasionally instructed in the use of the weapon which peculiarly belonged to the other class. Every foot soldier had at his side a sword for close fight. The dragoon was armed like a musketeer, and was also provided with a weapon which had, during many years, been gradually coming into use, and which the English then called a dagger, but which, from the time of our revolution, has been known among us by the French name of bayonet. The bayonet seems not to have been so formidable an instrument of destruction as it has since become; for it was inserted in the muzzle of the gun; and in action much time was lost while the soldier unfixed his bayonet in order to fire, and fixed it again in order to charge.

The regular army which was kept up in England at the beginning of the year 1685 consisted, all ranks included, of about seven thousand foot, and about seventeen hundred cavalry and dragoons. The whole charge amounted to about two hundred and ninety thousand pounds a year, less than a

19*

tenth part of what the military establishment of France then cost in time of peace. The daily pay of a private in the Life Guards was four shillings, in the Blues two shillings and sixpence, in the Dragoons eighteenpence, in the Foot Guards tenpence, and in the line eightpence. The discipline was lax, and indeed could not be otherwise. The common law of England knew nothing of courts martial, and made no distinction, in time of peace, between a soldier and any other subject; nor could the government then venture to ask even the most loyal Parliament for a Mutiny Bill. A soldier, therefore, by knocking down his colonel, incurred only the ordinary penalties of assault and battery, and by refusing to obey orders, by sleeping on guard, or by deserting his colours, incurred no legal penalty at all. Military punishments were doubtless inflicted during the reign of Charles the Second; but they were inflicted very sparingly, and in such a manner as not to attract public notice, or to produce an appeal to the courts of Westminster Hall.

Such an army as has been described was not very likely to enslave five millions of Englishmen. It would indeed have been hardly able to suppress an insurrection in London, if the train-bands of the City had joined the insurgents. Nor could the King expect that, if a rising took place in England, he would be able to obtain help from his other dominions. For, though both Scotland and Ireland supported separate military establishments, those establishments were not more than sufficient to keep down the Puritan malecontents of the former kingdom, and the Popish malecontents of the latter. The government had, however, an important military resource which must not be left unnoticed. There were in the pay of the United Provinces six fine regiments, formerly commanded by the brave Ossory. Of these regiments three had been raised in England and three in Scotland. Their native prince had reserved to himself the power of recalling them, if he needed their help against a foreign or domestic CHAP.
III. enemy. In the meantime they were maintained without any charge to him, and were kept under an excellent discipline, to which he could not have ventured to subject them.*

If the jealousy of the Parliament and of the nation made it The navy. impossible for the King to maintain a formidable standing army, no similar impediment prevented him from making England the first of maritime powers. Both Whigs and Tories were ready to applaud every step tending to increase the efficiency of that force which, while it was the best protection of the island against foreign enemies, was powerless against civil liberty. All the greatest exploits achieved within the memory of that generation by English soldiers had been achieved in war against English princes. The victories of our sailors had been won over foreign foes, and had averted havoc and rapine from our own soil. By at least half the nation the battle of Naseby was remembered with horror, and the battle of Dunbar with pride chequered by many painful feelings: but the defeat of the Armada, and the encounters of Blake with the Hollanders and Spaniards, were recollected with unmixed exultation by all parties. Ever since the Restoration, the Commons, even when most discontented and most parsimonious, had always been bountiful even to profusion where the interest of the navy was concerned. It had been represented to them, while Danby was minister, that many of the vessels in the royal fleet were old and unfit for sea; and, although the House was, at that time, in no giving mood, an aid of near six hundred thousand pounds had been granted for the building of thirty new men of war.

* Most of the materials which I have used for this account of the regular army will be found in the Historical Records of Regiments, published by command of King William the Fourth, and under the direction of the Adjutant General. See also Chamberlayne's State of England, 1684; Abridgment of the English Military Discipline, printed by especial command, 1685; Exercise of Foot, by their Majesties' command, 1690.

But the liberality of the nation had been made fruitless by the vices of the government. The list of the King's ships, it is true, looked well. There were nine first rates, fourteen second rates, thirty-nine third rates, and many smaller vessels. The first rates, indeed, were less than the third rates of our time; and the third rates would not now rank as very large frigates. This force, however, if it had been efficient, would in those days have been regarded by the greatest potentate as formidable. But it existed only on paper. When the reign of Charles terminated, his navy had sunk into degradation and decay, such as would be almost incredible if it were not certified to us by the independent and concurring evidence of witnesses whose authority is beyond exception. Pepys, the ablest man in the English Admiralty, drew up, in the year 1684, a memorial on the state of his department, for the information of Charles. A few months later Bonrepaux, the ablest man in the French Admiralty, having visited England for the especial purpose of ascertaining her maritime strength, laid the result of his inquiries before Lewis. The two reports are to the same effect. Bonrepaux declared that he found everything in disorder and in miserable condition, that the superiority of the French marine was acknowledged with shame and envy at Whitehall, and that the state of our shipping and dock-yards was of itself a sufficient guarantee that we should not meddle in the disputes of Europe. * Pepys informed his master that the naval administration was a prodigy of wastefulness, corruption, ignorance, and indolence, that no estimate could be trusted, that

---

* I refer to a despatch of Bonrepaux to Seignelay, dated Feb. $\frac{8}{18}$. 1686. It was transcribed for Mr. Fox from the French archives, during the peace of Amiens, and, with the other materials brought together by that great man, was intrusted to me by the kindness of the late Lady Holland, and of the present Lord Holland. I ought to add that, even in the midst of the troubles which have lately agitated Paris, I have found no difficulty in obtaining, from the liberality of the functionaries there, extracts supplying some chasms in Mr. Fox's collection.

no contract was performed, that no check was enforced.
The vessels which the recent liberality of Parliament had
enabled the government to build, and which had never been
out of harbour, had been made of such wretched timber that
they were more unfit to go to sea than the old hulls which had
been battered thirty years before by Dutch and Spanish
broadsides. Some of the new men of war, indeed, were so
rotten that, unless speedily repaired, they would go down at
their moorings. The sailors were paid with so little punctuality that they were glad to find some usurer who would
purchase their tickets at forty per cent discount. The commanders who had not powerful friends at court were even
worse treated. Some officers, to whom large arrears were
due, after vainly importuning the government during many
years, had died for want of a morsel of bread.

Most of the ships which were afloat were commanded by
men who had not been bred to the sea. This, it is true, was
not an abuse introduced by the government of Charles. No
state, ancient or modern, had, before that time, made a
complete separation between the naval and military services.
In the great civilised nations of the old world, Cimon and
Lysander, Pompey and Agrippa, had fought battles by sea
as well as by land. Nor had the impulse which nautical science
received at the close of the fifteenth century produced any
material improvement in the division of labour. At Flodden
the right wing of the victorious army was led by the Admiral
of England. At Jarnac and Moncontour the Huguenot ranks
were marshalled by the Admiral of France. Neither John
of Austria, the conqueror of Lepanto, nor Lord Howard of
Effingham, to whose direction the marine of England was
entrusted when the Spanish invaders were approaching our
shores, had received the education of a sailor. Raleigh,
highly celebrated as a naval commander, had served during
many years as a soldier in France, the Netherlands, and Ire-

land. Blake had dinstinguished himself by his skilful and valiant defence of an inland town before he humbled the pride of Holland and of Castile on the ocean. Since the Restoration the same system had been followed. Great fleets had been entrusted to the direction of Rupert and Monk; Rupert, who was renowned chiefly as a hot and daring cavalry officer, and Monk, who, when he wished his ship to change her course, moved the mirth of his crew by calling out, "Wheel to the left!"

But about this time wise men began to perceive that the rapid improvement, both of the art of war and of the art of navigation, made it necessary to draw a line between two professions which had hitherto been confounded. Either the command of a regiment or the command of a ship was now a matter quite sufficient to occupy the attention of a single mind. In the year 1672 the French government determined to educate young men of good family from a very early age specially for the sea service. But the English government, instead of following this excellent example, not only continued to distribute high naval commands among landsmen, but selected for such commands landsmen who, even on land, could not safely have been put in any important trust. Any lad of noble birth, any dissolute courtier for whom one of the King's mistresses would speak a word, might hope that a ship of the line, and with it the honour of the country and the lives of hundreds of brave men, would be committed to his care. It mattered not that he had never in his life taken a voyage except on the Thames, that he could not keep his feet in a breeze, that he did not know the difference between latitude and longitude. No previous training was thought necessary; or, at most, he was sent to make a short trip in a man of war, where he was subjected to no discipline, where he was treated with marked respect, and where he lived in a round of revels and amusements. If, in the intervals of feasting, drinking

and gambling, he succeeded in learning the meaning of a
few technical phrases and the names of the points of the compass, he was fully qualified to take charge of a three-decker.
This is no imaginary description. In 1666, John Sheffield,
Earl of Mulgrave, at seventeen years of age, volunteered to
serve at sea against the Dutch. He passed six weeks on
board, diverting himself, as well as he could, in the society
of some young libertines of rank, and then returned home
to take the command of a troop of horse. After this he was
never on the water till the year 1672, when he again joined
the fleet, and was almost immediately appointed Captain of
a ship of eighty-four guns, reputed the finest in the navy.
He was then twenty-three years old, and had not, in the
whole course of his life, been three months afloat. As soon
as he came back from sea he was made Colonel of a regiment
of foot. This is a specimen of the manner in which naval
commands of the highest importance were then given; and
a favourable specimen; for Mulgrave, though he wanted experience, wanted neither parts nor courage. Others were
promoted in the same way who not only were not good officers, but who were intellectually and morally incapable of
ever becoming good officers, and whose only recommendation
was that they had been ruined by folly and vice. The chief
bait which allured these men into the service was the profit
of conveying bullion and other valuable commodities from
port to port; for both the Atlantic and the Mediterranean
were then so much infested by pirates from Barbary that
merchants were not willing to trust precious cargoes to any
custody but that of a man of war. A Captain in this way
sometimes cleared several thousands of pounds by a short
voyage; and for this lucrative business he too often neglected
the interests of his country and the honour of his flag, made
mean submissions to foreign powers, disobeyed the most
direct injunctions of his superiors, lay in port when he was

ordered to chase a Sallee rover, or ran with dollars to Leghorn when his instructions directed him to repair to Lisbon. And all this he did with impunity. The same interest which had placed him in a post for which he was unfit maintained him there. No Admiral, bearded by these corrupt and dissolute minions of the palace, dared to do more than mutter something about a court martial. If any officer showed a higher sense of duty than his fellows, he soon found that he lost money without acquiring honour. One Captain, who, by strictly obeying the orders of the Admiralty, missed a cargo which would have been worth four thousand pounds to him, was told by Charles, with ignoble levity, that he was a great fool for his pains.

The discipline of the navy was of a piece throughout. As the courtly Captain despised the Admiralty, he was in turn despised by his crew. It could not be concealed that he was inferior in seamanship to every foremast man on board. It was idle to expect that old sailors, familiar with the hurricanes of the tropics and with the icebergs of the Arctic Circle, would pay prompt and respectful obedience to a chief who knew no more of winds and waves than could be learned in a gilded barge between Whitehall Stairs and Hampton Court. To trust such a novice with the working of a ship was evidently impossible. The direction of the navigation was therefore taken from the Captain and given to the Master: but this partition of authority produced innumerable inconveniences. The line of demarcation was not, and perhaps could not be, drawn with precision. There was therefore constant wrangling. The Captain, confident in proportion to his ignorance, treated the Master with lordly contempt. The Master, well aware of the danger of disobliging the powerful, too often, after a struggle, yielded against his better judgment; and it was well if the loss of ship and crew was not the consequence. In general the least mischievous

of the aristocratical Captains were those who completely abandoned to others the direction of the vessels, and thought
only of making money and spending it. The way in which
these men lived was so ostentatious and voluptuous that,
greedy as they were of gain, they seldom became rich. They
dressed as if for a gala at Versailles, ate off plate, drank the
richest wines, and kept harams on board, while hunger and
scurvy raged among the crews, and while corpses were daily
flung out of the port-holes.

Such was the ordinary character of those who were then
called gentlemen Captains. Mingled with them were to be
found, happily for our country, naval commanders of a very
different description, men whose whole life had been passed
on the deep, and who had worked and fought their way from
the lowest offices of the forecastle to rank and distinction.
One of the most eminent of these officers was Sir Christopher
Mings, who entered the service as a cabin boy, who fell
fighting bravely against the Dutch, and whom his crew,
weeping and vowing vengeance, carried to the grave. From
him sprang, by a singular kind of descent, a line of valiant
and expert sailors. His cabin boy was Sir John Narborough;
and the cabin boy of Sir John Narborough was Sir Cloudesley
Shovel. To the strong natural sense and dauntless courage
of this class of men England owes a debt never to be forgotten. It was by such resolute hearts that, in spite of much
maladministration, and in spite of the blunders of more
courtly admirals, our coasts were protected and the reputation of our flag upheld during many gloomy and perilous
years. But to a landsman these tarpaulins, as they were
called, seemed a strange and half savage race. All their
knowledge was professional; and their professional knowledge was practical rather than scientific. Off their own
element they were as simple as children. Their deportment
was uncouth. There was roughness in their very good na-

ture; and their talk, where it was not made up of nautical phrases, was too commonly made up of oaths and curses. Such were the chiefs in whose rude school were formed those sturdy warriors from whom Smollet, in the next age, drew Lieutenant Bowling and Commodore Trunnion. But it does not appear that there was in the service of any of the Stuarts a single naval officer such as, according to the notions of our times, a naval officer ought to be, that is to say, a man versed in the theory and practice of his calling, and steeled against all the dangers of battle and tempest, yet of cultivated mind and polished manners. There were gentlemen and there were seamen in the navy of Charles the Second. But the seamen were not gentlemen; and the gentlemen were not seamen.

The English navy at that time might, according to the most exact estimates which have come down to us, have been kept in an efficient state for three hundred and eighty thousand pounds a year. Four hundred thousand pounds a year was the sum actually expended, but expended, as we have seen, to very little purpose. The cost of the French marine was nearly the same; the cost of the Dutch marine considerably more.[*]

The
ordnance. The charge of the English ordnance in the seventeenth century was, as compared with other military and naval charges, much smaller than at present. At most of the garrisons there were gunners, and here and there, at an important

* My information respecting the condition of the navy, at this time, is chiefly derived from Pepys. His report, presented to Charles the Second in May 1684, has never, I believe, been printed. The manuscript is at Magdalene College, Cambridge. At Magdalene College is also a valuable manuscript containing a detailed account of the maritime establishments of the country in December 1684. Pepys's "Memoirs relating to the State of the Royal Navy for Ten Years, determined December 1688," and his diary and correspondence during his mission to Tangier, are in print. I have made large use of them. See also Sheffield's Memoirs, Teonge's Diary, Aubrey's Life of Monk, the Life of Sir Cloudesley Shovel, 1708, Commons' Journals, March 1. and March 20. 168⅝.

post, an engineer was to be found. But there was no regiment of artillery, no brigade of sappers and miners, no college in which young soldiers could learn the scientific part of war. The difficulty of moving field pieces was extreme. When, a few years later, William marched from Devonshire to London, the apparatus which he brought with him, though such as had long been in constant use on the Continent, and such as would now be regarded at Woolwich as rude and cumbrous, excited in our ancestors an admiration resembling that which the Indians of America felt for the Castilian harquebusses. The stock of gunpowder kept in the English forts and arsenals was boastfully mentioned by patriotic writers as something which might well impress neighbouring nations with awe. It amounted to fourteen or fifteen thousand barrels, about a twelfth of the quantity which it is now thought necessary to have always in store. The expenditure under the head of ordnance was on an average a little above sixty thousand pounds a year.[*]

The whole effective charge of the army, navy, and ordnance, was about seven hundred and fifty thousand pounds. The noneffective charge, which is now a heavy part of our Noneffective charge. public burdens, can hardly be said to have existed. A very small number of naval officers, who were not employed in the public service, drew half pay. No Lieutenant was on the list, nor any Captain who had not commanded a ship of the first or second rate. As the country then possessed only seventeen ships of the first and second rate that had ever been at sea, and as a large proportion of the persons who had commanded such ships had good posts on shore, the expenditure under this head must have been small indeed.[**] In the army, half

* Chamberlayne's State of England, 1684; Commons' Journals, March 1. and March 20. 168⅘. In 1833, it was determined, after full enquiry, that a hundred and seventy thousand barrels of gunpowder should constantly be kept in store; and this rule is still observed.

** It appears from the records of the Admiralty, that Flag officers were allowed half pay in 1668, Captains of first and second rates not till 1674.

pay was given merely as a special and temporary allowance to
a small number of officers belonging to two regiments, which
were peculiarly situated.* Greenwich Hospital had not been
founded. Chelsea Hospital was building: but the cost of that
institution was defrayed partly by a deduction from the pay of
the troops, and partly by private subscription. The King
promised to contribute only twenty thousand pounds for
architectural expenses, and five thousand a year for the
maintenance of the invalids.** It was no part of the plan that
there should be outpensioners. The whole noneffective
charge, military and naval, can scarcely have exceeded ten
thousand pounds a year. It now exceeds ten thousand pounds
a day.

Charge of
civil go-
vern-
ment.
Of the expense of civil government only a small portion
was defrayed by the crown. The great majority of the functionaries whose business was to administer justice and preserve order either gave their services to the public gratuitously, or were remunerated in a manner which caused no
drain on the revenue of the state. The sheriffs, mayors, and
aldermen of the towns, the country gentlemen who were in the
commission of the peace, the head-boroughs, bailiffs, and
petty constables, cost the King nothing. The superior courts
of law were chiefly supported by fees.

Our relations with foreign courts had been put on the most
economical footing. The only diplomatic agent who had the
title of Ambassador resided at Constantinople, and was partly
supported by the Turkey Company. Even at the court of
Versailles England had only an Envoy; and she had not even
an Envoy at the Spanish, Swedish, and Danish courts. The
whole expense under this head cannot, in the last year of the

---

* Warrant in the War Office Records, dated March 26. 1678.
** Evelyn's Diary, Jan. 27. 1682. I have seen a privy seal, dated May
17. 1683, which confirms Evelyn's testimony.

reign of Charles the Second, have much exceeded twenty
thousand pounds.*

In this frugality there was nothing laudable. Charles was, Great
as usual, niggardly in the wrong place, and munificent in the ministers
wrong place. The public service was starved that courtiers tiers.
might be pampered. The expense of the navy, of the ordnance, of pensions to needy old officers, of missions to
foreign courts, must seem small indeed to the present generation. But the personal favourites of the sovereign, his ministers, and the creatures of those ministers, were gorged
with public money. Their salaries and pensions, when compared with the incomes of the nobility, the gentry, the commercial and professional men of that age, will appear enormous. The greatest estates in the kingdom then very little
exceeded twenty thousand a year. The Duke of Ormond had
twenty-two thousand a year.** The Duke of Buckingham,
before his extravagance had impaired his great property, had
nineteen thousand six hundred a year.*** George Monk, Duke
of Albemarle, who had been rewarded for his eminent services
with immense grants of crown land, and who had been notorious both for covetousness and for parsimony, left fifteen
thousand a year of real estate, and sixty thousand pounds in
money which probably yielded seven per cent.† These three
Dukes were supposed to be three of the very richest subjects
in England. The Archbishop of Canterbury can hardly have
had five thousand a year.†† The average income of a temporal

* James the Second sent Envoys to Spain, Sweden, and Denmark;
yet in his reign the diplomatic expenditure was little more than 30,000*l.*
a year. See the Commons' Journals, March 20. 168⅘. Chamberlayne's
State of England, 1684, 1686.
   ** Carte's Life of Ormond.
   *** Pepys's Diary, Feb. 14. 166⅘.
   † See the Report of the Bath and Montague case, which was decided
by Lord Keeper Somers, in December, 1693.
   †† During three quarters of a year, beginning from Christmas 1689,
the revenues of the see of Canterbury were received by an officer appointed by the crown. That officer's accounts are now in the British

CHAP.
III.

peer was estimated, by the best informed persons, at about
three thousand a year, the average income of a baronet at
nine hundred a year, the average income of a member of the
House of Commons at less than eight hundred a year.* A
thousand a year was thought a large revenue for a barrister.
Two thousand a year was hardly to be made in the Court of
King's Bench, except by the crown lawyers.** It is evident,
therefore, that an official man would have been well paid if
he had received a fourth or fifth part of what would now be an
adequate stipend. In fact, however, the stipends of the
higher class of official men were as large as at present, and
not seldom larger. The Lord Treasurer, for example, had
eight thousand a year, and, when the Treasury was in commission, the junior Lords had sixteen hundred a year each.
The Paymaster of the Forces had a poundage, amounting to
about five thousand a year, on all the money which passed
through his hands. The Groom of the Stole had five thousand
a year, the Commissioners of the Customs twelve hundred a
year each, the Lords of the Bedchamber a thousand a year
each.*** The regular salary, however, was the smallest part
of the gains of an official man of that age. From the noblemen
who held the white staff and the great seal, down to the
humblest tide-waiter and gauger, what would now be called
gross corruption was practised without disguise and without
reproach. Titles, places, commissions, pardons, were daily
sold in market overt by the great dignitaries of the realm; and

---

Museum. (Lansdowne MSS. 885.) The gross revenue for the three
quarters was not quite four thousand pounds; and the difference between
the gross and the net revenue was evidently something considerable.
   * King's Natural and Political Conclusions. Davenant on the Balance of Trade. Sir W. Temple says, "The revenues of a House of
Commons have seldom exceeded four hundred thousand pounds." Memoirs, Third Part.
   ** Langton's Conversations with Chief Justice Hale, 1672.
   *** Commons' Journals, April 27. 1689; Chamberlayne's State of England, 1684.

every clerk in every department imitated, to the best of his power, the evil example.

During the last century no prime minister, however powerful, has become rich in office; and several prime ministers have impaired their private fortune in sustaining their public character. In the seventeenth century, a statesman who was at the head of affairs might easily, and without giving scandal, accumulate in no long time an estate amply sufficient to support a dukedom. It is probable that the income of the prime minister, during his tenure of power, far exceeded that of any other subject. The place of Lord Lieutenant of Ireland was supposed to be worth forty thousand pounds a year.[*] The gains of the Chancellor Clarendon, of Arlington, of Lauderdale, and of Danby, were enormous. The sumptuous palace to which the populace of London gave the name of Dunkirk House, the stately pavilions, the fish-ponds, the deer park and the orangery of Euston, the more than Italian luxury of Ham, with its busts, fountains, and aviaries, were among the many signs which indicated what was the shortest road to boundless wealth. This is the true explanation of the unscrupulous violence with which the statesmen of that day struggled for office,[*] of the tenacity with which, in spite of vexations, humiliations and dangers, they clung to it, and of the scandalous compliances to which they stooped in order to retain it. Even in our own age, formidable as is the power of opinion, and high as is the standard of integrity, there would be great risk of a lamentable change in the character of our public men, if the place of First Lord of the Treasury or Secretary of State were worth a hundred thousand pounds a year. Happily for our country the emoluments of the highest class of functionaries have not only not grown in proportion to the general growth of our opulence, but have positively diminished.

[*] See the Travels of the Grand Duke Cosmo.

The fact that the sum raised in England by taxation has, in a time not exceeding two long lives, been multiplied thirty-fold, is strange, and may at first sight seem appalling. But those who are alarmed by the increase of the public burdens may perhaps be reassured when they have considered the increase of the public resources. In the year 1685, the value of the produce of the soil far exceeded the value of all the other fruits of human industry. Yet agriculture was in what would now be considered as a very rude and imperfect state. The arable land and pasture land were not supposed by the best political arithmeticians of that age to amount to much more than half the area of the kingdom.* The remainder was believed to consist of moor, forest, and fen. These computations are strongly confirmed by the road books and maps of the seventeenth century. From those books and maps it is clear that many routes which now pass through an endless succession of orchards, hay-fields, and bean-fields, then ran through nothing but heath, swamp, and warren.** In the drawings of English landscapes made in that age for the Grand Duke Cosmo, scarce a hedgerow is to be seen, and numerous tracts, now rich with cultivation, appear as bare as Salisbury Plain.*** At Enfield, hardly out of sight of the smoke of the capital, was a region of five and twenty miles in circumference, which contained only three houses and scarcely any inclosed

---

* King's Natural and Political Conclusions. Davenant on the Balance of Trade.

** See the Itinerarium Angliæ, 1675, by John Ogilby, Cosmographer Royal. He describes great part of the land as wood, fen, heath on both sides, marsh on both sides. In some of his maps the roads through inclosed country are marked by lines, and the roads through uninclosed country by dots. The proportion of uninclosed country, which, if cultivated, must have been wretchedly cultivated, seems to have been very great. From Abingdon to Gloucester, for example, a distance of forty or fifty miles, there was not a single inclosure, and scarcely one inclosure between Biggleswade and Lincoln.

*** Large copies of these highly interesting drawings are in the noble collection bequeathed by Mr. Grenville to the British Museum.

fields. Deer, as free as in an American forest, wandered
there by thousands.* It is to be remarked, that wild animals
of large size were then far more numerous than at present.
The last wild boars, indeed, which had been preserved for
the royal diversion, and had been allowed to ravage the cultivated land with their tusks, had been slaughtered by the exasperated rustics during the license of the civil war. The last
wolf that has roamed our island had been slain in Scotland a
short time before the close of the reign of Charles the Second.
But many breeds, now extinct or rare, both of quadrupeds
and birds, were still common. The fox, whose life is, in
many counties, held almost as sacred as that of a human
being, was considered as a mere nuisance. Oliver Saint John
told the Long Parliament that Strafford was to be regarded,
not as a stag or a hare, to whom some law was to be given,
but as a fox, who was to be snared by any means, and knocked
on the head without pity. This illustration would be by no
means a happy one, if addressed to country gentlemen of our
time: but in Saint John's days there were not seldom great
massacres of foxes to which the peasantry thronged with all
the dogs that could be mustered: traps were set; nets were
spread; no quarter was given; and to shoot a female with cub
was considered as a feat which merited the gratitude of the
neighbourhood. The red deer were then as common in
Gloucestershire and Hampshire as they now are among the
Grampian Hills. On one occasion Queen Anne, on her way
to Portsmouth, saw a herd of no less than five hundred. The
wild bull with his white mane was still to be found wandering
in a few of the southern forests. The badger made his dark
and tortuous hole on the side of every hill where the copse-
wood grew thick. The wild cats were frequently heard by
night wailing round the lodges of the rangers of Whittlebury
and Needwood. The yellow-breasted martin was still pur-

* Evelyn's Diary, June 2, 1675.

sued in Cranbourne Chase for his fur, reputed inferior only to
that of the sable.   Fen eagles, measuring more than nine feet
between the extremities of the wings, preyed on fish along the
coast of Norfolk.   On all the downs, from the British Channel
to Yorkshire, huge bustards strayed in troops of fifty or sixty,
and were often hunted with greyhounds.   The marshes of
Cambridgeshire and Lincolnshire were covered during some
months of every year by immense clouds of cranes.   Some of
these races the progress of cultivation has extirpated.   Of
others the numbers are so much diminished that men crowd to
gaze at a specimen as at a Bengal tiger, or a Polar bear.*

The progress of this great change can nowhere be more
clearly traced than in the Statute Book.   The number of inclosure acts passed since King George the Second came to the
throne exceeds four thousand.   The area inclosed under the
authority of those acts exceeds, on a moderate calculation,
ten thousand square miles.   How many square miles, which
were formerly uncultivated or ill cultivated, have, during the
same period, been fenced and carefully tilled by the proprietors, without any application to the legislature, can only
be conjectured.   But it seems highly probable that a fourth
part of England has been, in the course of little more than a
century, turned from a wild into a garden.

Even in those parts of the kingdom which at the close of
the reign of Charles the Second were the best cultivated, the
farming, though greatly improved since the civil war, was not
such as would now be thought skilful.   To this day no
effectual steps have been taken by public authority for the
purpose of obtaining accurate accounts of the produce of the
English soil.   The historian must therefore follow, with some

* See White's Selborne; Bell's History of British Quadrupeds;
Gentleman's Recreation, 1686; Aubrey's Natural History of Wiltshire,
1685; Morton's History of Northamptonshire, 1712; Willoughby's Orni-
thology, by Ray, 1678; Latham's General Synopsis of Birds; and Sir
Thomas Browne's Account of Birds found in Norfolk.

misgivings, the guidance of those writers on statistics whose reputation for diligence and fidelity stands highest. At present an average crop of wheat, rye, barley, oats, and beans, is supposed considerably to exceed thirty millions of quarters. The crop of wheat would be thought wretched if it did not exceed twelve millions of quarters. According to the computation made in the year 1696 by Gregory King, the whole quantity of wheat, rye, barley, oats, and beans, then annually grown in the kingdom, was somewhat less than ten millions of quarters. The wheat, which was then cultivated only on the strongest clay, and consumed only by those who were in easy circumstances, he estimated at less than two millions of quarters. Charles Davenant, an acute and well informed though most unprincipled and rancorous politician, differed from King as to some of the items of the account, but came to nearly the same general conclusions. *

The rotation of crops was very imperfectly understood. It was known, indeed, that some vegetables lately introduced into our island, particularly the turnip, afforded excellent nutriment in winter to sheep and oxen: but it was not yet the practice to feed cattle in this manner. It was therefore by no means easy to keep them alive during the season when the grass is scanty. They were killed and salted in great numbers at the beginning of the cold weather; and, during several months, even the gentry tasted scarcely any fresh animal food, except game and river fish, which were consequently much more important articles in housekeeping than at present. It appears from the Northumberland Household Book that, in the reign of Henry the Seventh, fresh meat was never eaten even by the gentlemen attendant on a great Earl, except during the short interval between Midsummer and Michaelmas. But in the course of two centuries an improvement had taken place;

* King's Natural and Political Conclusions. Davenant on the Balance of Trade.

and under Charles the Second it was not till the beginning of November that families laid in their stock of salt provisions, then called Martinmas beef.*

The sheep and the ox of that time were diminutive when compared with the sheep and oxen which are now driven to our markets.** Our native horses, though serviceable, were held in small esteem, and fetched low prices. They were valued, one with another, by the ablest of those who computed the national wealth, at not more than fifty shillings each. Foreign breeds were greatly preferred. Spanish jennets were regarded as the finest chargers, and were imported for purposes of pageantry and war. The coaches of the aristocracy were drawn by grey Flemish mares, which trotted, as it was thought, with a peculiar grace, and endured better than any cattle reared in our island the work of dragging a ponderous equipage over the rugged pavement of London. Neither the modern dray horse nor the modern race horse was then known. At a much later period the ancestors of the gigantic quadrupeds, which all foreigners now class among the chief wonders of London, were brought from the marshes of Walcheren; the ancestors of Childers and Eclipse from the sands of Arabia. Already, however, there was among our nobility and gentry a passion for the amusements of the turf. The importance of improving our studs by an infusion of new blood was strongly felt; and with this view a considerable number of barbs had lately been brought into the country. Two men whose authority on such subjects was held in great esteem, the Duke of Newcastle and Sir John Fenwick, pronounced that the meanest hack ever imported from Tangier would produce a finer progeny than could be expected from the best sire of our native breed. They would not readily

---

* See the Almanacks of 1684 and 1685.

** See Mr. M'Culloch's Statistical Account of the British Empire, part III. chap. i. sec. 6.

have believed that a time would come when the princes and
nobles of neighbouring lands would be as eager to obtain
horses from England as ever the English had been to obtain
horses from Barbary.*

The increase of vegetable and animal produce, though
great, seems small when compared with the increase of our
mineral wealth. In 1685 the tin of Cornwall, which had, more
than two thousand years before, attracted the Tyrian sails
beyond the pillars of Hercules, was still one of the most valuable subterranean productions of the island. The quantity
annullay extracted from the earth was found to be, some years
later, sixteen hundred tons, probably about a third of what it
now is.** But the veins of copper which lie in the same region
were, in the time of Charles the Second, altogether neglected,
·nor did any landowner take them into the account in estima-
ting the value of his property. Cornwall and Wales at present yield annually near fifteen thousand tons of copper, worth
near a million and a half sterling; that is to say, worth about
twice as much as the annual produce of all English mines of all
descriptions in the seventeenth century.*** The first bed of
rock salt had been discovered not long after the Restoration in
Cheshire, but does not appear to have been worked in that
age. The salt which was obtained by a rude process from
brine pits was held in no high estimation. The pans in which
the manufacture was carried on exhaled a sulphurous stench;

* King and Davenant as before; The Duke of Newcastle on Horsemanship; Gentleman's Recreation, 1686. The "dappled Flanders mares"
were marks of greatness in the time of Pope, and even later.
    The vulgar proverb, that the grey mare is the better horse, origi-
nated, I suspect, in the preference generally given to the grey mares of
Flanders over the finest coach horses of England.
    ** See a curious note by Tonkin, in Lord De Dunstanville's edition of
Carew's Survey of Cornwall.
    *** Borlase's Natural History of Cornwall, 1758. The quantity of
copper now produced, I have taken from parliamentary returns. Davenant, in 1700, estimated the annual produce of all the mines of England
at between seven and eight hundred thousand pounds.

and, when the evaporation was complete, the substance
which was left was scarcely fit to be used with food. Physicians
attributed the scorbutic and pulmonary complaints which were
common among the English to this unwholesome condiment.
It was therefor seldom used by the upper and middle classes;
and there was a regular and considerable importation from
France. At present our springs and mines not only supply
our own immense demand, but send annually more than seven
hundred millions of pounds of excellent salt to foreign countries. *

Far more important has been the improvement of our iron
works. Such works had long existed in our island, but had
not prospered, and had been regarded with no favourable eye
by the government and by the public. It was not then the
practice to employ coal for smelting the ore; and the rapid
consumption of wood excited the alarm of politicians. As
early as the reign of Elizabeth there had been loud complaints
that whole forests were cut down for the purpose of feeding
the furnaces: and the Parliament had interfered to prohibit the
manufacturers from burning timber. The manufacture consequently languished. At the close of the reign of Charles the
Second, great part of the iron which was used in the country
was imported from abroad; and the whole quantity cast here
annually seems not to have exceeded ten thousand tons. At
present the trade is thought to be in a depressed state if less
than a million of tons are produced in a year.**

One mineral, perhaps more important than iron itself,
remains to be mentioned. Coal, though very little used in
any species of manufacture, was already the ordinary fuel

---

* Philosophical Transactions, No. 53. Nov. 1669, No. 66. Dec. 1670,
No. 103. May 1674, No. 156. Feb. 168¾.
** Yarranton, England's Improvement by Sea and Land, 1677; Porter's Progress of the Nation. See also a remarkably perspicuous history,
in small compass, of the English iron works, in Mr. M'Culloch's Statistical Account of the British Empire.

in some districts which were fortunate enough to possess large beds, and in the capital, which could easily be supplied by water carriage. It seems reasonable to believe that at least one half of the quantity then extracted from the pits was consumed in London. The consumption of London seemed to the writers of that age enormous, and was often mentioned by them as a proof of the greatness of the imperial city. They scarcely hoped to be believed when they affirmed that two hundred and eighty thousand chaldrons, that is to say, about three hundred and fifty thousand tons, were, in the last year of the reign of Charles the Second, brought to the Thames. At present near three millions and a half of tons are required yearly by the metropolis; and the whole annual produce cannot, on the most moderate computation, be estimated at less than thirty millions of tons. *

While these great changes have been in progress, the rent [Increase of rent.] of land has, as might be expected, been almost constantly rising. In some districts it has multiplied more than tenfold. In some it has not more than doubled. It has probably, on the average, quadrupled.

Of the rent, a large proportion was divided among the country gentlemen, a class of persons whose position and character it is most important that we should clearly understand; for by their influence and by their passions the fate of the nation was, at several important conjunctures, determined.

We should be much mistaken if we pictured to ourselves [The country gentlemen.] the squires of the seventeenth century as men bearing a close resemblance to their descendants, the county members and chairmen of quarter sessions with whom we are familiar. The modern country gentleman generally receives a liberal educa-

---

* See Chamberlayne's State of England, 1684, 1687; Angliæ Metropolis, 1691; M'Culloch's Statistical Account of the British Empire, Part III. chap. ii. (edition of 1847). In 1845 the quantity of coal brought into London appeared, by the parliamentary returns, to be 3,460,000 tons.

tion, passes from a distinguished school to a distinguished college, and has every opportunity to become an excellent scholar. He has generally seen something of foreign countries. A considerable part of his life has generally been passed in the capital; and the refinements of the capital follow him into the country. There is perhaps no class of dwellings so pleasing as the rural seats of the English gentry. In the parks and pleasure grounds, nature, dressed yet not disguised by art, wears her most alluring form. In the buildings, good sense and good taste combine to produce a happy union of the comfortable and the graceful. The pictures, the musical instruments, the library, would in any other country be considered as proving the owner to be an eminently polished and accomplished man. A country gentleman who witnessed the Revolution was probably in receipt of about a fourth part of the rent which his acres now yield to his posterity. He was, therefore, as compared with his posterity, a poor man, and was generally under the necessity of residing, with little interruption, on his estate. To travel on the Continent, to maintain an establishment in London, or even to visit London frequently, were pleasures in which only the great proprietors could indulge. It may be confidently affirmed that of the squires whose names were then in the Commissions of Peace and Lieutenancy not one in twenty went to town once in five years, or had ever in his life wandered so far as Paris. Many lords of manors had received an education differing little from that of their menial servants. The heir of an estate often passed his boyhood and youth at the seat of his family with no better tutors than grooms and gamekeepers, and scarce attained learning enough to sign his name to a Mittimus. If he went to school and to college, he generally returned before he was twenty to the seclusion of the old hall, and there, unless his mind were very happily constituted by nature, soon forgot his academical pursuits in rural business and pleasures.   His chief serious employment was the care of his property.   He examined samples of grain, handled pigs, and, on market days, made bargains over a tankard with drovers and hop merchants.   His chief pleasures were commonly derived from field sports and from an unrefined sensuality.   His language and pronunciation were such as we should now expect to hear only from the most ignorant clowns.   His oaths, coarse jests, and scurrilous terms of abuse, were uttered with the broadest accent of his province.   It was easy to discern, from the first words which he spoke, whether he came from Somersetshire or Yorkshire.   He troubled himself little about decorating his abode, and, if he attempted decoration, seldom produced anything but deformity.   The litter of a farm-yard gathered under the windows of his bed-chamber, and the cabbages and gooseberry bushes grew close to his hall door.   His table was loaded with coarse plenty; and guests were cordially welcomed to it.   But, as the habit of drinking to excess was general in the class to which he belonged, and as his fortune did not enable him to intoxicate large assemblies daily with claret or canary,   strong beer was the ordinary beverage. The quantity of beer consumed in those days was indeed enormous.   For beer then was to the middle and lower classes, not only all that beer now is, but all that wine, tea, and ardent spirits now are.   It was only at great houses, or on great occasions, that foreign drink was placed on the board. The ladies of the house, whose business it had commonly been to cook the repast, retired as soon as the dishes had been devoured,   and left the gentlemen to their ale and tobacco.   The coarse jollity of the afternoon was often prolonged till the revellers were laid under the table.

It was very seldom that the country gentleman caught glimpses of the great world; and what he saw of it tended rather to confuse than to enlighten his understanding.   His opinions respecting religion, government, foreign countries and former times, having been derived, not from study, from observation, or from conversation with enlightened companions, but from such traditions as were current in his own small circle, were the opinions of a child. He adhered to them, however, with the obstinacy which is generally found in ignorant men accustomed to be fed with flattery. His animosities were numerous and bitter. He hated Frenchmen and Italians, Scotchmen and Irishmen, Papists and Presbyterians, Independents and Baptists, Quakers and Jews. Towards London and Londoners he felt an aversion which more than once produced important political effects. His wife and daughter were in tastes and acquirements below a housekeeper or a still-room maid of the present day. They stitched and spun, brewed gooseberry wine, cured marigolds, and made the crust for the venison pasty.

From this description it might be supposed that the English esquire of the seventeenth century did not materially differ from a rustic miller or alehouse keeper of our time. There are, however, some important parts of his character still to be noted, which will greatly modify this estimate. Unlettered as he was and unpolished, he was still in some most important points a gentleman. He was a member of a proud and powerful aristocracy, and was distinguished by many both of the good and of the bad qualities which belong to aristocrats. His family pride was beyond that of a Talbot or a Howard. He knew the genealogies and coats of arms of all his neighbours, and could tell which of them had assumed supporters without any right, and which of them were so unfortunate as to be great grandsons of aldermen. He was a magistrate, and, as such, administered gratuitously to those who dwelt around him a rude patriarchal justice, which, in spite of innumerable blunders and of occasional acts of tyranny, was yet better than no justice at all. He was an officer

of the trainbands; and his military dignity, though it might
move the mirth of gallants who had served a campaign in
Flanders, raised his character in his own eyes and in the eyes
of his neighbours.   Nor indeed was his soldiership justly a
subject of derision.   In every county there were elderly
gentlemen who had seen service which was no child's play.
One had been knighted by Charles the First, after the battle
of Edgehill.   Another still wore a patch over the scar which
he had received at Naseby.   A third had defended his old
house till Fairfax had blown in the door with a petard.   The
presence of these old Cavaliers, with their old swords and
holsters, and with their old stories about Goring and Luns-
ford, gave to the musters of militia an earnest and warlike
aspect which would otherwise have been wanting.   Even those
country gentlemen who were too young to have themselves
exchanged blows with the cuirassiers of the Parliament had,
from childhood, been surrounded by the traces of recent
war, and fed with stories of the martial exploits of their
fathers and uncles.   Thus the character of the English esquire of the seventeenth century was compounded of two
elements which we are not accustomed to find united.   His
ignorance and uncouthness, his low tastes and gross phrases,
would, in our time, be considered as indicating a nature and
a breeding thoroughly plebeian.   Yet he was essentially a
patrician, and had, in large measure, both the virtues and
the vices which flourish among men set from their birth in
high place, and accustomed to authority, to observance, and
to self-respect.   It is not easy for a generation which is accustomed to find chivalrous sentiments only in company with
liberal studies and polished manners to image to itself a man
with the deportment, the vocabulary, and the accent of a
carter, yet punctilious on matters of genealogy and precedence, and ready to risk his life rather than see a stain cast
on the honour of his house.   It is however only by thus

joining together things seldom or never found together in our own experience, that we can form a just idea of that rustic aristocracy which constituted the main strength of the armies of Charles the First, and which long supported, with strange fidelity, the interest of his descendants.

The gross, uneducated, untravelled country gentleman was commonly a Tory: but, though devotedly attached to hereditary monarchy, he had no partiality for courtiers and ministers. He thought, not without reason, that Whitehall was filled with the most corrupt of mankind; that of the great sums which the House of Commons had voted to the crown since the Restoration part had been embezzled by cunning politicians, and part squandered on buffoons and foreign courtesans. His stout English heart swelled with indignation at the thought that the government of his country should be subject to French dictation. Being himself generally an old Cavalier, or the son of an old Cavalier, he reflected with bitter resentment on the ingratitude with which the Stuarts had requited their best friends. Those who heard him grumble at the neglect with which he was treated, and at the profusion with which wealth was lavished on the bastards of Nell Gwynn and Madam Carwell, would have supposed him ripe for rebellion. But all this ill humour lasted only till the throne was really in danger. It was precisely when those whom the sovereign had loaded with wealth and honours shrank from his side that the country gentlemen, so surly and mutinous in the season of his prosperity, rallied round him in a body. Thus, after murmuring twenty years at the misgovernment of Charles the Second, they came to his rescue in his extremity, when his own Secretaries of State and Lords of the Treasury had deserted him, and enabled him to gain a complete victory over the opposition; nor can there be any doubt that they would have shown equal loyalty to his brother James, if James would, even at the last moment, have refrained from outraging their strongest feeling. For there was one institution, and one only, which they prized even more than hereditary monarchy; and that institution was the Church of England. Their love of the Church was not, indeed, the effect of study or meditation. Few among them could have given any reason, drawn from Scripture or ecclesiastical history, for adhering to her doctrines, her ritual, and her polity; nor were they, as a class, by any means strict observers of that code of morality which is common to all Christian sects. But the experience of many ages proves that men may be ready to fight to the death, and to persecute without pity, for a religion whose creed they do not understand, and whose precepts they habitually disobey. *

The rural clergy were even more vehement in Toryism than the rural gentry, and were a class scarcely less important. It is to be observed, however, that the individual clergyman, as compared with the individual gentleman, then ranked much lower than in our days. The main support of the Church was derived from the tithe; and the tithe bore to the rent a much smaller ratio than at present. King estimated the whole income of the parochial and collegiate clergy at only four hundred and eighty thousand pounds a year; Davenant at only five hundred and forty-four thousand a year. It is certainly now more than seven times as great as the larger of these two sums. The average rent of the land has not, according to any estimate, increased proportionally. It follows that rectors and vicars must have been, as compared with the neighbouring knights and squires, much poorer in the seventeenth than in the nineteenth century.

The place of the clergyman in society had been completely changed by the Reformation. Before that event, ecclesiastics

* My notion of the country gentleman of the seventeenth century has been derived from sources too numerous to be recapitulated. I must leave my description to the judgment of those who have studied the history and the lighter literature of that age.

had formed the majority of the House of Lords, had, in wealth
and splendour, equalled, and sometimes outshone, the greatest
of the temporal barons, and had generally held the highest
civil offices. The Lord Treasurer was often a Bishop. The
Lord Chancellor was almost always so. The Lord Keeper of
the Privy Seal and the Master of the Rolls were ordinarily
churchmen. Churchmen transacted the most important diplomatic business. Indeed, almost all that large portion of the
administration which rude and warlike nobles were incompetent to conduct was considered as especially belonging to
divines. Men, therefore, who were averse to the life of camps,
and who were, at the same time, desirous to rise in the state,
ordinarily received the tonsure. Among them were sons of all
the most illustrious families, and near kinsmen of the throne,
Scroops and Nevilles, Bourchiers, Staffords, and Poles. To
the religious houses belonged the rents of immense domains,
and all that large portion of the tithe which is now in the hands
of laymen. Down to the middle of the reign of Henry the
Eighth, therefore, no line of life bore so inviting an aspect to
ambitious and covetous natures as the priesthood. Then came
a violent revolution. The abolition of the monasteries deprived the Church at once of the greater part of her wealth,
and of her predominance in the Upper House of Parliament.
There was no longer an Abbot of Glastonbury or an Abbot of
Reading seated among the peers, and possessed of revenues
equal to those of a powerful Earl. The princely splendour of
William of Wykeham and of William of Waynflete had disappeared. The scarlet hat of the Cardinal, the silver cross of the
Legate, were no more. The clergy had also lost the ascendency which is the natural reward of superior mental cultivation. Once the circumstance that a man could read had
raised a presumption that he was in orders. But, in an age
which produced such laymen as William Cecil and Nicholas
Bacon, Roger Ascham and Thomas Smith, Walter Mildmay

and Francis Walsingham, there was no reason for calling away
prelates from their dioceses to negotiate treaties, to super-
intend the finances, or to administer justice.   The spiritual
character not only ceased to be a qualification for high civil
office, but began to be regarded as a disqualification.   Those
worldly motives, therefore, which had formerly induced so
many able, aspiring, and high born youths to assume the ecclesiastical habit, ceased to operate.   Not one parish in two
hundred then afforded what a man of family considered as a
maintenance.   There were still indeed prizes in the Church:
but they were few; and even the highest were mean, when
compared with the glory which had once surrounded the
princes of the hierarchy.   The state kept by Parker and
Grindal seemed beggarly to those who remembered the imperial pomp of Wolsey, his palaces, which had become the
favourite abodes of royalty, Whitehall and Hampton Court,
the three sumptuous tables daily spread in his refectory, the
forty-four gorgeous copes in his chapel, his running footmen
in rich liveries, and his body guards with gilded pole-axes.
Thus the sacerdotal office lost its attraction for the higher
classes.   During the century which followed the accession of
Elizabeth, scarce a single person of noble descent took orders.
At the close of the reign of Charles the Second, two sons of
peers were Bishops; four or five sons of peers were priests, and
held valuable preferment: but these rare exceptions did not
take away the reproach which lay on the body.   The clergy
were regarded as, on the whole, a plebeian class.   And, indeed, for one who made the figure of a gentleman, ten were
mere menial servants.   A large proportion of those divines
who had no benefices, or whose benefices were too small to
afford a comfortable revenue, lived in the houses of laymen. It
had long been evident that this practice tended to degrade the
priestly character.   Laud had exerted himself to effect a
change; and Charles the First had repeatedly issued positive

orders that none but men of high rank should presume to keep
domestic chaplains. * But these injunctions had become obsolete. Indeed, during the domination of the Puritans, many
of the ejected ministers of the Church of England could obtain
bread and shelter only by attaching themselves to the households of royalist gentlemen; and the habits which had been
formed in those times of trouble continued long after the reestablishment of monarchy and episcopacy. In the mansions
of men of liberal sentiments and cultivated understandings,
the chaplain was doubtless treated with urbanity and kindness.
His conversation, his literary assistance, his spiritual advice,
were considered as an ample return for his food, his lodging,
and his stipend. But this was not the general feeling of the
country gentlemen. The coarse and ignorant squire who
thought that it belonged to his dignity to have grace said
every day at his table by an ecclesiastic in full canonicals,
found means to reconcile dignity with economy. A young
Levite — such was the phrase then in use — might be had for
his board, a small garret, and ten pounds a year, and might not
only perform his own professional functions, might not only be
the most patient of butts and of listeners, might not only be
always ready in fine weather for bowls, and in rainy weather
for shovel-board, but might also save the expense of a gardener,
or of a groom. Sometimes the reverend man nailed up the
apricots, and sometimes he curried the coach horses. He cast
up the farrier's bills. He walked ten miles with a message or a
parcel. He was permitted to dine with the family; but he was
expected to content himself with the plainest fare. He might fill
himself with the corned beef and the carrots: but, as soon as the
tarts and cheese-cakes made their appearance, he quitted his
seat, and stood aloof till he was summoned to return thanks for
the repast, from a great part of which he had been excluded. **

     * See Heylin's Cyprianus Anglicus.
     ** Eachard, Causes of the Contempt of the Clergy; Oldham, Satire

Perhaps, after some years of service, he was presented CHAP. III. to a living sufficient to support him: but he often found it necessary to purchase his preferment by a species of Simony, which furnished an inexhaustible subject of pleasantry to three or four generations of scoffers. With his cure he was expected to take a wife. The wife had ordinarily been in the patron's service; and it was well if she was not suspected of standing too high in the patron's favour. Indeed, the nature of the matrimonial connections which the clergymen of that age were in the habit of forming is the most certain indication of the place which the order held in the social system. An Oxonian, writing a few months after the death of Charles the Second, complained bitterly, not only that the country attorney and the country apothecary looked down with disdain on the country clergyman, but that one of the lessons most earnestly inculcated on every girl of honourable family was to give no encouragement to a lover in orders, and that, if any young lady forgot this precept, she was almost as much disgraced as by an illicit amour.* Clarendon, who assuredly bore no ill will to the Church, mentions it as a sign of the confusion of ranks which the great rebellion had produced, that some damsels of noble families had bestowed themselves on divines.** A waiting woman was generally considered as the most suitable helpmate for a parson. Queen Elizabeth, as head of the Church, had given what seemed to be a formal sanction to this prejudice, by issuing special orders that no

---

addressed to a Friend about to leave the University; Tatler, 255. 258. That the English clergy were a lowborn class, is remarked in the Travels of the Grand Duke Cosmo, Appendix A.

* "A causidico, medicastro, ipsaque artificum farragine, ecclesiæ rector aut vicarius contemnitur et fit ludibrio. Gentis et familiæ nitor sacris ordinibus pollutus censetur: fœminisque natalitio insignibus unicum inculcatur sæpius præceptum, ne modestiæ naufragium, faciant, aut, (quod idem auribus tam delicatulis sonat,) ne clerico se nuptas dari patiantur." Angliæ Notitia, by T. Wood, of New College, Oxford, 1686.

** Clarendon's Life, ii. 21.

clergyman should presume to marry a servant girl, without the consent of the master or mistress. * During several generations accordingly the relation between priests and handmaidens was a theme for endless jest; nor would it be easy to find, in the comedy of the seventeenth century, a single instance of a clergyman who wins a spouse above the rank of a cook.** Even so late as the time of George the Second, the keenest of all observers of life and manners, himself a priest, remarked that, in a great household, the chaplain was the resource of a lady's maid whose character had been blown upon, and who was therefore forced to give up hopes of catching the steward.***

In general the divine who quitted his chaplainship for a benefice and a wife found that he had only exchanged one class of vexations for another. Not one living in fifty enabled the incumbent to bring up a family comfortably. As children multiplied and grew, the household of the priest became more and more beggarly. Holes appeared more and more plainly in the thatch of his parsonage and in his single cassock. Often it was only by toiling on his glebe, by feeding swine, and by loading dung-carts, that he could obtain daily bread; nor did his utmost exertions always prevent the bailiffs from taking his concordance and his inkstand in execution. It was a white day on which he was admitted into the kitchen of a great house, and regaled by the servants with cold meat and ale. His children were brought up like the children of the neighbouring peasantry. His boys followed the plough; and his girls went out to service. Study he

* See the Injunctions of 1559, in Bishop Sparrow's Collection. Jeremy Collier, in his Essay on Pride, speaks of this injunction with a bitterness which proves that his own pride had not been effectually tamed.

** Roger and Abigail in Fletcher's Scornful Lady, Bull and the Nurse in Vanbrugh's Relapse, Smirk and Susan in Shadwell's Lancashire Witches, are instances.

*** Swift's Directions to Servants.

found impossible: for the advowson of his living would hardly have sold for a sum sufficient to purchase a good theological library; and he might be considered as unusually lucky if he had ten or twelve dog-eared volumes among the pots and pans on his shelves. Even a keen and strong intellect might be expected to rust in so unfavourable a tuation.

Assuredly there was at that time no lack in the English Church of ministers distinguished by abilities and learning. But it is to be observed that these ministers were not scattered among the rural population. They were brought together at a few places where the means of acquiring knowledge were abundant, and where the opportunities of vigorous intellectual exercise were frequent. * At such places were to be found divines qualified by parts, by eloquence, by wide knowledge of literature, of science, and of life, to defend their Church victoriously against heretics and sceptics, to command the attention of frivolous and worldly congregations, to guide the deliberations of senates, and to make religion respectable, even in the most dissolute of courts. Some laboured to fathom the abysses of metaphysical theology; some were deeply versed in biblical criticism; and some threw light on the darkest parts of ecclesiastical history. Some proved themselves consummate masters of logic. Some cultivated rhetoric with such assiduity and success that their discourses are still justly valued as models of style. These eminent men were to be found, with scarce a single exception, at the Universities, at the great Cathedrals, or in the capital. Barrow had lately died at Cambridge; and Pearson had gone thence to the episcopal bench. Cudworth and Henry More were still living there. South and Pococke, Jane and Aldrich,

---

* This distinction between country clergy and town clergy is strongly marked by Eachard, and cannot but be observed by every person who has studied the ecclesiastical history of that age.

were at Oxford. Prideaux was in the close of Norwich, and Whitby in the close of Salisbury. But it was chiefly by the London clergy, who were always spoken of as a class apart, that the fame of their profession for learning and eloquence was upheld. The principal pulpits of the metropolis were occupied about this time by a crowd of distinguished men, from among whom was selected a large proportion of the rulers of the Church. Sherlock preached at the Temple, Tillotson at Lincoln's Inn, Wake and Jeremy Collier at Gray's Inn, Burnet at the Rolls, Stillingfleet at St. Paul's Cathedral, Patrick at St. Paul's, Covent Garden, Fowler at St. Giles's, Cripplegate, Sharp at St. Giles's in the Fields, Tenison at St. Martin's, Sprat at St. Margaret's, Beveridge at St. Peter's in Cornhill. Of these twelve men, all of high note in ecclesiastical history, ten became Bishops, and four Archbishops. Meanwhile almost the only important theological works which came forth from a rural parsonage were those of George Bull, afterwards Bishop of St. David's; and Bull never would have produced those works, had he not inherited an estate, by the sale of which he was enabled to collect a library, such as probably no other country clergyman in England possessed. *

Thus the Anglican priesthood was divided into two sections, which, in acquirements, in manners, and in social position, differed widely from each other. One section, trained for cities and courts, comprised men familiar with all ancient and modern learning; men able to encounter Hobbes or Bossuet at all the weapons of controversy; men who could, in their sermons, set forth the majesty and beauty of Christianity with such justness of thought, and such energy of language, that the indolent Charles roused himself to listen,

---

* Nelson's Life of Bull. As to the extreme difficulty which the country clergy found in procuring books, see the Life of Thomas Bray, the founder of the Society for the Propagation of the Gospel.

and the fastidious Buckingham forgot to sneer; men whose address, politeness, and knowledge of the world qualified them to manage the consciences of the wealthy and noble; men with whom Halifax loved to discuss the interests of empires, and from whom Dryden was not ashamed to own that he had learned to write.* The other section was destined to ruder and humbler service. It was dispersed over the country, and consisted chiefly of persons not at all wealthier, and not much more refined, than small farmers or upper servants. Yet it was in these rustic priests, who derived but a scanty subsistence from their tithe sheaves and tithe pigs, and who had not the smallest chance of ever attaining high professional honours, that the professional spirit was strongest. Among those divines who were the boast of the Universities and the delight of the capital, and who had attained, or might reasonably expect to attain, opulence and lordly rank, a party, respectable in numbers, and more respectable in character, leaned towards constitutional principles of government, lived on friendly terms with Presbyterians, Independents, and Baptists, would gladly have seen a full toleration granted to all Protestant sects, and would even have consented to make alterations in the Liturgy, for the purpose of conciliating honest and candid Nonconformists. But such latitudinarianism was held in horror by the country parson. He was, indeed, prouder of his ragged gown than his superiors of their lawn and of their scarlet hoods. The very consciousness that there was little in his worldly circumstances to distinguish him from the villagers to whom he preached led him to hold immoderately high the dignity of that sacerdotal office which was his single title to reverence. Having lived in seclusion,

---

* "I have frequently heard him (Dryden) own with pleasure, that if he had any talent for English prose it was owing to his having often read the writings of the great Archbishop Tillotson." Congreve's Dedication of Dryden's Plays.

and having had little opportunity of correcting his opinions by
reading or conversation, he held and taught the doctrines of
indefeasible hereditary right, of passive obedience, and of
nonresistance in all their crude absurdity. Having been long
engaged in a petty war against the neighbouring dissenters,
he too often hated them for the wrongs which he had done
them, and found no fault with the Five Mile Act and the Conventicle Act, except that those odious laws had not a sharper
edge. Whatever influence his office gave him was exerted
with passionate zeal on the Tory side; and that influence was
immense. It would be a great error to imagine, because the
country rector was in general not regarded as a gentleman,
because he could not dare to aspire to the hand of one of the
young ladies at the manor house, because he was not asked
into the parlours of the great, but was left to drink and smoke
with grooms and butlers, that the power of the clerical body
was smaller than at present. The influence of a class is by no
means proportioned to the consideration which the members
of that class enjoy in their individual capacity. A Cardinal is
a much more exalted personage than a begging friar: but it
would be a grievous mistake to suppose that the College of
Cardinals has exercised a greater dominion over the public
mind of Europe than the Order of Saint Francis. In Ireland,
at present, a peer holds a far higher station in society than a
Roman Catholic priest: yet there are in Munster and Connaught few counties where a combination of priests would not
carry an election against a combination of peers. In the
seventeenth century the pulpit was to a large portion of the
population what the periodical press now is. Scarce any of
the clowns who came to the parish church ever saw a Gazette
or a political pamphlet. Ill informed as their spiritual pastor
might be, he was yet better informed than themselves: he
had every week an opportunity of haranguing them; and his
harangues were never answered. At every important con-

juncture, invectives against the Whigs and exhortations to CHAP.
III. obey the Lord's anointed resounded at once from many thousands of pulpits; and the effect was formidable indeed. Of all the causes which, after the dissolution of the Oxford Parliament, produced the violent reaction against the Exclusionists, the most potent seems to have been the oratory of the country clergy.

The power which the country gentlemen and the country clergymen exercised in the rural districts was in some measure The yeo-
manry. counterbalanced by the power of the yeomanry, an eminently manly and truehearted race. The petty proprietors who cultivated their own fields with their own hands, and enjoyed a modest competence, without affecting to have scutcheons and crests, or aspiring to sit on the bench of justice, then formed a much more important part of the nation than at present. If we may trust the best statistical writers of that age, not less than a hundred and sixty thousand proprietors, who with their families must have made up more than a seventh of the whole population, derived their subsistence from little freehold estates. The average income of these small landholders, an income made up of rent, profit, and wages, was estimated at between sixty and seventy pounds a year. It was computed that the number of persons who tilled their own land was greater than the number of those who farmed the land of others.* A large portion of the yeomanry had, from the time of the Reformation, leaned towards Puritanism, had, in the civil war, taken the side of the Parliament, had, after the Restoration, persisted in hearing Presbyterian and Independent preachers, had, at elections, strenuously supported the Exclusionists, and had continued, even after the discovery of the Rye House plot and the proscription of the Whig leaders, to regard Popery and arbitrary power with unmitigated hostility.

* I have taken Davenant's estimate, which is a little lower than King's.

Great as has been the change in the rural life of England since the Revolution, the change which has come to pass in the cities is still more amazing. At present a sixth part of the nation is crowded into provincial towns of more than thirty thousand inhabitants. In the reign of Charles the Second no provincial town in the kingdom contained thirty thousand inhabitants; and only four provincial towns contained so many as ten thousand inhabitants.

Next to the capital, but next at an immense distance, stood Bristol, then the first English seaport, and Norwich, then the first English manufacturing town. Both have since that time been far outstripped by younger rivals; yet both have made great positive advances. The population of Bristol has quadrupled. The population of Norwich has more than doubled.

Pepys, who visited Bristol eight years after the Restoration, was struck by the splendour of the city. But his standard was not high; for he noted down as a wonder the circumstance that, in Bristol, a man might look round him and see nothing but houses. It seems that, in no other place with which he was acquainted, except London, did the buildings completely shut out the woods and fields. Large as Bristol might then appear, it occupied but a very small portion of the area on which it now stands. A few churches of eminent beauty rose out of a labyrinth of narrow lanes built upon vaults of no great solidity. If a coach or a cart entered those alleys, there was danger that it would be wedged between the houses, and danger also that it would break in the cellars. Goods were therefore conveyed about the town almost exclusively in trucks drawn by dogs; and the richest inhabitants exhibited their wealth, not by riding in gilded carriages, but by walking the streets with trains of servants in rich liveries, and by keeping tables loaded with good cheer. The pomp of the christenings and burials far exceeded what was seen at any other place in England. The hospitality of the city was widely renowned, and especially the collations with which the sugar refiners regaled their visitors. The repast was dressed in the furnace, and was accompanied by a rich brewage made of the best Spanish wine, and celebrated over the whole kingdom as Bristol milk. This luxury was supported by a thriving trade with the North American plantations and with the West Indies. The passion for colonial traffic was so strong that there was scarce a small shopkeeper in Bristol who had not a venture on board of some ship bound for Virginia or the Antilles. Some of these ventures indeed were not of the most honourable kind. There was, in the Transatlantic possessions of the crown, a great demand for labour; and this demand was partly supplied by a system of crimping and kidnapping at the principal English seaports. Nowhere was this system found in such active and extensive operation as at Bristol. Even the first magistrates of that city were not ashamed to enrich themselves by so odious a commerce. The number of houses appears, from the returns of the hearth money, to have been, in the year 1685, just five thousand three hundred. We can hardly suppose the number of persons in a house to have been greater than in the City of London; and in the City of London we learn from the best authority that there were then fifty-five persons to ten houses. The population of Bristol must therefore have been about twenty-nine thousand souls.*

* Evelyn's Diary, June 27. 1654; Pepys's Diary, June 13. 1668; Roger North's Lives of Lord Keeper Guildford, and of Sir Dudley North; Petty's Political Arithmetic. I have taken Petty's facts, but, in drawing inferences from them, I have been guided by King and Davenant, who, though not abler men than he, had the advantage of coming after him. As to the kidnapping for which Bristol was infamous, see North's Life of Guildford, 121. 216., and the harangue of Jeffreys on the subject, in the Impartial History of his Life and Death, printed with the Bloody Assizes. His style was, as usual, coarse; but I cannot reckon the reprimand which he gave to the magistrates of Bristol among his crimes.

Norwich was the capital of a large and fruitful province. It was the residence of a Bishop and of a chapter. It was the chief seat of the chief manufacture of the realm. Some men distinguished by learning and science had recently dwelt there; and no place in the kingdom, except the capital and the Universities, had more attractions for the curious. The library, the museum, the aviary, and the botanical garden of Sir Thomas Browne, were thought by Fellows of the Royal Society well worthy of a long pilgrimage. Norwich had also a court in miniature. In the heart of the city stood an old palace of the Dukes of Norfolk, said to be the largest town house in the kingdom out of London. In this mansion, to which were annexed a tennis court, a bowling green, and a wilderness, stretching along the banks of the Wansum, the noble family of Howard frequently resided, and kept a state resembling that of petty sovereigns. Drink was served to guests in goblets of pure gold. The very tongs and shovels were of silver. Pictures by Italian masters adorned the walls. The cabinets were filled with a fine collection of gems purchased by that Earl of Arunded whose marbles are now among the ornaments of Oxford. Here, in the year 1671, Charles and his court were sumptuously entertained. Here, too, all comers were annually welcomed, from Christmas to Twelfth Night. Ale flowed in oceans for the populace. Three coaches, one of which had been built at a cost of five hundred pounds to contain fourteen persons, were sent every afternoon round the city to bring ladies to the festivities; and the dances were always followed by a luxurious banquet. When the Duke of Norfolk came to Norwich, he was greeted like a King returning to his capital. The bells of the Cathedral and of Saint Peter Mancroft were rung: the guns of the Castle were fired; and the Mayor and Aldermen waited on their illustrious fellow citizen with complimentary addresses. In the year 1693 the population of Norwich was found, by actual enume-

ration, to be between twenty-eight and twenty-nine thousand CHAP.
III.
souls.*

Far below Norwich, but still high in dignity and importance, were some other ancient capitals of shires. In that
age it was seldom that a country gentleman went up with his
family to London. The county town was his metropolis. He
sometimes made it his residence during part of the year. At
all events, he was often attracted thither by business and
pleasure, by assizes, quarter sessions, elections, musters of
militia, festivals, and races. There were the halls where the
judges, robed in scarlet and escorted by javelins and trum-
pets, opened the King's commission twice a year. There
were the markets at which the corn, the cattle, the wool, and
the hops of the surrounding country were exposed to sale.
There were the great fairs to which merchants came down
from London, and where the rural dealer laid in his annual
stores of sugar, stationery, cutlery, and muslin. There were
the shops at which the best families of the neighbourhood
bought grocery and millinery. Some of these places derived
dignity from interesting historical recollections, from cathedrals decorated by all the art and magnificence of the middle
ages, from palaces where a long succession of prelates had
dwelt, from closes surrounded by the venerable abodes of
deans and canons, and from castles which had in the old time
repelled the Nevilles or De Veres, and which bore more recent traces of the vengeance of Rupert or of Cromwell.

Conspicuous amongst these interesting cities were York, Other
the capital of the north, and Exeter, the capital of the country
towns.
west. Neither can have contained much more than ten thousand in habitants. Worcester, the queen of the cider land,
had about eight thousand; Nottingham probably as many.

* Fuller's Worthies; Evelyn's Diary, Oct. 17. 1671; Journal of E.
Browne, son of Sir Thomas Browne, Jan. 166¾; Blomefield's History of
Norfolk; History of the City and County of Norwich, 2 vols. 1768.

Gloucester, renowned for that resolute defence which had been
fatal to Charles the First, had certainly between four and five
thousand; Derby not quite four thousand. Shrewsbury was
the chief place of an extensive and fertile district. The court
of the marches of Wales was held there. In the language of the
gentry many miles round the Wrekin, to go to Shrewsbury
was to go to town. The provincial wits and beauties imitated,
as well as they could, the fashions of Saint James's Park, in
the walks along the side of the Severn. The inhabitants were
about seven thousand.*

The population of every one of these places has, since the
Revolution, much more than doubled. The population of
some has multiplied sevenfold. The streets have been almost
entirely rebuilt. Slate has succeeded to thatch, and brick to
timber. The pavements and the lamps, the display of wealth
in the principal shops, and the luxurious neatness of the dwellings occupied by the gentry would, in the seventeenth century, have seemed miraculous. Yet is the relative importance
of the old capitals of counties by no means what it was.
Younger towns, towns which are rarely or never mentioned
in our early history and which sent no representatives to our
early Parliaments, have, within the memory of persons still

* The population of York appears, from the return of baptisms and
burials, in Drake's History, to have been about 13,000 in 1730. Exeter
had only 17,000 inhabitants in 1801. The population of Worcester was
numbered just before the siege in 1646. See Nash's History of Wor-
cestershire. I have made allowance for the increase which must be supposed to have taken place in forty years. In 1740, the population of
Nottingham was found, by enumeration, to be just 10,000. See Dering's
History. The population of Gloucester may readily be inferred from
the number of houses which King found in the returns of hearth money,
and from the number of births and burials which is given in Atkyns's
History. The population of Derby was 4000 in 1712. See Wolley's MS.
History, quoted in Lyson's Magna Britannia. The population of Shrewsbury was ascertained, in 1695, by actual enumeration. As to the gaieties
of Shrewsbury, see Farquhar's Recruiting Officer. Farquhar's description is borne out by a ballad in the Pepysian Library, of which the
burden is " Shrewsbury for me."

living, grown to a greatness which this generation contem- CHAP.
plates with wonder and pride, not unaccompanied by awe and III.
anxiety.

The most eminent of these towns were indeed known in Man-
the seventeenth century as respectable seats of industry. Nay, chester.
their rapid progress and their vast opulence were then sometimes described in language which seems ludicrous to a man
who has seen their present grandeur. One of the most populous and prosperous among them was Manchester. It had
been required by the Protector to send one representative to
his Parliament, and was mentioned by writers of the time of
Charles the Second as a busy and opulent place. Cotton had,
during half a century, been brought thither from Cyprus and
Smyrna; but the manufacture was in its infancy. Whitney
had not yet taught how the raw material might be furnished in
quantities almost fabulous. Arkwright had yet not taught
how it might be worked up with a speed and precision which
seem magical. The whole annual import did not, at the end
of the seventeenth century, amount to two millions of pounds,
a quantity which would now hardly supply the demand of
forty-eight hours. That wonderful emporium, which in population and wealth far surpasses capitals so much renowned
as Berlin, Madrid, and Lisbon, was then a mean and ill built
market town, containing under six thousand people. It then
had not a single press. It now supports a hundred printing
establishments. It then had not a single coach. It now supports twenty coach-makers.*

Leeds was already the chief seat of the woollen manu- Leeds.
factures of Yorkshire: but the elderly inhabitants could still

* Blome's Britannia, 1673; Aikin's Country round Manchester; Manchester Directory, 1845; Baines, History of the Cotton Manufacture.
The best information which I have been able to find, touching the population of Manchester in the seventeenth century, is contained in a
paper drawn up by the Reverend R. Parkinson, and published in the
Journal of the Statistical Society for October, 1842.

CHAP.
III.
remember the time when the first brick house, then and long after called the Red House, was built. They boasted loudly of their increasing wealth, and of the immense sales of cloth which took place in the open air on the bridge. Hundreds, nay thousands of pounds, had been paid down in the course of one busy market day. The rising importance of Leeds had attracted the notice of successive governments. Charles the First had granted municipal privileges to the town. Oliver had invited it to send one member to the House of Commons. But from the returns of the hearth money it seems certain that the whole population of the borough, an extensive district which contains many hamlets, did not, in the reign of Charles the Second, exceed seven thousand souls. In 1841 there were more than a hundred and fifty thousand.*

Sheffield.
About a day's journey south of Leeds, on the verge of a wild moorland tract, lay an ancient manor, now rich with cultivation, then barren and uninclosed, which was known by the name of Hallamshire. Iron abounded there; and, from a very early period, the rude whittles fabricated there had been sold all over the kingdom. They had indeed been mentioned by Geoffrey Chaucer in one of his Canterbury Tales. But the manufacture appears to have made little progress during the three centuries which followed his time. This languor may perhaps be explained by the fact that the trade was, during almost the whole of this long period, subject to such regulations as the lord and his court leet thought fit to impose. The more delicate kinds of cutlery were either made in the capital, or brought from the Continent. It was not indeed till the reign of George the First that the English surgeons ceased to import from France those exquisitely fine blades which are required for operations on the human frame. Most of the Hallamshire forges were collected in a market town which

* Thoresby's Ducatus Leodensis: Whitaker's Loidis and Elmete; Wardell's Municipal History of the Borough of Leeds.

had sprung up near the castle of the proprietor, and which, in the reign of James the First, had been a singularly miserable place, containing about two thousand inhabitants, of whom a third were half starved and half naked beggars. It seems certain from the parochial registers that the population did not amount to four thousand at the end of the reign of Charles the Second. The effects of a species of toil singularly unfavourable to the health and vigour of the human frame were at once discerned by every traveller. A large proportion of the people had distorted limbs. This is that Sheffield which now, with is dependencies, contains a hundred and twenty thousand souls, and which sends forth its admirable knives, razors, and lancets to the farthest ends of the world. *

Birmingham had not been thought of sufficient importance to send a member to Oliver's Parliament. Yet the manufacturers of Birmingham were already a busy and thriving race. They boasted that their hardware was highly esteemed, not indeed as now, at Pekin and Lima, at Bokhara and Timbuctoo, but in London, and even as far off as Ireland. They had acquired a less honourable renown as coiners of bad money. In allusion to their spurious groats, the Tory party had fixed on demagogues, who hypocritically affected zeal against Popery, the nickname of Birminghams. Yet in 1685 the population, which is now little less than two hundred thousand, did not amount to four thousand. Birmingham buttons were just beginning to be known: of Birmingham guns nobody had yet heard; and the place whence, two generations later, the magnificent editions of Baskerville went forth to astonish all the librarians of Europe, did not contain a single regular shop were a Bible or an almanack could be bought. On market days a bookseller named Michael Johnson, the father of the great Samuel Johnson, came over

CHAP.
III.

Birmingham.

* Hunter's History of Hallamshire.

from Lichfield, and opened a stall during a few hours. This supply of literature was long found adequate to the demand. *

These four chief seats of our great manufactures deserve especial mention. It would be tedious to enumerate all the populous and opulent hives of industry which, a hundred and fifty years ago, were hamlets without a parish church, or desolate moors, inhabited only by grouse and wild deer. Nor has the change been less signal in those outlets by which the products of the English looms and forges are poured forth over the whole world. At present Liverpool contains about three hundred thousand inhabitants. The shipping registered at her port amounts to between four and five hundred thousand tons. Into her custom house has been repeatedly paid in one year a sum more than thrice as great as the whole income of the English crown in 1685. The receipts of her post office, even since the great reduction of the duty, exceed the sum which the postage of the whole kingdom yielded to the Duke of York. Her endless docks, quays and warehouses are among the wonders of the world. Yet even those docks and quays and warehouses seem hardly to suffice for the gigantic trade of the Mersey; and already a rival city is growing fast on the opposite shore. In the days of Charles the Second Liverpool was described as a rising town which had recently made great advances, and which maintained a profitable intercourse with Ireland and with the sugar colonies. The customs had multiplied eightfold within sixteen years, and amounted to what was then considered as the immense sum of fifteen thousand pounds annually. But the

Liver-
pool.

* Blome's Britannia, 1673; Dugdale's Warwickshire; North's Examen, 321.; Preface to Absalom and Achitophel; Hutton's History of Birmingham; Boswell's Life of Johnson. In 1690 the burials at Birmingham were 150, the baptisms 125. I think it probable that the annual mortality was little less than one in twenty-five. In London it was considerably greater. A historian of Nottingham, half a century later, boasted of the extraordinary salubrity of his town, where the annual mortality was one in thirty. See Dering's History of Nottingham.

population can hardly have exceeded four thousand: the ^{CHAP.} ^{III.} shipping was about fourteen hundred tons, less than the tonnage of a single modern Indiaman of the first class; and the whole number of seamen belonging to the port cannot be estimated at more than two hundred. *

Such has been the progress of those towns where wealth is Watering created and accumulated. Not less rapid has been the pro- places. gress of towns of a very different kind, towns in which wealth, created and accumulated elsewhere, is expended for purposes of health and recreation. Some of the most remarkable of these towns have sprung into existence since the time of the Stuarts. Cheltenham is now a greater city than any which the Cheltenham. kingdom contained in the seventeenth century, London alone excepted. But in the seventeenth century, and at the beginning of the eighteenth, Cheltenham was mentioned by local historians merely as a rural parish lying under the Cotswold Hills, and affording good ground, both for tillage and pasture. Corn grew and cattle browsed over the space now covered by that gay succession of streets and villas.** Brighton was described as a place which had once been Brighton. thriving, which had possessed many small fishing barks, and which had, when at the height of prosperity, contained above two thousand inhabitants, but which was sinking fast into decay. The sea was gradually gaining on the buildings, which at length almost entirely disappeared. Ninety years ago the ruins of an old fort were to be seen lying among the pebbles and seaweed on the beach; and ancient men could still point out the traces of foundations on a spot where a street of more than a hundred huts had been swallowed up by the waves.

* Blome's Britannia; Gregson's Antiquities of the County Palatine and Duchy of Lancaster, Part II.; Petition from Liverpool in the Privy Council Book, May 10. 1686. In 1690 the burials at Liverpool were 151, the baptisms 120. In 1844 the net receipt of the customs at Liverpool was 4,365,526l. 1s. 8d.

** Atkyns's Gloucestershire.

So desolate was the place after this calamity, that the vicarage
was thought scarcely worth having. A few poor fishermen,
however, still continued to dry their nets on those cliffs, on
which now a town, more than twice as large and populous as
the Bristol of the Stuarts, presents, mile after mile, its gay
and fantastic front to the sea. *

England, however, was not, in the seventeenth century,
destitute of watering places. The gentry of Derbyshire and
Buxton.
of the neighbouring counties repaired to Buxton, where they
were crowded into low wooden sheds, and regaled with
oat-cake, and with a viand which the hosts called mutton,
but which the guests strongly suspected to be dog.** Tun-
Tun-
bridge
Wells.
bridge Wells, lying within a day's journey of the capital, and
in one of the richest and most highly civilised parts of the
kingdom, had much greater attractions. At present we see
there a town which would, a hundred and sixty years ago,
have ranked, in population, fourth or fifth among the towns
of England. The brilliancy of the shops and the luxury of
the private dwellings far surpasses anything that England
could then show. When the court, soon after the Restoration, visited Tunbridge Wells, there was no town: but,
within a mile of the spring, rustic cottages, somewhat cleaner
and neater than the ordinary cottages of that time, were
scattered over the heath. Some of these cabins were moveable, and were carried on sledges from one part of the common to another. To these huts men of fashion, wearied with
the din and smoke of London, sometimes came in the summer
to breathe fresh air, and to catch a glimpse of rural life.
During the season a kind of fair was daily held near the
fountain. The wives and daughters of the Kentish farmers
came from the neighbouring villages with cream, cherries,

---

    * Magna Britannia; Grose's Antiquities; New Brighthelmstone Di-
rectory, 1770.
    ** Tour in Derbyshire, by Thomas Browne, son of Sir Thomas.

wheatears, and quails. To chaffer with them, to flirt with
them, to praise their straw hats and tight heels, was a
refreshing pastime to voluptuaries sick of the airs of actresses
and maids of honour. Milliners, toymen, and jewellers
came down from London, and opened a bazaar under the
trees. In one booth the politician might find his coffee and
the London Gazette; in another were gamblers playing deep
at basset; and, on fine evenings, the fiddles were in attendance, and there were morris dances on the elastic turf of
the bowling green. In 1685 a subscription had just been
raised among those who frequented the wells for building a
church, which the Tories, who then domineered everywhere,
insisted on dedicating to Saint Charles the Martyr.*

But at the head of the English watering places, without a
rival, was Bath. The springs of that city had been renowned Bath.
from the days of the Romans. It had been, during many
centuries, the seat of a Bishop. The sick repaired thither
from every part of the realm. The King sometimes held his
court there. Nevertheless, Bath was then a maze of only
four or five hundred houses, crowded within an old wall in the
vicinity of the Avon. Pictures of what were considered as
the finest of those houses are still extant, and greatly resemble
the lowest rag shops and pot-houses of Radcliffe Highway.
Even then, indeed, travellers complained of the narrowness
and meanness of the streets. That beautiful city which
charms even eyes familiar with the masterpieces of Bramante
and Palladio, and which the genius of Anstey and of Smollett,
of Frances Burney and of Jane Austen, has made classic
ground, had not begun to exist. Milsom Street itself was an
open field lying far beyond the walls; and hedgerows intersected the space which is now covered by the Crescent and

* Mémoires de Grammont; Hasted's History of Kent; Tunbridge
Wells, a Comedy, 1678; Causton's Tunbridgialia, 1688; Metellus, a poem
on Tunbridge Wells, 1693.

the Circus. The poor patients to whom the waters had been recommended lay on straw in a place which, to use the language of a contemporary physician, was a covert rather than a lodging. As to the comforts and luxuries which were to be found in the interior of the houses of Bath by the fashionable visitors who resorted thither in search of health or amusement, we possess information more complete and minute than can generally be obtained on such subjects. A writer who published an account of that city about sixty years after the Revolution has accurately described the changes which had taken place within his own recollection. He assures us that in his younger days the gentlemen who visited the springs slept in rooms hardly as good as the garrets which he lived to see occupied by footmen. The floors of the dining rooms were uncarpeted, and were coloured brown with a wash made of soot and small beer, in order to hide the dirt. Not a wainscot was painted. Not a hearth or a chimney-piece was of marble. A slab of common freestone and fire irons which had cost from three to four shillings were thought sufficient for any fire-place. The best apartments were hung with coarse woollen stuff, and were furnished with rush-bottomed chairs. Readers who take an interest in the progress of civilisation and of the useful arts will be grateful to the humble topographer who has recorded these facts, and will perhaps wish that historians of far higher pretensions had sometimes spared a few pages from military evolutions and political intrigues, for the purpose of letting us know how the parlours and bed-chambers of our ancestors looked. *

London. The position of London, relatively to the other towns

* See Wood's History of Bath, 1749; Evelyn's Diary, June 27. 1654; Pepys's Diary, June 12. 1668; Stukeley's Itinerarum Curiosum; Collinson's Somersetshire; Dr. Peirce's History and Memoirs of the Bath, 1713, book I. chap. viii. obs. 2. 1684. I have consulted several old maps and pictures of Bath, particularly one curious map which is surrounded by views of the principal buildings. It bears the date of 1717.

of the empire, was, in the time of Charles the Second, far
higher than at present. For at present the population of London is little more than six times the population of Manchester
or of Liverpool. In the days of Charles the Second the population of London was more than seventeen times the population of Bristol or of Norwich. It may be doubted whether
any other instance can be mentioned of a great kingdom in
which the first city was more than seventeen times as large as
the second. There is reason to believe that, in 1685, London
had been, during about half a century, the most populous
capital in Europe. The inhabitants, who are now at least
nineteen hundred thousand, where then probably little more
than half a million.* London had in the world only one commercial rival, now long outstripped, the mighty and opulent
Amsterdam. English writers boasted of the forest of masts
and yard-arms which covered the river from the Bridge to the
Tower, and of the stupendous sums which were collected at
the Custom House in Thames Street. There is, indeed, no
doubt that the trade of the metropolis then bore a far greater
proportion than at present to the whole trade of the country;
yet to our generation the honest vaunting of our ancestors
must appear almost ludicrous. The shipping which they
thought incredibly great appears not to have exceeded seventy thousand tons. This was, indeed, then more than a
third of the whole tonnage of the kingdom, but is now less
than a fourth of the tonnage of Newcastle, and is nearly
equalled by the tonnage of the steam vessels of the Thames.
The customs of London amounted, in 1685, to about three
hundred and thirty thousand pounds a year. In our time the
net duty paid annually, at the same place, exceeds ten millions.**

* According to King, 530,000.
** Macpherson's History of Commerce; Chalmers's Estimate; Chamberlayne's State of England, 1684. The tonnage of the steamers belonging to the port of London was, at the end of 1847, about 60,000 tons. The
customs of the port, from 1842 to 1845, very nearly averaged 11,000,000*l*.

Whoever examines the maps of London which were published towards the close of the reign of Charles the Second will see that only the nucleus of the present capital then existed. The town did not, as now, fade by imperceptible degrees into the country. No long avenues of villas, embowered in lilacs and laburnums, extended from the great centre of wealth and civilisation almost to the boundaries of Middlesex and far into the heart of Kent and Surrey. In the east, no part of the immense line of warehouses and artificial lakes which now spreads from the Tower to Blackwall had even been projected. On the west, scarcely one of those stately piles of building which are inhabited by the noble and wealthy was in existence; and Chelsea, which is now peopled by more than forty thousand human beings, was a quiet country village with about a thousand inhabitants.* On the north, cattle fed, and sportsmen wandered with dogs and guns, over the site of the borough of Marylebone, and over far the greater part of the space now covered by the boroughs of Finsbury and of the Tower Hamlets. Islington was almost a solitude; and poets loved to contrast its silence and repose with the din and turmoil of the monster London.** On the south the capital is now connected with its suburb by several bridges, not inferior in magnificence and solidity to the noblest works of the Cæsars. In 1685, a single line of irregular arches, overhung by piles of mean and crazy houses, and garnished, after a fashion worthy of the naked barbarians of Dahomy, with scores of mouldering heads, impeded the navigation of the river.

The City.
Of the metropolis, the City, properly so called, was the most important division. At the time of the Restoration it had been built, for the most part, of wood and plaster; the

* Lyson's Environs of London. The baptisms at Chelsea, between 1680 and 1690, were only forty-two a year.
** Cowley, Discourse of Solitude.

few bricks that were used were ill baked; the booths where
goods were exposed to sale projected far into the streets, and
were overhung by the upper stories. A few specimens of this
architecture may still be seen in those districts which were not
reached by the great fire. That fire had, in a few days,
covered a space of little less than a square mile with the ruins
of eighty-nine churches and of thirteen thousand houses.
But the City had risen again with a celerity which had excited
the admiration of neighbouring countries. Unfortunately,
the old lines of the streets had been to a great extent preserved; and those lines, originally traced in an age when even
princesses performed their journeys on horseback, were often
too narrow to allow wheeled carriages to pass each other with
ease, and were therefore ill adapted for the residence of
wealthy persons in an age when a coach and six was a fashionable luxury. The style of building was, however, far superior
to that of the City which had perished. The ordinary material
was brick, of much better quality than had formerly been
used. On the sites of the ancient parish churches had arisen
a multitude of new domes, towers, and spires which bore the
mark of the fertile genius of Wren. In every place save one
the traces of the great devastation had been completely effaced. But the crowds of workmen, the scaffolds and the
masses of hewn stone were still to be seen where the noblest
of Protestant temples was slowly rising on the ruins of the old
Cathedral of St. Paul.*

The whole character of the City has, since that time, undergone a complete change. At present the bankers, the mer-

* The fullest and most trustworthy information about the state of
the buildings of London at this time is to be derived from the maps and
drawings in the British Museum and in the Pepysian Library. The badness of the bricks in the old buildings of London is particularly mentioned in the Travels of the Grand Duke Cosmo. There is an account
of the works at St. Paul's in Ward's London Spy. I am almost ashamed
to quote such nauseous balderdash; but I have been forced to descend
even lower, if possible, in search of materials.

chants, and the chief shopkeepers repair thither on six morn-
ings of every week for the transaction of business: but they
reside in other quarters of the metropolis, or at suburban
country seats surrounded by shrubberies and flower gardens.
This revolution in private habits has produced a political revolution of no small importance. The City is no longer regarded
by the wealthiest traders with that attachment which every
man naturally feels for his home. It is no longer associated
in their minds with domestic affections and endearments.
The fireside, the nursery, the social table, the quiet bed are
not there. Lombard Street and Threadneedle Street are
merely places where men toil and accumulate. They go
elsewhere to enjoy and to expend. On a Sunday, or in an
evening after the hours of business, some courts and alleys,
which a few hours before had been alive with hurrying feet
and anxious faces, are as silent as the glades of a forest. The
chiefs of the mercantile interests are no longer citizens.
They avoid, they almost contemn, municipal honours and
duties. Those honours and duties are abandoned to men
who, though useful and highly respectable, seldom belong to
the princely commercial houses of which the names are renowned throughout the world.

In the seventeenth century the City was the merchant's
residence. Those mansions of the great old burghers which
still exist have been turned into counting houses and warehouses: but it is evident that they were originally not inferior
in magnificence to the dwellings which were then inhabited by
the nobility. They sometimes stand in retired and gloomy
courts, and are accessible only by inconvenient passages: but
their dimensions are ample, and their aspect stately. The
entrances are decorated with richly carved pillars and cano-
pies. The staircases and landing places are not wanting in
grandeur. The floors are sometimes of wood, tessellated
after the fashion of France. The palace of Sir Robert

Clayton, in the Old Jewry, contained a superb banqueting
room wainscoated with cedar, and adorned with battles of
gods and giants in fresco.* Sir Dudley North expended four
thousand pounds, a sum which would then have been important to a Duke, on the rich furniture of his reception rooms in
Basinghall Street.** In such abodes, under the last Stuarts,
the heads of the great firms lived splendidly and hospitably.
To their dwelling place they were bound by the strongest ties
of interest and affection. There they had passed their youth,
had made their friendships, had courted their wives, had seen
their children grow up, had laid the remains of their parents
in the earth, and expected that their own remains would be
laid. That intense patriotism which is peculiar to the members of societies congregated within a narrow space was, in
such circumstances, strongly developed. London was, to
the Londoner, what Athens was to the Athenian of the age of
Pericles, what Florence was to the Florentine of the fifteenth
century. The citizen was proud of the grandeur of his city,
punctilious about her claims to respect, ambitious of her
offices, and zealous for her franchises.

At the close of the reign of Charles the Second the pride
of the Londoners was smarting from a cruel mortification.
The old charter had been taken away; and the magistracy had
been remodelled. All the civic functionaries were Tories;
and the Whigs, though in numbers and in wealth superior to
their opponents, found themselves excluded from every local
dignity. Nevertheless, the external splendour of the municipal government was not diminished, nay, was rather increased
by this change. For, under the administration of some Puritans who had lately borne rule, the ancient fame of the city
for good cheer had declined: but under the new magistrates,
who belonged to a more festive party, and at whose boards

* Evelyn's Diary, Sept. 20. 1672.
** Roger North's Life of Sir Dudley North.

guests of rank and fashion from beyond Temple Bar were
often seen, the Guildhall and the halls of the great companies
were enlivened by many sumptuous banquets. During these
repasts, odes, composed by the poet laureate of the corporation, in praise of the King, the Duke, and the Mayor, were
sung to music. The drinking was deep, the shouting loud.
An observant Tory, who had often shared in these revels, has
remarked that the practice of huzzaing after drinking healths
dates from this joyous period. *

The magnificence displayed by the first civic magistrate
was almost regal. The gilded coach, indeed, which is now
annually admired by the crowd, was not yet a part of his
state. On great occasions he appeared on horseback, attended by a long cavalcade inferior in magnificence only to
that which, before a coronation, escorted the sovereign from
the Tower to Westminster. The Lord Mayor was never seen
in public without his rich robe, his hood of black velvet, his
gold chain, his jewel, and a great attendance of harbingers
and guards.** Nor did the world find anything ludicrous in
the pomp which constantly surrounded him. For it was not
more than proportioned to the place which, as wielding the
strength and representing the dignity of the City of London,
he was entitled to occupy in the state. That City, being then
not only without equal in the country, but without second,
had, during five and forty years, exercised almost as great
an influence on the politics of England as Paris has, in our
own time, exercised on the politics of France. In intelligence
London was greatly in advance of every other part of the
kingdom. A government, supported and trusted by London,

* North's Examen. This most amusing writer has preserved a specimen of the sublime raptures in which the Pindar of the City indulged: —
      " The worshipful Sir John Moor!
        After age that name adore! "
** Chamberlayne's State of England, 1684; Angliæ Metropolis, 1690;
Seymour's London, 1734.

could in a day obtain such pecuniary means as it would have taken months to collect from the rest of the island. Nor were the military resources of the capital to be despised. The power which the Lord Lieutenants exercised in other parts of the kingdom was in London intrusted to a Commission of eminent citizens. Under the orders of this Commissions were twelve regiments of foot and two regiments of horse. An army of drapers' apprentices and journeymen tailors, with common councilmen for captains and aldermen for colonels, might not indeed have been able to stand its ground against regular troops; but there were then very few regular troops in the kingdom. A town, therefore, which could send forth, at an hour's notice, twenty thousand men, abounding in natural courage, provided with tolerable weapons, and not altogether untinctured with martial discipline, could not but be a valuable ally and a formidable enemy. It was not forgotten that Hampden and Pym had been protected from lawless tyranny by the London trainbands; that, in the great crisis of the civil war, the London trainbands had marched to raise the siege of Gloucester; or that, in the movement against the military tyrants which followed the downfall of Richard Cromwell, the London trainbands had borne a signal part. In truth, it is no exaggeration to say that, but for the hostility of the City, Charles the First would never have been vanquished, and that, without the help of the City, Charles the Second could scarcely have been restored.

These considerations may serve to explain why, in spite of that attraction which had, during a long course of years, gradually drawn the aristocracy westward, a few men of high rank had continued, till a very recent period, to dwell in the vicinity of the Exchange and of the Guildhall. Shaftesbury and Buckingham, while engaged in bitter and unscrupulous opposition to the government, had thought that they could nowhere carry on their intrigues so conveniently or so securely as under the protection of the City magistrates and the City militia. Shaftesbury had therefore lived in Aldersgate Street, at a house which may still easily be known by pilasters and wreaths, the graceful work of Inigo. Buckingham had ordered his mansion near Charing Cross, once the abode of the Archbishops of York, to be pulled down; and, while streets and alleys which are still named after him were rising on that site, chose to reside in Dowgate.*

Fashion-
able part
of the
capital.
These, however, were rare exceptions. Almost all the noble families of England had long migrated beyond the walls. The district where most of their town houses stood lies between the City and the regions which are now considered as fashionable. A few great men still retained their hereditary hotels between the Strand and the river. The stately dwellings on the south and west of Lincoln's Inn Fields, the Piazza of Covent Garden, Southampton Square, which is now called Bloomsbury Square, and King's Square in Soho Fields, which is now called Soho Square, were among the favourite spots. Foreign princes were carried to see Bloomsbury Square, as one of the wonders of England.** Soho Square, which had just been built, was to our ancestors a subject of pride with which their posterity will hardly sympathize. Monmouth Square had been the name while the fortunes of the Duke of Monmouth flourished; and on the southern side towered his mansion. The front, though ungraceful, was lofty and richly adorned. The walls of the principal apartments were finely sculptured with fruit, foliage, and armorial bearings, and were hung with embroidered satin.*** Every trace of this magnificence has long disap-

* North's Examen, 116. Wood, Ath. Ox. Shaftesbury. The Duke of B.'s Litany.
** Travels of the Grand Duke Cosmo.
*** Chamberlayne's State of England, 1684; Pennant's London; Smith's Life of Nollekens.

peared; and no aristocratical mansion is to be found in that
once aristocratical quarter.   A little way north from Holborn,
and on the verge of the pastures and cornfields, rose two
celebrated palaces, each with an ample garden.   One of
them, then called Southampton House, and subsequently
Bedford House, was removed about fifty years ago to make
room for a new city, which now covers, with its squares,
streets, and churches, a vast area, renowned in the seventeenth century for peaches and snipes.   The other, Montague
House, celebrated for its frescoes and furniture, was, a few
months after the death of Charles the Second, burned to the
ground, and was speedily succeeded by a more magnificent
Montague House, which, having been long the repository
of such various and precious treasures of art, science, and
learning as were scarce ever before assembled under a single
roof, has just given place to an edifice more magnificent
still.*

Nearer to the court, on a space called Saint James's
Fields, had just been built Saint James's Square and Jermyn
Street.   Saint James's Church had recently been opened for
the accommodation of the inhabitants of this new quarter.**
Golden Square, which was in the next generation inhabited
by lords and ministers of state, had not yet been begun.
Indeed the only dwellings to be seen on the north of Piccadilly
were three or four isolated and almost rural mansions, of
which the most celebrated was the costly pile erected by
Clarendon, and nicknamed Dunkirk House.   It had been
purchased after its founder's downfall by the Duke of Albemarle.   The Clarendon Hotel and Albemarle Street still preserve the memory of the site.

He who then rambled to what is now the gayest and most
crowded part of Regent Street found himself in a solitude,

* Evelyn's Diary, Oct. 10. 1683, Jan. 19. 168⅘.
** Stat. 1 Jac. I. c. 22.   Evelyn's Diary, Dec. 7. 1684.

and was sometimes so fortunate as to have a shot at a wood-
cock.* On the north the Oxford road ran between hedges.
Three or four hundred yards to the south were the garden
walls of a few great houses which were considered as quite
out of town. On the west was a meadow renowned for a
spring from which, long afterwards, Conduit Street was
named. On the east was a field not to be passed without a
.shudder by any Londoner of that age. There, as in a place
far from the haunts of men, had been dug, twenty years
before, when the great plague was raging, a pit into which
the dead carts had nightly shot corpses by scores. It was
popularly believed that the earth was deeply tainted with
infection, and could not be disturbed without imminent risk
to human life. No foundations were laid there till two generations had passed without any return of the pestilence, and
till the ghastly spot had long been surrounded by buildings.**

We should greatly err if we were to suppose that any of
the streets and squares then bore the same aspect as at present. The great majority of the houses, indeed, have, since
that time, been wholly, or in great part, rebuilt. If the most
fashionable parts of the capital could be placed before us,
such as they then were, we should be disgusted by their
squalid appearance, and poisoned by their noisome atmosphere. In Covent Garden a filthy and noisy market was held
close to the dwellings of the great. Fruit women screamed,
carters fought, cabbage stalks and rotten apples accumulated
in heaps at the thresholds of the Countess of Berkshire and
of the Bishop of Durham.***

* Old General Oglethorpe, who died in 1785, used to boast that he
had shot birds here in Anne's reign. See Pennant's London, and the
Gentleman's Magazine for July, 1785.
** The pest field will be seen in maps of London as late as the end of
George the First's reign.
*** See a very curious plan of Covent Garden made about 1690, and
engraved for Smith's History of Westminster. See also Hogarth's Morning, painted while some of the houses in the Piazza were still occupied
by people of fashion.

The centre of Lincoln's Inn Fields was an open space where the rabble congregated every evening, within a few yards of Cardigan House and Winchester House, to hear mountebanks harangue, to see bears dance, and to set dogs at oxen. Rubbish was shot in every part of the area. Horses were exercised there. The beggars were as noisy and importunate as in the worst governed cities of the Continent. A Lincoln's Inn mumper was a proverb. The whole fraternity knew the arms and liveries of every charitably disposed grandee in the neighbourhood, and, as soon as his lordship's coach and six appeared, came hopping and crawling in crowds to persecute him. These disorders lasted, in spite of many accidents, and of some legal proceedings, till, in the reign of George the Second, Sir Joseph Jekyll, Master of the Rolls, was knocked down and nearly killed in the middle of the square. Then at length palisades were set up, and a pleasant garden laid out.*

Saint James's Square was a receptacle for all the offal and cinders, for all the dead cats and dead dogs of Westminster. At one time a cudgel player kept the ring there. At another time an impudent squatter settled himself there, and built a shed for rubbish under the windows of the gilded saloons in which the first magnates of the realm, Norfolks, Ormonds, Kents, and Pembrokes, gave banquets and balls. It was not till these nuisances had lasted through a whole generation, and till much had been written about them, that

* London Spy; Tom Brown's Comical View of London and Westminster; Turner's Propositions for the employing of the Poor, 1678; Daily Courant and Daily Journal of June, 7. 1733; Case of Michael v. Allestree, in 1676, 2 Levinz. p. 172. Michael had been run over by two horses which Allestree was breaking in Lincoln's Inn Fields. The declaration set forth that the defendant "porta deux chivals ungovernable en un coach, et improvide, incaute, et absque debita consideratione ineptitudinis loci la eux drive pur eux faire tractable et apt pur un coach, quels chivals, pur ceo que, per leur ferocite, ne poient estre rule, curre sur le plaintiff et le noie."

the inhabitants applied to Parliament for permission to put up rails, and to plant trees.*

When such was the state of the region inhabited by the most luxurious portion of society, we may easily believe that the great body of the population suffered what would now be considered as insupportable grievances. The pavement was detestable; all foreigners cried shame upon it. The drainage was so bad that in rainy weather the gutters soon became torrents. Several facetious poets have commemorated the fury with which these black rivulets roared down Snow Hill and Ludgate Hill, bearing to Fleet Ditch a vast tribute of animal and vegetable filth from the stalls of butchers and greengrocers. This flood was profusely thrown to right and left by coaches and carts. To keep as far from the carriage road as possible was therefore the wish of every pedestrian. The mild and timid gave the wall. The bold and athletic took it. If two roisterers met, they cocked their hats in each other's faces, and pushed each other about till the weaker was shoved towards the kennel. If he was a mere bully he sneaked off, muttering that he should find a time. If he was pugnacious, the encounter probably ended in a duel behind Montague House.**

The houses were not numbered. There would indeed have been little advantage in numbering them; for of the coachmen, chairmen, porters, and errand boys of London, a very small proportion could read. It was necessary to use marks which the most ignorant could understand. The shops

---

* Stat. 12 Geo. I. c. 25; Commons' Journals, Feb. 25. March 2. 1724; London Gardener, 1712; Evening Post, March 23. 1731. I have not been able to find this number of the Evening Post; I therefore quote it on the faith of Mr. Malcolm, who mentions it in his History of London.

** Lettres sur les Anglois, written early in the reign of William the Third; Swift's City Shower; Gay's Trivia. Johnson used to relate a curious conversation which he had with his mother about giving and taking the wall.

were therefore distinguished by painted signs, which gave
a gay and grotesque aspect to the streets. The walk from
Charing Cross to Whitechapel lay through an endless succession of Saracens' Heads, Royal Oaks, Blue Bears, and
Golden Lambs, which disappeared when they were no longer
required for the direction of the common people.

When the evening closed in, the difficulty and danger
of walking about London became serious indeed. The garret
windows were opened, and pails were emptied, with little regard
to those who were passing below. Falls, bruises, and broken
bones were of constant occurrence. For, till the last year of
the reign of Charles the Second, most of the streets were left
in profound darkness. Thieves and robbers plied their trade
with impunity: yet they were hardly so terrible to peaceable
citizens as another class of ruffians. It was a favourite amusement of dissolute young gentlemen to swagger by night about
the town, breaking windows, upsetting sedans, beating quiet
men, and offering rude caresses to pretty women. Several
dynasties of these tyrants had, since the Restoration, domineered over the streets. The Muns and Tityre Tus had
given place to the Hectors, and the Hectors had been recently
succeeded by the Scourers. At a later period arose the Nicker,
the Hawcubite, and the yet more dreaded name of Mohawk.[*]
The machinery for keeping the peace was utterly contemptible. There was an Act of Common Council which

Police of London.

* Oldham's Imitation of the 3d Satire of Juvenal, 1682; Shadwell's
Scourers, 1690. Many other authorities will readily occur to all who are
acquainted with the popular literature of that and the succeeding generation. It may be suspected that some of the Tityre Tus, like good
Cavaliers, broke Milton's windows shortly after the Restoration. I am
confident that he was thinking of those pests of London when he dictated
the noble lines, —
    "And in luxurious cities, when the noise
    Of riot ascends above their loftiest towers,
    And injury and outrage, and when night
    Darkens the streets, then wander forth the sons
    Of Belial, flown with insolence and wine."

23 *

CHAP.
III.   provided that more than a thousand watchmen should be
constantly on the alert in the city, from sunset to sunrise, and
that every inhabitant should take his turn of duty.   But this
Act was negligently executed.   Few of those who were summoned left their homes; and those few generally found it
more agreeable to tipple in alehouses than to pace the
streets. *

Lighting
of
London.   It ought to be noticed that, in the last year of the reign of
Charles the Second, began a great change in the police of
London, a change which has perhaps added as much to the
happiness of the body of the people as revolutions of much
greater fame.   An ingenious projector, named Edward
Heming, obtained letters patent conveying to him, for a term
of years, the exclusive right of lighting up London.   He
undertook, for a moderate consideration, to place a light
before every tenth door, on moonless nights, from Michaelmas to Lady Day', and from six to twelve of the clock.
Those who now see the capital all the year round, from dusk
to dawn, blazing with a splendour compared with which the
illuminations for La Hogue and Blenheim would have looked
pale, may perhaps smile to think of Heming's lanterns, which
glimmered feebly before one house in ten during a small part
of one night in three.   But such was not the feeling of his
contemporaries.   His scheme was enthusiastically applauded,
and furiously attacked.   The friends of improvement extolled him as the greatest of all the benefactors of his city.
What, they asked, were the boasted inventions of Archi-
medes, when compared with the achievement of the man who
had turned the nocturnal shades into noon day?   In spite of
these eloquent eulogies the cause of darkness was not left
undefended.   There were fools in that age who opposed the
introduction of what was called the new light as strenuously
as fools in our age have opposed the introduction of vaccina-

* Seymour's London.

tion and railroads, as strenuously as the fools of an age _{CHAP.}

anterior to the dawn of history doubtless opposed the intro-

duction of the plough and of alphabetical writing. Many
years after the date of Heming's patent there were extensive
districts in which no lamp was seen.*

We may easily imagine what, in such times, must have _{White-}
been the state of the quarters of London which were peopled _{friars.}
by the outcasts of society. Among those quarters one had
attained a scandalous preeminence. On the confines of the
City and the Temple had been founded, in the thirteenth
century, a House of Carmelite Friars, distinguished by their
white hoods. The precinct of this house had, before the Reformation, been a sanctuary for criminals, and still retained
the privilege of protecting debtors from arrest. Insolvents
consequently were to be found in every dwelling, from cellar
to garret. Of these a large proportion were knaves and
libertines, and were followed to their asylum by women more
abandoned than themselves. The civil power was unable to
keep order in a district swarming with such inhabitants; and
thus Whitefriars became the favourite resort of all who wished
to be emancipated from the restraints of the law. Though
the immunities legally belonging to the place extended only
to cases of debt, cheats, false witnesses, forgers, and highwaymen found refuge there. For amidst a rabble so desperate
no peace officer's life was in safety. At the cry of "Rescue"
bullies with swords and cudgels, and termagant hags with
spits and broomsticks, poured forth by hundreds; and the
intruder was fortunate if he escaped back into Fleet Street,
hustled, stripped, and pumped upon. Even the warrant of
the Chief Justice of England could not be executed without
the help of a company of musketeers. Such relics of the
barbarism of the darkest ages were to be found within a short

* Angliæ Metropolis, 1690, Sect. 17. entitled, "Of the new lights."
Seymour's London.

walk of the chambers where Somers was studying history and
law, of the chapel where Tillotson was preaching, of the
coffee house where Dryden was passing judgment on poems
and plays, and of the hall where the Royal Society was
examining the astronomical system of Isaac Newton.[*]

Each of the two cities which made up the capital of England had its own centre of attraction. In the metropolis of
commerce the point of convergence was the Exchange; in
the metropolis of fashion the Palace. But the Palace did
not retain its influence so long as the Exchange. The Revolution completely altered the relations between the court and
the higher classes of society. It was by degrees discovered
that the King, in his individual capacity, had very little to
give; that coronets and garters, bishoprics and embassies,
lordships of the Treasury and tellerships of the Exchequer,
nay, even charges in the royal stud and bed-chamber, were
really bestowed, not by him, but by his advisers. Every
ambitious and covetous man perceived that he would consult
his own interest far better by acquiring the dominion of a
Cornish borough, and by rendering good service to the
ministry during a critical session, than by becoming the com-
panion, or even the minion, of his prince. It was therefore
in the antechambers, not of George the First and of George
the Second, but of Walpole and of Pelham, that the 'daily
crowd of courtiers was to be found. It is also to be remarked
that the same revolution which made it impossible that our
Kings should use the patronage of the state, merely for the
purpose of gratifying their personal predilections, gave us
several Kings unfitted by their education and habits to be
gracious and affable hosts. They had been born and bred on
the Continent. They never felt themselves at home in our
island. If they spoke our language, they spoke it inelegantly

* Stowe's Survey of London; Shadwell's Squire of Alsatia; Ward's
London Spy; Stat. 8 & 9 Gul. III. cap. 27.

and with effort. Our national character they never fully understood. Our national manners they hardly attempted to acquire. The most important part of their duty they performed
better than any ruler who had preceded them: for they governed strictly according to law: but they could not be the
first gentlemen of the realm, the heads of polite society. If
ever they unbent, it was in a very small circle where hardly an
English face was to be seen; and they were never so happy as
when they could escape for a summer to their native land.
They had indeed their days of reception for our nobility and
gentry; but the reception was mere matter of form, and became at last as solemn a ceremony as a funeral.

Not such was the court of Charles the Second. Whitehall,
when he dwelt there, was the focus of political intrigue and of
fashionable gaiety. Half the jobbing and half the flirting of
the metropolis went on under his roof. Whoever could make
himself agreeable to the prince, or could secure the good
offices of the mistress, might hope to rise in the world without
rendering any service to the government, without being even
known by sight to any minister of state. This courtier got a
frigate, and that a company; a third the pardon of a rich
offender; a fourth, a lease of crown land on easy terms. If the
King notified his pleasure that a briefless lawyer should be
made a judge, or that a libertine baronet should be made a
peer, the gravest counsellors, after a little murmuring, submitted.* Interest, therefore, drew a constant press of suitors
to the gates of the palace; and those gates always stood wide.
The King kept open house every day, and all day long, for the
good society of London, the extreme Whigs only excepted.
Hardly any gentleman had any difficulty in making his way to
the royal presence. The levee was exactly what the word im-

* See Sir Roger North's account of the way in which Wright was
made a judge, and Clarendon's account of the way in which Sir George
Savile was made a peer.

ports. Some men of quality came every morning to stand round their master, to chat with him while his wig was combed and his cravat tied, and to accompany him in his early walk through the Park. All persons who had been properly introduced might, without any special invitation, go to see him dine, sup, dance, and play at hazard, and might have the pleasure of hearing him tell stories, which indeed he told remarkably well, about his flight from Worcester, and about the misery which he had endured when he was a state prisoner in the hands of the canting meddling preachers of Scotland. Bystanders whom His Majesty recognised often came in for a courteous word. This proved a far more successful kingcraft than any that his father or grandfather had practised. It was not easy for the most austere republican of the school of Marvel to resist the fascination of so much good humour and affability: and many a veteran Cavalier, in whose heart the remembrance of unrequited sacrifices and services had been festering during twenty years, was compensated in one moment for wounds and sequestrations by his sovereign's kind nod, and "God bless you, my old friend!"

Whitehall naturally became the chief staple of news. Whenever there was a rumour that anything important had happened or was about to happen, people hastened thither to obtain intelligence from the fountain head. The galleries presented the appearance of a modern club room at an anxious time. They were full of people inquiring whether the Dutch mail was in, what tidings the express from France had brought, whether John Sobiesky had beaten the Turks, whether the Doge of Genoa was really at Paris. These were matters about which it was safe to talk aloud. But there were subjects concerning which information was asked and given in whispers. Had Halifax got the better of Rochester? Was there to be a Parliament? Was the Duke of York really going to Scotland? Had Monmouth really been summoned from the Hague? Men

tried to read the countenance of every minister as he went
through the throng to and from the royal closet.   All sorts of
auguries were drawn from the tone in which His Majesty spoke
to the Lord President, or from the laugh with which His Majesty honoured a jest of the Lord Privy Seal; and in a few hours
the hopes and fears inspired by such slight indications had
spread to all the coffee-houses from St. James's to the
Tower. *

The coffee-house must not be dismissed with a cursory
mention.   It might indeed at that time have been not im-
properly called a most important political institution.   No Parliament had sat for years.   The municipal council of the City
had ceased to speak the sense of the citizens.   Public meetings,
harangues, resolutions, and the rest of the modern machinery
of agitation had not yet come into fashion.   Nothing resembling
the modern newspaper existed.   In such circumstances the
coffee-houses were the chief organs through which the public
opinion of the metropolis vented itself.

The first of these establishments had been set up, in the
time of the Commonwealth, by a Turkey merchant, who had
acquired among the Mahometans a taste for their favourite
beverage.   The convenience of being able to make appoint-
ments in any part of the town, and of being able to pass evenings socially at a very small charge, was so great that the
fashion spread fast.   Every man of the upper or middle class
went daily to his coffee-house to learn the news and to discuss
it.   Every coffee-house had one or more orators to whose eloquence the crowd listened with admiration, and who soon became, what the journalists of our own time have been called, a
fourth Estate of the realm.   The court had long seen with un-

* The sources from which I have drawn my information about the
state of the court are too numerous to recapitulate.   Among them are
the Despatches of Barillon, Citters, Ronquillo, and Adda, the Travels of
the Grand Duke Cosmo, the Diaries of Pepys, Evelyn, and Teonge, and
the Memoirs of Grammont and Reresby.

CHAP.
III.

easiness the growth of this new power in the state. An attempt had been made, during Danby's administration, to close the coffee-houses. But men of all parties missed their usual places of resort so much that there was an universal outcry. The government did not venture, in opposition to a feeling so strong and general, to enforce a regulation of which the legality might well be questioned. Since that time ten years had elapsed, and during those years the number and influence of the coffee-houses had been constantly increasing. Foreigners remarked that the coffee-house was that which especially distinguished London from all other cities; that the coffee-house was the Londoner's home, and that those who wished to find a gentleman commonly asked, not whether he lived in Fleet Street or Chancery Lane, but whether he frequented the Grecian or the Rainbow. Nobody was excluded from these places who laid down his penny at the bar. Yet every rank and profession, and every shade of religious and political opinion, had its own head quarters. There were houses near Saint James's Park where fops congregated, their heads and shoulders covered with black or flaxen wigs, not less ample than those which are now worn by the Chancellor and by the Speaker of the House of Commons. The wig came from Paris; and so did the rest of the fine gentleman's ornaments, his embroidered coat, his fringed gloves, and the tassel which upheld his pantaloons. The conversation was in that dialect which, long after it had ceased to be spoken in fashionable circles, continued, in the mouth of Lord Foppington, to excite the mirth of theatres.* The atmosphere was like that of a perfumer's shop. Tobacco in any other form than that of richly scented snuff was held in abomination. If any clown, ignorant

---

* The chief peculiarity of this dialect was that, in a large class of words, the O was pronounced like A. Thus stork was pronounced stark. See Vanbrugh's Relapse. Lord Sunderland was a great master of this court tune, as Roger North calls it; and Titus Oates affected it in the hope of passing for a fine gentleman. Examen, 77, 254.

of the usages of the house, called for a pipe, the sneers of the whole assembly and the short answers of the waiters soon convinced him that he had better go somewhere else. Nor, indeed, would he have had far to go. For, in general, the coffee-rooms reeked with tobacco like a guard-room; and strangers sometimes expressed their surprise that so many people should leave their own firesides to sit in the midst of eternal fog and stench. Nowhere was the smoking more constant than at Will's. That celebrated house, situated between Covent Garden and Bow Street, was sacred to polite letters. There the talk was about poetical justice and the unities of place and time. There was a faction for Perrault and the moderns, a faction for Boileau and the ancients. One group debated whether Paradise Lost ought not to have been in rhyme. To another an envious poetaster demonstrated that Venice Preserved ought to have been hooted from the stage. Under no roof was a greater variety of figures to be seen, Earls in stars and garters, clergymen in cassocks and bands, pert Templars, sheepish lads from the Universities, translators and index makers in ragged coats of frieze. The great press was to get near the chair where John Dryden sate. In winter that chair was always in the warmest nook by the fire; in summer it stood in the balcony. To bow to him, and to hear his opinion of Racine's last tragedy or of Bossu's treatise on epic poetry, was thought a privilege. A pinch from his snuff-box was an honour sufficient to turn the head of a young enthusiast. There were coffee-houses where the first medical men might be consulted. Doctor John Radcliffe, who, in the year 1685, rose to the largest practice in London, came daily, at the hour when the Exchange was full, from his house in Bow Street, then a fashionable part of the capital, to Garraway's, and was to be found, surrounded by surgeons and apothecaries, at a particular table. There were Puritan coffee-houses where no oath was heard, and where lank-haired men discussed election and reprobation through their noses; Jew coffee-houses where dark eyed money changers from Venice and from Amsterdam greeted each other; and Popish coffee-houses where, as good Protestants believed, Jesuits planned, over their cups, another great fire, and cast silver bullets to shoot the King. *

These gregarious habits had no small share in forming the character of the Londoner of that age. He was, indeed, a different being from the rustic Englishman. There was not then the intercourse which now exists between the two classes. Only very great men were in the habit of dividing the year between town and country. Few esquires came to the capital thrice in their lives. Nor was it yet the practice of all citizens in easy circumstances to breathe the fresh air of the fields and woods during some weeks of every summer. A cockney, in a rural village, was stared at as much as if he had intruded into a Kraal of Hottentots. On the other hand, when the lord of a Lincolnshire or Shropshire manor appeared in Fleet Street, he was as easily distinguised from the resident population as a Turk or a Lascar. His dress, his gait, his accent, the manner in which he stared at the shops, stumbled into the gutters, ran against the porters, and stood under the waterspouts, marked him out as an excellent subject for the operations of swindlers and banterers. Bullies jostled him into the kennel. Hackney coachmen splashed him from head to foot. Thieves explored with perfect security the huge pockets of his horseman's coat, while he stood entranced by the splendour of the Lord Mayor's show. Money-droppers, sore from the cart's tail,

---

* Lettres sur les Anglois; Tom Brown's Tour; Ward's London Spy; The Character of a Coffee-House, 1673; Rules and Orders of the Coffee-House, 1674; Coffee-Houses vindicated, 1675; A Satyr against Coffee; North's Examen, 138.; Life of Guildford, 152.; Life of Sir Dudley North, 149.; Life of Dr. Radcliffe, published by Curll in 1715. The liveliest description of Will's is in the City and Country Mouse. There is a remarkable passage about the influence of the coffee-house orators in Halstead's Succinct Genealogies, printed in 1685.

introduced themselves to him, and appeared to him the most
honest friendly gentlemen that he had ever seen. Painted
women, the refuse of Lewkner Lane and Whetstone Park,
passed themselves on him for countesses and maids of honour.
If he asked his way to Saint James's, his informants sent him
to Mile End. If he went into a shop, he was instantly discerned to be a fit purchaser of everything that nobody else
would buy, of second-hand embroidery, copper rings, and
watches that would not go. If he rambled into any fashionable coffee-house, he became a mark for the insolent derision
of fops and the grave waggery of Templars. Enraged and
mortified, he soon returned to his mansion, and there, in the
homage of his tenants, and the conversation of his boon companions, found consolation for the vexations and humiliations
which he had undergone. There he once more felt himself a
great man; and he saw nothing above him except when at the
assizes he took his seat on the bench near the Judge, or when
at the muster of the militia he saluted the Lord Lieutenant.

The chief cause which made the fusion of the different elements of society so imperfect was the extreme difficulty which
our ancestors found in passing from place to place. Of all
inventions, the alphabet and the printing press alone excepted,
those inventions which abridge distance have done most for
the civilisation of our species. Every improvement of the
means of locomotion benefits mankind morally and intellectually as well as materially, and not only facilitates the inter-
change of the various productions of nature and art, but tends
to remove national and provincial antipathies, and to bind together all the branches of the great human family. In the
seventeenth century the inhabitants of London were, for
almost every practical purpose, farther from Reading than
they now are from Edinburgh, and farther from Edinburgh
than they now are from Vienna.

The subjects of Charles the Second were not, it is true,

quite unacquainted with that principle which has, in our own
time, produced an unprecedented revolution in human affairs,
which has enabled navies to advance in the face of wind and
tide, and battalions, attended by all their baggage and artillery, to traverse kingdoms at a pace equal to that of the fleetest
race horse. The Marquess of Worcester had recently observed the expansive power of moisture rarefied by heat.
After many experiments he had succeeded in constructing a
rude steam engine, which he called a fire water work, and
which he pronounced to be an admirable and most forcible
instrument of propulsion.* But the Marquess was suspected
to be a madman, and known to be a Papist. His inventions,
therefore, found no favourable reception. His fire water work
might, perhaps, furnish matter for conversation at a meeting
of the Royal Society, but was not applied to any practical purpose. There were no railways, except a few made of timber,
from the mouths of the Northumbrian coal pits to the banks of
the Tyne.** There was very little internal communication by
water. A few attempts had been made to deepen and embank
the natural streams, but with slender success. Hardly a
single navigable canal had been even projected. The English
of that day were in the habit of talking with mingled admiration and despair of the immense trench by which Lewis the
Fourteenth had made a junction between the Atlantic and the
Mediterranean. They little thought that their country would,
in the course of a few generations, be intersected, at the cost
of private adventurers, by artificial rivers making up more
than four times the length of the Thames, the Severn, and the
Trent together.

Badness
of the
roads.
It was by the highways that both travellers and goods
generally passed from place to place. And those highways
appear to have been far worse than might have been expected

* Century of Inventions, 1663. No. 68.
** North's Life of Guildford, 136.

from the degree of wealth and civilisation which the nation had even then attained.   On the best lines of communication the ruts were deep, the descents precipitous, and the way often such as it was hardly possible to distinguish, in the dusk, from the uninclosed heath and fen which lay on both sides.   Ralph Thoresby, the antiquary, was in danger of losing his way on the great North road, between Barnby Moor and Tuxford, and actually lost his way between Doncaster and York.*   Pepys and his wife, travelling in their own coach, lost their way between Newbury and Reading.   In the course of the same tour they lost their way near Salisbury, and were in danger of having to pass the night on the plain.**   It was only in fine weather that the whole breadth of the road was available for wheeled vehicles.   Often the mud lay deep on the right and the left;   and only a narrow track of firm ground rose above the quagmire.***   At such times obstructions and quarrels were frequent, and the path was sometimes blocked up during a long time by carriers, neither of whom would break the way. It happened, almost every day, that coaches stuck fast, until a team of cattle could be procured from some neighbouring farm, to tug them out of the slough.   But in bad seasons the traveller had to encounter inconveniences still more serious. Thoresby, who was in the habit of travelling between Leeds and the capital, has recorded, in his Diary, such a series of perils and disasters as might suffice for a journey to the Frozen Ocean or to the Desert of Sahara.   On one occasion he learned that the floods were out between Ware and London, that passengers had to swim for their lives, and that a higgler had perished in the attempt to cross.   In consequence of these tidings he turned out of the high road, and was conducted across some meadows, where it was necessary for him

---

* Thoresby's Diary, Oct. 21. 1680, Aug. 3. 1712.
** Pepys's Diary, June 12. and 16. 1668.
*** Ibid. Feb. 28. 1660.

to ride to the saddle skirts in water.[*] In the course of another journey he narrowly escaped being swept away by an inundation of the Trent. He was afterwards detained at Stamford four days, on account of the state of the roads, and then ventured to proceed only because fourteen members of the House of Commons, who were going up in a body to Parliament with guides and numerous attendants, took him into their company.[**] On the roads of Derbyshire travellers were in constant fear for their necks, and were frequently compelled to alight and lead their beasts.[***] The great route through Wales to Holyhead was in such a state that, in 1685, a viceroy, going to Ireland, was five hours in travelling fourteen miles, from Saint Asaph to Conway. Between Conway and Beaumaris he was forced to walk great part of the way; and his lady was carried in a litter. His coach was, with great difficulty, and by the help of many hands, brought after him entire. In general, carriages were taken to pieces at Conway, and borne, on the shoulders of stout Welsh peasants, to the Menai Straits.[†] In some parts of Kent and Sussex none but the strongest horses could, in winter, get through the bog, in which, at every step, they sank deep. The markets were often inaccessible during several months. It is said that the fruits of the earth were sometimes suffered to rot in one place, while in another place, distant only a few miles, the supply fell far short of the demand. The wheeled carriages were, in this district, generally pulled by oxen.[††] When Prince George of Denmark visited the stately mansion of Petworth in wet weather, he was six hours in going nine miles; and it was

[*] Thoresby's Diary, May 17. 1695.
[**] Ib. Dec. 27. 1708.
[***] Tour in Derbyshire, by J. Browne, son of Sir Thomas Browne, 1662. Cotton's Angler, 1676.
[†] Correspondence of Henry Earl of Clarendon, Dec. 30. 1685, Jan. 1. 1686.
[††] Postlethwaite's Dict., Roads. History of Hawkhurst, in the Bibliotheca Topographica Britannica.

necessary that a body of sturdy hinds should be on each side of his coach, in order to prop it. Of the carriages which conveyed his retinue several were upset and injured. A letter from one of his gentlemen in waiting has been preserved, in which the unfortunate courtier complains that, during fourteen hours, he never once alighted, except when his coach was overturned or stuck fast in the mud. *

One chief cause of the badness of the roads seems to have been the defective state of the law. Every parish was bound to repair the highways which passed through it. The peasantry were forced to give their gratuitous labour six days in the year. If this was not sufficient, hired labour was employed, and the expense was met by a parochial rate. That a route connecting two great towns, which have a large and thriving trade with each other, should be maintained at the coast of the rural population scattered between them is obviously unjust; and this injustice was peculiarly glaring in the case of the great North road, which traversed very poor and thinly inhabited districts, and joined very rich and populous districts. .Indeed it was not in the power of the parishes of Huntingdonshire to mend a highway worn by the constant traffic between the West Riding of Yorkshire and London. Soon after the Restoration this grievance attracted the notice of Parliament; and an act, the first of our many turnpike acts, was passed, imposing a small toll on travellers and goods, for the purpose of keeping some parts of this important line of communication in good repair.** This innovation, however, excited many murmurs; and the other great avenues to the capital were long left under the old system. A change was at length affected, but not without much difficulty. For unjust and absurd taxation to which men are accustomed is often borne far more willingly than the most reasonable impost

* Annals of Queen Anne, 1703. Appendix, No. 3.
** 15 Car. II. c. 1.

which is new. It was not till many toll bars had been violently
pulled down', till the troops had in many districts been forced
to act against the people, and till much blood had been
shed, that a good system was introduced.* By slow degrees
reason triumphed over prejudice; and our island is now
crossed in every direction by near thirty thousand miles of
turnpike road.

On the best highways heavy articles were, in the time of
Charles the Second, generally conveyed from place to place
by stage waggons. In the straw of these vehicles nestled a
crowd of passengers, who could not afford to travel by coach
or on horseback, and who were prevented by infirmity, or by
the weight of their luggage, from going on foot. The expense of transmitting heavy goods in this way was enormous.
From London to Birmingham the charge was seven pounds a
ton; from London to Exeter twelve pounds a ton.** This
was about fifteen pence a ton for every mile, more by a third
than was afterwards charged on turnpike roads, and fifteen
times what is now demanded by railway companies. The cost
of conveyance amounted to a prohibitory tax on many useful
articles. Coal in particular was never seen except in the
districts where it was produced, or in the districts to which it
could be carried by sea, and was indeed always known in the
south of England by the name of sea coal.

On byroads, and generally throughout the country north
of York and west of Exeter, goods were carried by long
trains of packhorses. These strong and patient beasts, the
breed of which is now extinct, were attended by a class of
men who seem to have borne much resemblance to the Spanish
muleteers. A traveller of humble condition often found it

---

* The evils of the old system are strikingly set forth in many petitions which appear in the Commons' Journal of 172⅜. How fierce an opposition was offered to the new system may be learned from the Gentleman's Magazine of 1749.
** Postlethwaite's Dict., Roads.

convenient to perform a journey mounted on a pack-saddle
between two baskets, under the care of these hardy guides.
The expense of this mode of conveyance was small. But the
caravan moved at a foot's pace; and in winter the cold was
often insupportable. *

The rich commonly travelled in their own carriages, with
at least four horses. Cotton, the facetious poet, attempted
to go from London to the Peak with a single pair, but found
at Saint Albans that the journey would be insupportably
tedious, and altered his plan.** A coach and six is in our
time never seen, except as part of some pageant. The frequent mention therefore of such equipages in old books is
likely to mislead us. We attribute to magnificence what was
really the effect of a very disagreeable necessity. People, in
the time of Charles the Second, travelled with six horses,
because with a smaller number there was great danger of
sticking fast in the mire. Nor were even six horses always
sufficient. Vanbrugh, in the succeeding generation, described
with great humour the way in which a country gentleman,
newly chosen a member of Parliament, went up to London.
On that occasion all the exertions of six beasts, two of which
had been taken from the plough, could not save the family
coach from being imbedded in a quagmire.

Public carriages had recently been much improved. During the years which immediately followed the Restoration, a
diligence ran between London and Oxford in two days. The
passengers slept at Beaconsfield. At length, in the spring of
1669, a great and daring innovation was attempted. It was
announced that a vehicle, described as the Flying Coach,
would perform the whole journey between sunrise and sunset.
This spirited undertaking was solemnly considered and sanc-

* Loidis and Elmete. Marshall's Rural Economy of England. In
1739 Roderic Random came from Scotland to Newcastle on a pack-horse.
** Cotton's Epistle to J. Bradshaw.

tioned by the Heads of the University, and appears to have excited the same sort of interest which is excited in our own time by the opening of a new railway. The Vicechancellor, by a notice affixed in all public places, prescribed the hour and place of departure. The success of the experiment was complete. At six in the morning the carriage began to move from before the ancient front of All Souls College: and at seven in the evening the adventurous gentlemen who had run the first risk were safely deposited at their inn in London.[*] The emulation of the sister University was moved; and soon a diligence was set up which in one day carried passengers from Cambridge to the capital. At the close of the reign of Charles the Second, flying carriages ran thrice a week from London to the chief towns. But no stage coach, indeed no stage waggon, appears to have proceeded further north than York, or further west than Exeter. The ordinary day's journey of a flying coach was about fifty miles in the summer; but in winter, when the ways were bad and the nights long, little more than thirty. The Chester coach, the York coach, and the Exeter coach generally reached London in four days during the fine season, but at Christmas not till the sixth day. The passengers, six in number, were all seated in the carriage. For accidents were so frequent that it would have been most perilous to mount the roof. The ordinary fare was about twopence halfpenny a mile in summer, and somewhat more in winter.[**]

This mode of travelling, which by Englishmen of the present day would be regarded as insufferably slow, seemed to our ancestors wonderfully and indeed alarmingly rapid. In a work published a few months before the death of Charles the

Second, the flying coaches are extolled as far superior to any
similar vehicles ever known in the world. Their velocity is
the subject of special commendation, and is triumphantly
contrasted with the sluggish pace of the continental posts.
But with boasts like these was mingled the sound of complaint
and invective. The interests of large classes had been un-
favourably affected by the establishment of the new dili-
gences; and, as usual, many persons were, from mere stu-
pidity and obstinacy, disposed to clamour against the innovation, simply because it was an innovation. It was vehemently
argued that this mode of conveyance would be fatal to the
breed of horses and to the noble art of horsemanship; that
the Thames, which had long been an important nursery of
seamen, would cease to be the chief thoroughfare from London up to Windsor and down to Gravesend; that saddlers
and spurriers would be ruined by hundreds; that numerous
inns, at which mounted travellers had been in the habit of
stopping, would be deserted, and would no longer pay any
rent; that the new carriages were too hot in summer and too
cold in winter; that the passengers were grievously annoyed
by invalids and crying children; that the coach sometimes
reached the inn so late that it was impossible to get supper,
and sometimes started so early that it was impossible to get
breakfast. On these grounds it was gravely recommended
that no public carriage should be permitted to have more than
four horses, to start oftener than once a week, or to go more
than thirty miles a day. It was hoped that, if this regulation
were adopted, all except the sick and the lame would return
to the old mode of travelling. Petitions embodying such
opinions as these were presented to the King in council from
several companies of the City of London, from several provincial towns, and from the justices of several counties. We
smile at these things. It is not impossible that our descendants, when they read the history of the opposition offered by

cupidity and prejudice to the improvements of the nineteenth century, may smile in their turn. *

In spite of the attractions of the flying coaches, it was still usual for men who enjoyed health and vigour, and who were not encumbered by much baggage, to perform long journeys on horseback. If the traveller wished to move expeditiously he rode post. Fresh saddle horses and guides were to be procured at convenient distances along all the great lines of road. The charge was threepence a mile for each horse, and fourpence a stage for the guide. In this manner, when the ways were good, it was possible to travel, for a considerable time, as rapidly as by any conveyance known in England, till vehicles were propelled by steam. There were as yet no post chaises; nor could those who rode in their own coaches ordinarily procure a change of horses. The King, however, and the great officers of state were able to command relays. Thus Charles commonly went in one day from Whitehall to Newmarket, a distance of about fifty-five miles through a level country; and this was thought by his subjects a proof of great activity. Evelyn performed the same journey in company with the Lord Treasurer Clifford. The coach was drawn by six horses, which were changed at Bishop Stortford and again at Chesterford. The travellers reached Newmarket at night. Such a mode of conveyance seems to have been considered as a rare luxury confined to princes and ministers. **

Highway-
men.
Whatever might be the way in which a journey was performed, the travellers, unless they were numerous and well armed, ran considerable risk of being stopped and plundered. The mounted highwayman, a marauder known to our genera-

---

* John Cresset's Reasons for suppressing Stage Coaches, 1672. These reasons were afterwards inserted in a tract, entitled "The Grand Concern of England explained, 1673." Cresset's attack on stage coaches called forth some answers which I have consulted.
** Chamberlayne's State of England, 1684. North's Examen, 105. Evelyn's Diary, Oct. 9, 10. 1671.

tion only from books, was to be found on every main road.
The waste tracts which lay on the great routes near London
were especially haunted by plunderers of this class. Hounslow
Heath, on the great Western Road, and Finchley Common,
on the great Northern Road, were perhaps the most celebrated of these spots. The Cambridge scholars trembled
when they approached Epping Forest, even in broad daylight.
Seamen who had just been paid off at Chatham were often
compelled to deliver their purses on Gadshill, celebrated near
a hundred years earlier by the greatest of poets as the scene
of the depredations of Poins and Falstaff. The public authorities seem to have been often at a loss how to deal with the
plunderers. At one time it was announced in the Gazette that
several persons, who were strongly suspected of being highwaymen, but against whom there was not sufficient evidence,
would be paraded at Newgate in riding dresses: their horses
would also be shown: and all gentlemen who had been robbed
were invited to inspect this singular exhibition. On another
occasion a pardon was publicly offered to a robber if he would
give up some rough diamonds, of immense value, which he
had taken when he stopped the Harwich mail. A short time
after appeared another proclamation, warning the innkeepers
that the eye of the government was upon them. Their criminal connivance, it was affirmed, enabled banditti to infest
the roads with impunity. That these suspicions were not
without foundation, is proved by the dying speeches of some
penitent robbers of that age, who appear to have received
from the innkeepers services much resembling those which
Farquhar's Boniface rendered to Gibbet. *

It was necessary to the success and even to the safety of
the highwayman that he should be a bold and skilful rider,

* See the London Gazette, May 14. 1677, August 4. 1687, Dec. 5. 1687.
The last confession of Augustin King, who was the son of an eminent
divine, and had been educated at Cambridge, but was hanged at Col-
chester in March 1688, is highly curious.

and that his manners and appearance should be such as suited the master of a fine horse. He therefore held an aristocratical position in the community of thieves, appeared at fashionable coffee-houses and gaming-houses, and betted with men of quality on the race ground. * Sometimes, indeed, he was a man of good family and education. A romantic interest therefore attached, and perhaps still attaches, to the names of freebooters of this class. The vulgar eagerly drank in tales of their ferocity and audacity, of their occasional acts of generosity and good nature, of their amours, of their miraculous escapes, of their desperate struggles, and of their manly bearing at the bar and in the cart. Thus it was related of William Nevison, the great robber of Yorkshire, that he levied a quarterly tribute on all the northern drovers, and, in return, not only spared them himself, but protected them against all other thieves; that he demanded purses in the most courteous manner; that he gave largely to the poor what he had taken from the rich; that his life was once spared by the royal clemency, but that he again tempted his fate, and at length died, in 1685, on the gallows of York.** It was related how Claude Duval, the French page of the Duke of Richmond, took to the road, became captain of a formidable gang, and had the honour to be named first in a royal proclamation against notorious offenders; how at the head of his troop he stopped a lady's coach, in which there was a booty of four hundred pounds; how he took only one hundred, and suffered the fair owner to ransom the rest by dancing a coranto with

---

* *Aimwell.* Pray Sir, han't I seen your face at Will's coffee-house?
  Gibbet. Yes, Sir, and at White's too. — Beaux' Stratagem.
** Gent's History of York. Another marauder of the same description, named Biss, was hanged at Salisbury in 1695. In a ballad which is in the Pepysian Library, he is represented as defending himself thus before the Judge:

> "What say you now, my honoured Lord,'
> What harm was there in this?
> Rich, wealthy misers were abhorred
> By brave, freehearted Biss."

him on the heath; how his vivacious gallantry stole away the hearts of all women; how his dexterity at sword and pistol made him a terror to all men; how, at length, in the year 1670, he was seized when overcome by wine; how dames of high rank visited him in prison, and with tears interceded for his life; how the King would have granted a pardon, but for the interference of Judge Morton, the terror of highwaymen, who threatened to resign his office unless the law were carried into full effect; and how, after the execution, the corpse lay in state with all the pomp of scutcheons, wax lights, black hangings and mutes, till the same cruel Judge, who had intercepted the mercy of the crown, sent officers to disturb the obsequies.* In these anecdotes there is doubtless a large mixture of fable; but they are not on that account unworthy of being recorded; for it is both an authentic and an important fact that such tales, whether false or true, were heard by our ancestors with eagerness and faith.

All the various dangers by which the traveller was beset Inns. were greatly increased by darkness. He was therefore commonly desirous of having the shelter of a roof during the night; and such shelter it was not difficult to obtain. From a very early period the inns of England had been renowned. Our first great poet had described the excellent accommodation which they afforded to the pilgrims of the fourteenth century. Nine and twenty persons, with their horses, found room in the wide chambers and stables of the Tabard in Southwark. The food was of the best, and the wines such as drew the company on to drink largely. Two hundred years later, under the reign of Elizabeth, William Harrison gave a lively description of the plenty and comfort of the great hostelries. The Continent of Europe, he said, could show nothing like them. There were some in which two or three

* Pope's Memoirs of Duval, published immediately after the execution. Oates's Εἰκὼν βασιλικὴ, Part. I.

hundred people, with their horses, could without difficulty be
lodged and fed.   The bedding, the tapestry, above all, the
abundance of clean and fine linen was matter of wonder.
Valuable plate was often set on the tables.   Nay, there were
signs which had cost thirty or forty pounds.   In the seventeenth century England abounded with excellent inns of every
rank.   The traveller sometimes, in a small village, lighted on
a public house such as Walton has described, where the brick
floor was swept clean, where the walls were stuck round with
ballads, where the sheets smelt of lavender, and where a
blazing fire, a cup of good ale, and a dish of trouts fresh from
the neighbouring brook, were to be procured at small charge.
At the larger houses of entertainment were to be found beds
hung with silk, choice cookery, and claret equal to the best
which was drunk in London. *   The innkeepers too, it was
said, were not like other innkeepers.   On the Continent the
landlord was the tyrant of those who crossed the threshold.
In England he was a servant.   Never was an Englishman
more at home than when he took his ease in his inn.   Even
men of fortune, who might in their own mansions have
enjoyed every luxury, were often in the habit of passing their
evenings in the parlour of some neighbouring house of public
entertainment.   They seem to have thought that comfort and
freedom could in no other place be enjoyed in equal perfection.   This feeling continued during many generations to
be a national peculiarity.   The liberty and jollity of inns long
furnished matter to our novelists and dramatists.   Johnson
declared that a tavern chair was the throne of human felicity;
and Shenstone gently complained that no private roof, however friendly, gave the wanderer so warm a welcome as that
which was to be found at an inn.

* See the prologue to the Canterbury Tales, Harrison's Historical
Description of the Island of Great Britain, and Pepys's account of his
tour in the summer of 1668. The excellence of the English inns is noticed
in the Travels of the Grand Duke Cosmo.

Many conveniences, which were unknown at Hampton
Court and Whitehall in the seventeenth century, are to be
found in our modern hotels. Yet on the whole it is certain
that the improvement of our houses of public entertainment
has by no means kept pace with the improvement of our roads
and of our conveyances. Nor is this strange; for it is evident
that, all other circumstances being supposed equal, the inns
will be best where the means of locomotion are worst. The
quicker the rate of travelling, the less important is it that
there should be numerous agreeable resting places for the
traveller. A hundred and sixty years ago a person who came
up to the capital from a remote county generally required
twelve or fifteen meals, and lodging for five or six nights
by the way. If he were a great man, he expected the meals
and lodging to be comfortable, and even luxurious. At
present we fly from York or Exeter to London by the light of
a single winter's day. At present, therefore, a traveller
seldom interrupts his journey merely for the sake of rest and
refreshment. The consequence is that hundreds of excellent
inns have fallen into utter decay. In a short time no good
houses of that description will be found, except at places
where strangers are likely to be detained by business or
pleasure.

The mode in which correspondence was carried on between distant places may excite the scorn of the present
generation; yet it was such as might have moved the admiration and envy of the polished nations of antiquity, or of the
contemporaries of Raleigh and Cecil. A rude and imperfect
establishment of posts for the conveyance of letters had been
set up by Charles the First, and had been swept away by the
civil war. Under the Commonwealth the design was resumed.
At the Restoration the proceeds of the Post Office, after all
expenses had been paid, were settled on the Duke of York.
On most lines of road the mails went out and came in only on

the alternate days. In Cornwall, in the fens of Lincolnshire, and among the hills and lakes of Cumberland, letters were received only once a week. During a royal progress a daily post was despatched from the capital to the place where the court sojourned. There was also daily communication between London and the Downs; and the same privilege was sometimes extended to Tunbridge Wells and Bath at the seasons when those places were crowded by the great. The bags were carried on horseback day and night at the rate of about five miles an hour. *

The revenue of this establishment was not derived solely from the charge for the transmission of letters. The Post Office alone was entitled to furnish post horses; and, from the care with which this monopoly was guarded, we may infer that it was found profitable.** If, indeed, a traveller had waited half an hour without being supplied, he might hire a horse wherever he could.

To facilitate correspondence between one part of London and another was not originally one of the objects of the Post Office. But, in the reign of Charles the Second, an enterprising citizen of London, William Dockwray, set up, at great expense, a penny post, which delivered letters and parcels six or eight times a day in the busy and crowded streets near the Exchange, and four times a day in the outskirts of the capital. This improvement was, as usual, strenuously resisted. The porters complained that their interests were attacked, and tore down the placards in which the scheme was announced to the public. The excitement caused by Godfrey's death, and by the discovery of Coleman's papers, was then at the height. A cry was therefore raised that the penny post was a Popish contrivance. The

---

* Stat. 12 Car. II. c. 35. Chamberlayne's State of England, 1684. Angliæ Metropolis, 1690. London Gazette, June 22. 1685, August 15. 1687.
** London Gazette, Sept. 14. 1685.

great Doctor Oates, it was affirmed, had hinted a suspicion
that the Jesuits were at the bottom of the scheme, and that the
bags, if examined, would be found full of treason. * The
utility of the enterprise was, however, so great and obvious
that all opposition proved fruitless. As soon as it became
clear that the speculation would be lucrative, the Duke of
York complained of it as an infraction of his monopoly, and
the courts of law decided in his favour.**

The revenue of the Post Office was from the first constantly increasing. In the year of the Restoration a committee
of the House of Commons, after strict inquiry, had estimated
the net receipt at about twenty thousand pounds. At the
close of the reign of Charles the Second, the net receipt was
little short of fifty thousand pounds; and this was then
thought a stupendous sum. The gross receipt was about
seventy thousand pounds. The charge for conveying a single
letter was twopence for eighty miles, and threepence for a
longer distance. The postage increased in proportion to the
weight of the packet.*** At present a single letter is carried
to the extremity of Scotland or of Ireland for a penny; and
the monopoly of post horses has long ceased to exist. Yet
the gross annual receipts of the department amount to more
than eighteen hundred thousand pounds, and the net receipts
to more than seven hundred thousand pounds. It is, therefore, scarcely possible to doubt that the number of letters
now conveyed by mail is seventy times the number which
was so conveyed at the time of the accession of James the
Second.

No part of the load which the old mails carried out was News-
more important than the newsletters. In 1685 nothing like papers.
the London daily paper of our time existed, or could exist.

* Smith's Current Intelligence, March 30. and April 3. 1680.
** Angliæ Metropolis, 1690.
*** Commons' Journals, Sept. 4. 1660, March 1. 168⅗. Chamberlayne,
684. Davenant on the Public Revenue, Discourse IV.

Neither the necessary capital nor the necessary skill was to
be found.   Freedom too was wanting, a want as fatal as that
of either capital or skill.   The press was not indeed at that
moment under a general censorship.   The licensing act, which
had been passed soon after the Restoration, had expired in
1679.   Any person might therefore print, at his own risk, a
history, a sermon, or a poem, without the previous approbation of any public officer; but the Judges were unanimously
of opinion that this liberty did not extend to Gazettes, and
that, by the common law of England, no man, not authorised
by the crown, had a right to publish political news. *   While
the Whig party was still formidable, the government thought
it expedient occasionally to connive at the violation of this
rule.   During the great battle of the Exclusion Bill, many
newspapers were suffered to appear, the Protestant Intelligence, the Current Intelligence, the Domestic Intelligence,
the True News, the London Mercury.**   None of these was
published oftener than twice a week.   None exceeded in size
a single small leaf.   The quantity of matter which one of
them contained in a year was not more than is often found in
two numbers of the Times.   After the defeat of the Whigs it
was no longer necessary for the King to be sparing in the use
of that which all his Judges had pronounced to be his undoubted prerogative.   At the close of his reign no newspaper
was suffered to appear without his allowance: and his allowance was given exclusively to the London Gazette.   The
London Gazette came out only on Mondays and Thursdays.
The contents generally were a royal proclamation, two or
three Tory addresses, notices of two or three promotions, an
account of a skirmish between the imperial troops and the
Janissaries on the Danube, a description of a highwayman,

---

* London Gazette, May 5. and 17. 1680.
** There is a very curious, and, I should think, unique collection of
these papers in the British Museum.

an announcement of a grand cock-fight between two persons of honour, and an advertisement offering a reward for a strayed dog. The whole made up two pages of moderate size. Whatever was communicated respecting matters of the highest moment was communicated in the most meagre and formal style. Sometimes, indeed, when the government was disposed to gratify the public curiosity respecting an important transaction, a broadside was put forth giving fuller details than could be found in the Gazette: but neither the Gazette nor any supplementary broadside printed by authority ever contained any intelligence which it did not suit the purposes of the court to publish. The most important parliamentary debates, the most important state trials, recorded in our history, were passed over in profound silence. * In the capital the coffee-houses supplied in some measure the place of a journal. Thither the Londoners flocked, as the Athenians of old flocked to the market place, to hear whether there was any news. There men might learn how brutally a Whig had been treated the day before in Westminster Hall, what horrible accounts the letters from Edinburgh gave of the torturing of Covenanters, how grossly the Navy Board had cheated the crown in the victualling of the fleet, and what grave charges the Lord Privy Seal had brought against the Treasury in the matter of the hearth money. But people who lived at a distance from the great theatre of political contention could be kept regularly informed of what was passing there only by means of newsletters. To prepare such letters became a calling in London, as it now is among the natives of India. The newswriter rambled from coffee-room to coffee-room, collecting reports, squeezed himself into the Sessions House at the Old Bailey if there was an interesting trial, nay,

News-
letters.

* For example, there is not a word in the Gazette about the important parliamentary proceedings of November 1685, or about the trial and acquittal of the seven Bishops.

perhaps obtained admission to the gallery of Whitehall, and noticed how the King and Duke looked. In this way he gathered materials for weekly epistles destined to enlighten some county town or some bench of rustic magistrates. Such were the sources from which the inhabitants of the largest provincial cities, and the great body of the gentry and clergy, learned almost all that they knew of the history of their own time. We must suppose that at Cambridge there were as many persons curious to know what was passing in the world as at almost any place in the kingdom, out of London. Yet at Cambridge, during a great part of the reign of Charles the Second, the Doctors of Laws and the Masters of Arts had no regular supply of news except through the London Gazette. At length the services of one of the collectors of intelligence in the capital were employed. That was a memorable day on which the first newsletter from London was laid on the table of the only coffee-room in Cambridge.* At the seat of a man of fortune in the country the newsletter was impatiently expected. Within a week after it had arrived it had been thumbed by twenty families. It furnished the neighbouring squires with matter for talk over their October, and the neighbouring rectors with topics for sharp sermons against Whiggery or Popery. Many of these curious journals might doubtless still be detected by a diligent search in the archives of old families. Some are to be found in our public libraries; and one series, which is not the least valuable part of the literary treasures collected by Sir James Mackintosh, will be occasionally quoted in the course of this work.**

* Roger North's Life of Dr. John North. On the subject of news-letters, see the Examen, 133.

** I take this opportunity of expressing my warm gratitude to the family of my dear and honoured friend Sir James Mackintosh for confiding to me the materials collected by him at a time when he meditated a work similar to that which I have undertaken. I have never seen, and I do not believe that there anywhere exists, within the same compass, so noble a collection of extracts from public and private archives. The

It is scarcely necessary to say that there were then no provincial newspapers. Indeed, except in the capital and at the two Universities, there was scarcely a printer in the kingdom. The only press in England north of Trent appears to have been at York.*

It was not only by means of the London Gazette that the government undertook to furnish political instruction to the people. That journal contained a scanty supply of news without comment. Another journal, published under the patronage of the court, consisted of comment without news. This paper, called the Observator, was edited by an old Tory pamphleteer named Roger Lestrange. Lestrange was by no means deficient in readiness and shrewdness; and his diction, though coarse, and disfigured by a mean and flippant jargon which then passed for wit in the green room and the tavern, was not without keenness and vigour. But his nature, at once ferocious and ignoble, showed itself in every line that he penned. When the first Observators appeared there was some excuse for his acrimony. For the Whigs were then powerful; and he had to contend against numerous adversaries, whose unscrupulous violence might seem to justify unsparing retaliation. But in 1685 all opposition had been crushed. A generous spirit would have disdained to insult a party which could not reply, and to aggravate the misery of prisoners, of exiles, of bereaved families: but from the malice of Lestrange the grave was no hiding place, and the house of mourning no sanctuary. In the last month of the reign of Charles the Se-

---

judgment with which Sir James, in great masses of the rudest ore in history, selected what was valuable, and rejected what was worthless, can be fully appreciated only by one who has toiled after him in the same mine.

* Life of Thomas Gent. A complete list of all printing houses in 1724 will be found in Nichols's Literary Anecdotes of the eighteenth century. There had then been a great increase within a few years in the number of presses; and yet there were thirty-four counties in which there was no printer, one of those counties being Lancashire.

cond, William Jenkyn, an aged dissenting pastor of great
note, who had been cruelly persecuted for no crime but that
of worshipping God according to the fashion generally followed throughout Protestant Europe, died of hardships and
privations in Newgate. The outbreak of popular sympathy
could not be repressed. The corpse was followed to the grave
by a train of a hundred and fifty coaches. Even courtiers
looked sad. Even the unthinking King showed some signs of
concern. Lestrange alone set up a howl of savage exultation,
laughed at the weak compassion of the Trimmers, proclaimed
that the blasphemous old impostor had met with a most
righteous punishment, and vowed to wage war, not only to
the death, but after death, with all the mock saints and martyrs.* Such was the spirit of the paper which was at this time
the oracle of the Tory party, and especially of the parochial
clergy.

Scarcity
of books
in country
places.
Literature which could be carried by the post bag then
formed the greater part of the intellectual nutriment rumi-
nated by the country divines and country justices. The difficulty and expense of conveying large packets from place to
place was so great, that an extensive work was longer in
making its way from Paternoster Row to Devonshire or Lancashire than it now is in reaching Kentucky. How scantily a
rural parsonage was then furnished, even with books the most
necessary to a theologian, has already been remarked. The
houses of the gentry were not more plentifully supplied. Few
knights of the shire had libraries so good as may now perpe-
tually be found in a servants' hall, or in the back parlour of a
small shopkeeper. An esquire passed among his neighbours
for a great scholar, if Hudibras and Baker's Chronicle, Tarl-
ton's Jests and the Seven Champions of Christendom, lay in
his hall window among the fishing rods and fowling pieces.

* Observator, Jan. 29. and 31. 1685. Calamy's Life of Baxter. Non-
conformist Memorial.

No circulating library, no book society then existed even in the capital: but in the capital those students who could not afford to purchase largely had a resource. The shops of the great booksellers, near Saint Paul's Churchyard, were crowded every day and all day long with readers; and a known customer was often permitted to carry a volume home. In the country there was no such accommodation; and every man was under the necessity of buying whatever he wished to read.*

As to the lady of the manor and her daughters, their literary stores generally consisted of a prayer book and a receipt book. But in truth they lost little by living in rural seclusion. For, even in the highest ranks, and in those situations which afforded the greatest facilities for mental improvement, the English women of that generation were decidedly worse educated than they have been at any other time since the revival of learning. At an earlier period they had studied the masterpieces of ancient genius. In the present day they seldom bestow much attention on the dead languages; but they are familiar with the tongue of Pascal and Moliere, with the tongue of Dante and Tasso, with the tongue of Goethe and Schiller; nor is there any purer or more graceful English than that which accomplished women now speak and write. But, during the latter part of the seventeenth century, the culture of the female mind seems to have been almost entirely neglected. If a damsel had the least smattering of literature she was regarded as a prodigy. Ladies highly born, highly bred, and naturally quick witted, were unable to write a line in their mother tongue without solecisms

Female education.

---

* Cotton seems, from his Angler, to have found room for his whole library in his hall window; and Cotton was a man of letters. Even when Franklin first visited London in 1724, circulating libraries were unknown there. The crowd at the booksellers' shops in Little Britain is mentioned by Roger North in his life of his brother John.

and faults of spelling such as a charity girl would now be ashamed to commit.*

The explanation may easily be found. Extravagant licentiousness, the natural effect of extravagant austerity, was now the mode: and licentiousness had produced its ordinary effect, the moral and intellectual degradation of women. To their personal beauty, it was the fashion to pay rude and impudent homage. But the admiration and desire which they inspired were seldom mingled with respect, with affection, or with any chivalrous sentiment. The qualities which fit them to be companions, advisers, confidential friends, rather repelled than attracted the libertines of Whitehall. In that court a maid of honour, who dressed in such a manner as to do full justice to a white bosom, who ogled significantly, who danced voluptuously, who excelled in pert repartee, who was not ashamed to romp with Lords of the Bedchamber and Captains of the Guards, to sing sly verses with sly expression, or to put on a page's dress for a frolic, was more likely to be followed and admired, more likely to be honoured with royal attentions, more likely to win a rich and noble husband than Jane Grey or Lucy Hutchinson would have been. In such circumstances the standard of female attainments was necessarily low; and it was more dangerous to be above that standard than to be beneath it. Extreme ignorance and frivolity were thought less unbecoming in a lady than the slightest tincture of pedantry. Of the too celebrated women whose faces we still admire on the walls of Hampton Court, few indeed were in the habit of reading anything more valuable than

---

* One instance will suffice. Queen Mary had good natural abilities, had been educated by a Bishop, was fond of history and poetry, and was regarded by very eminent men as a superior woman. There is, in the library at the Hague, a superb English Bible which was delivered to her when she was crowned in Westminster Abbey. In the title page are these words in her own hand, "This book was given the King and I, at our crownation. Marie R."

acrostics, lampoons, and translations of the Clelia and the Grand Cyrus.

The literary acquirements, even of the accomplished gen- tlemen of that generation, seem to have been somewhat less solid and profound than at an earlier or a later period. Greek learning, at least, did not flourish among us in the days of Charles the Second, as it had flourished before the civil war, or as it again flourished long after the Revolution. There were undoubtedly scholars to whom the whole Greek literature, from Homer to Photius, was familiar: but such scholars were to be found almost exclusively among the clergy resident at the Universities, and even at the Universities were few, and were not fully appreciated. At Cambridge it was not thought by any means necessary that a divine should be able to read the Gospels in the original.* Nor was the standard at Oxford higher. When, in the reign of William the Third, Christ Church rose up as one man to defend the genuineness of the Epistles of Phalaris, that great college, then considered as the first seat of philology in the kingdom, could not muster such a stock of Attic learning as is now possessed by several youths at every great public school. It may easily be supposed that a dead language, neglected at the Universities, was not much studied by men of the world. In a former age the poetry and eloquence of Greece had been the delight of Raleigh and Falkland. In a later age the poetry and eloquence of Greece were the delight of Pitt and Fox, of Windham and Grenville. But during the latter part of the seventeenth century there was in England scarcely one eminent statesman who could read with enjoyment a page of Sophocles or Plato.

Good Latin scholars were numerous. The language of Rome, indeed, had not altogether lost its imperial character,

* Roger North tells us that his brother John, who was Greek professor at Cambridge, complained bitterly of the general neglect of the Greek tongue among the academical clergy.

and was still, in many parts of Europe, almost indispensable
to a traveller or a negotiator. To speak it well was therefore
a much more common accomplishment than in our time; and
neither Oxford nor Cambridge wanted poets who, on a great
occasion, could lay at the foot of the throne happy imitations
of the verses in which Virgil and Ovid had celebrated the
greatness of Augustus.

Yet even the Latin was giving way to a younger rival.
France united at that time almost every species of ascendency.
Her military glory was at the height. She had vanquished
mighty coalitions. She had dictated treaties. She had subjugated great cities and provinces. She had forced the
Castilian pride to yield her the precedence. She had summoned Italian princes to prostrate themselves at her foot-stool.
Her authority was supreme in all matters of good breeding,
from a duel to a minuet. She determined how a gentleman's
coat must be cut, how long his peruke must be, whether his
heels must be high or low, and whether the lace on his hat
must be broad or narrow. In literature she gave law to the
world. The fame of her great writers filled Europe. No
other country could produce a tragic poet equal to Racine,
a comic poet equal to Moliere, a trifler so agreeable as La
Fontaine, a rhetorician so skilful as Bossuet. The literary
glory of Italy and of Spain had set; that of Germany had not
yet dawned. The genius, therefore, of the eminent men
who adorned Paris shone forth with a splendour which was
set off to full advantage by contrast. France, indeed, had
at that time an empire over mankind, such as even the Roman
Republic never attained. For, when Rome was politically
dominant, she was in arts and letters the humble pupil of
Greece. France had, over the surrounding countries, at
once the ascendency which Rome had over Greece, and the
ascendency which Greece had over Rome. French was fast
becoming the universal language, the language of fashionable

society, the language of diplomacy. At several courts princes and nobles spoke it more accurately and politely than their mother tongue. In our island there was less of this servility than on the Continent. Neither our good nor our bad qualities were those of imitators. Yet even here homage was paid, awkwardly indeed and sullenly, to the literary supremacy of our neighbours. The melodious Tuscan, so familiar to the gallants and ladies of the court of Elizabeth, sank into contempt. A gentleman who quoted Horace or Terence was considered in good company as a pompous pedant. But to garnish his conversation with scraps of French was the best proof which he could give of his parts and attainments.* New canons of criticism, new models of style came into fashion. The quaint ingenuity which had deformed the verses of Donne, and had been a blemish on those of Cowley, disappeared from our poetry. Our prose became less majestic, less artfully involved, less variously musical than that of an earlier age, but more lucid, more easy, and better fitted for controversy and narrative. In these changes it is impossible not to recognise the influence of French precept and of French example. Great masters of our language, in their most dignified compositions, affected to use French words, when English words, quite as expressive and melodious, were at hand:** and from France was imported the tragedy in rhyme, an exotic which, in our soil, drooped, and speedily died.

---

* Butler, in a satire of great asperity, says,

> "For, though to smatter words of Greek
> And Latin be the rhetorique
> Of pedants counted, and vainglorious,
> To smatter French is meritorious."

** The most offensive instance which I remember is in a poem on the coronation of Charles the Second by Dryden, who certainly could not plead poverty as an excuse for borrowing words from any foreign tongue: —

> "Hither in summer evenings you repair
> To taste the fraicheur of the cooler air."

CHAP.
III.

Immora-
lity of the
polite
literature
of Eng-
land.
It would have been well if our writers had also copied
the decorum which their great French contemporaries, with
few exceptions, preserved; for the profligacy of the English
plays, satires, songs, and novels of that age is a deep blot
on our national fame. The evil may easily be traced to its
source. The wits and the Puritans had never been on friendly
terms. There was no sympathy between the two classes.
They looked on the whole system of human life from different
points and in different lights. The earnest of each was the
jest of the other. The pleasures of each were the torments
of the other. To the stern precisian even the innocent sport
of the fancy seemed a crime. To light and festive natures
the solemnity of the zealous brethren furnished copious
matter of ridicule. From the Reformation to the civil war,
almost every writer, gifted with a fine sense of the ludicrous,
had taken some opportunity of assailing the straight haired,
snuffling, whining saints, who christened their children out
of the Book of Nehemiah, who groaned in spirit at the sight
of Jack in the Green, and who thought it impious to taste
plum porridge on Christmas day. At length a time came
when the laughers began to look grave in their turn. The
rigid, ungainly zealots, after having furnished much good
sport during two generations, rose up in arms, conquered,
ruled, and, grimly smiling, trod down under their feet the
whole crowd of mockers. The wounds inflicted by gay and
petulant malice were retaliated with the gloomy and implacable malice peculiar to bigots who mistake their own
rancour for virtue. The theatres were closed. The players
were flogged. The press was put under the guardianship of
austere licensers. The Muses were banished from their own
favourite haunts, Cambridge and Oxford. Cowley, Crashaw,
and Cleveland were ejected from their fellowships. The
young candidate for academical honours was no longer required to write Ovidian epistles or Virgilian pastorals, but

was strictly interrogated by a synod of lowering Supralapsarians as to the day and hour when he experienced the new birth. Such a system was of course fruitful of hypocrites. Under sober clothing and under visages composed to the expression of austerity lay hid during several years the intense desire of license and of revenge. At length that desire was gratified. The Restoration emancipated thousands of minds from a yoke which had become insupportable. The old fight recommenced, but with an animosity altogether new. It was now not a sportive combat, but a war to the death. The Roundhead had no better quarter to expect from those whom he had persecuted than a cruel slave driver can expect from insurgent slaves still bearing the marks of his collars and his scourges.

The war between wit and Puritanism soon became a war between wit and morality. The hostility excited by a grotesque caricature of virtue did not spare virtue herself. Whatever the canting Roundhead had regarded with reverence was insulted. Whatever he had proscribed was favoured. Because he had been scrupulous about trifles, all scruples were treated with derision. Because he had covered his failings with the mask of devotion, men were encouraged to obtrude with Cynic impudence all their most scandalous vices on the public eye. Because he had punished illicit love with barbarous severity, virgin purity and conjugal fidelity were to be made a jest. To that sanctimonious jargon which was his Shibboleth, was opposed another jargon not less absurd and much more odious. As he never opened his mouth except in scriptural phrase, the new breed of wits and fine gentlemen never opened their mouths without uttering ribaldry of which a porter would now be ashamed, and without calling on their Maker to curse them, sink them, confound them, blast them, and damn them.

It is not strange, therefore, that our polite literature, when it revived with the revival of the old civil and ecclesiastical polity, should have been profoundly immoral. A few

eminent men, who belonged to an earlier and better age,
were exempt from the general contagion. The verse of
Waller still breathed the sentiments which had animated a
more chivalrous generation. Cowley, distinguished as a
loyalist and as a man of letters, raised his voice courageously
against the immorality which disgraced both letters and
loyalty. A mightier poet, tried at once by pain, danger,
poverty, obloquy and blindness, meditated, undisturbed by
the obscene tumult which raged all around him, a song so
sublime and so holy that it would not have misbecome the lips
of those ethereal Virtues whom he saw, with that inner eye
which no calamity could darken, flinging down on the jasper
pavement their crowns of amaranth and gold. The vigorous
and fertile genius of Butler, if it did not altogether escape
the prevailing infection, took the disease in a mild form.
But these were men whose minds had been trained in a world
which had passed away. They gave place in no long time to
a younger generation of wits; and of that generation, from
Dryden down to Durfey, the common characteristic was
hard-hearted, shameless, swaggering licentiousness, at once
inelegant and inhuman. The influence of these writers was
doubtless noxious, yet less noxious than it would have been
had they been less depraved. The poison which they administered was so strong that it was, in no long time, rejected
with nausea. None of them understood the dangerous art
of associating images of unlawful pleasure with all that is
endearing and ennobling. None of them was aware that a
certain decorum is essential even to voluptuousness, that
drapery may be more alluring than exposure, and that the
imagination may be far more powerfully moved by delicate
hints which impel it to exert itself than by gross descriptions
which it takes in passively.

The spirit of the Antipuritan reaction pervades almost the
whole polite literature of the reign of Charles the Second.

But the very quintessence of that spirit will be found in the comic drama. The play-houses, shut by the meddling fanatic in the day of his power, were again crowded. To their old attractions new and more powerful attractions had been added. Scenery, dresses, and decorations such as would now be thought mean or absurd, but such as would have been esteemed incredibly magnificent by those who, early in the seventeenth century, sate on the filthy benches of the Hope, or under the thatched roof of the Rose, dazzled the eyes of the multitude. The fascination of sex was called in to aid the fascination of art: and the young spectator saw, with emotions unknown to the contemporaries of Shakspeare and Jonson, tender and sprightly heroines personated by lovely women. From the day on which the theatres were reopened they became seminaries of vice; and the evil propagated itself. The profligacy of the representations soon drove away sober people. The frivolous and dissolute who remained required every year stronger and stronger stimulants. Thus the artists corrupted the spectators, and the spectators the artists, till the turpitude of the drama became such as must astonish all who are not aware that extreme relaxation is the natural effect of extreme restraint, and that an age of hypocrisy is, in the regular course of things, followed by an age of impudence.

Nothing is more characteristic of the times than the care with which the poets contrived to put all their loosest verses into the mouths of women. The compositions in which the greatest license was taken were the epilogues. They were almost always recited by favourite actresses; and nothing charmed the depraved audience so much as to hear lines grossly indecent repeated by a beautiful girl, who was supposed to have not yet lost her innocence.*

Our theatre was indebted in that age for many plots and

* Jeremy Collier has censured this odious practice with his usual force and keenness.

characters to Spain, to France, and to the old English masters:
but whatever our dramatists touched they tainted. In their
imitations the houses of Calderon's stately and high spirited
Castilian gentlemen became sties of vice, Shakspeare's Viola
a procuress, Moliere's Misanthrope a ravisher, Moliere's
Agnes an adulteress. Nothing could be so pure or so heroic
but that it became foul and ignoble by transfusion through
those foul and ignoble minds.

Such was the state of the drama; and the drama was the
department of polite literature in which a poet had the best
chance of obtaining a subsistence by his pen. The sale of
books was so small that a man of the greatest name could
expect only a pittance for the copyright of the best performance. There cannot be a stronger instance than the fate
of Dryden's last production, the Fables. That volume was
published when he was universally admitted to be the chief of
living English poets. It contains about twelve thousand lines.
The versification is admirable; the narratives and descriptions full of life. To this day Palamon and Arcite, Cymon
and Iphigenia, Theodore and Honoria, are the delight both
of critics and of school-boys. The collection includes Alexander's Feast, the noblest ode in our language. For the copyright Dryden received two hundred and fifty pounds, less
than in our days has sometimes been paid for two articles in a
review.* Nor does the bargain seem to have been a hard one.
For the book went off slowly; and the second edition was not
required till the author had been ten years in his grave. By
writing for the theatre it was possible to earn a much larger
sum with much less trouble. Southern made seven hundred
pounds by one play.** Otway was raised from beggary to
temporary affluence by the success of his Don Carlos.***
Shadwell cleared a hundred and thirty pounds by a single

* The contract will be found in Sir Walter Scott's edition of Dryden.
** See the Life of Southern, by Shiels.
*** See Rochester's Trial of the Poets.

representation of the Squire of Alsatia.* The consequence
was that every man who had to live by his wit wrote plays,
whether he had any internal vocation to write plays or not.
It was thus with Dryden. As a satirist he has rivalled Juvenal.
As a didactic poet he perhaps might, with care and meditation, have rivalled Lucretius. Of lyric poets he is, if not the
most sublime, the most brilliant and spirit-stirring. But nature, profuse to him of many rare gifts, had denied him the
dramatic faculty. Nevertheless all the energies of his best
years were wasted on dramatic composition. He had too
much judgment not to be aware that in the power of exhibit-
ing character by means of dialogue he was deficient. That
deficiency he did his best to conceal, sometimes by surprising and amusing incidents, sometimes by stately declamation, sometimes by harmonious numbers, sometimes
by ribaldry but too well suited to the taste of a profane and
licentious pit. Yet he never obtained any theatrical success
equal to that which rewarded the exertions of some men far
inferior to him in general powers. He thought himself fortunate if he cleared a hundred guineas by a play; a scanty
remuneration, yet apparently larger than he could have
earned in any other way by the same quantity of labour.**

The recompense which the wits of that age could obtain
from the public was so small, that they were under the necessity of eking out their incomes by levying contributions on
the great. Every rich and good-natured lord was pestered by
authors with a mendicancy so importunate, and a flattery so
abject, as may in our time seem incredible. The patron to
whom a work was inscribed was expected to reward the writer
with a purse of gold. The fee paid for the dedication of a
book was often much larger than the sum which any publisher
would give for the copyright. Books were therefore fre-

* Some Account of the English Stage.
** Life of Southern, by Shiels.

quently printed merely that they might be dedicated. This traffic in praise produced the effect which might have been expected. Adulation pushed to the verge, sometimes of nonsense, and sometimes of impiety, was not thought to disgrace a poet. Independence, veracity, self-respect, were things not required by the world from him. In truth, he was in morals something between a pandar and a beggar.

To the other vices which degraded the literary character was added, towards the close of the reign of Charles the Second, the most savage intemperance of party spirit. The wits, as a class, had been impelled by their old hatred of Puritanism to take the side of the court, and had been found useful allies. Dryden, in particular, had done good service to the government. His Absalom and Achitophel, the greatest satire of modern times, had amazed the town, had made its way with unprecedented rapidity even into rural districts, and had, wherever it appeared, bitterly annoyed the Exclusionists, and raised the courage of the Tories. But we must not, in the admiration which we naturally feel for noble diction and versification, forget the great distinctions of good and evil. The spirit by which Dryden and several of his compeers were at this time animated against the Whigs deserves to be called fiendish. The servile Judges and Sheriffs of those evil days could not shed blood so fast as the poets cried out for it. Calls for more victims, hideous jests on hanging, bitter taunts on those who, having stood by the King in the hour of danger, now advised him to deal mercifully and generously by his vanquished enemies, were publicly recited on the stage, and, that nothing might be wanting to the guilt and the shame, were recited by women, who, having long been taught to discard all modesty, were now taught to discard all compassion. *

* If any reader thinks my expressions too severe, I would advise him to read Dryden's Epilogue to the Duke of Guise, and to observe that it was spoken by a woman.

It is a remarkable fact that, while the lighter literature of

England was thus becoming a nuisance and a national disgrace, the English genius was effecting in science a revolution
which will, to the end of time, be reckoned among the highest achievements of the human intellect. Bacon had sown
the good seed in a sluggish soil and an ungenial season. He
had not expected an early crop, and in his last testament had
solemnly bequeathed his fame to the next age. During a
whole generation his philosophy had, amidst tumults, wars,
and proscriptions, been slowly ripening in a few well constituted minds. While factions were struggling for dominion
over each other, a small body of sages had turned away with
benevolent disdain from the conflict, and had devoted themselves to the nobler work of extending the dominion of man
over matter. As soon as tranquillity was restored, these
teachers easily found attentive audience. For the discipline
through which the nation had passed had brought the public
mind to a temper well fitted for the reception of the Veru-
lamian doctrine. The civil troubles had stimulated the
faculties of the educated classes, and had called forth a restless activity and an insatiable curiosity, such as had not before
been known among us. Yet the effect of those troubles was
that schemes of political and religious reform were generally
regarded with suspicion and contempt. During twenty years
the chief employment of busy and ingenious men had been to
frame constitutions with first magistrates, without first magistrates, with hereditary senates, with senates appointed by
lot, with annual senates, with perpetual senates. In these
plans nothing was omitted. All the detail, all the nomen-
clature, all the ceremonial of the imaginary government was
fully set forth, Polemarchs and Phylarchs, Tribes and Ga-
laxies, the Lord Archon and the Lord Strategus. Which
ballot boxes were to be green and which red, which balls
were to be of gold and which of silver, which magistrates were

to wear hats and which black velvet caps with peaks, how the mace was to be carried and when the heralds were to uncover, these, and a hundred more such trifles, were gravely considered and arranged by men of no common capacity and learning.* But the time for these visions had gone by; and, if any steadfast republican still continued to amuse himself with them, fear of public derision and of a criminal information generally induced him to keep his fancies to himself. It was now unpopular and unsafe to mutter a word against the fundamental laws of the monarchy: but daring and ingenious men might indemnify themselves by treating with disdain what had lately been considered as the fundamental laws of nature. The torrent which had been dammed up in one channel rushed violently into another. The revolutionary spirit, ceasing to operate in politics, began to exert itself with unprecedented vigour and hardihood in every department of physics. The year 1660, the era of the restoration of the old constitution, is also the era from which dates the ascendency of the new philosophy. In that year the Royal Society, destined to be a chief agent in a long series of glorious and salutary reforms, began to exist.** In a few months experimental science became all the mode. The transfusion of blood, the ponderation of air, the fixation of mercury, succeeded to that place in the public mind which had been lately occupied by the controversies of the Rota. Dreams of perfect forms of government made way for dreams of wings with which men were to fly from the Tower to the Abbey, and of double-keeled ships which were never to founder in the fiercest storm. All classes were hurried along by the prevailing sentiment. Cavalier and Roundhead, Churchman and Puritan were for once allied. Divines, jurists, statesmen, nobles, princes, swelled the triumph of the Baconian philosophy.

* See particularly Harrington's Oceana.
** See Sprat's History of the Royal Society.

Poets sang with emulous fervour the approach of the golden
age. Cowley, in lines weighty with thought and resplendent
with wit, urged the chosen seed to take possession of the
promised land flowing with milk and honey, that land which
their great deliverer and law-giver had seen, as from the sum-
mit of Pisgah, but had not been permitted to enter.* Dryden,
with more zeal than knowledge, joined his voice to the general
acclamation, and foretold things which neither he nor any-
body else understood. The Royal Society, he predicted,
would soon lead us to the extreme verge of the globe, and
there delight us with a better view of the moon.** Two able
and aspiring prelates, Ward, Bishop of Salisbury, and Wilkins,
Bishop of Chester, were conspicuous among the leaders of the
movement. Its history was eloquently written by a younger
divine, who was rising to high distinction in his profession,
Thomas Sprat, afterwards Bishop of Rochester. Both Chief
Justice Hale and Lord Keeper Guildford stole some hours
from the business of their courts to write on hydrostatics.
Indeed it was under the immediate directions of Guildford
that the first barometers ever exposed to sale in London were
constructed.*** Chemistry divided, for a time, with wine and
love, with the stage and the gaming table, with the intrigues
of a courtier and the intrigues of a demagogue, the attention
of the fickle Buckingham. Rupert has the credit of having
invented mezzotinto; and from him is named that curious
bubble of glass which has long amused children and puzzled
philosophers. Charles himself had a laboratory at Whitehall,
and was far more active and attentive there than at the council
board. It was almost necessary to the character of a fine

* Cowley's Ode to the Royal Society.
** " Then we upon the globe's last verge shall go,
    And view the ocean leaning on the sky;
  Fro m thence our rolling neighbours we shall know,
    And on the lunar world securely pry."
                                    Annus Mirabilis, 164.
*** North's Life of Guildford.

gentleman to have something to say about air-pumps and tele-
scopes; and even fine ladies, now and then, thought it becoming to affect a taste for science, went in coaches and six
to visit the Gresham curiosities, and broke forth into cries of
delight at finding that a magnet really attracted a needle,
and that a microscope really made a fly look as large as a
sparrow. *

In this, as in every great stir of the human mind, there was
doubtless something which might well move a smile. It is the
universal law that whatever pursuit, whatever doctrine, becomes fashionable, shall lose a portion of that dignity which it
had possessed while it was confined to a small but earnest minority, and was loved for its own sake alone. It is true that
the follies of some persons who, without any real aptitude for
science, professed a passion for it, furnished matter of contemptuous mirth to a few malignant satirists who belonged to
the preceding generation, and were not disposed to unlearn
the lore of their youth.** But it is not less true that the great
work of interpreting nature was performed by the English of
that age as it had never before been performed in any age by
any nation. The spirit of Francis Bacon was abroad, a spirit
admirably compounded of audacity and sobriety. There was
a strong persuasion that the whole world was full of secrets of
high moment to the happiness of man, and that man had, by
his Maker, been intrusted with the key which, rightly used,
would give access to them. There was at the same time a conviction that in physics it was impossible to arrive at the knowledge of general laws except by the careful observation of particular facts. Deeply impressed with these great truths, the
professors of the new philosophy applied themselves to their

* Pepys's Diary, May 30. 1667.
** Butler was, I think, the only man of real genius who, between the
Restoration and the Revolution, showed a bitter enmity to the new philosophy, as it was then called. See the Satire on the Royal Society, and
the Elephant in the Moon.

task, and, before a quarter of a century had expired, they had given ample earnest of what has since been achieved. Already a reform of agriculture had been commenced. New vegetables were cultivated. New implements of husbandry were employed. New manures were applied to the soil. * Evelyn had, under the formal sanction of the Royal Society, given instruction to his countrymen in planting. Temple, in his intervals of leisure, had tried many experiments in horticulture, and had proved that many delicate fruits, the natives of more favoured climates, might, with the help of art, be grown on English ground. Medicine, which in France was still in abject bondage, and afforded an inexhaustible subject of just ridicule to Molière, had in England become an experimental and progressive science, and every day made some new advance, in defiance of Hippocrates and Galen. The attention of speculative men had been, for the first time, directed to the important subject of sanitary police. The great plague of 1665 induced them to consider with care the defective architecture, draining, and ventilation of the capital. The great fire of 1666 afforded an opportunity for effecting extensive improvements. The whole matter was diligently examined by the Royal Society; and to the suggestions of that body must be partly attributed the changes which, though far short of what the public welfare required, yet made a wide difference between the new and the old London, and probably put a final close to the ravages of pestilence in our country.** At the same time one of the founders of the society, Sir William Petty, created the science of political arithmetic, the humble but indispensable handmaid of political philosophy. No kingdom of nature was left unexplored. To that period belong the che-

---

* The eagerness with which the agriculturists of that age tried experiments and introduced improvements, is well described by Aubrey, Natural History of Wiltshire, 1685.
** Sprat's History of the Royal Society.

mical discoveries of Boyle, and the earliest botanical researches of Sloane. It was then that Ray made a new classification of birds and fishes, and that the attention of Woodward was first drawn towards fossils and shells. One after another phantoms which had haunted the world through ages of darkness fled before the light. Astrology and alchymy became jests. Soon there was scarcely a county in which some of the Quorum did not smile contemptuously when an old woman was brought before them for riding on broomsticks or giving cattle the murrain. But it was in those noblest and most arduous departments of knowledge in which induction and mathematical demonstration cooperate for the discovery of truth, that the English genius won in that age the most memorable triumphs. John Wallis placed the whole system of statics on a new foundation. Edmund Halley investigated the properties of the atmosphere, the ebb and flow of the sea, the laws of magnetism, and the course of the comets; nor did he shrink from toil, peril, and exile in the course of science. While he, on the rock of Saint Helena, mapped the constellations of the southern hemisphere, our national observatory was rising at Greenwich; and John Flamsteed, the first astronomer royal, was commencing that long series of observations which is never mentioned without respect and gratitude in any part of the globe. But the glory of these men, eminent as they were, is cast into the shade by the transcendent lustre of one immortal name. In Isaac Newton two kinds of intellectual power, which have little in common, and which are not often found together in a very high degree of vigour, but which nevertheless are equally necessary in the most sublime departments of physics, were united as they have never been united before or since. There may have been minds as happily constituted as his for the cultivation of pure mathematical science; there may have been minds as happily constituted for the cultivation of science purely experimental: but in no other mind have the demonstrative faculty and the inductive faculty coexisted in such supreme excellence and perfect harmony.   Perhaps in an age of Scotists and Thomists even his intellect might have run to waste, as many intellects ran to waste which were inferior only to his. Happily the spirit of the age on which his lot was cast, gave the right direction to his mind; and his mind reacted with tenfold force on the spirit of the age.   In the year 1685 his fame, though splendid, was only dawning; but his genius was in the meridian. His great work, that work which effected a revolution in the most important provinces of natural philosophy, had been completed, but was not yet published, and was just about to be submitted to the consideration of the Royal Society.

It is not very easy to explain why the nation which was so far before its neighbours in science should in art have been far behind them all.   Yet such was the fact.   It is true that in architecture, an art which is half a science, an art in which none but a geometrician can excel, an art which has no standard of grace but what is directly or indirectly dependent on utility, an art of which the creations derive a part, at least, of their majesty from mere bulk, our country could boast of one truly great man, Christopher Wren; and the fire which laid London in ruins had given him an opportunity, unprecedented in modern history, of displaying his powers.   The austere beauty of the Athenian portico, the gloomy sublimity of the Gothic arcade, he was, like almost all his contemporaries, incapable of emulating, and perhaps incapable of appreciating: but no man, born on our side of the Alps, has imitated with so much success the magnificence of the palacelike churches of Italy.   Even the superb Lewis has left to posterity no work which can bear a comparison with Saint Paul's.   But at the close of the reign of Charles the Second there was not a single English painter or statuary whose name is now remembered. This sterility is somewhat mysterious; for painters and statuaries were by no means a despised or an ill paid class. Their social position was at least as high as at present. Their gains, when compared with the wealth of the nation and with the remuneration of other descriptions of intellectual labour, were even larger than at present. Indeed the munificent patronage which was extended to artists drew them to our shores in multitudes. Lely, who has preserved to us the rich curls, the full lips, and the languishing eyes of the frail beauties celebrated by Hamilton, was a Westphalian. He had died in 1680, having long lived splendidly, having received the honour of knighthood, and having accumulated a good estate out of the fruits of his skill. His noble collection of drawings and pictures was, after his decease, exhibited by the royal permission in the Banqueting House at Whitehall, and was sold by auction for the almost incredible sum of twenty-six thousand pounds, a sum which bore a greater proportion to the fortunes of the rich men of that day than a hundred thousand pounds would bear to the fortunes of the rich men of our time. * Lely was succeeded by his countryman Godfrey Kneller, who was made first a knight and then a baronet, and who, after keeping up a sumptuous establishment, and after losing much money by unlucky speculations, was still able to bequeath a large fortune to his family. The two Vandeveldes, natives of Holland, had been tempted by English liberality to settle here, and had produced for the King and his nobles some of the finest sea pieces in the world. Another Dutchman, Simon Varelst, painted glorious sunflowers and tulips for prices such as had never before been known. Verrio, a Neapolitan, covered ceilings and staircases with Gorgons and Muses, Nymphs and Satyrs, Virtues and Vices, Gods quaffing nectar, and laurelled princes riding in triumph. The income which he derived from his performances enabled him to keep one of the most expensive tables in England. For his pieces at Windsor alone he received

* Walpole's Anecdotes of Painting. London Gazette, May 31. 1683. North's Life of Guildford.

seven thousand pounds, a sum then sufficient to make a gentleman of moderate wishes perfectly easy for life, a sum greatly
exceeding all that Dryden, during a literary life of forty years,
obtained from the booksellers. * Verrio's chief assistant and
successor, Lewis Laguerre, came from France. The two most
celebrated sculptors of that day were also foreigners. Cibber,
whose pathetic emblems of Fury and Melancholy still adorn
Bedlam, was a Dane. Gibbons, to whose graceful fancy and
delicate touch many of our palaces, colleges, and churches owe
their finest decorations, was a Dutchman. Even the designs
for the coin were made by French medallists. Indeed, it was
not till the reign of George the Second that our country could
glory in a great painter; and George the Third was on the
throne before she had reason to be proud of any of her
sculptors.

It is time that this description of the England which
Charles the Second governed should draw to a close. Yet
one subject of the highest moment still remains untouched.
Nothing has as yet been said of the great body of the people,
of those who held the ploughs, who tended the oxen, who
toiled at the looms of Norwich and squared the Portland stone
for Saint Paul's. Nor can very much be said. The most
numerous class is precisely the class respecting which we have
the most meagre information. In those times philanthropists
did not yet regard it as a sacred duty, nor had demagogues
yet found it a lucrative trade, to expatiate on the distress of
the labourer. History was too much occupied with courts
and camps to spare a line for the hut of the peasant or for the
garret of the mechanic. The press now often sends forth in a
day a greater quantity of discussion and declamation about
the condition of the working man than was published during
the twenty-eight years which elapsed between the Restoration

* The great prices paid to Varelst and Verrio are mentioned in Walpole's Anecdotes of Painting.

and the Revolution. But it would be a great error to infer from the increase of complaint that there has been any increase of misery.

State of
the com-
mon
people.
     The great criterion of the state of the common people is the amount of their wages; and, as four fifths of the common people were, in the seventeenth century, employed in agriculture, it is especially important to ascertain what were then the wages of agricultural industry. On this subject we have the means of arriving at conclusions sufficiently exact for our purpose.

Agricul-
tural
wages.
     Sir William Petty, whose mere assertion carries great weight, informs us that a labourer was by no means in the lowest state who received for a day's work fourpence with food, or eightpence without food. Four shillings a week therefore were, according to Petty's calculation, fair agricultural wages.*

That this calculation was not remote from the truth we have abundant proof. About the beginning of the year 1685 the Justices of Warwickshire, in the exercise of a power entrusted to them by an act of Elizabeth, fixed, at their quarter sessions, a scale of wages for the county, and notified that every employer who gave more than the authorised sum, and every working man who received more, would be liable to punishment. The wages of the common agricultural labourer, from March to September, were fixed at the precise sum mentioned by Petty, namely four shillings a week without food. From September to March the wages were to be only three and sixpence a week.**

But in that age, as in ours, the earnings of the peasant were very different in different parts of the kingdom. The wages of Warwickshire were probably about the average, and those of the counties near the Scottish border below it:

* Petty's Political Arithmetic.
** Stat. 5 Eliz. c. 4. Archæologia, vol. xi.

but there were more favoured districts. In the same year, 1685, a gentleman of Devonshire, named Richard Dunning, published a small tract, in which he described the condition of the poor of that county. That he understood his subject well it is impossible to doubt; for a few months later his work was reprinted, and was, by the magistrates assembled in quarter sessions at Exeter, strongly recommended to the attention of all parochial officers. According to him, the wages of the Devonshire peasant were, without food, about five shillings a week.*

Still better was the condition of the labourer in the neighbourhood of Bury St. Edmund's. The magistrates of Suffolk met there in the spring of 1682 to fix a rate of wages, and resolved that, where the labourer was not boarded, he should have five shillings a week in winter, and six in summer.**

In 1661 the justices at Chelmsford had fixed the wages of the Essex labourer, who was not boarded, at six shillings in winter and seven in summer. This seems to have been the highest remuneration given in the kingdom for agricultural labour between the Restoration and the Revolution; and it is to be observed that, in the year in which this order was made, the necessaries of life were immoderately dear. Wheat was at seventy shillings the quarter, which would even now be considered as almost a famine price.***

These facts are in perfect accordance with another fact which seems to deserve consideration. It is evident that, in a country where no man can be compelled to become a soldier, the ranks of an army cannot be filled if the government offers much less than the wages of common rustic labour. At

* Plain and easy Method showing how the Office of Overseer of the Poor may be managed, by Richard Dunning; 1st edition, 1685; 2d edition, 1686.
** Cullum's History of Hawsted.
*** Ruggles on the Poor.

present the pay and beer money of a private in a regiment of the line amount to seven shillings and sevenpence a week. This stipend, coupled with the hope of a pension, does not attract the English youth in sufficient numbers; and it is found necessary to supply the deficiency by enlisting largely from among the poorer population of Munster and Connaught. The pay of the private foot soldier in 1685 was only four shillings and eightpence a week; yet it is certain that the government in that year found no difficulty in obtaining many thousands of English recruits at very short notice. The pay of the private foot soldier in the army of the Commonwealth had been seven shillings a week, that is to say, as much as a corporal received under Charles the Second;* and seven shillings a week had been found sufficient to fill the ranks with men decidedly superior to the generality of the people. On the whole, therefore, it seems reasonable to conclude that, in the reign of Charles the Second, the ordinary wages of the peasant did not exceed four shillings a week; but that, in some parts of the kingdom, five shillings, six shillings, and, during the summer months, even seven shillings were paid. At present a district where a labouring man earns only seven shillings a week is thought to be in a state shocking to humanity. The average is very much higher; and, in prosperous counties, the weekly wages of husbandmen amount to twelve, fourteen, and even sixteen shillings.

Wages of manufacturers.
The remuneration of workmen employed in manufactures has always been higher than that of the tillers of the soil. In the year 1680, a member of the House of Commons remarked that the high wages paid in this country made it impossible for our textures to maintain a competition with the produce of the Indian looms. An English mechanic, he said, instead of slaving like a native of Bengal for a piece of copper, exacted

* See, in Thurloe's State Papers, the memorandum of the Dutch Deputies, dated August $\frac{2}{12}$. 1653.

a shilling a day.* Other evidence is extant, which proves
that a shilling a day was the pay to which the English manu-
facturer then thought himself entitled, but that he was often
forced to work for less. The common people of that age
were not in the habit of meeting for public discussion, of
haranguing, or of petitioning Parliament. No newspaper
pleaded their cause. It was in rude rhyme that their love and
hatred, their exultation and their distress found utterance.
A great part of their history is to be learned only from their
ballads. One of the most remarkable of the popular lays
chaunted about the streets of Norwich and Leeds in the time
of Charles the Second may still be read on the original broadside. It is the vehement and bitter cry of labour against
capital. It describes the good old times when every artisan
employed in the woollen manufacture lived as well as a farmer.
But those times were past. Sixpence a day was now all that
could be earned by hard labour at the loom. If the poor
complained that they could not live on such a pittance, they
were told that they were free to take it or leave it. For so
miserable a recompense were the producers of wealth compelled to toil, rising early and lying down late, while the
master clothier, eating, sleeping, and idling, became rich
by their exertions. A shilling a day, the poet declares, is
what the weaver would have, if justice were done.** We may

---

* The orator was Mr. John Basset, member for Barnstaple. See
Smith's Memoirs of Wool, chapter lxviii.
** This ballad is in the British Museum. The precise year is not
given; but the Imprimatur of Roger Lestrange fixes the date sufficiently
for my purpose. I will quote some of the lines. The master clothier is
introduced speaking as follows: —

"In former ages we used to give,
So that our workfolks like farmers did live;
But the times are changed, we will make them know.
    *   *   *
We will make them to work hard for sixpence a day,
Though a shilling they deserve if they had their just pay;
If at all they murmur and say 't is too small,
We bid them choose whether they 'll work at all."

therefore conclude that, in the generation which preceded
the Revolution, a workman employed in the great staple
manufacture of England thought himself fairly paid if he
gained six shillings a week.

Labour of
children
in facto-
ries.
It may here be noticed that the practice of setting children
prematurely to work, a practice which the state, the legitimate
protector of those who cannot protect themselves, has, in our
time, wisely and humanely interdicted, prevailed in the seventeenth century to an extent which, when compared with the
extent of the manufacturing system, seems almost incredible.
At Norwich, the chief seat of the clothing trade, a little
creature of six years old was thought fit for labour.   Several
writers of that time, and among them some who were considered as eminently benevolent, mention, with exultation,
the fact that in that single city boys and girls of very tender
age created wealth exceeding what was necessary for their
own subsistence by twelve thousand pounds a year.*   The
more carefully we examine the history of the past, the more
reason shall we find to dissent from those who imagine that
our age has been fruitful of new social evils.   The truth is that
the evils are, with scarcely an exception, old.   That which is
new is the intelligence which discerns and the humanity which
remedies them.

Wages of
different
classes of
artisans.
When we pass from the weavers of cloth to a different
class of artisans, our inquiries will still lead us to nearly the
same conclusions.   During several generations, the Commissioners of Greenwich Hospital have kept a register of the

And thus we do gain all our wealth and estate,
By many poor men that work early and late.
Then hey for the clothing trade! It goes on brave;
We scorn for to toyl and moyl, nor yet to slave.
Our workmen do work hard, but we live at ease,
We go when we will, and we come when we please."
    * Chamberlayne's State of England; Petty's Political Arithmetic,
chapter viii. ; Dunning's Plain and Easy Method; Firmin's Proposition
for the Employing of the Poor.   It ought to be observed that Firmin was
an eminent philanthropist.

wages paid to different classes of workmen who have been employed in the repairs of the building. From this valuable record it appears that, in the course of a hundred and twenty years, the daily earnings of the bricklayer have risen from half a crown to four and tenpence, those of the mason from half a crown to five and threepence, those of the carpenter from half a crown to five and fivepence, and those of the plumber from three shillings to five and sixpence.

It seems clear, therefore, that the wages of labour, estimated in money, were, in 1685, not more than half of what they now are; and there were few articles important to the working man of which the price was not, in 1685, more than half of what it now is. Beer was undoubtedly much cheaper in that age than at present. Meat was also cheaper, but was still so dear that hundreds of thousands of families scarcely knew the taste of it. * In the cost of wheat there has been very little change. The average price of the quarter, during the last twelve years of Charles the Second, was fifty shillings. Bread, therefore, such as is now given to the inmates of a workhouse, was then seldom seen, even on the trencher of a yeoman or of a shopkeeper. The great majority of the nation lived almost entirely on rye, barley, and oats.

The produce of tropical countries, the produce of the mines, the produce of machinery, was positively dearer than at present. Among the commodities for which the labourer would have had to pay higher in 1685 than his posterity pay in 1848 were sugar, salt, coals, candles, soap, shoes, stockings, and generally all articles of clothing and all articles of bedding. It may be added, that the old coats and blankets would have been, not only more costly, but less serviceable than the modern fabrics.

* King in his Natural and Political Conclusions roughly estimated the common people of England at 880,000 families. Of these families 440,000, according to him, ate animal food twice a week. The remaining 440,000 ate it not at all, or at most not oftener than once a week.

It must be remembered that those labourers who were able to maintain themselves and their families by means of wages were not the most necessitous members of the community. Beneath them lay a large class which could not subsist without some aid from the parish. There can hardly be a more important test of the condition of the common people than the ratio which this class bears to the whole society. At present the men, women, and children who receive relief appear from the official returns to be, in bad years, one tenth of the inhabitants of England, and, in good years, one thirteenth. Gregory King estimated them in his time at more than a fifth; and this estimate, which all our respect for his authority will scarcely prevent us from calling extravagant, was pronounced by Davenant eminently judicious.

We are not quite without the means of forming an estimate for ourselves. The poor rate was undoubtedly the heaviest tax borne by our ancestors in those days. It was computed, in the reign of Charles the Second, at near seven hundred thousand pounds a year, much more than the produce either of the excise or of the customs, and little less than half the entire revenue of the crown. The poor rate went on increasing rapidly, and appears to have risen in a short time to between eight and nine hundred thousand a year, that is to say, to one sixth of what it now is. The population was then less than a third of what it now is. The minimum of wages, estimated in money, was half of what it now is; and we can therefore hardly suppose that the average allowance made to a pauper can have been more than half of what it now is. It seems to follow that the proportion of the English people which received parochial relief then must have been larger than the proportion which receives relief now. It is good to speak on such questions with diffidence: but it has certainly never yet been proved that pauperism was a less heavy burden or a less serious social evil during the last quarter of the CHAP.
III. seventeenth century than it is in our own time. *

In one respect it must be admitted that the progress of civilisation has diminished the physical comforts of a portion of the poorest class. It has already been mentioned that, before the Revolution, many thousands of square miles, now inclosed and cultivated, were marsh, forest, and heath. Of this wild land much was, by law, common, and much of what was not common by law was worth so little that the proprietors suffered it to be common in fact. In such a tract, squatters and trespassers were tolerated to an extent now unknown. The peasant who dwelt there could, at little or no charge, procure occasionally some palatable addition to his hard fare, and provide himself with fuel for the winter. He kept a flock of geese on what is now an orchard rich with apple blossoms. He snared wild fowl on the fen which has long since been drained and divided into corn fields and turnip fields. He cut turf among the furze bushes on the moor which is now a meadow bright with clover and renowned for butter and cheese. The progress of agriculture and the increase of population necessarily deprived him of these privileges. But against this disadvantage a long list of advantages is to be set off. Of the blessings which civilisation and philosophy bring with them a large proportion is common to all ranks, and

Benefits
derived
by the
common
people
from the
progress
of civili-
sation.

---

* Fourteenth Report of the Poor Law Commissioners, Appendix B. No. 2. Appendix C. No. 1. 1848. Of the two estimates of the poor rate mentioned in the text one was formed by Arthur Moore, the other, some years later, by Richard Dunning. Moore's estimate will be found in Davenant's Essay on Ways and Means; Dunning's in Sir Frederic Eden's valuable work on the poor. King and Davenant estimate the paupers and beggars in 1696, at the incredible number of 1,330,000 out of a population of 5,500,000. In 1846 the number of persons who received relief appears from the official returns to have been only 1,332,089 out of a population of about 17,000,000. It ought also to be observed that, in the official returns, a pauper is very likely to be reckoned more than once.

I would advise the reader to consult De Foe's pamphlet entitled "Giving Alms no Charity," and the Greenwich tables which will be found in Mr. M'Culloch's Commercial Dictionary under the head Prices.

would, if withdrawn, be missed as painfully by the labourer as by the peer. The market place which the rustic can now reach with his cart in an hour was, a hundred and sixty years ago, a day's journey from him. The street which now affords to the artisan, during the whole night, a secure, a convenient, and a brilliantly lighted walk was, a hundred and sixty years ago, so dark after sunset that he would not have been able to see his hand, so ill paved that he would have run constant risk of breaking his neck, and so ill watched that he would have been in imminent danger of being knocked down and plundered of his small earnings. Every bricklayer who falls from a scaffold, every sweeper of a crossing who is run over by a carriage, may now have his wounds dressed and his limbs set with a skill such as, a hundred and sixty years ago, all the wealth of a great lord like Ormond, or of a merchant prince like Clayton, could not have purchased. Some frightful diseases have been extirpated by science; and some have been banished by police. The term of human life has been lengthened over the whole kingdom, and especially in the towns. The year 1685 was not accounted sickly; yet in the year 1685 more than one in twenty-three of the inhabitants of the capital died.[*] At present only one inhabitant of the capital in forty dies annually. The difference in salubrity between the London of the nineteenth century and the London of the seventeenth century is very far greater than the difference between London in an ordinary season and London in the cholera.

Still more important is the benefit which all orders of society, and especially the lower orders, have derived from the mollifying influence of civilisation on the national character. The groundwork of that character has indeed been the same through many generations, in the sense in which the groundwork of the character of an individual may be said to be the

---

[*] The deaths were 23,222. — Petty's Political Arithmetic.

same when he is a rude and thoughtless school-boy and when
he is a refined and accomplished man.   It is pleasing to reflect
that the public mind of England has softened while it has
ripened, and that we have, in the course of ages, become,
not only a wiser, but also a kinder people.   There is scarcely
a page of the history or lighter literature of the seventeenth
century which does not contain some proof that our ancestors
were less humane than their posterity.   The discipline of
workshops, of schools, of private families, though not more
efficient than at present, was infinitely harsher.   Masters,
well born and bred, were in the habit of beating their servants.   Pedagogues knew no way of imparting knowledge but
by beating their pupils.   Husbands, of decent station, were
not ashamed to beat their wives.   The implacability of hostile
factions was such as we can scarcely conceive.   Whigs were
disposed to murmur because Stafford was suffered to die without seeing his bowels burned before his face.   Tories reviled
and insulted Russell as his coach passed from the Tower to
the scaffold in Lincoln's Inn Fields.*   As little mercy was
shown by the populace to sufferers of a humbler rank.   If an
offender was put into the pillory, it was well if he escaped
with life from the shower of brickbats and paving stones.**   If
he was tied to the cart's tail, the crowd pressed round him,
imploring the hangman to give it the fellow well, and make
him howl.***   Gentlemen arranged parties of pleasure to Bride-
well on court days, for the purpose of seeing the wretched
women who beat hemp there whipped.†   A man pressed to
death for refusing to plead, a woman burned for coining, excited less sympathy than is now felt for a galled horse or an
overdriven ox.   Fights compared with which a boxing match

* Burnet, i. 560.
** Muggleton's Acts of the Witnesses of the Spirit.
*** Tom Brown describes such a scene in lines which I do not venture
to quote.
† Ward's London Spy.

is a refined and humane spectacle were among the favourite
diversions of a large part of the town. Multitudes assembled
to see gladiators hack each other to pieces with deadly weapons, and shouted with delight when one of the combatants
lost a finger or an eye. The prisons were hells on earth, seminaries of every crime and of every disease. At the assizes
the lean and yellow culprits brought with them from their cells
to the dock an atmosphere of stench and pestilence which
sometimes avenged them signally on bench, bar, and jury. But
on all this misery society looked with profound indifference.
Nowhere could be found that sensitive and restless compassion which has, in our time, extended a powerful protection
to the factory child, to the Hindoo widow, to the negro slave,
which pries into the stores and water-casks of every emigrant
ship, which winces at every lash laid on the back of a drunken
soldier, which will not suffer the thief in the hulks to be ill
fed or overworked, and which has repeatedly endeavoured
to save the life even of the murderer. It is true that compassion ought, like all other feelings, to be under the government
of reason, and has, for want of such government, produced
some ridiculous and some deplorable effects. But the more
we study the annals of the past the more shall we rejoice that
we live in a merciful age, in an age in which cruelty is abhorred, and in which pain, even when deserved, is inflicted
reluctantly and from a sense of duty. Every class doubtless
has gained largely by this great moral change: but the class
which has gained most is the poorest, the most dependent,
and the most defenceless.

Delusion
which
leads men
to over-
rate the
happiness
of pre-
ceding
genera-
tions.
The general effect of the evidence which has been submitted to the reader seems hardly to admit of doubt. Yet, in
spite of evidence, many will still image to themselves the England of the Stuarts as a more pleasant country than the England in which we live. It may at first sight seem strange that
society, while constantly moving forward with eager speed,

should be constantly looking backward with tender regret. But these two propensities, inconsistent as they may appear, can easily be resolved into the same principle. Both spring from our impatience of the state in which we actually are. That impatience, while it stimulates us to surpass preceding generations, disposes us to overrate their happiness. It is, in some sense, unreasonable and ungrateful in us to be constantly discontented with a condition which is constantly improving. But, in truth, there is constant improvement precisely because there is constant discontent. If we were perfectly satisfied with the present, we should cease to contrive, to labour, and to save with a view to the future. And it is natural that, being dissatisfied with the present, we should form a too favourable estimate of the past.

In truth we are under a deception similar to that which misleads the traveller in the Arabian desert. Beneath the caravan all is dry and bare: but far in advance, and far in the rear, is the semblance of refreshing waters. The pilgrims hasten forward and find nothing but sand where, an hour before, they had seen a lake. They turn their eyes and see a lake where, an hour before, they were toiling through sand. A similar illusion seems to haunt nations through every stage of the long progress from poverty and barbarism to the highest degrees of opulence and civilisation. But, if we resolutely chase the mirage backward, we shall find it recede before us into the regions of fabulous antiquity. It is now the fashion to place the golden age of England in times when noblemen were destitute of comforts the want of which would be intolerable to a modern footman, when farmers and shopkeepers breakfasted on loaves the very sight of which would raise a riot in a modern workhouse, when men died faster in the purest country air than they now die in the most pestilential lanes of our towns, and when men died faster in the lanes of our towns than they now die on the coast of Guiana. We

27 *

CHAP.
III.

too shall, in our turn, be outstripped, and in our turn be envied. It may well be, in the twentieth century, that the peasant of Dorsetshire may think himself miserably paid with fifteen shillings a week; that the carpenter at Greenwich may receive ten shillings a day; that labouring men may be as little used to dine without meat as they now are to eat rye bread; that sanitary police and medical discoveries may have added several more years to the average length of human life; that numerous comforts and luxuries which are now unknown, or confined to a few, may be within the reach of every diligent and thrifty working man.   And yet it may then be the mode to assert that the increase of wealth and the progress of science have benefited the few at the expense of the many, and to talk of the reign of Queen Victoria as the time when England was truly merry England, when all classes were bound together by brotherly sympathy, when the rich did not grind the faces of the poor, and when the poor did not envy the splendour of the rich.

INDEX

TO

THE FIRST VOLUME.

END OF THE FIRST VOLUME.

PRINTED BY BERNH. TAUCHNITZ JUN.

Made in the USA
Lexington, KY
30 May 2014